OXFORD THEOLOGICAL MONOGRAPHS

OXFORD THEOLOGICAL MONOGRAPHS

THE MACARIAN LEGACY
The Place of Macarius-Symeon in the Eastern Christian Tradition
Marcus Plested (2004)

PSALMODY AND PRAYER IN THE WRITINGS OF EVAGRIUS PONTICUS
Luke Dysinger, OSB (2004)

ORIGEN ON THE SONG OF SONGS AS THE SPIRIT OF SCRIPTURE
The Bridegroom's Perfect Marriage-Song
J. Christopher King (2004)

AN INTERPRETATION OF HANS URS VON BALTHASAR
Eschatology as Communion
Nicholas J. Healy (2005)

DURANDUS OF ST POURÇAIN
A Dominican Theologian in the Shadow of Aquinas
Isabel Iribarren (2005)

THE TROUBLES OF TEMPLELESS JUDAH
Jill Middlemas (2005)

TIME AND ETERNITY IN MID-THIRTEENTH-CENTURY THOUGHT
Rory Fox (2006)

THE SPECIFICATION OF HUMAN ACTIONS IN ST THOMAS AQUINAS
Joseph Pilsner (2006)

THE WORLDVIEW OF PERSONALISM
Origins and Early Development
Jan Olof Bengtsson (2006)

THE EUSEBIANS
The Polemic of Athanasius of Alexandria and the Construction of the 'Arian Controversy'
David M. Gwynn (2006)

CHRIST AS MEDIATOR
A study of the Theologies of Eusebius of Caesarea, Marcellus of Ancyra, and Anthanasius of Alexandria
Jon M. Robertson (2007)

RIGHTEOUS JEHU AND HIS EVIL HEIRS
The Deuteronomist's Negative Perspective on Dynastic Succession
David T. Lamb (2007)

Fundamentalism and Evangelicals

HARRIET A. HARRIS

This book has been printed digitally and produced in a standard specification in order to ensure its continuing availability

OXFORD
UNIVERSITY PRESS

Great Clarendon Street, Oxford OX2 6DP

Oxford University Press is a department of the University of Oxford.
It furthers the University's objective of excellence in research, scholarship,
and education by publishing worldwide in

Oxford New York

Auckland Cape Town Dar es Salaam Hong Kong Karachi
Kuala Lumpur Madrid Melbourne Mexico City Nairobi
New Delhi Shanghai Taipei Toronto
With offices in
Argentina Austria Brazil Chile Czech Republic France Greece
Guatemala Hungary Italy Japan South Korea Poland Portugal
Singapore Switzerland Thailand Turkey Ukraine Vietnam

Oxford is a registered trade mark of Oxford University Press
in the UK and in certain other countries

Published in the United States
by Oxford University Press Inc., New York

Reprinted 2009

ISBN 978-0-19-953253-7

PREFACE TO THE PAPERBACK EDITION

In the decade since this book was first published, fundamentalism has become yet more strongly associated with terrorism and violence. Over the same period, the fundamentalist tendencies of mainstream evangelicals have become more dilute; though not all evangelicals will agree. I wish here to say something about these two developments, and how this book's analysis of fundamentalism sheds light on them.

The world changed after September 11, 2001, probably more so for Muslims than for members of any other faith. Muslims around the world have been radicalized, that is, made to think about their roots and identity. It has become almost a catchphrase for Muslims in the UK to say: 'before, I was a Brit who happened to be Muslim, now I am a British Muslim'.

Being radicalized involves being sent back to one's roots so as to investigate, and newly interpret and assert one's identity. This does not itself make one a fundamentalist. Fundamentalists are people who have been radicalized in particular ways; ways that are primitivist and anxious for certainty.

Fundamentalists are primitivists, meaning that they wish to live in accord with the beliefs and practices of the earliest followers of their faith – for Muslims, the Prophet and his first four successors; for Protestant fundamentalists, the earliest Christians of New Testament times; for Sinhalese Buddhists, inhabitants of a mythical narrative, when the Buddha visited Sri Lanka by supernatural powers and consecrated the land. Being primitivists, they idealize the earliest years and bypass much of the tradition of the intervening years. Fundamentalists are typically not traditionalists, because engaging with tradition means engaging with change and development. An acknowledgement of change and development does not sit well with the fundamentalist concern for certainty.

Not all radicals crave certainty. Many people return to their roots without expecting or wanting to find certainty there. Fundamentalists, however, believe that by going right back to the beginning, and disregarding the ways their religion developed down the centuries, they gain possession of something unfaltering. They regard this unfaltering entity as the foundation, or fundament, of their faith. For Protestant fundamentalists it is the Bible, which they hold to be without error. For Muslim fundamentalists it is the Qur'an and hadith, principally, and a particular school of interpretation.

'Fundamentalism' is most at home within Protestant Christianity, where there is a history of distrust of both tradition and interpretation. Protestant fundamentalists believe that they simply go 'back to the Bible', and that anyone can understand the plain sense of scripture. They view interpretation as interfering with the immediacy of God's revelation. By contrast, I had thought, Muslim 'fundamentalists' are always conscious of belonging to a particular school of law, and thereby situate themselves within an interpretive tradition.

However, a view has emerged amongst Sunni Muslims that the earliest generation - the *Salaf* (the ancestors) - provides the supreme model of Islam, and that later history is a corruption rather than a legitimate development of the faith. This is significantly like the primitivism of Protestant fundamentalists. The ancestry of the Muslim view can be traced back to Ahmad ibn Hanbal in the ninth century. Descendants of this way of thinking include the eighteenth-century Wahabbi movement in Arabia, and several later groups sometimes collectively known as the Salafiyya. The Salafist approach to scripture is strikingly similar to that of Protestant fundamentalists; both abjure traditional scholarship, and believe that the meaning of scripture is plain and immediately accessible. Muslims reflecting this Salafist approach are currently involved in separatist or violent responses to the Western world. Fifteen of the nineteen suicide hijackers of September 11, 2001, were Saudi citizens, and therefore influenced by Wahabbism. Salafist tendencies are found in radical Muslim groups that call for the establishment of an Islamic state governed by *shar'ia* (divine law). Many of these groups are offshoots of the Muslim Brotherhood, founded in Egypt in 1927 by Hasan al-Banna. Today, Tariq Ramadan, al-Ban na's grandson, combats the militant separatism of these groups, and their use of scripture. He reminds Salafists that when they appeal to scripture they are always interpreting: 'There can be no revealed Text unless there is human intellect up to the task of reading and interpreting it' (Ramadan 2004: 20). His point is one that has been made in battles over the Bible within Protestant Christianity, and it highlights the similarities between Salafist and Protestant fundamentalist approaches to scripture. Muslims, Christians, and members of any faith, feel greatly empowered, and even justified to use force, if they believe that they have immediate access to unfaltering, divinely revealed truth, and that others are diluting that truth and failing to live by it.

The second development I would like to mention, since this book was first published, is one that has occurred quietly, and with barely an upset. Mainstream Protestant evangelicals have become less fundamentalist, at least in Britain. That said, the evangelical world has become even more diverse than it was before, and within it some groups have become increasingly fundamentalist, particularly in reaction against female or gay ordained ministry. The fundamentalist patterns of thought described in the book remain in the evangelical bloodstream; particularly a belief that the Bible is the foundation of faith, and therefore needs to be reliable in the sense of not making factual mistakes. But these patterns of thought have become diluted within mainstream evangelicalism through influences that evangelicals would not have tolerated in previous decades.

This is interesting because at the end of the twentieth century a significant number of evangelicals explored new methods and theories of interpretation, in an attempt, partly, to break out of the fundamentalist mould. They protested that because they engaged with hermeneutics, it really was not fair to keep accusing them of being fundamentalist. Others were reasserting conservative doctrines of inerrancy in resistance to certain hermeneutical trends. But philosophical hermeneutics did not move evangelicals away from fundamentalist base-camp. The inerrantists need not have worried on that front. Evangelical spokesmen who courted hermeneutical theories, such as John Stott, did not change their method of interpretation nor their stance on the nature of biblical truth, in any significant way.

However, other influences have crept up on evangelicals and modified their fundamentalist tendencies: charismaticism; an interest in worship that engages the senses and the emotions, and not only the mind; an enthusiasm for the power of story and drama; and an increasing sacramentalism.

A brief aside: a number of evangelical reviewers of this book assumed that I had studied under James Barr, and also wondered how, as an 'outsider', I had come to know the evangelical world so well. In fact, I never studied under Barr. He was a generous conversation partner, and external examiner. I agreed with him on a number of points, including his view that charismatic and Pentecostal expressions of faith had the potential to undermine fundamentalism. I also shared his suspicions that these forms of faith might themselves be taken over by fundamentalist patterns of thought. I myself had been a member of both charismatic and conservative evangelical congregations, both of which were fundamentalist in their biblical teaching. This involvement is how I came to know the evangelical world from the inside, and to understand the fundamentalist mentality.

I have argued throughout this book that evangelicals harbour fundamentalist tendencies to varying degrees. Charismatic evangelicals are no exception. In fundamentalist mode, they prepare detailed arguments in defence of scripture's accuracy and consistency. In charismatic mode, they understand the authority of scripture experientially, by the way scripture works in their lives. This also makes them more open to the power of story and to narrative theology, where the emphasis falls not on the historicity of scripture so much as on the paradigms that scripture offers for living a life of faith. Charismatics have an affinity with the Holiness tradition, whose doctrine of assurance rests on biblical promises and the experience of life in Christ, rather than on what can be proved from the Bible.

Both the fundamentalist and the charismatic mode sit side-by-side in Nicky Gumbel's phenomenally successful *Alpha* course; an evangelistic programme that characterizes the charismaticized evangelical mainstream of the 1990s and 2000s. Significantly, no one seems to mind. Evangelicals are pragmatic, and *Alpha* works well as an evangelistic tool. But at other times and places in the twentieth century, it would not have been possible to conflate these two approaches. The mainstream evangelical world was heavily suspicious of Pentecostals and charismatics for much of the twentieth century, because of their emphasis on experience and feeling.

Evangelical apologists insisted that we should be guided by fact and reason, because feelings could not be trusted. The self-proclaimed fundamentalists of the 1920s attacked liberals for putting experience before reason, and they viewed Pentecostals in the same light. Still, by the 1990s, charismaticism had become the norm amongst evangelicals. This, or more properly, the increasingly experiential culture of which charismaticism is a part, is silently undercutting fundamentalism, even though most charismatics sign up to a fundamentalist doctrine of scripture.

Not that evangelicals need to be charismatic to slough off fundamentalism. They already have the relevant experiential resources within their lineage, and within their own personal experiences of conversion, forgiveness, prayer, and worship. But charismatic Christianity has significantly changed the landscape, and opened evangelicals up to a range of attitudes and practices that the more fundamentalist-minded find very uncomfortable. Speaking in tongues, and using the body in worship transcend reason. They are expressions of faith beyond the control of the mind. There is a recognized trend of evangelicals moving through charismaticism into more sacramental worship. If as charismatics they have spiritualized the everyday world and attributed mundane happenings to the work of demons and powers, it is not a big leap to believe that divine grace is channelled through mundane objects, or to enjoy the ceremonial around those objects. Raising their hands to a chorus is not a million miles from crossing themselves or genuflecting. 'Alternative worship' services sprung up in the mid- and late-1990s, some of which inserted a high mass, or even Benediction, into a post-charismatic mix of rave and ambient music, flashing lights and images, icons, words projected on to walls, and poetry readings.

I am beginning to conflate categories, because many who engage in alternative worship regard themselves as 'post-evangelical', and are specifically post-charismatic. Their experience of charismatic Christianity has put them off church. Charismatic Christianity can be just as hierarchical, authoritarian, and biblically naïve as the fundamentalist expressions of faith described in this book. But it has played a significant part in loosening up a cerebral, apologetic approach to faith. Evangelicals earlier in the twentieth century realized its subversive potential when they rejected Pentecostal and charismatic movements.

Evangelicals have engaged in decades of heated dispute over biblical authority, and put most of their scholarly energy into defending the Bible, or in to arguing over whether or not they are fundamentalist. Yet, after all the ink that has been spilled, the jobs lost, and even the lives lost in the twentieth-century battles over the Bible, charismatic, narrative, and sacramental influences are moving evangelicals to another place, perhaps without them fully noticing; and, at least, without them greatly objecting.

H.A.H.

Oxford, 2007

ACKNOWLEDGEMENTS

I HAVE many people to thank for helping me bring this work to fruition. First and foremost, James Barr, John Barton, Keith Ward, and Trevor Williams, inspired and supported me through the doctoral stage and beyond. A number of people, too many to mention them all, have kindly endured interviews, sent me material, or read earlier work of mine which has made its way into this book: Nancy Ammerman, David Beck, Eugenio Biagini, David and Gloria Hague, Barry Hankins, Theodore Letis, George Marsden, Joe and Linette Martin, Basil Mitchell, Alister McGrath, Mark Noll, Gillian Peele, Steve Shaw, John Shortt, David Smith, David C. C. Watson, and the late John Wenham.

I should also like to thank those who have welcomed me into their own fundamentalist and evangelical worlds and aided my understanding of their faith, particularly the faculty and students of Bob Jones University, Liberty University, and Wheaton College, and Richard Russell and Stephen Perks who introduced me to the varied world of neo-Calvinist evangelicalism.

Others generously enabled me to benefit from ongoing research programmes, notably Scott Appleby and Martin Marty of The Fundamentalism Project, and Larry Eskridge and Mark Noll of The Institute for the Study of American Evangelicals. Pew Charitable Trusts and the Billy Graham Center at Wheaton College provided financial assistance.

I am indebted to those who have read parts of the book and offered valuable, and I hope well-heeded, advice for its improvement: David Bebbington, Grayson Carter, and Ian Rennie on the historical sections; Daniel Robinson on Common Sense Realism; Jonathan Chaplin, Peter Heslam, John Peck, and Richard Russell on the Kuyperian elements; and Tony Nuttall on hermeneutics. I am extremely grateful to them all.

My deepest thanks go to my parents Claude and Judy Rawson for their calm and abiding support, and to my husband Mark who has lived with this study since we married and whose interest in it has been my constant encouragement. This book is dedicated to them.

CONTENTS

LIST OF FIGURES

Introduction

Fundamentalism and Evangelicalism

> Although *logically* fundamentalism is only one circle within the several that constitute evangelicalism . . . numerically it is much the most populous: let's say, something well over ninety per cent of world evangelicalism is fundamentalistic, and, even for many of those not included in that percentage, fundamentalism commonly remains the ideological standard by which it is determined what is evangelical and what is conservative.
>
> (Barr 1991*a*: 144)

Fundamentalism is a historical movement closely related to evangelicalism. It may be understood as a subset or extremist element of evangelicalism. However, it is not sufficient to say only this. Many evangelicals this century share with fundamentalists basic assumptions about the nature of biblical truth and authority, and for this reason are often described as fundamentalists themselves. Confusion over the label 'fundamentalist' arises partly because the term is used both to denote the historical movement and to describe a certain way of thinking.

Students of fundamentalism disagree over the appropriate usage of the label. Some reserve the designation only for the original fundamentalists who coined the term and for those of their heirs who still accept it. Such is the practice of most historians of Protestant fundamentalist and evangelical movements in the United States, including George M. Marsden, Mark A. Noll, and Joel E. Carpenter. These three scholars are themselves evangelicals who acknowledge the influence of fundamentalist attitudes upon subsequent American evangelicalism. Marsden explains, in his work *Fundamentalism and American Culture: The Shaping of Twentieth-Century Evangelicalism* 1870–1925 (1980), generally accepted as the authoritative history of fundamentalism, that:

> Most of the . . . groups that had been touched by the fundamentalist experience of the 1920s re-emerged in a new post-fundamentalist coalition. Their basic attitude toward culture is suggested by their successful appropriation of the more culturally respectable term "evangelical." Yet although this new evangelical sub-culture repudiated "fundamentalist" as too exclusivist in implication, "fundamentalistic" remains a useful adjective to describe many of its conspicuous and controversial traits. (Marsden 1980: 195)

Scholars whose approach to fundamentalism is not primarily historical employ the term to describe evangelicalism in so far as it reflects fundamentalist ways of thinking. Such has been the practice of James Barr, the most prominent critic of British fundamentalism. Barr built upon the convention of the 1950s where critics of the then resurgent conservative evangelical movement in England attacked it as fundamentalist. Others have since continued this practice on both sides of the Atlantic. In America, Kathleen Boone (1989: 7–10), a literary theorist examining the 'discourse' of fundamentalism, and Morris Ashcraft (1982: 32–3), writing on 'The Theology of Fundamentalism', both accept Barr's judgement that 'fundamentalism' is the most useful general term for the phenomenon they describe. In Britain, John Barton criticized the biblicism of fundamentalism in his Bampton lectures of 1988. More recently Martyn Percy (1996: 12) has rejected Barr's 'cognitive approach' to fundamentalism and has provided a theological, psychosocial interpretation of fundamentalism and revivalism as an entire 'cultural-linguistic system'.

By contrast, historical studies enable distinctions to be drawn between fundamentalism and evangelicalism at particular points in history, where new movements and trends have developed. A brief historical outline, to be further elaborated in Chapter 1, will indicate how this is so. Fundamentalism developed out of nineteenth-century Anglo-American evangelicalism. It was a strange coalition of diverse evangelical groups who rallied against the common enemy of theological liberalism. In particular, they were unified in upholding the truth of scripture—which they conceived primarily in terms of factual reliability—against the theories of higher criticism. In the middle decades of the twentieth century, fundamentalists became increasingly separatist. There was a counter-reaction from a new generation who called themselves 'new evangelicals', and who came to dominate the

American evangelical scene. As heirs of the fundamentalist tradition they perpetuated the fundamentalist doctrine of an error-free Bible within mainstream evangelical thought, even while they modified that doctrine in various ways.

Separatism remains the central distinguishing feature of self-proclaimed fundamentalists in the United States.[1] British evangelicals were spared a fundamentalist episode of the scale and ferocity of that in the US in the 1920s, and hence no large-scale movement comparable to separatist fundamentalism has developed in Britain. British conservative evangelicalism, often called 'fundamentalism' by its critics, has much in common with mainstream American evangelicalism, and has both influenced and been influenced by new evangelicalism. There exists today an interdenominational, international evangelicalism, described variously as the evangelical 'denomination' (Barr 1977: 22; Marsden 1984*a*), 'coalition' (Ellingsen 1988: 123–34), or 'mainstream' (Hunter 1987: 9), with which separatist fundamentalists rarely co-operate, but which has been affected by earlier fundamentalism and which displays fundamentalistic characteristics.

The term 'evangelicalism' in this book may be taken to refer to this mainstream, which is dominated by new evangelicals and their heirs in the United States and by conservative evangelicals in Britain.[2] However, use of the term should not be taken to imply

[1] Often the term 'militant-separatism' is used. It requires some explanation because the most violent groups are often not the most separatist, but are those 'neo-fundamentalists' who co-operate with a variety of religious and political conservatives in campaigns such as the crusade against abortion. Older-style, separatist fundamentalists refuse to co-operate even with evangelicals and neo-fundamentalists. They take a belligerent tone in their polemic against other Christians, and are proud of their 'militant' zeal to preserve purity in doctrine and practice. They are separatist in lifestyle and may adhere to certain dress-codes, and may forbid such pursuits as cinema-going and the playing of popular music. They are also doctrinally separatist, refusing association with those who hold different views from their own, hence the many schisms in their ranks.

[2] Conservative evangelicalism has expanded worldwide in recent decades, affecting Europe, Australia, Africa, Latin America, the Far East, and the former Soviet Union. In Germany, the term *evangelikal* has been coined to distinguish the new movement from *Evangelisch* Lutheranism. This expansion is due not only to American and British evangelists and missionary organizations, but increasingly to the work of indigenous missionaries. Some American fundamentalist and evangelical institutions are now being funded by non-American sources. Carl McIntire's Faith Theological Seminary is heavily dependent on Korean money and James Packer now holds the Sangwoo Youtong Chee chair in Theology at Regent College, Vancouver. It is not possible to do credit to the range and diversity of evangelicalism across the continents in this study. I have chosen to concentrate on evangelicalism in Britain and the United States, which I regard as seminal to conservative

that there is a unified, easily identifiable evangelical position, even on scripture. The founders of the Institute for the Study of American Evangelicals (ISAE) deliberately chose the term 'evangelicals' over 'evangelicalism' so as to do justice to the diversity within evangelical ranks.[3] That said, the majority of evangelicals are conscious of their shared identity which they express often in terms of their submission to the authority of scripture. They claim not to be 'selective' in their use of scripture but to take the whole of the Bible as relevant and normative. These are the sorts of evangelical I have in mind in this book. Their views on scripture will be my main focus, though I make reference to some wider theological and social issues, particularly where these relate to evangelical use of the Bible.

Marsden (e.g. 1980: 4, 102–3, 141, 164–70, 228) cites militancy as the key feature distinguishing fundamentalism from non-fundamentalist evangelicalism. It has been the practice since the early 1980s to extend the fundamentalist label to resurgent religious movements worldwide, many of which are militant. Militancy thus assumes prominence as a major characteristic of fundamentalism, but only in historical and comparative studies. It is barely mentioned in the conceptual studies of Barr, Barton, and Boone, or even in Percy's discussion of fundamentalism as a religion of power.[4] Marsden traces fundamentalist militancy to a Calvinistic zeal to root out error and preserve doctrinal purity. This zeal, if not its militant pursuit, is to Barr (1980*a*: 82) a telling sign of fundamentalist attitudes among evangelicals, over whom the 'emphasis on a traditional rational orthodoxy has completely triumphed'.

Comparative studies of fundamentalism in other religions (including Roman Catholicism) have so far made little contact with the Protestant debate over the relation between evangelicalism and fundamentalism. Indeed, within the Protestant discussion, one might think in terms of a '*tendency toward fundamentalism*' (Boone 1989: 10), which is exhibited by militant and irenic groups alike.

evangelical movements across the world. For an introductory discussion of evangelical movements outside North America see Ellingsen (1988: 107–22).

[3] ISAE was founded in 1982 by evangelical historians Mark Noll and Nathan Hatch as a centre for research at Wheaton College, Illinois.

[4] Percy's case-study is of the work and writings of John Wimber, a major charismatic leader of the 1980s.

In global discussion, 'fundamentalism' often denotes similar militant tendencies among theologically diverse groups, or even among groups which are not expressly religious. Comparative usage of the term 'fundamentalism' is discussed in the Appendix.

The practice of extending the fundamentalist label beyond its original referent is questioned by those who resist the term, whether Protestant evangelicals or members of non-Protestant religions. It becomes a matter for debate how far their self-perception and self-designations should be accepted. As William Shepard argues, those 'who accept a label are privileged in relation to it': 'That is, one should not *lightly* exclude from a category such as fundamentalism those who accept the label for themselves nor *lightly* apply it to those who do not. One may do so, but only with very good and considered reason' (1992: 280). Decisions about terminology, however, involve more complications than the already perplexing task of discerning who is and who is not justified in disowning the fundamentalist label. 'Fundamentalism' is regarded neither as unconditionally negative nor unconditionally positive by its supposed subjects. Typically it is a term accepted under some conditions and rejected under others. Many evangelicals will say that they are fundamentalist in so far as they defend the fundamentals of their faith, but will reject various other connotations of the term. A critique of the kind offered by James Barr leaves such evangelicals feeling that they are unjustifiably tarnished with a negative fundamentalist image. They react by attempting to distinguish themselves from fundamentalists. Leading evangelical spokesmen have listed what they perceive to be their main differences from fundamentalism. Such lists can be found in John Stott's response to David Edwards in the 'liberal–evangelical dialogue' *Essentials* (Edwards and Stott 90–1), in the Evangelical Alliance publication, 'Who Do Evangelicals Think They Are?' (Calver, *et al.*: n.d. 6), and in Derek J. Tidball's *Who Are the Evangelicals?* (1994: 17–18). All follow the same eight-point pattern. The Evangelical Alliance tabulates the distinctions as in Table 1.

The extent to which fundamentalist ways of thinking have influenced evangelicalism will affect the legitimacy of these distinctions.

The last four points draw upon differences that have emerged as evangelicals in the States have distanced themselves from their

TABLE 1. *Distinctions between fundamentalists and evangelicals*

Fundamentalists	Evangelicals
Are suspicious of scholarship and science. Tend to be anti-intellectual.	Encourage academic study in order to develop a deeper understanding of faith.
Have a 'mechanical' view of how the Bible was written.	Believe it essential to understand the culture and circumstances in which the Bible was written.
Believe the Authorized (King James) Version of the Bible as the only inspired translation.	Value the Authorized Version, but believe there are now more accurate translations.
Have a literalistic approach to interpreting the Bible.	See the Bible as a rich collection of history, poetry, prophecy, metaphor, and symbol—to be understood accordingly.
Reject involvement with Christians who do not accept their views.	Will not negotiate on the essentials of the Christian faith, but believe secondary differences do not prevent co-operation with others.
Often allow their culture to influence their beliefs. Thus, some support racial intolerance, 'prosperity teaching', and politically 'right-wing' views.	Seek to allow the Bible to question and challenge culture—including their own.
Have denied, until recently, that the Christian gospel has social implications.	Believe that Christians have a duty to be 'salt and light' in society.
Insist on certain views concerning the Second Coming of Christ.	Believe there are legitimate differences of interpretation about the details of the return of the Lord Jesus Christ to this earth.

fundamentalist roots. Alister McGrath (1994*a*: 112–13), who distinguishes evangelicalism from fundamentalism by a similar set of arguments, suggests that between fundamentalism and evangelicalism there is 'an overlap of beliefs (such as the authority of Scripture), which can too easily mask profound differences in outlook and temperament'. By 'differences in outlook and temperament' he seems to mean a siege mentality and a narrow commitment to premillennial dispensationalism.[5] These differences are dealt with in points five and eight of the Evangelical Alliance list. They provide the most promising distinctions between self-designated fundamentalists and evangelicals in the United States. Most self-proclaimed fundamentalists in the States today are strict in their separation from non-fundamentalist Christians. Many also, particularly in the southern states, are dispensationalists.

However, social practice and millennial beliefs are not the grounds on which a critic such as Barr calls evangelicals 'fundamentalist'. Barr (1977: 198) is little interested in separatism and does not count dispensationalism as part of the fundamentalist 'orthodoxy' he is describing. The conception of biblical authority is, however, central to his concerns. Therefore, while British evangelicals can legitimately claim not to be fundamentalist in the separatist sense, and can show themselves to be flexible regarding eschatology, they do not thereby escape the charge of fundamentalism. Critics remain unconvinced that evangelical approaches to scripture differ significantly from a fundamentalist approach. The first four points in the Evangelical Alliance table attempt to address this issue but they do so unsatisfactorily. They offer a picture of fundamentalism which is no less distorted than the unfriendly caricatures which dominated perceptions of fundamentalism from the 1920s to the 1960s, and which portrayed it as a wholly anti-intellectual and culturally backward phenomenon.[6] Since evangelicals do not generally like to be called 'fundamentalist' they have described as fundamentalist a position to the right of their own from which they can distance themselves. Self-designated fundamentalists would not accept this portrayal, and

[5] Dispensationalists believe in Christ's imminent return to earth, the 'rapture' of Christians to meet him in the clouds, and a seven-year period of divine judgement upon the world which they refer to as 'the tribulation'. See ss. 1.1, 4.3 below.

[6] See s. 1.4.3 below.

would identify more readily with the evangelical position as described in the table.

Self-proclaimed fundamentalists would not admit to being anti-intellectualist any more than would evangelicals. Those, such as old-style fundamentalist Allan A. MacRae or the new-style fundamentalist Norman L. Geisler, who are at separated fundamentalist institutions, are not obviously less well-educated in biblical studies and philosophy than are evangelical scholars. Like the British evangelical Martyn Lloyd-Jones, fundamentalists want to keep 'reason and scholarship in their place', as '*servants* and not masters' (Lloyd-Jones [1971] 1992: 48). Like Lloyd-Jones's friend and compatriot James Packer, they reject a 'mechanical' view of scripture and would at the same time accept Packer's image of 'dictation' as a metaphor signifying 'not the method or psychology of God's guidance . . . but simply the fact and result of it' (Packer 1958*a*: 79). All conservatives used the Authorized Version until modern translations by evangelically minded interpreters appeared.[7] A few groups still insist upon the Authorized Version, but the official doctrine of most fundamentalists and evangelicals has been influenced by the Princeton doctrine of inerrancy, according to which only the original autographs are fully inspired and inerrant. No one from either camp admits to taking a solely literalistic approach in interpreting scripture, though fundamentalists and evangelicals have both described their approach in shorthand as literal. Thus Carl Henry, a leading theologian of the new evangelicals, describes the issue between Barr and evangelicals as that between 'the literal sense of an errant Bible . . . versus the literal truth of an inerrant Bible' (1979*b*: 122).

McGrath (1994*a*: 112–13) constructs a straw-man when he states that 'fundamentalism is totally hostile to the notion of biblical criticism, in any form'. Fundamentalism in fact accords with evangelicalism which, according to McGrath, 'accepts the principle of biblical criticism (although insisting that it be applied responsibly)'. The difference between the two positions becomes a matter of what sorts of biblical criticism are accepted, and how its responsible application is defined. Here we will discover no hard-and-fast distinctions between fundamentalism and evangelicalism, but

[7] Notably the New International Version and the New American Standard Version. For statistics on preferred Bible translations see Noll (1986: 218).

rather varying degrees of acceptance of different forms of criticism. Moreover, both fundamentalists and evangelicals have a notion of true criticism as that which reflects the correct presuppositions about scripture and which yields conservative interpretations. Only where evangelicals can demonstrate that their attitudes towards scripture are genuinely different from fundamentalist attitudes, can their protests carry real weight.

While evangelicals attempt to distance themselves from fundamentalism, their critics refuse to acknowledge a significant difference. Evangelicalism, though a far wider and older tradition than fundamentalism, has been so influenced by fundamentalist forms of thought, especially in biblical apologetics, that evangelicals have difficulty clarifying their position in distinction from fundamentalist tendencies. James Barr argues that now 'the fundamentalist view of Scripture is the only one, effectively, that is *distinctively* evangelical' (Barr 1991*a*: 146; cf. 1980*a*: 67). Therefore, in so far as evangelicals agree with fundamentalists over what it is to defend the authority of scripture, they will seem fundamentalist to a critic such as Barr.

Being essentially conservative, evangelicals tend to view excess zeal in the fundamentalist direction as less theologically dangerous than excessive liberalizing. While they object to fundamentalist extremes in temperament, they are in basic theological agreement with those to the right of them, and share the same criticisms of non-evangelical theology. Donald Bloesch, an American evangelical, would have it noted that he criticizes fundamentalism 'from the right, i.e., from the perspective of evangelical and catholic tradition, not of modernity' (1994: 98). Evangelicals share the same opponents as fundamentalists and therefore stand with their 'more conservative brothers and sisters in affirming the fundamental doctrines of the faith' (Bloesch 1994: 98). They tend to regard all non-evangelical, Protestant theology as liberal, much to the chagrin of their critics (Barr 1977: 19–20, 100–1, 164–5; Barton 1988: 1). They recognize neo-orthodoxy as a distinct movement, but theologically they have generally regarded it as a variation of liberalism or modernism. Hence, Cornelius Van Til entitled his attack on Barth's theology *The New Modernism* (1947), and J. I. Packer (1958*a*: 151–60) termed the Biblical Theology movement the 'New Liberalism'. Secular humanism has received attention in the last couple of decades. It is rejected as a philosophy based upon non-biblical principles (e.g. F. Schaeffer 1981), and is fought in the public realm as a political issue (e.g. Falwell 1980). However, liberalism remains dominant in the consciousness of evangelicals. Liberal tendencies are held responsible for causing the decline into secularism by 'destroying the power of the Scriptures to confront the spirit of our age' (F. Schaeffer 1984: 36–8). Evangelical suspicions of any alien thought-forms are usually voiced as suspicions of liberal elements.[8]

Multifarious fundamentalist and evangelical movements are united by their distinctive conception of biblical authority which distinguishes their position from that of all non-evangelical theologies. Kenneth Kantzer (1975: 39), a new-evangelical theologian, describes the 'principle of biblical authority' as 'the watershed between most other movements within the broad stream of contemporary Protestantism and the movement (or movements) of twentieth-century Protestantism known as fundamentalism, which is a term often poorly used for the purpose it is intended to serve, or evangelicalism or conservative Protestantism'. Where the fundamentalist influence is present, the authority of the Bible is defended primarily by reference to its factual reliability. This emphasis in evangelical apologetics conceals the rich variety of ways in which evangelicals experience scripture to be an authority for their faith and life. It also betrays a conception of facts as stated entities which are independent of judgement. Evangelicals can experience difficulty within themselves or with their colleagues when they ascribe an interpretative role to the biblical authors. The fundamentalist impulse is to imagine the authors producing factual reports oblivious of God's control over their words. A truer evangelical outlook would allow that the Holy Spirit quickened the spirits of the biblical authors in ways to which evangelicals could themselves relate from their own, lowlier experiences of

[8] At the same time, non-evangelical scholars often do not note distinctions within conservative theology. David Tracy uses 'fundamentalism' as 'roughly equivalent' to 'supernaturalism' (1975: 24, 135, 145 n.93) and generalizes both as literalism (ibid. 126, 239). John Barton (1988: ix–2) uses the terms 'fundamentalism', 'biblicist', 'Bible-centred' and 'conservative' seemingly interchangeably. Moreover, while evangelicals suspect neo-orthodoxy of being liberal, critics of neo-orthodoxy and of conservative evangelicalism find affinities between the two. Barton (ibid. 82) claims that 'living the Christian life from day to day we shall, if we are Christians of a Neo-orthodox turn of mind, treat the Bible as the Word of God without qualification and rely on it as an infallible and inerrant source of doctrine and ethical guidance'.

God speaking. 'It is time we recognized the dynamic nature of the world of biblical narrative', Vinay Samuel (1996: 55) urges, in a recent Anglican evangelical consultation on scripture, 'especially as it is expressed by a community of disciples who recognize the role of the Holy Spirit in making that world dynamic and empowering'.

Evangelicals enjoy a highly personal, experiential religion (something for which they also often receive criticism!). They testify to scripture 'coming alive' once they have 'accepted Christ as their saviour'. Their belief that God speaks personally to them through scripture forms a major aspect of their spirituality. Yet they typically advocate a 'double approach' to scripture (e.g. Stott 1996: 25–6), which, in effect, divorces a devotional from a factual style of reading. They have frequently come to argue that scripture must be justified as entirely or substantially true with respect to facts before one can claim to have knowledge about Christ, and that accurate knowledge of facts about him must logically if not temporally precede one's faith-relation to him.

The Fundamentalist Mentality

James Barr has been the most influential critic to ascribe a fundamentalist mentality to evangelicals. He has caused much upset among British evangelicals, who generally assume that he simply identifies them as fundamentalists. However, Barr's critique is more subtle, because it distinguishes what he considers to be true evangelicalism from the damaging effects of a fundamentalist ideology. Evangelicalism, full of the delights of a personal faith, has lost its openness, freedom, and spontaneity to a mentality which Barr describes as basically rationalistic.

Martyn Percy also views fundamentalism as a '*tendency*, a habit of mind', but by this he means something wider and more complex than what he describes as Barr's (1996: 10, 11) 'habit of treating fundamentalism as a (primarily) credal phenomenon'. He likens fundamentalism to a culture or a language, and calls it a 'form of life'. He employs psychosocial analysis of a kind which Barr largely ignores and sometimes explicitly rejects. I have found Barr's approach more helpful than has Percy. I do not read Barr as offering something so clear-cut as a cognitive or noetic account of fundamentalism, but rather as trying to describe a way of thinking which is not wholly susceptible to systematic presentation. (It is noteworthy that Barr does not risk claiming to define fundamentalism as Percy (1996: 13) does.) Percy aims to give a comprehensive account of the mind-set of people within certain types of fundamentalist communities, particularly charismatic communities. Barr attacks a way of thinking which he ascribes to many evangelicals whether or not they can be said to be members of fundamentalist communities. Barr thereby bypasses the question of which sorts of communities deserve the name 'fundamentalist'. The flexibility this produces enables us to recognize that many evangelicals share a fundamentalist mentality in Barr's sense without participating in the entire 'form of life' that Percy identifies. While evangelicals feel frustrated that under Barr's type of critique they can never escape the fundamentalist label, such a critique leaves room for us to recognize that few evangelicals are fundamentalist through and through.

Barr means several things by fundamentalist rationalism: a priority given to reason in verifying the truth of scripture by testing its evidences; a greater concern to provide evidence for the authenticity of biblical passages than to discover their religious significance; and a methodological principle according to which reason draws conclusions from biblical 'facts' or propositions (e.g. 1977: 93, 173–5, 272–5). Several scholars have followed Barr in characterizing fundamentalism as rationalistic. Kathleen Boone (1989: 11–12) argues that fundamentalists emphasize rational apprehension of the biblical text over subjective apprehension of the divine. Richard Tapper and Nancy Tapper (1987: 55) take Barr to mean that fundamentalists play down emotion, the miraculous, supernatural, and mystical, and are accommodating to modern science. Martin Marty (1992: 6 and n. 5) says 'fundamentalism is very rationalistic' in that it takes the 'task of the theologian . . . [to be] to co-ordinate the historical and literary "facts" of the Bible and order them systematically'.

When fundamentalists are described as rationalistic the claim is not that they stress the power of a priori reason to grasp theological truth. Rather, fundamentalists are said to base theological truth on evidences. Barr (1977: 272) sometimes uses the term 'empirical rationalism', which is more appropriate. Others have also noted that fundamentalist assumptions reflect the empirical rationalism of the early Enlightenment, and many have emphasized the particular influence of Scottish Common Sense philosophy. This influence, which has been in terms of broad sweeps of thought rather than of specific philosophical arguments, has been described as 'evidentialist' or 'Baconian' (e.g. Marsden 1980: 15–18, 55–6, 110–16, 215–21; Noll 1985). Some commentators have conflated these descriptions with the word 'rationalist' (e.g. Ellingsen 1985; Marty 1992: 6; Volf 1992: 102).

'Rationalism' is the most ambiguous of these three terms for describing what commentators are attempting to convey, namely, the fundamentalist assumptions that Christian truth must be founded on evidences and that theological method should be modelled on the inductive method set out by Francis Bacon. 'Evidentialist' and 'Baconian' better capture these two characteristics. However, 'rationalism' in a more traditional sense is operative in fundamentalist views of scripture. Behind the fundamentalist conviction that scripture contains no errors is a deductive argument that God inspired the scriptures and God cannot err. The Bible is free from error because rationally, given the Protestant scholastic doctrine of verbal inspiration, it can contain no errors. This deductive argument is at odds with fundamentalist attempts to validate scripture inductively. The tension created by this dual deductive–inductive approach leads to the tendency that James Barr most condemns, of fundamentalist-minded evangelicals determining that their biblical scholarship will yield only conservative results.

The Scottish Common Sense philosophy has influenced fundamentalist thought, but its influence is neither specific nor comprehensive. It is not specific because fundamentalist theologians have not engaged with the arguments of Common Sense philosophers, and the philosophy does not lead obviously in a fundamentalist direction. It is not comprehensive because many fundamentalist characteristics—even those which have parallels in Common Sense philosophy—derive from aspects of the Christian tradition which predate that philosophy. For example, the Puritans had regarded religious truth as open to empirical verification; the Reformers and Protestant scholastics were suspicious of reason; the Reformers, Tyndale, and Wyclif before them had championed the right of the plain man to interpret scripture; and throughout

Christian history there have been exegetes emphasizing the literal sense of the text, Luther being a prominent example.[9]

Common Sense philosophy provided a framework within which to produce a conservative biblical apologetic in a scientific age. Besides passing on a veneration for Bacon's inductive method, Common Sense philosopher Thomas Reid gave assurance that external reality was just as it appeared to be. Conservative biblicists found in this a philosophical parallel for their insistence on the perspicuity of scripture. Reid's views on memory, that what we remember is not the *idea* of a past event but the past event itself, and on the reliability of testimony gave fundamentalists the means to insist that what we know from scripture is not an idea of the events recorded therein but the events themselves. Thus they developed an apologetic against Kantian and Hegelian views which were affecting biblical criticism in Germany, that truth was in some way a function of human mental activity.

Common Sense Realism was the governing philosophy of American theologians, indeed of much of American life, in the nineteenth century. By the end of that century the majority of theologians, except for the most biblically conservative, were abandoning their Common Sense theories for more idealist and Romantic notions of truth. The assumptions of Common Sense philosophy permeated Princeton theology. The doctrine of inerrancy advocated by scholars at Princeton Theological Seminary provided the most intellectual statement of the fundamentalist movement, and has dominated the evangelical understanding of scripture ever since. A doctrine of inerrancy implies that biblical

[9] I shall not be describing the fundamentalist approach to scripture as that which takes scripture literally. All fundamentalists and evangelicals recognize some figurative language in scripture. This aside, the meaning of 'literal' has been neither constant nor uncontroversial in Christian tradition, and fundamentalist interpretation today is not equivalent to literalistic interpretations in the past. For example, in the immediate pre- and post-Reformation period the prophetic-literal sense was distinguished from the carnal, rabbinical, or historical-literal sense, as that by which scripture was read Christologically (McGrath 1987: 152–74). A prophetic-literal sense might be associated with exactitude in the rendering of spiritual realities, in contradistinction from a physical or empirical interpretation (Barr 1989: 412). A fundamentalist approach to scripture does not have a monopoly on literalism in the prophetic or spiritual sense. Even regarding the physical sense, a fundamentalist approach may oblige one to reject a literal reading in the interests of safeguarding scripture from error. So, while Barr (1977: 42) interprets the author of Genesis 1 as intending to convey that the world was created in six days, evangelicals commonly argue that Genesis 1 intends to communicate spiritual but not physical truths about the origins of our world.

authority would be undermined if any error were to be found in scripture, and that only an error-free Bible can provide a sure foundation for the Christian faith.

Fundamentalists and many evangelicals today retain the ideal of a factually inerrant Bible, but in order to preserve the error-free status of scripture they depart from factual interpretations of many biblical passages. The degree to which they surrender factual readings varies, and there is now much diversity within fundamentalist and evangelical ranks. Not all evangelicals think in a fundamentalist way about the Bible, but very many do in some aspect or to some degree. It would be implausible to attempt to draw a clear line between those who do and those who do not, because the fundamentalist mentality is both too pervasive and too variable. To speak generally for the moment, pending further clarification in the main body of the book, evangelicals manifest this mentality when they reveal something of the following attitudes: a commitment to a priori reasoning that scripture cannot contain any error because it is inspired by God; an almost contrary commitment to demonstrating empirically that scripture is indeed inspired because it contains no error; a feeling that in moving away from either commitment one is making concessions to modern scholarship; and a hesitancy to make such concessions lest they detract from the authority of the Bible and so threaten the very foundations of the Christian faith.

An Outline of the Book

This book both acknowledges historical and social distinctions between fundamentalist and evangelical movements, and argues that evangelicals often reflect a fundamentalist mentality with respect to the Bible. Chapter 1 traces the major influences upon the fundamentalist movement of the 1920s, and upon the various evangelical and fundamentalist movements that emerged subsequently. Chapter 2 considers a British approach to fundamentalism—that of James Barr. While evangelicals make two major sets of distinctions—between themselves and fundamentalists, and between themselves and liberals—Barr attempts to distinguish evangelicals who are not fundamentalist from evangelicals who are. Barr (1981: p. xiv) describes the fundamentalist quality of the evangelicals whom he studies as the 'rationalism of pure conservative ideology'. The philosophical roots of the fundamentalist mentality are investigated in Chapter 3, with particular attention given to Scottish Common Sense Realism. I distinguish between rationalism, as the use of a priori arguments, and a reliance on reason to test Christian evidences. The Common Sense philosophy has contributed to an apologetic based on the testing of evidences. The development of such an apologetic alongside deductive arguments for the truth of scripture is traced in Chapter 4 through Princeton theology, turn-of-the-century traditional and radical evangelical movements, early fundamentalism, and contemporary fundamentalism and evangelicalism.

In Chapter 5 the fundamentalist mentality among evangelicals is depicted in an imaginary dialogue between evangelicals and their critics over the nature of biblical authority. Evangelicals commonly understand themselves to be waging a battle against subjectivism, which they identify with attempts to judge the Word of God by human reason and emotion. Their critics, meanwhile, argue that evangelicals impose a particular tradition upon scripture which actually prevents it from speaking with its own voice. The second half of the chapter contains a discussion of the tension created for evangelicals by the fundamentalist reliance on reason and evidences, since evangelicals retain a very personal understanding of the way in which God speaks to them. It is argued that despite the influence of fundamentalist ways of thinking, evangelicalism does not become a wholly dry or formal religion. The fundamentalist influence is most powerful in apologetics for the faith, and in the doctrine and interpretation of scripture.

The last three chapters consider two potential alternatives to fundamentalist notions of biblical truth: from the Dutch neo-Calvinist philosophy, and from phenomenological hermeneutics. Evangelicals have accepted influence from both of these areas, and have as a result been encouraged to recognize the role of their personal presuppositions in interpreting scripture. Neo-Calvinism advances the theory that all views of the world stem from basic presuppositions which are religious in nature, be they theistic or anti-theistic. Hermeneutical philosophy emphasizes the cultural forces at work in both the writers and interpreters of biblical texts. The Dutch influence is the most significant. It has given rise to a branch of evangelical thought which challenges mainstream evangelicalism and its fundamentalist assumptions, but which has received minimal attention from critics of evangelicalism and fundamentalism. However, where neo-Calvinism and fundamentalist evangelicalism meet, I conclude that fundamentalist patterns of thought do usually prevail. I further suggest that hermeneutical philosophy has not significantly tempered a fundamentalist disposition. In so far as evangelicals resist modifying their concepts of biblical truth and authority, fundamentalist assumptions remain intact.

A Note on Terminology

For the most part Barr's (1980*a*: 67) critique describes a broad cross-section of evangelicalism that is distinct from separatist and dispensationalist fundamentalism, and is fundamentalist in its '*ideology*'. This ideology has pervaded conservative evangelicalism and renders ineffectual many attempts by evangelicals to distance themselves from fundamentalism. Barr preserves the term 'evangelical' for a position unspoilt by fundamentalist patterns of thought. I use the term 'evangelical' where Barr would usually use 'fundamentalist',[10] while acknowledging that twentieth-century evangelicalism has been affected by the fundamentalist phenomenon. I maintain that a predominant feature of much contemporary evangelicalism is a fundamentalist mentality.

I will employ the term 'fundamentalist' in three main ways, each of which should be clear from the context. I will use it when referring to the fundamentalist mentality which prevails in contemporary evangelicalism. Secondly, I will retain the label 'fundamentalist' for those involved in the controversies with 'modernism' in the 1920s. Thirdly, I will call 'fundamentalist' particular separatist groups who regard themselves as fundamentalist (and I do not, by virtue of this label, judge that self-proclaimed fundamentalists lack the advantages of a personal, evangelical faith). In this third sense, 'fundamentalist' is as specific a designation as are the terms 'new evangelical', 'dispensationalist', 'neo-Calvinist', 'reconstructionist', and other names of

[10] However, occasionally I use the term 'fundamentalist' as Barr and other critics do when engaging with their critiques, as required by the context.

particular movements and groups within the broad fundamentalist–evangelical spectrum. Such terms will be used as the adherents to the respective positions would use them, and the terminology will develop with the book as each position is described.

1

The Relation of Fundamentalism to Evangelicalism: A Historical Approach

> We here and now move that a new word be adopted to describe the men among us who insist that the landmarks shall not be removed . . . We suggest that those who still cling to the great fundamentals and who mean to do battle royal for the fundamentals shall be called 'Fundamentalists'.[1]

Fundamentalists became named and self-conscious as such in the 1920s. This was the decade of the fundamentalist–modernist controversies in the American denominations, and of the anti-evolution crusade which culminated in the infamous Scopes Trial of 1925. The fundamentalism of the 1920s was a complicated coalition. It is best understood by considering not only its activism in that decade but also its roots which go back into the eighteenth and nineteenth centuries.

The following account traces the development of fundamentalism and its effects upon later movements. The influences which shaped the thought of the first fundamentalists throw light on the attitudes of their various fundamentalist and evangelical heirs. Fundamentalism is commonly assumed to be an emotional and uneducated position. However, students of fundamentalism rejected this verdict long ago. As the story of fundamentalism is told in this chapter, so is the story of how it has been seen by others. Throughout the century, interpretations of fundamentalism have been revised at each new period of its strength, decline, and re-emergence. Scholars have progressed from regarding it as a culturally backward, anti-intellectual phenomenon driven by psychological and economic forces, to crediting it with theological motivation and attributing to it an intellectual heritage in eighteenth-century philosophy.

Ever since the fundamentalist episode of the 1920s evangelicals

[1] Curtis Lee Laws, 'Convention Side Lights', *Watchman-Examiner*, 1 July 1920, p. 834.

have grappled with the problem of terminology. We discover in the following pages a multitude of positive and negative reactions to the term 'fundamentalism'. We also discover that many distinct fundamentalist and evangelical groups, despite their diversity, share a sense of identity. They perceive their task as being to defend the faith by defending the authority of the Bible. While they vary somewhat in their notions of biblical truth and authority they are in more agreement than their sometimes acrimonious debates and schisms would suggest.

1.1. The Roots of Fundamentalism

The fundamentalism of the 1920s was an awkward coalition of diverse movements and groups who represented a range of theological opinion. The remarkable nature of the coalition may be illustrated by the strange situation in which J. Gresham Machen (1881–1937) found himself. Machen was the professor of New Testament at Princeton Theological Seminary and was credited as the greatest intellectual spokesman for fundamentalism. He found an unconventional set of allies in William Jennings Bryan, who became the leading anti-evolutionist crusader, James M. Gray, dean of the dispensationalist Moody Bible Institute, and the popular revivalist, Billy Sunday. Machen was invited to speak at the premillennialist Winona Lake Bible Conference. He defended Billy Sunday when the evangelist spoke at Princeton in 1915. In the 1920s Gray intimated that Machen should succeed him at the Moody Institute, while Bryan's admirers hoped that he might accept the presidency of the Bryan Memorial University (Marsden 1980: 138). Machen suffered these associations and the 'distasteful' term 'fundamentalism' for the sake of the battle at hand:

> Do you suppose, gentlemen, that I do not detect faults in many popular defenders of supernatural Christianity? Do you suppose that I do not regret my being called, by a term that I greatly dislike, a 'Fundamentalist'? Most certainly I do. But in the presence of a great common foe, I have little time to be attacking my brethren who stand with me in defense of the Word of God. I must continue to support an unpopular cause. (Machen in 1926, quoted in Stonehouse 1954: 337–8)

The foe was theological modernism.

In the 1960s Paul Carter wrote a revised assessment of fundamentalism, describing it as a theological rather than sociological phenomenon. He concluded that 'the movement [was] a defense, under fire, of an existing orthodoxy' (1968: 214 n. 81). Around the same time, Ernest Sandeen was researching the theological roots of fundamentalism. Unlike Carter, Sandeen emphasized the innovative nature of fundamentalism. In *The Roots of Fundamentalism* (1970) and related writings, Sandeen traced its origins to the Anglo-American millenarian movement of the nineteenth century. He went so far as to argue that fundamentalism was 'only the millenarian movement renamed' (1970*a*: 59), albeit in alliance with 'Princeton-oriented Calvinists' (1967: 82).

Both positions are oversimplifications. George Marsden establishes that the fundamentalist coalition of the 1920s comprised both denominational traditionalists and advocates of theologically innovative doctrines (1980: 102). Sandeen uncovered only one substantial root to fundamentalism. Marsden suggests that had Sandeen begun by 'examining the tree itself', fundamentalism from the 1920s onwards, 'he would have been forced to recognize that Fundamentalism was too complex a movement to be defined largely in terms of only one of its predecessors' (Marsden 1971: 144–5).[2] Marsden argues that one of the most obvious and important roots was the evangelical tradition in nineteenth-century England and America. Of particular relevance was the revivalist heritage (Marsden 1980: 43–8, 223–5). This heritage was evident in the biblicist and primitivist impulse in fundamentalism, in the drive for personal and mass evangelism, and in the combined stress upon emotion, personal commitment to Christ, and purity of doctrine.

Of the innovative strands within fundamentalism the most significant were the holiness and millenarian movements. They contributed distinct theological emphases, notably on holy living and

[2] Bradley Longfield deals a further blow to Sandeen's thesis that fundamentalism was the product of a union between millenarianism and Princeton theology. He shows that Charles Erdman and Robert Speer, millenarians on the Princeton Faculty, promoted peace and compromise, while J. Gresham Machen, Clarence E. Macartney, and William Jennings Bryan, none of them premillennialist, led the fundamentalist cause among the Presbyterians (1991: 220). Of the three, only Machen came to separate from the Presbyterian Church. Moreover, one of the strongest dispensationalists within the Northern Presbyterian Church, Donald G. Barnhouse, pastor of Tenth Presbyterian Church in Philadelphia, remained within the denomination.

on premillennial expectations of the Second Coming. More significantly, they provided an organizational structure for fundamentalism in the form of conferences and Bible institutes. These organs were established initially for the propagation of premillennialist ideas, but they came to embrace the theology of the holiness movement and later of the wider fundamentalist movement. The Bible institutes became headquarters for the fundamentalist effort, and were especially significant after the 1920s when many fundamentalists separated from the denominations (Cole [1931] 1963: 42–5, 246–51; Sandeen 1970*b*: 181–3, 241; Carpenter 1980: 66–8).

The millenarian and holiness movements developed through interaction between British and American evangelicals in the nineteenth century.[3] Millenarian interest revived in Britain after the French Revolution, and was pursued in the question of the restoration of the Jews. The London Society for Promoting Christianity Amongst Jews was founded early in the nineteenth century and attracted both Dissenters and evangelicals within the Church of England. In the 1810s and 1820s groups of evangelicals, some with secessionist tendencies, were meeting in homes around Britain to study unfulfilled prophecies. This period of millennial speculation contributed to a fragmentation of English evangelicalism in the late 1820s, remnants of which are still apparent today (G. L. Carter 1990; Oliver 1978: 68–98). In 1826 Edward Irving founded the London-based Society for the Investigation of Prophecy. Henry Drummond, a Tory MP, invited this group to meet at his Surrey home. Thus began the Albury Prophetic Conferences, which were held annually between 1826 and 1830. William Wilberforce and Thomas Chalmers declined Drummond's invitation to the Albury Conference. The moderate journal *The Christian Observer* recoiled at the appearance of charismatic gifts. The Moderate evangelicals, represented by Wilberforce, Hannah More, and Charles Simeon, feared enthusiasm and promoted moral and social reform and missionary endeavours. They increasingly distanced themselves from those gripped by millennial fervour.

Lady Powerscourt attended the first Albury meeting and was encouraged by Irving and Drummond to convene similar confer-

[3] For information on British millenarianism I am grateful to Grayson L. Carter. For a detailed account see his doctoral thesis, 'Evangelical Seceders from the Church of England, c. 1800–1850' (1990).

ences on her estate in Ireland. The Powerscourt Conferences began in 1827. John Nelson Darby (1800–82) exercised a powerful influence over these conferences, and he there developed his distinctive system of interpreting scripture within a framework of seven ages or dispensations. Darby resigned from his curacy in 1828, left the Church of Ireland and began holding 'Separatist' gatherings in Dublin. Soon he was bringing his views and practices to England. He met Francis Newman (John Henry Newman's younger brother) when Newman was private tutor in the home of Darby's brother-in-law, Edward Pennefather. On Newman's invitation, Darby came to Oxford in 1830. He gained a following there, and was encouraged by Benjamin Wiles Newton to visit Plymouth where believers were meeting in a fashion similar to the Dublin Brethren. Darby thus became involved in founding the Plymouth Brethren.[4]

There was a further millenarian revival in the second half of the century in Britain which greatly affected the United States (Sandeen 1970*b*: 145). Conferences were held at Mildmay Park in 1878, 1879, and 1886, organized by Revd William Pennefather, which coincided with the first of the big American prophetic conferences. The Niagara Conference was the mother of the American conferences, known during its years as the Believers' Meeting for Bible Study (Sandeen 1970*b*: 132). The conference was founded in 1878 by a group of men associated with the millenarian periodical, *Waymarks in the Wilderness*. The form of premillennialism most widely represented at this and other American conferences was Darby's dispensational premillennialism.

Dispensationalism was more successful in the United States than in Britain.[5] It received widest endorsement among Calvinists,

[4] The Brethren movement has no single source. Important figures in its founding were Anthony Norris Groves, Henry Craik, and George Müller. The movement had centres in Plymouth and Bristol. Darby had connections with the Plymouth group, which split over his doctrine of separation in 1845. This division occasioned the permanent divide between Exclusive and Open Brethren (G. L. Carter 1990: 272–321; Fiedler 1994: 169–72).

[5] Darby's system placed all the events prophesied in Revelation in the future. In Britain the historicist approach of Henry Gratten Guinness, which interpreted Revelation in the light of historical events, modified Darby's influence even after the publication of the *Scofield Reference Bible* in 1909 (Bebbington 1988: 108–9). *The Scofield Bible* became the standard text to be used by millions of fundamentalist dispensationalists this century. It defines a dispensation as 'a period of time during which man is tested in respect of obedience to some *specific* revelation of the will of God' (5 n. 4), and lists the dispensations as Innocence (Gen. 1: 28); Conscience (Gen. 3: 23); Human Government (Gen. 8: 20); Promise (Gen. 12: 1); Law

perhaps because of its emphasis upon God's sovereignty and will in determining the course of history. However, holiness teachings prepared the way for its wider acceptance. The holiness doctrine accorded with dispensationalism's view of the church age as the age of the Spirit (Marsden 1980: 72). Holiness–dispensationalist co-operation was a crucial factor in the emergence of fundamentalism. It was facilitated by the development of non-Methodist holiness teaching (Bebbington 1989: 164–5). The holiness concept of 'entire sanctification' had derived from revivalism and Wesleyan Methodism and was an obstacle to Calvinists. By the end of the century the alternative Keswick doctrine of repeated consecrations or fillings with the Holy Spirit became dominant.

It was the revivalist Dwight L. Moody (1837–99) who was largely responsible for bringing together holiness advocates and premillennial dispensationalists. This he did through his Northfield Conferences, founded in 1880. These conferences were predominantly informed by the holiness teaching Moody had received in England from the Keswick Movement. Through having conducted revivals in Britain in the early 1880s he was able to invite British speakers, such as F. B. Meyer, G. Campbell Morgan, and J. E. K. Studd. However, many of the speakers were premillennialists, including James H. Brookes from St Louis who was a central figure in the Niagara Conference. According to Sandeen (1970*b*: 175), by 1886 premillennialist leaders had virtually taken over the conference.

Premillennialist and holiness movements became so closely associated that many prominent leaders such as A. J. Gordon, A. T. Pierson, Charles G. Trumbull, editor of *The Sunday School Times* who converted to Keswick in 1910, and C. I. Scofield, editor of the *Scofield Reference Bible*, identified with both. An American Keswick movement was founded in 1913 (Sandeen 1970*b*: 180). Among its leaders was W. H. Griffith Thomas, an English Anglican then teaching at Wycliffe College, Toronto.

(Exod. 19: 18); Grace (John 1: 17); Kingdom (Eph. 1: 10). According to this schema, the present age is under the dispensation of Grace which began with the death and resurrection of Christ, with the surprising result that Christ's teachings are relegated to the dispensation of law. The *New Scofield Bible* (1967, compiled by a series of editors) gave Christ's teachings greater prominence. Kathleen Boone regards this as an apologetical move enabling the authority of Christ to be invoked in defence of inerrancy (1989: 80). For an account of dispensationalist teaching see Weber (1987: 16–24) and Marsden (1980: 51–4).

The prophetic and Bible conferences brought together an increasing variety of conservatives who were unified in their effort to resist liberalizing theological and social trends. Most surprising was the alliance with conservative scholars. The Princeton professors were not comfortable with dispensationalist and holiness teachings, yet they spoke at conferences in the 1890s. A. A. Hodge (1823–86) invited A. T. Pierson to special services at Princeton. William Erdman, a leading dispensationalist, sent his son Charles to Princeton, where he became professor of practical theology. Benjamin Warfield (1851–1921) did attack holiness teaching when the Keswick Conferences came to Princeton from 1916 to 1918. However, by 1919 the controversy with modernism pre-empted other concerns, and conservatives of all sorts closed ranks (Marsden 1980: 98–9).

1.2. Pre-Fundamentalist Developments

A list of five fundamentals of the faith and a set of pamphlets called *The Fundamentals* have been judged, somewhat mistakenly, to capture the essence of 1920s fundamentalism. Both existed before any formal fundamentalist coalition had been organized.

1.2.1. *The Five Points of Fundamentalism*

Fundamentalists were unified by the concern to defend the faith but they remained doctrinally diverse. The so-called 'five points of fundamentalism' did not provide a blueprint for fundamentalists as many scholars have assumed. The first historian of fundamentalism, Stewart G. Cole ([1931] 1963: 34), emphasized the role of the conferences in the initial stages of fundamentalism, and wrongly attributed the five points of fundamentalism to the 1895 Niagara Conference. His mistake was repeated by subsequent historians (Handy 1954: 390; Gasper 1963: 11; P. Carter 1968: 188), and not corrected until exposed by Sandeen (1970*b*: pp. xiv–xv). Sandeen points out that the Niagara Conference of 1895 passed a fourteen-point declaration, and that the only five-point declaration which did influence the fundamentalist movement was that adopted by the Presbyterian General Assembly in 1910, and reaffirmed in 1916 and 1923.[6] The Presbyterian five points were: the inerrancy of scripture; the Virgin Birth of Christ; his substitutionary atonement; his bodily resurrection; the authenticity of the miracles.

Norman Furniss, who provided the second major historical account of the fundamentalist movement, regarded the five points as the '*sine qua non* of fundamentalism' (1954: 13). Sandeen, however, correctly perceived that fundamentalists had no preference for five over above another number of articles (1970*b*: pp. xiv–xv). There was no sense of there being such a thing as the five points of fundamentalism until the 1920s (Marsden 1980: 117), and then the particular points differed from those given by the Presbyterian Church. In the more popularly known version of the 1920s, premillennialism replaced the authenticity of miracles. The deity of Christ was listed second and his resurrection and second coming were combined in the fifth point (ibid. 117, 262 n. 30). Neither list was intended as a statement of the essentials of Christianity so much as a reaffirmation of doctrines that were under attack at the time.

1.2.2. *The Fundamentals*

Furniss (1954: 12–13) further added to the confusion by stating that *The Fundamentals* 'expatiated on the "Five Points"' so that the 'conservatives' creed was now reduced to clear essentials'. *The Fundamentals* were the most significant fruit of pre-war conservative co-operation. They were a set of twelve volumes published from Chicago probably between 1909 and 1915. Copies were sent to 'every pastor, evangelist, missionary, theological professor, theological student, Sunday school superintendent, Y.M.C.A. and Y.W.C.A. secretary in the English speaking world' of whom the addresses could be obtained (Foreword, vol. i). The expense was borne by two Christian laymen, Milton and Lyman Stewart, oil tycoons from California. The Stewarts were premillennialists, as was A. C. Dixon, who was selected to edit the series. However, premillennialist elements and other potentially divisive issues were kept to a minimum in the publications (Sandeen 1970*b*: 201, 205–

[6] Cole ([1931] 1963: 98–9) in fact thought that the five points were adopted both at Niagara and at the 1910 General Assembly.

6; Marsden 1980: 119). The contributors—scholars, missionaries, and clergymen—overlooked their differences for the sake of presenting a 'new statement of the fundamentals of Christianity' (Forewords, vols. i and ii).

The volumes did not expound a fundamentalist creed, nor present anything so systematic as five-point fundamentalism. About a third of the articles dealt with scripture, another third concerned traditional doctrines, and the rest comprised attacks on Darwinism, refutations of particular cults, writings on missions, and personal testimonies. The crucial issue was perceived, in George Marsden's (1980: 120) words, as that of 'the authority of God in Scripture in relation to the authority of modern science, particularly science in the form of higher criticism of Scripture'. Some of the contributors were entirely anti-critical, such as Franklin Johnson, who accepted no middle ground between higher criticism and the doctrine of inspiration (e.g. F. Johnson n.d.: ii. 67–8). Anti-critical views were adopted not only by populist writers but also by more learned scholars such as F. Bettex, an emeritus professor from Stuttgart, and David Heagle, a Ph.D. who taught at Ewing College, Illinois. A quarter of the authors were British, including James Orr, Robert Anderson, and W. H. Griffith Thomas. They rejected only the naturalistic assumptions of higher criticism, a stance shared by the Canadian Dyson Hague. Most contributors rejected the idea that criticism could be neutral (Noll 1986: 41). A typical proposal was that the 'special divine authority' of scripture 'be taken into account by the linguistic and historical critic' (Caven n.d.: iv. 55). They cast aspersions on the 'assured results' of higher criticism (Johnson n.d.: ii. 49; Anderson n.d.: ii. 70), as did later evangelicals who questioned the supposed objectivity of historical criticism (cf. Manley 1926: 20; Packer 1958*a*: 141).[7]

The beginnings of fundamentalism are often traced to these publications (e.g. Cole [1931] 1963: 53, 229; Furniss 1954: 13; Handy 1954: 390–1; Gasper 1963: 12; Packer 1958*a*: 28; S. Bruce 1987: 179), but the association can be misleading. The volumes did not have a huge impact, and were moderate in style and irenic in intention. They took on significance in retrospect, as a symbol for fundamentalists in the 1920s of conservative unity and opposition

[7] Barr (1977: 141) notes that this phrase 'has always excited the wrath of conservatives'.

to modernism (Sandeen 1970*b*: 206–7; Marsden 1980: 119). However, less sympathetic historians have not regarded *The Fundamentals* as temperate in nature. Cole ([1931] 1963: 52–3, 60–1) perceived them as aggressive and as a vehicle for the self-exaltation of the editors. Handy (1954: 390, 391) judged that they 'yielded no ground at all to critical scholars', and that 'their anti-evolution, anti-liberal, anti-social-gospel tone . . . provided a rallying point for the conservatively inclined, and won many of them to an extreme position'. Carter (1968: 194) gave a more balanced assessment: 'in sharp contrast to the anxieties and angers of the radical right of a later day, the tone of these essays is in general quite as much marked by love for God and man as it is by hate for the devil and Modernists'.

The Fundamentals, it is fair to say, reflected a strong stand against the new trends of higher criticism and evolutionary thought but did not display any of the aggression against modernists in the churches that marked the fundamentalism of the 1920s. For this reason many self-designated evangelicals, even in Britain, are happy to be associated with *The Fundamentals*, but not with the subsequent fundamentalism (e.g. D. Johnson 1955; Stott 1956: 1–2; Packer 1958*a*: 29–40). Full-fledged fundamentalism developed after World War I and was markedly more militant. Its belligerence signalled the divergence of fundamentalism from pre-war evangelicalism (Marsden 1980: 141) and occasioned disparity between British and American evangelicals.

1.3. The First Fundamentalist Organizations

The war precipitated a sense of cultural crisis. Groups who were already co-operating in their defence of the Bible and traditional doctrines came together with new urgency. William Bell Riley (1861–1947), a premillennialist Baptist, emerged as the leader of militant fundamentalism. In 1919 he founded 'the first explicitly fundamentalist organization' (Marsden 1980: 157–8), the interdenominational World's Christian Fundamentals Association (WCFA). Conservatism gained importance over denominational identity. Most of those connected with WCFA were premillennialists, although, as Cole argued, WCFA shifted its emphasis from premillennialism to Christian essentials to antievolutionism, to keep abreast with popular themes (Cole [1931] 1963: 302).

At the first WCFA meeting there seems to have been a reference to the concern among the Baptists over a new periodical called the *Baptist.* The periodical had been established at the 1919 Northern Baptist convention in order to counteract the conservative, independently owned *Watchman-Examiner.* It was the proposal for this periodical which prompted Curtis Lee Laws to call the pre-convention conference in 1920 where he introduced the term 'fundamentalist'.[8] However, WCFA was not fully representative of all who made a stand for the fundamentals. Some denominational conservatives, Laws included, did not co-operate with Riley's group (Marsden 1980: 168–9). Laws adhered neither to premillennialism nor to the doctrine of biblical inerrancy, both of which were in the creed of WCFA. He founded the National Federation of Fundamentalists of the Northern Baptists.

The militancy of WCFA undermined its effectiveness. It was the only all-inclusive fellowship yet it could not keep its competing factions together (Cole [1931] 1963: 325). Despite setting up five committees (Sandeen 1970*b*: 243–47), WCFA produced little fruit and lost momentum in the later 1920s. Riley resigned in 1930 and was succeeded by Paul Rood, but the Association had run its course. The individualism of the leaders was the primary disintegrating force. Its speakers continued to fight in their denominations but gave less momentum to WCFA.

1.4. The Fundamentalist Offensive

At the time of their greatest strength, the early 1920s, fundamentalists operated both denominationally and interdenominationally. They fought on two fronts: against liberalism in the denominations and Darwinism in schools (Marsden 1980: 164–95).

1.4.1. *The Fundamentalist–Modernist Controversies*

The fundamentalist–modernist controversies were denominational disputes. They were fiercest in the Northern Presbyterian

[8] See the quotation with which this chapter begins.

and Northern Baptist denominations, though parallel disputes broke out in other churches. Marsden (ibid. 164–5) suggests that in these denominations, modernists were matched by conservatives of equal strength. Elsewhere liberals had gained virtual control, as in Congregationalism, or else conservatives were so strong that no protracted controversy was possible, as in the Southern churches.

It is probable, moreover, that fundamentalist zeal was most likely to develop among Presbyterian and Baptist conservatives, who displayed greater concern for doctrinal purity than did most other conservatives.[9] Their Calvinist heritage committed them to a propositional notion of truth, and it was among Calvinists in particular that doctrines of inerrancy were established. The Presbyterian doctrine, formalized by B. B. Warfield and A. A. Hodge at Princeton Seminary, became the most influential. Earlier in the nineteenth century Robert Haldane from Scotland and Alexander Carson from Ulster developed arguments in defence of an error-free Bible. Both were Baptists, though Haldane had been Church of Scotland.[10] Doctrines of inerrancy were well suited to the dispensationalist scheme, which received its strongest support from Presbyterians and Calvinist Baptists (Sandeen 1970*b*: 163–4; Marsden 1980: 46), and which relied upon accurate correspondence between biblical statements and the factual state of affairs.

A landmark in the fundamentalist–modernist controversies was Harold Emerson Fosdick's sermon of 1922 called 'Shall the Fundamentalists Win?'. This sermon particularly affected Baptist and Presbyterian conservatives because Fosdick was a Baptist serving as associate pastor in the First Presbyterian Church of New York. Baptist conservatives were already divided by 1922 and so made no unified response. Moderate conservatives such as Curtis Lee Laws and J. C. Massee would not support Riley's insistence that doctrinal standards be imposed upon Baptists. Militants followed Riley in founding the ultra-conservative Baptist Bible Union, to

[9] There had been discord between conservative and moderate factions of the Northern Presbyterian Church in recent decades as evidenced not only by the heresy trials of the 1890s against Charles A. Briggs, Henry Preserved Smith, and Arthur Cushman McGiffert (Ahlstrom 1972: 812–16; Marsden 1980: 117), but also by the formulation of the five points in 1910 and the presentation to the church by 150 clergy of a 'Back to the Fundamentals' statement in 1915 (Cole [1931] 1963: 100).

[10] See s. 3.3 below.

rival Laws's group (Marsden 1980: 172). Presbyterian conservatives, by contrast, rallied in defence against Fosdick's sermon. Clarence E. Macartney responded with a sermon asking 'Shall Unbelief Win?', in which he argued that Fosdick's naturalistic understanding of Christianity differed from the traditional faith. He also led the Philadelphia Presbytery in a failed attempt to persuade the 1922 General Assembly to take action against the New York preacher (Beale 1986: 154; Marsden 1980: 173).

As Macartney's sermon indicates, fundamentalists portrayed their fight with modernism as a battle between two rival versions of religion. J. Gresham Machen, in *Christianity and Liberalism* (1923), presented liberalism as a new religion and something other than Christianity. Shailer Mathews, of the Chicago Divinity School, wrote *The Faith of Modernism* (1924) clearly in response to Machen. This clash of religious systems was brought to the general public in the Fundamentalist–Modernist Debates staged in New York in 1923–4. Charles Francis Potter, a Unitarian, challenged John Roach Straton to a debate after Straton had held a series of fundamentalist rallies in his church. Straton was pastor of Calvary Baptist Church in New York City, and was known as the 'fundamentalist Pope'. The sessions which followed were the most widely publicized events of the conflict between fundamentalists and modernists prior to the Scopes Trial. The judges' opinion was more favourable towards Straton.[11]

In early 1925 fundamentalists looked set to win major victories in their denominations, but disunity blighted their efforts. Militant fundamentalists, such as Macartney (Presbyterian) and Riley (Baptist), wanted to separate from the denominations, while more moderate conservatives, such as Charles Erdman (Presbyterian) and J. C. Massee (Baptist), were losing their will to fight and now wanted peace and co-operation. The main body of fundamentalist adherents hesitated to follow the radicals, and the movement was left in a shambles. By late 1925 there was a desire among Northern Baptist liberals and fundamentalists to have done with the

[11] There were to be five debates in all, on the subjects: The Battle over the Bible; Evolution versus Creation; The Virgin Birth—Fact or Fiction?; Was Christ both God and Man?; and Utopia—By Man's Effort or Christ's Return? It seems that the fifth did not happen. Transcripts of the other four have been republished under the title *Fundamentalist Versus Modernist* (Carpenter 1988). Straton won the second and fourth debate unanimously. Potter won the first and third, but in a split vote.

controversy. Their Convention's magazine, the *Baptist*, began to print articles by fundamentalists, and fundamentalists declared in *Watchman-Examiner* that they had failed to ally themselves with the rank-and-file conservatives in the denomination (no. 15, 1927: 1639, cited in Furniss 1954: 118).

Dispute lingered on among the Presbyterians, and moved to Princeton Seminary. There Machen criticized Erdman's tolerance of liberals (Stonehouse 1954: 371–91; Marsden 1980: 183; Longfield 1991: 131–2). Machen eventually left Princeton in 1929, together with the Old Testament scholars Robert Dick Wilson and Oswald T. Allis, and the young professor of apologetics Cornelius Van Til. That year they founded Westminster Theological Seminary in Philadelphia. Machen was expelled from the Northern Presbyterian Church in 1936 over an argument concerning foreign missions. He formed the Presbyterian Church in America, taking with him J. Oliver Buswell, then president of Wheaton College, and Carl McIntire, who was to become a leading separatist fundamentalist in the 1940s. This church split again after Machen's death in 1937, when McIntire founded the Bible Presbyterian Church. The Westminster faculty suffered division in the same year. Some of its members joined McIntire in founding Faith Theological Seminary, also in Philadelphia.[12]

1.4.2. *The Crusade Against Evolution*

While battle raged in the denominations, momentum was gathering in the crusade against evolution. William Jennings Bryan adopted and widely publicized the anti-Darwinian cause. The crusade swept through the south and became identified in people's minds with fundamentalism. Traditional religion in the south readily allied itself with fundamentalism, and southern regions provided new, rural constituencies for the fundamentalist movement (Marsden 1980: 170).

Fundamentalism thus came to be seen as a southern, rural, anti-

[12] Princeton graduates Allan A. MacRae, Paul Woolley, R. B. Kuiper, and Ned Stonehouse joined the Westminster faculty. Through Van Til, Kuiper, and Stonehouse, Dutch ideas at variance with those of Old Princeton came to dominate the Seminary, resulting in the 1937 schism. Faith Theological Seminary itself suffered divisions when Covenant Theological Seminary was founded in 1955 in St Louis, and Biblical School of Theology in 1971 in Hatfield, Penn. See s. 7.3 below.

intellectual, and anti-scientific phenomenon. This was a powerful but distorting image. Fundamentalism developed principally in the north, where liberalism was most in evidence, and was defended as an intellectual and scientific position. Some militant figures in the denominations were involved in the anti-evolution crusade, including Riley, Straton, and the one Southern Baptist fundamentalist of the era, J. Frank Norris. Yet anti-evolution was not itself a key issue in the denominational controversies, and was usually absent from lists of fundamental doctrines (Marsden 1980: 169–70). Nor did it receive support from scholars associated with the fundamentalist movement. Warfield had absorbed biological evolution into his understanding of divine providence ([1911*a*] [1915]).[13] Machen would not treat evolution as a major issue, and refused Bryan's request for assistance at the Scopes Trial (Longfield 1991: 70, 154; Stonehouse 1954: 401–2).

The Scopes Trial marked the peak of the anti-evolution crusade. In 1925 in Dayton, Tennessee, the State of Tennessee prosecuted the schoolteacher John Scopes for teaching evolution. Clarence Darrow, a renowned lawyer from New York City, went down to Dayton to defend Scopes. He took with him scientists and theologians, many, including Shailer Mathews, from the University of Chicago. Bryan, 'the personification of the agrarian myth himself' (Marsden 1980: 185), was the prosecuting lawyer.

Bryan won the trial but it was a pyrrhic victory. Darrow made the provocative move of calling Bryan as a witness for the defence (Scopes Trial Transcript, p. 734). It became apparent that Bryan could not cite any serious scientist in support of his suppositions about the age of the earth, and in fact did not himself have thoughts on its possible dating (pp. 774–5, 783–7). He did not think that the Bible committed him to a literal six-day creation but he

[13] See also Warfield's 'Lectures on Anthropology' (1888), and his review of James Orr's *God's Image in Man* (*Princeton Theological Review*, 4 (1906)). In these writings David Livingstone (1987: 118–20) finds an increasing acceptance of evolutionary theory. While Warfield was stricter than Orr on inerrancy (see ss. 2.2.3 and 4.2 below), he did not follow Orr in asserting the entirely supernatural origin of Adam—body and soul. His disagreement with Orr was philosophical and scientific and did not centre on the question of biblical reliability. Warfield accepted the physical evolution of man but insisted that God oversaw the whole process and provided the human soul by miraculous intervention. Orr hoped for some system which would synthesize evolution and special creation, but he insisted that body and soul were so unified in man that one could not originate distinct from the other. See Orr's Stone Lectures, *God's Image in Man* (1905), esp. 46–53, 151–4.

refused to give answers on issues over which scripture is silent. He believed that the defence had 'no other purpose than ridiculing every person who believes in the Bible' (p. 775). Darrow adopted an increasingly derisory tone, as did unsympathetic journalists who reported the spectacle. The fundamentalist position was discredited in public opinion.

After 1925 the liberal versus fundamentalist situation came to be viewed as a high-brow versus low-brow, north–south, urban–rural dispute (Marsden 1980: 184–91). The northern press, who flocked to Dayton, found the Scopes Trial a delightful opportunity to ridicule southern religion and parade the progressive, open-minded attitudes of the north. H. L. Mencken wrote an anti-eulogy to Bryan, who died a few days after the close of the trial, describing him as motivated by a hatred for 'city men', whom he knew 'were laughing at him—if not at his baroque theology, then at least at his alpaca pantaloons'.[14]

1.4.3. *Perceptions of Early Fundamentalists*

The 'Menckenesque' image of fundamentalists as 'gaping primates of the upland valleys' (quoted in Marsden 1980: 187) was perpetuated in the early histories. The liberal opponents of fundamentalism in the 1920s regarded the issue between themselves and fundamentalists as 'not so much religious as due to different degrees of sympathy with the social and cultural forces of the day'.[15] Fundamentalism was interpreted as a culture-lag: as a form of resistance from rural-minded, semi-educated Christians to urbanization and immigration, and to threatening new ideas in theology and science. H. Richard Niebuhr's sociological account became normative, according to which fundamentalism was 'closely related to the conflict between rural and urban cultures in America' (1932: 527). Norman Furniss (1954: 29) reinterpreted Niebuhr's thesis in terms of the ignorant versus the educated: 'it was apparently ignorance of the meaning of modernism and evolution, ignorance then blanketing much of rural America, that brought about the attack, not antagonism toward the cities'.

[14] Mencken, *Prejudices: Fifth Series* (1926), quoted in Marsden (1980: 187).
[15] Mathews, *The Faith of Modernism* (1924), quoted in Marsden (1980: 185).

The first historian of fundamentalism, Stewart Cole (1931), gave more of a psychological than sociological interpretation of the movement. Cole was a scholar of liberal sympathies writing in the aftermath of the controversies. He concentrated on the power-struggles in the denominations, and contended that attempts to offer theological rather than psychological explanations had missed the point. Liberals, he said, had fallaciously examined the doctrinal deliverances of fundamentalists 'in the light of current principles of biblical and scholarly procedure', rather than using the 'psychological method to account for the real meaning of such values' ([1931] 1963: 328, 329). Cole's own understanding of fundamentalists was that:

> Psychologically, a fundamental became such for them, because it bore a vital relation to some desired outcome in a controversial situation . . . [E]ven *the* essentials were subject to change as the seasonal problems of discordant parties necessitated. The permanent factor in orthodoxy has not been a residuum of so-called revealed truth . . . but an insistence upon loyalty to such tangible forms of authority as would anchor a conventional believer in any clash of Christian interests, and the vigorous defense of such forms (as long as they gave promise of denominational control) in opposition to the more democratic ideals of religious liberals. (p. 324)

In the late 1960s more sympathetic portrayals of fundamentalism began to appear. Ernest Sandeen was one of the first historians to give a theological interpretation of fundamentalism. He was a graduate of Wheaton College and had been raised a fundamentalist Christian himself. From his acquaintance with fundamentalists he found 'incongruous' the 'standard descriptions of Fundamentalism as a political struggle to maintain the control of some denomination or as a battle to destroy evolution' (Sandeen 1971: 228). Meanwhile, Paul Carter reversed his verdict of the 1950s that fundamentalism was 'a spent or dying force' (1968: 180). Having to explain a resurgence of fundamentalism since the late 1950s, Carter suggested that

> the Fundamentalists may after all have been doing just what they thought they were doing: not merely defending a political ideology . . . not only defending an economic system . . . not simply defending the countryside against the city . . . not even essentially defending ignorance against intellect . . . but also, and chiefly, defending what

the Fundamentalists honestly believed was all that gave meaning to human life, 'the faith once delivered to the saints'. (p. 212)

Marsden generally resists anti-intellectual and sociological interpretations of fundamentalism, though he considers that 'rapid social and intellectual changes' spawned 'certain Fundamentalist attitudes in cultural backwaters' (1971: 149). For the most part Marsden suggests that fundamentalism derives from a religious heritage which puts great emphasis upon ideas. It was the basic assumption that ideas in themselves are important that generated the fundamentalist zeal to expose and denounce error. He reinterprets much of the presumed anti-intellectualism of fundamentalism and its apparent anti-scientific stance as a clash of intellectual traditions (1980: 7–8 and *passim*; 1984*c*). Rather than being 'indiscriminately anti-scientific', fundamentalists reflected a 'striking commitment to the assumptions and procedures of the first scientific revolution' (1984*c*: 97). Their 'confidence in objective scientific certainty' (1984*c*: 99), including the belief that the facts of both science and scripture could be readily apprehended, appeared anomalous to the more subjectivist outlook of much twentieth-century thought. Fundamentalists rejected modernism and Darwinism as unscientific, hypothetical systems and claimed that their own beliefs were consistent with true science.

The Scopes Trial is best understood as incorporating both popular and intellectual fundamentalist elements, as is implied in Harvey Cox's (1984: 56) interpretation:

The liberals granted that the Genesis account of Creation might be 'religiously valid' but insisted it was not science. For ordinary fundamentalists these liberals were wrong to 'deny the Bible' and that was that, while scholarly fundamentalists would add that the critics of the Scopes verdict were mistaken at a more basic philosophical level in accepting such a dichotomy between science and faith.

Bryan resisted claims that fundamentalists were pitching religion against science. He described the question at the Scopes Trial as being 'between religion and irreligion' (Trial transcript, p. 434). His more general contention, as he fought evolution, was that scripture was scientific whereas Darwinism was not.

Fundamentalism was an idea-based movement which was exercised over the importance of right belief. It attracted a mixture of intellectualist and anti-intellectual sentiment—for it equated right belief with the old faith which simple folk had not forsaken. It remained strongest where there existed a Calvinist heritage. Conservatives from traditions which put less emphasis upon dogma, notably those from Wesleyan traditions, were not usually fundamentalist. There was no official fundamentalist creed to identify the movement, and no set of doctrines to which all fundamentalists in the 1920s would have subscribed. The diverse parties in the fundamentalist coalition were unified by their concern to defend the faith, a task which they conceived primarily in terms of upholding the truth of scripture against the false theories of modernizers.

1.4.4. *Retreat and Rearmament*

> From 1920 to 1925 fundamentalism was a broad and nationally influential coalition of conservatives, but after 1925 it was composed of less flexible and more isolated minorities often retreating into separatism, where they could regroup their considerable forces.
>
> (Marsden 1980: 164)

Moderate fundamentalists of the early 1920s made peace with their denominations; militant fundamentalists withdrew. To the outside world they seemed to disappear. Cole reported that at the time of his writing, in 1931, most of the organizations were defunct (Cole [1931] 1963: 324–5). In fact fundamentalists were establishing their own cultural and institutional network which enabled them to survive and later to re-emerge as a significant force (Carpenter 1980). Thus, 'although the rest of American Protestantism floundered in the 1930s, fundamentalist groups, or those at least with fundamentalist sympathies, increased' (Marsden 1980: 194).

Fundamentalism was changing. Having failed to purge the leading denominations it now worked through local congregations and independent agencies, Bible schools, and mission organizations. Bible schools flourished more than ever before (Gasper 1963: 93–6). They became the 'regional and national coordinating centers for the movement' with Moody Bible Institute as 'the national giant' (Carpenter 1980: 67). Throughout the 1930s they organized conferences and developed publishing and broadcasting enterprises.

Radio gave new impetus to the movement. Charles E. Fuller first started broadcasting in 1925 in California, and had a network of stations by 1933. The title of his radio broadcast, the 'Old-Fashioned Revival Hour', has been fondly echoed in Jerry Falwell's 'Old-Time Gospel Hour'. From the late 1930s onwards there was an outburst of evangelistic effort from new organizations, including Youth for Christ, High School Christian Clubs, and Inter-Varsity Christian Fellowship (Gasper 1963: p. vi). Fundamentalist education was organized on primary, secondary, and tertiary levels (ibid. pp. vii, 93–115). Wheaton College near Chicago was the fastest growing liberal arts college for a while in the 1930s, and was educating future evangelical leaders such as Carl Henry and Billy Graham. J. Oliver Buswell, president of Wheaton from 1926 to 1940, concentrated on raising its academic standard and the college became known as the 'Harvard of the Bible Belt' (Carpenter 1980: 69).

Fundamentalism was also taking on a more southern feel. Headquarters were developed in the south around such leading figures as Bob Jones (1883–1968) and John R. Rice (1896–1980). New institutions of learning, including Bob Jones College (now Bob Jones University) and the dispensationalist stronghold Dallas Theological Seminary, became significant centres for branches of the movement.

Fundamentalism after 1925 took various forms. It remained within the denominations but was also a force of separation for those who formed their own denominations or independent churches. By the 1960s, few besides the separatists called themselves fundamentalist. There were also holiness, pentecostal, and other denominations which were not purely fundamentalist but which recognized an affinity with fundamentalism. Other traditions and immigrant churches, such as the Christian Reformed Church,[16] were affected by fundamentalist influences. Later in the century the Lutheran Church–Missouri Synod and the Southern Baptist Convention suffered their own fundamentalist schisms (Carpenter 1984: 275–7; Ellingsen 1988: 106, 114–15; Marsden 1980: 194–5). Thus, evangelical groups which had been little con-

[16] See Ch. 7.

nected with the fundamentalism of the early 1920s came to develop fundamentalist characteristics.

1.5. Separatist Fundamentalists and New Evangelicals

In the middle of the century a rift developed among second-generation fundamentalists. Carl McIntire, a central figure in the Presbyterian schisms, opposed any co-operation with non-fundamentalists. He founded the American Council of Christian Churches (ACCC) in 1941 as a fundamentalist alternative to the Federal Council of Churches. A number of fundamentalists who were unhappy with the militant and separatist direction that their movement had taken declined association with McIntire's organization. In 1942 they formed the more inclusive National Association of Evangelicals (NAE).[17]

Differences of opinion arose as to the usefulness of the term 'fundamentalism'. Harold J. Ockenga, the first president of the NAE, coined the term 'new evangelical' to describe the emergent moderate fundamentalists. Bernard Ramm was one of the new-evangelical theologians. He stated in the official journal of the NAE that 'fundamentalism' had been given an 'odious connotation' by men with 'much zeal, enthusiasm, and conviction, yet lacking in education or cultural breadth, and many times highly individualistic'. He continued: 'Many times they were dogmatic beyond evidence, or were intractable of disposition, or were obnoxiously anti-cultural, anti-scientific, and anti-educational. Hence the term came to mean one who was bigoted, an obscurantist, a fidest [*sic*], a fighter, and anti-intellectual.'[18] John F. Walvoord, president of Dallas Theological Seminary, represented a contrary line of thought. He sympathized with the new-evangelical cause and with the anxiety over the connotations of the term 'fundamentalism', but was disturbed that the name 'fundamentalist' had been dropped: 'In modern literature the term

[17] Louis Gasper (1963) was the first historian to give an account of developments in the organized fundamentalist movement since 1930, which he did with particular reference to these two distinct groups. Gasper gave a more sympathetic account of fundamentalism than did his predecessors, but his history is rarely cited.

[18] *United Evangelical Action*, 15 Mar. 1951, quoted in Gasper (1963: 151 n. 57).

fundamentalist carried with it clear, historical and theological meaning', whereas 'the term *evangelical* lends itself to manipulation by the modern liberal'.[19]

The new evangelicals did not see themselves as betraying a fundamentalist theology but as reversing the withdrawal from intellectual engagement and social responsibility. As Ockenga describes the situation, 'Younger fundamentalists . . . [w]hile remaining theologically committed to orthodoxy . . . were reaching for a new position ecclesiastically and sociologically' (Ockenga 1978: 38). In *The Uneasy Conscience of Modern Fundamentalism* (1947), Carl F. H. Henry delivered one of the earliest and most direct self-criticisms of the fundamentalist position. He still spoke of fundamentalism as 'our position' and assured his readers that

> the 'uneasy conscience' of which I write is not one troubled about the great Biblical verities, which I consider the only outlook capable of resolving our problems, but rather one distressed by the frequent failure to apply them effectively to crucial problems confronting the modern mind. It is application of, not a revolt against, fundamentals of the faith, for which I plead. (Preface)

Henry has since become the recognized representative of mainstream evangelical theology in America.[20]

Some separatists, including Bob Jones and John R. Rice, maintained connections with the NAE into the 1950s. In that decade Billy Graham's successful evangelistic campaigns were bringing fundamentalists back into the headlines. A significant factor in the widening gap between fundamentalists and new evangelicals was Graham's decision to co-operate with liberals and Roman Catholics in the work of evangelism (Carpenter 1984: 286). This lost him the support of the ACCC, of Bob Jones University where he had studied for a year, and of John Rice who edited the fundamentalist newspaper *The Sword of the Lord*. Meanwhile, the new evangelicals in consultation with Graham were organizing an alternative evangelical journal, *Christianity Today*, which was intended to be more intellectual and less oppositional than fundamentalist publications (Marsden 1987: 157–65). The first issue appeared in October 1956 under the editorship of Carl Henry. In the second year of the

[19] Walvoord, 'What's Right About Fundamentalism', *Eternity*, June 1957, quoted ibid. 120.

[20] See esp. Woodbridge (1993).

journal, Henry declared the 'modernist-fundamentalist conflict' dead (10 June 1957, pp. 3–6, 25).

The conflict between separatist fundamentalism and new evangelicalism, however, gained force. Edward J. Carnell, the most controversial of the new-evangelical theologians, used the 'liberal' mouthpiece *Christian Century* to berate fundamentalism for its cultic nature.[21] He attacked fundamentalists for their ungracious practice of limiting the true church to those who possessed true doctrine, and for their failure 'to connect their convictions with the wider problems of the general culture' (Carnell 1958: 142–3). He wanted to preserve 'orthodoxy' while escaping fundamentalism. John Rice interpreted Carnell as being 'very anxious to please modernists, unbelieving scientists, and the men of this world'.[22] He called *Christianity Today* moderate, meaning that it frequently published articles by modernists, 'although they claim to believe the Bible, they are buddy-buddies with the infidels who spit on the blood of Jesus, deny the inspiration of the Bible and the blood atonement, while they despise us fundamentalists'.[23]

Generally, separatist fundamentalists have attacked evangelicals less for theological deviance than for their principle of cooperation. Two professors of history at Bob Jones University have written histories of fundamentalism which provide an inside perspective on the breach within the movement. The first, George Dollar, described new evangelicalism as a 'new mood or attitude, not basically a theology' (1973: 192). He regarded it as a 'national menace' for spreading 'a permissive attitude on personal and ecclesiastical separation, a new interest in social issues, an openness to worldly standards, and a new toleration of the Ecumenical Movement' (ibid.). Dollar's successor, David Beale, describes the 'broad, non-militant, evangelical movement that emerged in the 1950s' as differing from fundamentalism 'primarily in practice rather than in theology' (1986: 10).

Yet fundamentalists in the United States do regard the issue between themselves and evangelicals as theological in so far as they take the principle of separation to be fundamental. Bob Jones (1978: 4) attacks those who 'claim to be fundamental but who do

[21] 'Post-Fundamentalist Faith', Summer 1959, and 'Orthodoxy: Cultic vs. Classical', Mar. 1960, repr. in Nash (1969: 45–7, 40–5 respectively).

[22] *The Sword of the Lord*, 30 Oct. 1959, quoted in Nelson (1987: 109).

[23] Rice, *Here Are More Questions . . .*, ii (1973), 147, cited in Boone (1989: 8).

not practice biblical principles in the alliances and fellowships and whose influence is, therefore, unscriptural'. He derisively labels them 'fudgymentalists': 'Scripture clearly enjoins two sorts of separation. . . (1) the ecclesiastical separation, which the "fudgymentalists" ignore; and (2) personal separation from sin and the world, which they usually profess to follow. Both are enjoined by Scripture, and no man has a right to profess to obey one but to ignore the other.' Contravention of the principle of separation is considered as grave as the rejection of more traditional fundamentals. Consequently, when Billy Graham accepted sponsorship from people who were not 'born again' and 'Bible-believing', Bob Jones questioned his very belief in the Bible as the Word of God:

> I cannot see how Billy Graham says he believes the Bible is the Word of God ([h]e knows that all we know about Jesus Christ, His virgin birth, His incarnation, His vicarious blood atonement, His bodily resurrection, and His coming again, is what is clearly taught in the Word of God.) [*sic*] and can be sponsored by preachers who do not believe these fundamentals and give to these preachers the same recognition that he gives to God's faithful, sacrificing servants who refuse to compromise. (1957: 4)

Separatist fundamentalism is still a very real presence in American life. Its Bible schools continue to advertise themselves with such slogans as 'Separated, Independent, Fundamental', '"Fundamental" and "Premillennial"', offering a 'Dynamic Biblicism' and 'a sound academic program built upon the old-time fundamentals of the Bible'.[24] Educational institutions which come under the new-evangelical umbrella have a very different feel and a higher academic profile. They include Fuller Theological Seminary in Pasadena, California; Northern Baptist Theological Seminary, Trinity Theological Seminary and Wheaton College, all in the Chicago area; and Gordon College and Gordon-Conwell Theological Seminary in Wenham, Massachusetts. Fuller Theological Seminary was founded by Charles E. Fuller in 1947 to represent the new-evangelical movement. Harold Ockenga was its first president, and Ed Carnell, Carl Henry, and Harold Lindsell were among its leading scholars.

New evangelicals occasioned a renaissance in fundamentalist

[24] Advertisements in *The Sword of the Lord*, June 1984.

scholarship, which separatists regarded as further evidence of their concern to impress liberals. Many acquired doctorates from reputable universities, notably Harvard.[25] With such theological training, they became increasingly concerned about the systematization and academic defence of doctrine. Their writings were more informed, but no less conservative than previous fundamentalist works. Initially there was no departure from the doctrine of inerrancy but only fresh attempts to bolster the doctrine with intellectual apologetics. Their scholarship came to shape evangelical debate in the United States, and a wide range of positions developed.

Being of fundamentalist descent, new evangelicals are partly responsible for fundamentalist aspects of contemporary evangelical apologetics, particularly the ongoing preoccupation with inerrancy. They now regard themselves simply as evangelicals, as Ockenga's article, 'From Fundamentalism, through New Evangelicalism, to Evangelicalism' (1978), indicates. They dominate the North-American evangelical scene and, as Marsden says, have 'attempted to speak or to set standards for evangelicals generally' (Marsden 1984*b*: p. xvi). As a result, the evangelical mainstream is conceived of primarily in new-evangelical terms. Hence Clark Pinnock, a Canadian Baptist, defines evangelicalism as 'the approach that arose out of the fundamentalist-modernist debates' of the 1920s, and describes evangelicals as 'postfundamentalists with a college education' (Pinnock 1990*a*: p. x).[26]

[25] R. L. Nelson (1982; 1987: 54–72) argues that Harvard was chosen by fundamentalists over against other institutions because it was historicist and did not go the way of neo-orthodoxy.

[26] The title 'post-fundamentalist' is sometimes used to denote evangelicals who are of a principally fundamentalist heritage. It differentiates them from 19th-c. evangelicals and from 20th-c. evangelical groups who have been relatively untouched by the fundamentalist–modernist controversies, notably Wesleyan holiness and pentecostal groups (Dayton 1976: 137–41; Nelson 1987: 8, 232 n. 3). Donald W. Dayton objects to evangelicalism being too strongly associated with Reformed traditions (Dayton 1976; Dayton 1991: 49–51, 245–51). New evangelicals such as Bernard Ramm, Harold J. Ockenga, and Harold Lindsell have tended to describe evangelical theology in exclusively Reformed terms (Ramm 1973; Carpenter 1984: 288). Dayton attempts to raise the profile of pentecostal and holiness strands within evangelicalism. Against Marsden's thesis he argues that 'modern post-fundamentalist evangelicalism is not rooted historically in the "evangelical mainstream" of the 19th century but in its most innovative and radically sectarian side' (Marsden and Dayton 1977: 208). Marsden responds, as he did to Sandeen regarding fundamentalism, that radical sectarian movements provide 'only one of many strands in the present-day evangelical heritage' (p. 211).

There now exists a broad interdenominational evangelicalism, which both Barr and Marsden refer to as an evangelical denomination (Barr 1977: 20, 22; Marsden 1984*b*). Its members exhibit varying degrees of fundamentalist influence. Separatist fundamentalists have strained relations with this evangelical coalition. They 'remain a part of the consciously evangelical movement, at least in the sense of paying the closest attention to it and often addressing it' (Marsden 1984*b*: p. xiv), sometimes as its most vehement critics. Their very animosity towards the less separatist evangelicals reflects a recognition that evangelicals are their closest cousins or, in the opinion of Bob Jones University, 'fallen brethren'.[27]

1.6. Neo-Fundamentalists

Since the late 1970s another type has emerged whom some call 'neo-fundamentalists' (Beale 1986: 6, 9, 267–8; Marsden 1983*b*; Wuthnow 1988: 195–7; Kurtz 1988). They claim the fundamentalist designation but in their fight against secular humanism they co-operate with people outside the narrowly fundamentalist fold. Their broad political coalitions such as the Moral Majority and Operation Rescue have been dominated by fundamentalist and evangelical Christians, but they have also comprised Roman Catholics, Jehovah's Witnesses, and Mormons among others. The Moral Majority (MM), which operated from 1979 to 1989, was organized primarily for the purpose of political lobbying on such issues as abortion, the Equal Rights Amendment, prayer in schools, and textbook legislation. Operation Rescue (OR) was established in 1988 as an interventionist pro-life group. Unlike the Moral Majority it has scorned the civil political process. Pat Robertson's Christian Coalition, established in the late 1980s, focuses on local politics as a way to influence politics at the national level. All of these groups would come under the umbrella label 'New Christian Right' (NCR), which constitutes a 'second wave of highly visible fundamentalist politicking and cultural presence' (Marty and Appleby 1992: 70).[28]

[27] The description given to evangelicals in a chart defining different types of Christianity (received from Bob Jones University, untitled, n.d.).

[28] The emergence of the NCR has received much attention. See particularly, Danzig (1962); Clabaugh (1974); Lipset and Raab (1981); Leibman and Wuthnow (1983); Bromley

Jerry Falwell, founder of the Moral Majority, has been the figure most representative of this development. He is treated with suspicion by separatists, who regard neo-fundamentalists as part of the broader evangelical movement (Beale 1986: 9–10, 267–8). The 'neo-fundamentalist' designation undermines Falwell's claims to represent true fundamentalism.[29] The issue is again one of separation. Bob Jones Jr. condemned Falwell as 'the most dangerous man in America today as far as Biblical Christianity is concerned', because he 'uses such good things as morality and reform in an attempt to deceive Christians into alliance with apostasy'.[30] Bob Jones III (1980: 28) advised 'God's people' to 'turn their back upon the Moral Majority and seek the soul-satisfying contentment of being a scriptural minority'. Falwell (1981: 162), for his part, has termed this more extreme separatist position 'hyper-fundamentalism'.

1.7. The British Scene

Churches in Britain experienced nothing as dramatic as the American fundamentalist–modernist controversies. Nor did British evangelicals develop a militant and separatist mentality to such a degree or on such a large scale as those in America. However, divergence in conservative and liberal opinion occasioned some rifts within mainstream evangelicalism in the late nineteenth and early twentieth centuries. Of particular significance in British evangelical history were the Baptist Down Grade Controversy, and the split within student evangelicalism which led to the formation of Inter-Varsity Fellowship (IVF).

and Shupe (1984); Peele (1984); S. Bruce (1988); Capps (1990). Literature written since the late 1980s on fundamentalism worldwide typically compares politically active fundamentalists in America with resurgent groups in other religions (see the Appendix for details). On the diversity of fundamentalist and evangelical political views see Neuhaus and Cromartie (1987); G. S. Smith (1989); Skillen (1990); Gay (1991).

[29] The term 'pseudo-neo-fundamentalism' has also been used against him (David Sproul, *An Open Letter to Jerry Falwell* (1976), cited in Falwell 1981: 160–1). It is an indication of how complex the battle over terminology has become that Sproul applied this term to Falwell because Falwell invited Harold Lindsell to speak on inerrancy at Liberty Baptist College (now Liberty University). Lindsell is treated with suspicion by fundamentalists because he had been one of the pioneering new evangelicals in the 1950s. However, Lindsell has since called on evangelicals to reclaim the name 'fundamentalism' in order to dissociate themselves from those who have lapsed over inerrancy (Lindsell 1979: 319–21).

[30] Letter 10 June 1980, sent to 'Preacher Boy' graduates of BJU and printed by Falwell in *Moral Majority Report*, 14 July 1980, p. 6.

C. H. Spurgeon (1834–92) withdrew from the Baptist Union in the Down Grade Controversy of 1887–8, an incident which 'helped prepare the way for sharper divisions among Evangelicals in the following century' (Bebbington 1989: 146). Spurgeon gave his support to a series of anonymous articles against modern theological trends entitled 'The Down Grade', published in his church magazine. His conservative stance, perpetuated through the training of Baptist ministers at Spurgeon's College in London, inspired American as well as British conservatives. A. C. Dixon, first editor of *The Fundamentals*, came to London to take charge of Spurgeon's Tabernacle from 1911 to 1919 (Marsden 1977: 222).

Cambridge Inter-Collegiate Christian Union (CICCU) was a crucial precursor to IVF. It was founded in 1877, in the Moody–Keswick era, for the purpose of evangelism, prayer, and missionary commitment. Its constitution affirmed 'the fundamental truths of Christianity', including the infallibility of scripture, and decreed non-cooperation with liberals. OICCU, the Oxford equivalent, followed in 1889. In the 1890s the Inter-University Christian Union (later the British College Christian Union) had emerged to co-ordinate such student bodies. This took the name Student Christian Movement (SCM) in 1905. SCM developed a wide and diverse clientele, which included Anglo-Catholics and intellectual enquirers into the Christian faith. CICCU separated from SCM in 1910 having protested about invitations to speakers who accepted higher-critical views (Hastings [1986] 1991: 87–91). In withdrawing, CICCU declared 'its first and final reference to the authority of Holy Scripture as its inerrant guide in all matters concerned with faith and morals' (Pollock 1953: 178). Inter-Varsity Fellowship of Christian Unions (IVF) was formally established as a conservative student body in 1928, organized largely by a London medical student, Douglas Johnson (Bebbington 1989: 259).

British evangelical historian David Bebbington (ibid. 227) gives details of isolated rifts between 1913 and 1928 which he regards as 'storms in a teacup' compared with the controversies in the States.[31] In 1913 Methodist conservatives complained about the

[31] Cf Bebbington (1993), where he suggests that those involved in the controversies from 1913 onwards represent a British trend which is entitled to the name 'fundamentalist': it arose at the same time as its American counterpart, looked to some of the same men for leadership, and displayed similar traits. Its participants were 'contentious by conviction and often by temperament' and 'formed the extremist fringe of the Evangelical movement' (p. 420).

appointment, in the previous year, of George Jackson to Didsbury College, because he had argued that biblical criticism was to be respected. Their protests were to no avail (Bebbington 1989: 217). More disruptive was the rift in the Church Missionary Society (CMS) in the 1920s, caused by suspicion that higher-critical views were being taught among missionaries. The conservatives wanted a concordat laying down belief in revelation, inspiration, and the authority of scripture to be observed. When it was decided that adherence to the Nicene Creed and Article IV of the Church of England was sufficient, conservatives founded their own Bible Churchmen's Missionary Society (BCMS) (Bebbington 1989: 217–18; Marsden 1977: 221). In 1920 the Keswick Convention closed its ranks against pantheistic teaching and ideas from German higher criticism (Bebbington 1989: 218–20). A Baptist Bible Union was launched in 1919 by James Mountain, in reaction against a proposal to create a Free Church Federation among Nonconformists. Mountain feared that an inadequate creed would be adopted. The Union hoped to precipitate an exodus from the churches, but it disbanded in 1925 (ibid. 220; Marsden 1977: 222–3). In America William Bell Riley's group of the same name, founded in 1922, eventually became a separate denomination.[32]

Moderate conservatives in Britain refused to identify with fundamentalism. They recognized that 'the divergence between what are known, on the one hand, as the Fundamentalists, and, on the other, as the Modernists, exceeds, in the United States, anything known in this country'.[33] For the first few decades of the twentieth century conservative evangelicals in Britain were mostly of the 'non-controversialist Keswick variety' (Marsden 1980: 222). In the 1920s American fundamentalist leaders were suspicious of Keswick tolerance. Riley called it 'carelessness'.[34] British conservatives who visited America, on the other hand, deplored the damage caused by the aggression of fundamentalists there (Bebbington 1989: 222; 1990: 323–6). Most importantly, moderate conservatives withdrew support from the Bible League, which was the power base of the militants. The Bible League was created in 1892

[32] The General Association of Regular Baptist Churches (GARBC) was founded in 1932 by a Chicago pastor, Howard C. Fulton. Riley himself did not leave the Northern Baptist Convention until 1947, the year of his death (Beale 1986: 273).

[33] *Life of Faith*, 20 May 1925, p. 573, quoted in Bebbington (1989: 220–1).

[34] *Christian Fundamentalist*, 2 (1928), 7, quoted in Marsden (1977: 220).

'to promote the Reverent Study of the Holy Scriptures, and to resist the varied attacks made upon their Inspiration, Infallibility, and Sole Sufficiency as the Word of God'.[35] In 1923 moderate conservatives, who were worried that the League would adopt American fundamentalist tactics, backed a new Fraternal Union for Bible Testimony. This was decisive, Bebbington argues, in shaping the future course of evangelicalism in Britain (1989: 223).

American historians George Marsden (1980: 223–4) and Mark Noll (1986: 86–8) attribute British moderation partly to the role of the universities, the established church, and pre-revivalist traditions of Nonconformist groups in Britain in restraining revivalism. In America these agencies were not available. American Protestants united behind a principle of *sola scriptura*, having no strong institutional church and rejecting the relevance of tradition. Revivalism was uninhibited, and fostered biblicism and primitivism. This explanation coheres with Marsden's thesis that fundamentalism developed out of revivalism and was not only a product of co-operation between premillennialists and inerrantists.

A further significant factor in British restraint was the broad influence of Romantic thought upon the outlook of British evangelicals (Bebbington 1989: esp. 80–1, 167–9). The Keswick holiness teaching in particular shared the sentimental piety of the Romantic movement. Here was an area of evangelicalism where emotion triumphed over reason. Holiness spirituality reflected Romantic emphases on feeling and intuition and on moments of intense experience. The everyday world was imbued with spiritual significance. Furthermore, holiness advocates adopted the Romantic admiration for the power of the individual will. They thought they could achieve the state of perfection as a matter of the will. They viewed sin not objectively but in relation to the individual's knowledge, 'the measure of light he had received'.[36] Such ethical relativism was not far removed from the emphasis on historical experience in shaping interpretations of the world. British evangelicals were somewhat accustomed to historical relativist ideas.

These ideas enabled greater acceptance of the concepts of natural and historical development on which Darwinism and higher

[35] *Record*, 25 June 1909, p. 673, quoted in Bebbington (1989: 187).
[36] H. W. Webb-Peploe, *Record*, 18 Jan. 1889, p. 56, quoted in Bebbington (1989: 168).

criticism were based, than did the philosophical tradition of American evangelicals which was so conducive to fundamentalism (Marsden 1977: 228–32; 1980: 225–7; Bebbington 1989: 166–7, 226–8; D. F. Wright 1980: 93). At the same time they encouraged the idea that biblical criticism was itself not a neutral pursuit. Few British evangelicals opposed Darwinism or higher criticism outright, but they objected to 'naturalistic' and 'rationalistic' assumptions (Glover 1954: 25; D. F. Wright 1980; Cameron 1984).[37] G. T. Manley distrusted modern criticism on the grounds that some of its adherents have been 'professed rationalists' with a 'prejudice against the supernatural' (1925: 147). James Orr (n.d.: ix. 33, 35) let 'criticism have its rights', but rejected 'futile, rationalistic criticism' which begins with a denial of the supernatural. W. H. Griffith Thomas (n.d.: viii. 6) declared higher criticism 'legitimate' and 'necessary' while denouncing its 'illegitimate, unscientific and unhistorical use'. Reflecting this attitude, John Stott argued in the 1950s that one should be both a fundamentalist and a higher critic (1956: 3). British evangelicals did not regard the cleavage between conservative and critical approaches to scripture as absolute. They accepted a developmental approach to biblical history which they understood in terms of progressive revelation (D. F. Wright 1980). They rejected not the idea of development but the removal of God from the process, which in biblical studies reduced scripture to a train of human thoughts.

1.8. Anglo-American Evangelicalism

The immediate formative history behind most contemporary British evangelicalism lies in the development of IVF. If evangelicalism was weak in the 1920s, lacking in inspiration and suffering from 'a pettiness in the atmosphere of party', it began to revive after the establishment of IVF in 1928 (Hastings [1986] 1991: 200, 453). By 1939 the Christian Union was active in most British universities and attracted over a thousand students to its

[37] The Victoria Institute, founded in 1865 to defend 'the great truths revealed in Holy Scripture . . . against the oppositions of Science, falsely so called', attracted many who were sceptical towards Darwinism, notably Philip Henry Gosse (1810–88). However, it was not officially opposed to evolution, and did not welcome George McCready Price's 'peculiarly American brand of antievolutionism' in the 1920s (Numbers 1992: 141).

international conference in Cambridge. It had its own publishing house, the Inter-Varsity Press, and headquarters in Bedford Square. The foundations were being laid for a dramatic expansion of evangelicalism in the post-war years.

The 1950s was another decade marked by controversy for conservative evangelicalism, but one which significantly shaped the growing movement.[38] It was then that John Stott, Michael Green, and James Packer emerged as the young evangelical spokesmen. The developments taking place within British evangelicalism coincided with the rise of new evangelicalism in the States, the two movements identifying and interacting with one another (Bebbington 1994: 368–9; Hastings [1986] 1991: 453–5). CICCU played a role in bridging the Atlantic divide. The Presbyterian fundamentalist preacher Donald Barnhouse preached CICCU's first major mission after the war and Billy Graham preached the mission of 1955. John Stott led the CICCU missions of 1952 and 1958 (and the OICCU missions of 1954 and 1957).

There again emerged an Anglo-American evangelicalism resembling that which had existed prior to the rise of fundamentalism. This new trans-Atlantic coalition developed in contradistinction to fundamentalism and yet was not unaffected by it. American evangelicals contributed much in the area of evangelism, which was essential to the rise of post-war evangelicalism. Billy Graham's Greater London Crusade in Harringay in 1954 was attended by more than 1,300,000 people during its three months (Hastings, ibid. 454–5). His subsequent British crusades, in 1966–7, 1984–5, and 1990, have less dramatically but still significantly increased evangelical recruitment. America provided not only individual evangelists, but also evangelistic organizations and training in evangelistic techniques.[39]

British evangelicals provided more in the way of biblical scholarship.[40] They made conscious efforts to raise the intellectual

[38] The term 'conservative evangelical' is frequently used in Britain and has less currency elsewhere. It originally distinguished the conservative from the 'liberal' evangelical, but today it is used almost synonymously with the general evangelical label. A distinct liberal evangelical position was defended in Britain between the 1920s and 1960s. Liberal evangelicals did not defend scripture as infallible, but emphasized that the mind of Christ rather than the letter of scripture was authoritative (Hylson-Smith 1988: 241–55).

[39] See s. 5.3.2 below.

[40] For an account of the influence of British evangelical scholarship in America see Noll 1986: 91–121. British evangelical writings were made available to Americans by Eerdmans publishing house (Noll 1986: 101–5) and by IVP, which began production in America in 1946 (Wells 1994: 395).

standard of evangelical research, especially in the area of biblical studies (Gasque 1973; Bebbington 1989: 259–61; Wenham 1989). One of the earliest initiatives was the Tyndale Fellowship for Biblical Research, which began informally in 1938. Tyndale lectures were given at the annual IVF conference from 1942 onwards. F. F. Bruce gave the inaugural address on 'The Speeches in the Acts of the Apostles'. Tyndale House was opened in Cambridge as a residential library for IVF in 1945. F. F. Bruce, W. J. Martin, and J. W. Wenham were involved in the Tyndale enterprise. Bruce and Martin were both Open Brethren. The Brethren were immensely supportive of pan-denominational evangelical work. One Brethren member, John Laing, financially supported IVF, Tyndale House, and London Bible College. London Bible College opened in 1943. Like IVF it was spearheaded by Douglas Johnson. It remains to this day an interdenominational college, training graduates in Christian work. In 1942 the CMS Secretary Max Warren founded the Evangelical Fellowship for Theological Literature (EFTL), a largely liberal evangelical body which also included such conservatives as T. C. Hammond and J. W. Wenham (Bebbington 1989: 253). The Theological Students' Fellowship (TSF) was founded in 1933 and appointed a full-time director in 1962. TSF has sought to establish groups or contacts in universities and theological colleges, and to promote evangelical literature among theological students. Clark Pinnock, who had studied under F. F. Bruce, led in the founding of the North American TSF in 1974 (Noll 1986: 106). The *TSF Bulletin*, its English counterpart *Themelios*, and the *Tyndale Bulletin* have been described as 'the finest regular sources of serious evangelical writing on the modern study of the Bible in the English-speaking world' (ibid. 106).

There are some British evangelicals who feel that Tyndale and similar inter-war initiatives, which developed a view of scripture in dialogue with biblical criticism, concentrated too heavily on problems in the biblical documents and that an evangelical dogmatic approach to the nature of scripture was not restored until the 1950s (Cameron 1984; Wright 1980). In the 1950s one particular line came to dominate—that of James Packer, whose doctrine of scripture was heavily influenced by Warfield. Packer responded to Gabriel Hebert's critique, *Fundamentalism and the Church of God* (1957*a*), with a defence of biblical authority which he entitled *'Fundamentalism' and the Word of God* (1958*a*). Mark Noll describes Packer's volume as 'the most intelligent reassertion of biblical inerrancy since Warfield and Hodge' (1986: 104). The theology of Old Princeton had inspired British evangelical writers earlier in the century (Wenham 1989: 210–11), but Packer's book secured its prominence.[41] Packer also reflected Warfield's attitude towards holiness doctrine. He rejected as Pelagian the Keswick teaching which had shaped British evangelicalism for almost a century (1955).

Packer and Martyn Lloyd-Jones were together regarded as adding 'intellectual muscle' (McGrath 1994*b*: 36) to post-war evangelicalism in Britain. They organized the annual Puritan Conference in Westminster Chapel while Lloyd-Jones was serving as joint Minister there. At its height in the early 1960s the Puritan Conference was attracting over 300 people, most of them young (Bebbington 1989: 261–2). Lloyd-Jones lent his support to the Banner of Truth Trust, which was publishing Reformed literature including works from Princeton.[42] Differences between British and American evangelical apologetic narrowed, as the 'Princeton-Westminster' approach became the 'majority report' of post-war evangelicalism in Britain (Cameron 1984: 130). While some British evangelicals protest that their heritage lies more with Orr than with Warfield (Dunn 1982; France 1991), others find similarities between Warfield's writings and the nineteenth-century British position of J. Bannerman and W. Lee (D. F. Wright 1980: 102; Cameron 1984: 159). For the most part British evangelicals are grateful to Packer for aiding the recovery of a dogmatically (deductively) confident evangelical theology (D. F. Wright 1980: 105; cf. Wenham 1989: 213).

As in the States so in Britain, it was the Reformed wing who, for the sake of doctrinal purity, came to threaten conservative unity. Martyn Lloyd-Jones ([1971] 1992: 23) became alarmed at the ecumenical spirit developing among evangelicals, which he attributed

[41] Some British evangelical scholars have since tried to move evangelicals away from Warfield's style of apologetic, but it still remains dominant (see s. 2.2.3 below). For example, John Stott draws on Warfield and Packer in his recent statement on scripture for the Evangelical Fellowship in the Anglican Communion (1996: 24–5).

[42] The Banner of Truth was established as a Trust in 1957. Its founders included Iain H. Murray and Sidney Norton, then ministers of St John's Church, north Oxford. *Banner of Truth* magazine began in 1955 and a publishing programme in 1957. The object of the organization is to advance the Reformed faith, and it publishes mostly Reformed and Puritan writings. The Trust was originally based in London but moved to Edinburgh in 1972. For a history of the Trust see Murray (1993).

partly to the tolerance exhibited by Billy Graham. He regarded ecumenism as dangerous because 'based on doctrinal indifferentism' (p. 68). He discouraged evangelicals from the view that 'leaving their denomination is . . . the greatest of all sins' (pp. 52–3). At the 1966 National Assembly of Evangelicals he urged evangelicals to separate from liberals and form an official evangelical denomination. This proposal was opposed by John Stott and rejected at the first National Evangelical Anglican Congress at Keele in 1967 (Bebbington 1989: 267; 1994: 370; McGrath 1993*a*: 16–17). Thus British evangelicals retained their non-separatist nature. They have flourished since the late 1960s, with John Stott acclaimed nationally and internationally as a 'touchstone of Evangelical respectability' (Hastings [1986] 1991: 615). However, Lloyd-Jones ([1971] 1992: 29) felt that at Keele they had undermined their own identity by becoming as 'concerned as anybody else about church union with bodies that are not at all evangelical'.

1.9. British 'Fundamentalism'?

> For thirty-five years now I have felt it right to repudiate the label 'fundamentalist' . . . In an exchange of letters with Professor James Barr in 1978, after the publication of his book *Fundamentalism*, I complained that he seemed to lump us all together. He denied this, but added that 'the overlap was very great'. Now you write, David, that I have a 'lingering inclination towards fundamentalism', and that you hope to wean me away from my 'near-fundamentalism'.[13]

> We evangelicals are Bible people. We believe that God has spoken fully and finally in his son Jesus Christ and in the biblical witness to Christ. We believe that scripture is precisely the written speech of God, and that because it is God's word it has supreme authority over the Church.
>
> The supremity [*sic*] of scripture has always been and always will be the first hallmark of an evangelical. We deplore the cavalier and sometimes arrogant attitudes to holy scripture which are flaunted in the Church today. We see these as derogatory to the Lord Jesus Christ, whose attitude was one of humble reverent submission to scripture.[14]

[13] John Stott in response to David L. Edwards, in Edwards and Stott (1988: 89).
[14] John Stott, quoted in a 1990s Evangelical Alliance publication, Calver *et al.* (n.d.: 4).

The term 'fundamentalism' has different connotations in Britain from those it has in the United States. To most American minds, evangelicals are clearly distinguishable from fundamentalists, from whom they underwent a historical separation. Billy Graham would be taken to epitomize the non-fundamentalist evangelical stance. In Britain evangelicals are termed 'fundamentalist' if they are thought to reflect fundamentalist attitudes. In the 1950s the fundamentalist epithet was applied to British evangelicalism with particular vehemence. This was the period of conservative evangelical growth and the renewed Reformed influence. Ironically it was a Billy Graham crusade which then occasioned the use of the term.

In 1955 CICCU invited Graham to lead a mission which was to be held in Cambridge University Church. Canon Luce complained in a letter to *The Times* that fundamentalism 'ignores the conclusions of modern scholarship', and therefore ought not 'claim a hearing at Cambridge' (15 August 1955, p. 7). This sparked the so-called 'fundamentalist debates' in the letter pages of *The Times*, which lasted several weeks. One letter, from the Secretary of the Christian Evidence Society, expressed hope 'that we may be spared the reopening of the controversies of a generation ago' (20 August, p. 7). The connection with the fundamentalist controversies raises the question of definition, which only John Stott addressed. 'It is surprising', he wrote, 'that your correspondents . . . have not paused to define the term "fundamentalism"', a term which Graham 'has publicly denied on more than one occasion' (25 August, p. 14). Stott argued that the term, respectable in its origins, has become 'almost a synonym for obscurantism' so that it is 'neither true nor fair to dub every conservative evangelical a "fundamentalist"' (ibid.). He reiterated this point in an article on fundamentalism, published in *Fundamentalism and Evangelism* (1956). He identified with the stance taken in *The Fundamentals*, but distanced conservative evangelicals from subsequent 'extremes and extravagances, particularly in the United States' (pp. 1, 2).

Critics of the resurgent conservative evangelicalism in the 1950s took IVF to be typically fundamentalist. IVF was the most formative force behind British evangelicalism. It was not fundamentalist by American standards. As George Marsden (1977: 221) writes, IVF placed 'far more emphasis on the personal piety and evangelism reminiscent of the Moody-Keswick era . . . than on the doctrinal militancy of the fundamentalist era'. Its 'ties to America were confined largely to the moderate variety of fundamentalism eventually known as "neo-evangelicalism"'. New (or neo-) evangelicalism was the movement with which Graham identified, and CICCU as a part of IVF had organized the Graham mission. British evangelicals wanted to share with new evangelicals a dissociation from the term 'fundamentalist'. Packer (1958*c*) wrote an article entitled 'Fundamentalism: The British Scene' for the new-evangelical journal, *Christianity Today*. He put the word 'fundamentalism' in quotation marks: 'though it is the term which critics habitually use, the majority of British conservatives have never espoused it, do not like it, and prefer, with Dr. Carl F. H. Henry, to call themselves evangelicals, on the ground that this term is more scriptural, meaningful, and less encrusted with unhelpful associations' (p. 3).

British evangelicals regard themselves as fundamentalists only in that they defend the fundamentals of the faith. Packer emphasized this in the 1950s (Packer 1958*a*: 29). Stott reiterated the point after the blow of Barr's critique in the late 1970s. He accepted only the 'original meaning' of 'fundamentalism', as insistence on 'fundamental doctrines' (1978: 45). I. Howard Marshall (1992: 9), in the light of current interest in fundamentalism worldwide, claims that if 'fundamentalism' retained the meaning of upholding and defending 'the fundamentals of the faith . . . many of us today would be happy to use it'. David Bebbington reflects this opinion. He supplies historical arguments in support of a distinction between fundamentalism and British evangelicalism (1989: 275–6). Having chronicled British evangelicalism from the 1730s to the present he argues that because 'Evangelicalism has changed so much over time, any attempt to equate it with "Fundamentalism" is doomed to failure' (ibid.). Bebbington interprets Barr as making this mistake, at least with regard to conservative evangelicalism. However, Barr is making a different kind of point from any Bebbington considers. Barr is attempting to combat the imposition of a conservative ideology upon scripture. He is concerned to present true evangelicalism as something unspoilt by fundamentalist influences.

Through the history recounted in this chapter it should be possible to distinguish the type of claim made by Barr from the type of claim made by Bebbington. Evangelicalism predated fundamentalism and is likely to survive beyond it. Various evangelical movements co-operated in the fundamentalist coalition of the 1920s, and various evangelical movements emerged out of that fundamentalist episode. Clearly evangelicalism is too wide a phenomenon to be equated with fundamentalism. Moreover, British evangelicals have not exhibited militant or separatist attitudes to the same degree as American fundamentalists. Yet these considerations do not make it inappropriate to suggest that contemporary evangelicals are 'fundamentalist' in Barr's sense. Barr's principal argument is that many evangelicals reflect a fundamentalist mentality regarding scripture. From the account provided in this chapter of the relation between fundamentalism and evangelicalism we can begin to see what is entailed by such a charge. We have found in fundamentalism a biblical apologetic tailored to the scientific age. We have discovered a tendency to deny that methods of biblical criticism and scientific investigation are truly objective when they challenge what scripture seems plainly to be saying. We have suggested that many evangelicals have assimilated a fundamentalist style of apologetic partly through the influence of new evangelicals in America and of Packer in Britain. To propose, however, that evangelicals share certain fundamentalist ways of thinking is not to equate evangelicalism with fundamentalism. Bearing this in mind, we turn to Barr's critique.

2
The Relation of Fundamentalism to Evangelicalism: A British Critique

2.1. James Barr's Critique of Fundamentalism

In the 1960s, James Barr was drawing attention to the need for a fresh study of fundamentalism which would recognize its full complexity (1966: 202). His own critique in the book he called *Fundamentalism* (1977) has since proved the most influential assessment of the phenomenon in Britain and the one to have caused greatest consternation among evangelicals. His approach differs markedly from that taken in the primarily historical studies reviewed in the previous chapter. He is little concerned with historical distinctions between fundamentalism and evangelicalism, and avoids making political, sociological, and psychological generalizations about fundamentalists (1977: 90, 108–9, 317–18, 325, 331–2; 1980*a*: 69). He regards fundamentalism as insufficiently advanced in theology to receive a straightforward theological appraisal (1977: 160–86; 1984: 118, 148–55). The problem with fundamentalism, he argues, is not that it threatens theology and biblical study—it does little to impede them—but that it has placed itself outside the real task of theology and biblical study, and so has to have special study devoted to it (1977: 336–7).

In his earliest discussion of fundamentalism, in *Old and New in Interpretation* (1966), Barr described its most distinctive aspect as its 'very extreme character of *tradition*'—its reliance being not on the Bible as such but 'on traditional stances into which biblical insights are fitted' (p. 203). Barr's main case against fundamentalism is that it makes zeal for orthodoxy more important than evangelical experience, and distorts scripture by imposing a conservative tradition upon it (1980*a*: 67, 68; 1980*b*: 71, 74; 1984: 149, 176–7; 1986*a*: 29). His response to the problem of fundamentalism comes across most clearly in his pastoral work *Escaping from Fundamentalism* (1984). He shows great seriousness about the Bible and an interest in what the Bible itself says, as fundamentalists themselves aim to do, and suggests that it does not say what fundamentalists think it says (1984: 174–5).

2.1.1. *'Fundamentalism', 'Conservative Evangelicalism', and 'Evangelicalism'*

Although Barr implicates many conservative evangelicals in his writings on fundamentalism, describing them as 'fundamentalist' while knowing that they will object to the term, he does not simply equate fundamentalism with conservative evangelicalism. Still less does he identify fundamentalism with evangelicalism *per se*, but rather regards it as 'a threat to the heart of evangelical religion' (1984: 159). Nevertheless he applies the term 'fundamentalism' more widely than many self-designated evangelicals find comfortable. Wherever Barr discerns the imposition of a conservative ideology upon scripture he finds the offenders fundamentalistic, regardless of any particular distinctions they themselves make. He finds that Oliver Barclay's history of CICCU gives an 'excellent insider's account of the kind of movement taken as typical fundamentalism by me': one that champions an 'uncompromising conservative stand' and that interprets its weaknesses as 'failures to stick to the proper conservative line' (1981: p. xiv).

Barr means to capture 'a certain basic personal religious and existential attitude' which he calls fundamentalism and which, if belonging to any self-termed conservative evangelicals, implicates them also in his critique. That this 'pathological condition of Christianity' affects only some conservative evangelicals is an indication that not all conservative evangelicals are fundamentalist, but 'the overlap is very great' (1977: 5). In places, Barr strongly implies an actual identification:

> I merely observe that there is a central and 'orthodox' sort of conservative evangelicalism, which aspires to hold itself close to the traditional positions of the mainstream churches, considering that these traditions would have remained totally satisfactory if they had not been spoiled by deviation into 'modern' theology and biblical criticism. It is this 'orthodox' fundamentalism that is taken as the typical pattern in this book. (ibid. 8)

The overriding implication of *Fundamentalism* is that conservative evangelicals are in fact fundamentalists but that they reject the term because of its pejorative connotations: 'By what term would "fundamentalists" prefer to be called? The term favoured at present, at least in Great Britain, is "conservative evangelical"' (ibid. 2). He disallows this shift in terminology for three reasons. First, he regards the designation 'conservative evangelical' to be 'technical and esoteric', and to be preferred only on grounds of politeness.

> We are talking about a problem which is felt by almost all persons who are at all, even marginally, concerned with religion; and of such persons there are fifty who know and use the term 'fundamentalism' for every one who has any idea what is meant by 'conservative evangelicalism' . . . The fact is that 'fundamentalism' is the normal designation in common English for the phenomenon which we propose to discuss. (ibid. 2–3)

Secondly, he believes that the terms 'fundamentalism' and 'conservative evangelicalism' differ in their frames of reference, the latter being more related to the politics of church parties whereas the former identifies a particular mentality and theological make-up. Barr's terminology suggests that one claims to be conservative evangelical primarily on church political rather than on theological grounds. The question remains: 'how far do those who, within one frame of reference, are conservative evangelicals, and who prefer to be so termed, in fact show the characteristics which within another frame of reference are commonly taken to constitute fundamentalism?' (ibid. 3).

Thirdly, Barr insists on the need to see evidence of a substantial difference in ideas and practice between the position of many conservative evangelicals and that of fundamentalism before a difference of terms can be considered useful. 'The question is not', he says, 'whether they dissociate themselves from the term, but whether they in their religious practice and biblical interpretation show substantial difference from the characteristics suggested by it' (ibid. 3–4).

> Unless evangelicalism turns clearly away from inerrancy, infallibility and the other accompanying features, people as a whole will continue to call much evangelicalism 'fundamentalist' . . . Where there is the ascription of ultimacy, inerrancy and infallibility to a sacred book, along with militancy, exclusivism and the assumption of orthodoxy, 'fundamentalism' is

the normal English word for that phenomenon and suits it very well. (1991*a*: 143)

In *Fundamentalism,* Barr (1977: 3) suggests an image of two overlapping circles to describe the relationship between fundamentalism and conservative evangelicalism: 'The people who are fundamentalists are commonly also conservative evangelicals; but this does not mean that the two designations specify exactly the same features'. The terms designate different frames of reference. In a later article he uses an image of three concentric circles: 'The outermost and largest we may call Evangelical; the intermediate we will call Conservative Evangelical; and the innermost we will call Fundamentalist' (1986*a*: 24). Barr (1991*a*: 142 n. 1) regards this as his clearest account of the distinction between the three positions. He associates evangelicalism with European pietism and subsequent revivalism, the main emphasis being upon personal conversion and inward experience. 'Evangelicalism', he notes, 'is not always and necessarily conservative' (1986*a*: 25). Its conservative form insists upon maintenance of traditional Protestant orthodoxies, including such principles as the total depravity of man and the absolute centrality of scripture, and holds that 'one cannot be truly Evangelical unless one is also *conservative* in opposing all sorts of modern ideas and modes of interpretation'. Fundamentalism consists of those 'who insist that even this conservative position is not maintainable except upon the basis of the complete inerrancy, infallibility and absolute centrality of the Bible' (ibid.).

The image of the three concentric circles affords a sharper contrast between fundamentalism and conservative evangelicalism than that given in *Fundamentalism.* However, it undermines Barr's more general critique, which is based on the perceptive discernment of a fundamentalist mentality pervading conservative evangelicalism and conservative scholarship, and which is reflected in his more recent judgement that 'well over ninety percent of world evangelicalism is fundamentalistic' (1991*a*: 144).

Barr's (1981: p. xix) distinction between fundamentalism and non-conservative evangelicalism is the really functional distinction for his critique, and provides a backdrop against which to understand his disapproval of the conservative variety. Non-conservative evangelicalism 'conserves the true essence of evangelical faith', whereas the fundamentalistic aspects of conservative evangelical thought are antithetical to true evangelicalism. The basis of evangelicalism is the gospel, which is threatened by fundamentalist exclusivism and eclipsed by fundamentalist 'rationalism': 'evangelicalism . . . has a choice before it between two leading principles. One is that of personal religion with the primacy of faith; the other is that of orthodoxy reinforced by rationalist argumentation. To me the heart of evangelical religion lies in the former; fundamentalism, seeking to defend the evangelical tradition, ends by losing the very centre of it' (1980*a*: 82). For example, student fundamentalism 'seems to have systematically lost or eradicated the major features that a generation ago softened the rationalism of pure conservative ideology . . . [and which] made it much more biblical, and also made it really evangelical' (1981: p. xiv).

Fundamentalism 'does not admit that there is room for a non-conservative evangelical faith' (ibid. p. xix). Barr alerts fundamentalists to this possibility. He reassures those wanting to escape from fundamentalism that they can remain evangelical: 'the evangelical religion is *not* dependent on the fundamentalist view of scripture, and that . . . view of scripture is actually contrary to much of the evangelical tradition and harmful to it' (1984: 157). In fact, 'the only way of maintaining a consistently evangelical position is if one carefully avoids the non-evangelical modes of thinking that are essential to the conservative evangelical position' (1977: 61). Hence those who feel themselves moving away from a fundamentalist view of the Bible should not feel disqualified from evangelicalism (ibid. 157–9).

2.1.2. *Fundamentalist Characteristics*

No simple definition of fundamentalism can be given, so Barr (1977: 1) offers instead an 'extended description' which unfolds throughout his critique. As a preliminary he sets out the most pronounced fundamentalist characteristics: a strong emphasis on biblical inerrancy; a strong hostility to modern theology and to the methods, results, and implications of modern critical biblical study; and an assurance that those of other religious viewpoints are not really 'true Christians' (ibid.). His main focus of attention is the fundamentalist view of scripture. However, Barr denies that the core of fundamentalism is the Bible. Rather, it is a particular kind of religion which fundamentalists believe follows from the acceptance of biblical authority, but which in fact they impose upon scripture thus skewing its meaning: 'In other words, fundamentalism is based on a particular kind of religious tradition, and uses the form, rather than the reality, of biblical authority to provide a shield for this tradition' (p. 11). The dominant stream in this tradition is the religious experience of the evangelical revivals. The revivals encouraged a distinction between belonging to a church and being saved through hearing the gospel (pp. 11–12). As a result, many churchgoers have been denounced as 'nominal' Christians. Criticism of the formality, externality, and hypocrisy of churches is not peculiar to fundamentalism, but for fundamentalists being a 'true Christian' is the 'cornerstone of all Christian experience' (p. 13). Moreover, true Christianity is tested at the doctrinal level: the true Christian is one who adheres to conservative evangelical doctrine (pp. 13–14).

It may seem confusing that Barr regards both a certain view of scripture and a particular religious pattern as somehow basic to fundamentalism. In fact he finds that in fundamentalism there is a 'reciprocal relation between the Bible and the religious tradition', and that the Bible can become dominant (p. 37). On the one hand, the religious tradition is ultimate. Fundamentalists 'do not use the Bible to question and re-check this tradition, they just accept that this tradition is the true interpretation of the Bible'. The position on inerrancy protects this tradition by preventing 'modes of interpretation that might make the Bible mean something else'. On the other hand, while so protecting scripture, fundamentalism finds that 'in its intellectual and apologetic work . . . it gradually has to alter and even abandon essential elements in the very religious tradition from which it started out'. When this happens, the Bible has become 'the supreme controlling factor' (ibid.).

Other features of fundamentalism picked out by Barr include a trans-denominational nature, coupled with an exclusivism towards non-evangelicals of all denominations (pp. 18–22); an anxiety to preserve 'sound' doctrine and a refusal to hear speakers of unsound views (pp. 23–4); a depiction of sin as universal and metaphysical, and an insistence on the substitutionary nature of atonement (pp. 25–8); a heavy emphasis upon the divinity of Christ (pp. 28, 169–72); often a 'low' church style with the emphasis being upon the priesthood of all believers rather than on scholarly training and ordination (pp. 30–1); a view of the sacraments as inessential to Christian identity or evangelical unity (p. 31); an emphasis on personal prayer aided by the Holy Spirit, especially for preaching the gospel and for understanding scripture (pp. 31–3); and an evangelistic zeal (pp. 33–6). Most important is the place of the Bible, which is regarded as 'part of the religion itself' and which in the fundamentalist mind 'functions as a sort of correlate of Christ' (p. 36). Not that fundamentalists view the Bible as Saviour, but it is the '"inscripturated" entity, the given form of words in which God has made himself known', and 'the accessible and articulate reality, available empirically for checking and verification' (ibid.).

Theologically, Barr argues, fundamentalism is underdeveloped. It has doctrines rather than a theology (p. 162), borrowing from older Protestant orthodoxies in a piecemeal fashion with little regard for the complex interrelations worked out in these systems (pp. 166–7). This reflects a lack of awareness of the history of doctrine (pp. 16, 168–9; cf. 1984: pp. ix, 148–55). Fundamentalism affirms 'essentials' and compiles check-lists to test non-conservative theologies (pp. 167–8). Conservative evangelicalism relates itself to older doctrines through formalization (p. 175). The doctrines of scripture, the virgin birth, the Trinity and the 'fact of sin' are highly formalized, affirmed because assumed to be in the Bible, and employed as test-cases for the soundness of any theology encountered (pp. 175–9, 268–9).

Barr regards inerrancy as the 'point of conflict between fundamentalists and others' (p. 40). His main criticism of fundamentalism is that this doctrine distorts scripture: 'My argument is simply and squarely that fundamentalist interpretation, because it insists that the Bible cannot err, not even in historical regards, has been forced to interpret the Bible wrongly' (1980*a*: 79). Whereas for mainstream Christianity a scriptural passage functions as part of the faith relation to Christ, the general principle of fundamentalism is inerrancy. Handling of biblical materials becomes a '*rational* deduction from the already accepted principle of infallibility' (pp. 79–80). Fundamentalists even sacrifice literal interpretation in order to 'avoid imputing error to the Bible' (1977: 40, 46–54).

Although Barr sees inerrancy as such a central issue in fundamentalism he does not mean any particular theory of inerrancy, of which there are many. As with 'fundamentalism' so with 'inerrancy' Barr is best understood as referring to a general mentality rather than to a tightly defined position. He regards in-house debates over inerrancy and infallibility as 'simply stirrings of the dust within the total fundamentalist conceptuality' (1981: p. xx). Some pretend to introduce flexibility into inerrancy, but this still confirms that inerrancy is their basic approach. No actual instance of biblical error is admitted (1977: 54–5, 346–7 n. 17). Even talking about inerrancy accommodates us 'to the fundamentalist way of perceiving the matter' (p. 55).

Linked to the inerrantist mentality is an assumption that the truth of biblical statements is judged by correspondence to external reality (pp. 49–51, 55–6). Barr contends that fundamentalists are more concerned with the factual truth of a passage than with its religious significance. Their interpretations of seemingly historical narratives focus almost entirely on whether the events took place materially and physically (p. 93). In this respect their outlook is peculiarly modern, imposing upon the Bible an understanding of the nature of truth derived from natural science (pp. 173–5). Fundamentalists do not reflect a historic Christian veneration for the Bible. They share the outlook of an eighteenth-century Anglo-Saxon philosophy of reason, providing evidences to verify biblical statements (pp. 209, 272–5). They are opposing not so much a Harnackian liberalism, as a seventeenth- and eighteenth-century deism. The Deists assumed that an attack on the verbal form of the Bible would undermine Christianity as a revealed religion (pp. 165–6). Fundamentalists have not understood their opponents well enough to realize that they do not hold to a rationalist position (1980*a*: 70–1).

In a sense 'rationalism' is the definitive feature of fundamentalism for Barr, for it is what distinguishes it from real evangelicalism. He regards fundamentalism as basically intellectualist, a rationalist not a fideist position, and 'perhaps the only really rationalist position widely operative within Christianity today' (ibid. 70). Barr's criticism of the 'domino mentality', which accompanies the doctrine of inerrancy, displays his conviction that rationalism has driven out a personal faith. The domino theory is the theory that if any point in scripture becomes uncertain, then other parts will be doubted and soon there will be no grounds left for assurance and no faith left in Jesus Christ:

This argument does not depend on faith; on the contrary, it displays the absence of faith. It depends on a rational nexus. If in fact one's faith is in a person, in Jesus Christ, and if one knows that person as a person, then that faith is not going to be overturned by any changes in the meaning or certainty of one part of scripture or another. (1980*a*: 80)

In general terms Barr seems to mean by 'rationalism' a concern to 'prove' the authority of scripture in ways that would appeal to reason. For the fundamentalist nothing short of inerrancy would provide the necessary proof: 'the fundamentalist as a rational man cannot see how scripture can be inspired unless it is historically inerrant' (ibid. 70). More specifically, he means an 'empirical rationalism' preserved since the eighteenth century and untouched by Kantian and post-Kantian developments (1977: 272–6). This is an important specification, for the characteristics Barr identifies as rationalist are related not to deductive argumentation but to the empirical verification of biblical truth, and to inductive reasoning in theology.

He illustrates this empirical rationalist way of thinking by reference to the Princeton theologians Charles Hodge and Benjamin Warfield. He identifies as particular features of Hodge's rationalism an unbounded confidence in reason, a notion of biblical facts akin to that of scientific fact, a belief in the ultimate harmony of science and religion, and an emphasis upon fact as opposed to theory (pp. 272–4). These notions engendered an apologetic in which seemingly scriptural errors were explained as the result of falsely accepting philosophy or science as fact rather than as theory.

Barr does not claim that all fundamentalists think like Hodge, or that they give conscious thought to these matters, but he finds remarkable agreement between aspects of Hodge's philosophy and modern conservative interpretation. For example, fundamentalists offer apologetics for the resurrection based upon historical 'evidences', they favour 'facts' over speculative 'theories', they 'accommodate' biblical narratives to scientific discoveries once these are recognized as fact, and they accord biblical passages asserting inspiration the status of fact from which they justify a full doctrine of inspiration (p. 275).

Barr rarely mentions militancy, so often picked out as an essential feature of fundamentalism by other scholars. He does include it in some later articles (1986*a*; 1991*a*; 1991*b*), perhaps as he has been more greatly influenced by comparative studies of the fundamentalist phenomenon. Indeed his first mention of militancy is not directly connected with Christian fundamentalism but with analogous movements in other religions (1986*a*: 24). He later locates militancy in the evangelistic and restorationist drives present in Christian fundamentalism (1991*b*: 33). Nowhere does he suggest, with George Marsden, that fundamentalists are to be distinguished from evangelicals by their belligerent attitude towards other forms of Christianity. Barr, playing down the distinction Marsden upholds and paying little attention to hardline American groups, paints a less aggressive picture of fundamentalism.

2.1.3. *Conservative Scholarship*

While Barr does not object to conservative conclusions being drawn in biblical research, he does oppose any attempt to determine prior to scholarly investigation that the conclusions will be conservative. He regards himself as conservative for showing caution against rash innovations (1980*a*: 71; 1977: 157), but he attacks conservative scholarship which is fundamentalistic, that is, which imposes a conservative ideology upon the study of the Bible.

The attack on conservative scholarship is the most uncompromising part of Barr's study. Barr remains generally tolerant of conservative belief at a grass-roots level (1977: 226, 260–1, 341). He perceives 'a sizeable gap between official conservative evangelical doctrine and the actual religious perception of things by conservative people themselves' (p. 261). He primarily attacks a corporate identity, an ideology (pp. 318, 322–3), the blame for which lies not with the conservatism of the majority of evangelicals but with their polemicists. Barr claims he would not have written the book *Fundamentalism* were it not for the way in which fundamentalist scholars eclipsed the existentialist, Barthian elements of the evangelicalism he knew in his student days (1980*a*: 82).[1] The Christian Union in Edinburgh was not then centred upon inerrancy but upon the doctrinal content of the Bible. It refused apologetical attempts to 'prove' the reliability of the biblical material and put greater emphasis upon a personal faith (ibid. 81). Even Barr's

[1] Barr chronicles elsewhere (1988: 17) the loss of Barthian insight among evangelicals. Biblical theology, he argues, failed to make 'any deep impression on inherited conservative attitudes', and so its decline little affected the conservative evangelical constituency.

earlier drafts of *Fundamentalism* were kinder; 'it was my increasing reading in the current literature, the literature, shall we say, from the fifties to the present day, that increasingly determined my mind against this movement' (p. 82). Indeed his earliest account of fundamentalism was markedly more sympathetic, concluding that it 'seems likely that all forms of religious tradition or theological expression are capable of being turned into a kind of human security from the authority which these forms invoke' (1966: 206).

Barr's main objection to conservative scholarship is its non-impartial nature (1977: 120–1, 127–8). He accuses R. T. France of thinking in terms of 'a partisan contest, in which successes have to be marked up for the side: can evangelical scholars "win"? he asks, and he is very worried about this' (1991*a*: 142). Conservative scholarship is propagandistic (1977: 123, 127) and either dogmatic or inconsistent. A dogmatic approach to biblical scholarship was a feature of old fundamentalist arguments. Arguments which look critically at the biblical evidence are a more recent development (ibid. 85–9, 124–8). The dogmatic approach would base the Davidic authorship of Psalm 110 on the testimony of Jesus himself. The newer approach 'attempts . . . to show by ancient near-eastern evidence, by linguistic data and so on, that the Psalm cannot be late and must be "very early"' (p. 88). Barr calls it the 'maximal-conservative' approach. On the one hand, this approach is evidence of improvement in evangelical scholarship, for it employs the historical-critical method. On the other hand, it is more abhorrent than the old fundamentalist dogmatism which was at least consistent with its own principles when it rejected historical-criticism (1977: 88–9). Conservative scholars who practise maximal-conservatism are dishonest on two counts. First, they are aware that they share the 'same universe of discourse with critical scholars' but they keep this hidden from their fundamentalist readership (p. 125). Second, they claim to work with the evidence 'but all evidence is slanted in favour of maximum approximation to the norm' (p. 89). Despite being critical, the maximal-conservative approach demands conservative interpretations.

Barr believes that 'fundamentalism' is changing rapidly, and predicts that it will shift its stand on a number of issues in the next few decades (ibid. 325–6; 1984: 154–5). He thus rejects the fundamentalist claim to represent a changeless 'narrow line of testimony throughout the ages' (1984: 155). Use of the maximal-conservative argument is itself a sign of change (1977: 88). Another change is that fundamentalists now want recognition, especially in biblical scholarship (ibid. 343). However, Barr finds little development in arguments against non-fundamentalists over the last hundred years (ibid. 316). To the criticism that the books he quoted in *Fundamentalism* are no longer representative he responds, first, by insisting that they are and, second, by pointing out that it is ludicrous in a conservative movement to claim that books which are six or eight years old are out of date (1980*a*: 83–4). The changes he perceives are not in fundamentalist polemics but more in interpretative methods, and he suspects these developments to be the outcome of fundamentalist attempts to gain academic respectability while preserving the inerrancy of scripture.

Commitment to the inerrancy of scripture has occasioned the maximally conservative approach in evangelical scholarship. A belief in inerrancy conveys most clearly the empirical rationalist assumptions which contribute to the fundamentalist mentality. It is these philosophical assumptions that receive attention in this study, rather than the theological antecedents to fundamentalism, or the sociological and psychological factors in the creation of the fundamentalist mind. The relevant features of the fundamentalist mentality receive fuller discussion in Chapter 4 after their philosophical roots have been described. There also, we shall see how diverse the concept of inerrancy has become, and how broad and complex the evangelical identity now is even in relation to that one doctrine.

2.2. Barr and his Evangelical Critics

2.2.1. *Frustration and Misunderstanding*

Evangelicals recognize that Barr is describing 'our' position (Stott 1978: 44), but they object that the picture he presents is 'distorted' (Tidball 1994: 26) and 'the "feel" is wrong' (Goldingay 1977*b*: 297). Carl Henry anticipates that: 'Few if any fundamentalists anywhere on earth will see themselves reflected in the mirror Barr holds up' (Henry 1978*a*: 23). Barr's feeling about such objections is that evangelicals simply refuse to recognize themselves in his characterization of fundamentalism. He says that those he is describing think of fundamentalists as people more extreme than themselves, perhaps in a different country (1980*a*: 67–8; 1991*a*: 144).

One can sense the frustration of conservative evangelicals as they try to rebut Barr's critique. Barr usually forestalls them, though not always fully, and they frequently incriminate themselves. This makes for an unsatisfactory interchange in which Barr is more able to score clever points against evangelicals than he is to gain their trust. A pivotal point in evangelical responses to Barr is that Barr has confused evangelicalism with fundamentalism. As we discussed in the Introduction, evangelicals are at pains to distinguish themselves from fundamentalists. Their attempts are like water off a duck's back to Barr, who began his analysis with a discussion of how fundamentalists do not like to be labelled as such (1977: 2–5). It would not be sufficient for Barr to answer objections to his portrayal of fundamentalism solely on terminological grounds. If he has got the feel of conservative evangelicalism wrong, then whether or not conservative evangelicals resist being depicted as fundamentalists is by the by. Yet in objecting to the terminology evangelicals are, according to Barr, behaving in a fundamentalist way.

The insistence on the term 'fundamentalism' is taken by evangelicals as one example of Barr's highly polemical tone which they find so unhelpful (Goldingay 1977*b*: 298; Bush 1978; Stott 1978: 44). They interpret Barr's vehemence as a reaction against his own previously held evangelical beliefs. Pinnock (1979: 31; cf. 1990*b*: 41) judges Barr 'Less than candid about his own past', while Sheppard (1983: 3) suggests he 'may be projecting a repudiation of his own earlier fundamentalism into his assessment of others who do not share his continuing historical conservatism'. Barr, however, denies them even this triumph. He contrasts the Christian Union he knew as a student at Edinburgh with the fundamentalism that has taken over such groups (1980*a*: 81–2). He finds that 'all that had made my own experience of evangelicalism tolerable, creative and enjoyable' has been replaced by the 'emphasis on a traditional rational orthodoxy' (p. 82).

Barr is able to steal much thunder from his evangelical critics because many of their objections display the very tendencies he identifies as fundamentalist. It is a common problem that evangelicals have not wrestled with his critique sufficiently to realize that he does not share the fundamentalist conception of truth and obsession with error. Daniel Estes attributes to Barr the position that 'the Bible itself implies and even requires an errantist position' (Estes 1986: 94). Carl Henry (1979*b*: 166) argues that 'Barr's alternative of an errant Bible . . . lend[s] itself to an almost infinite variety of liberal and rationalistic formulations'. He thus justifies Barr's suspicion that fundamentalists treat all opponents as rationalists. Indeed, Henry (ibid. 354) contends that Barr's 'agenda contains little more than one will find in pamphlets from the Rationalist Press and the writings of Tom Paine'. Similarly, when Henry (1978*c*: 32) speaks of Barr's 'whole-souled devotion to liberal criticism' and John Goldingay (1977*b*: 304) describes Barr's 'unqualified' acceptance of the historical-critical method as an instance of '"liberalism" failing to be self critical', they substantiate Barr's (1977: 164) charge that fundamentalists indiscriminately dismiss non-conservative theological stances as liberal.

John Stott provides a typical example of an inadequate evangelical rejoinder to Barr's critique. Barr (1980*a*: 80) names Stott as one of fundamentalism's '*gurus*'. Stott responded to *Fundamentalism* in an article for *Christianity Today* called 'Are Evangelicals Fundamentalists?' (1978). In this article, Stott makes an unsatisfactory distinction between fundamentalists and evangelicals in order to place his own position on the evangelical side. He argues that fundamentalists overlook the human aspect of scripture whilst evangelicals remember the double authorship (p. 46). This distinction is insufficient because all fundamentalists claim to recognize the human side of scripture and would consider anyone who did not recognize it to be more extreme than themselves. Barr would be justified in dismissing this argument unless convincing evidence could be found in the interpretative methods employed by evangelicals that the human side really is acknowledged. Stott suggests that evangelicals pay close attention to 'context, structure, grammar, and vocabulary' (p. 46). In some senses they do, and fundamentalists are equally as rigorous. Indeed, the dispensationalist schema adopted by many self-proclaimed fundamentalists is itself dependent upon painstaking attention to these details.[2] The major difficulty is that evangelicals such as Stott pay attention to the human aspect of scripture within a double authorship framework. Stott acknowledges that it was 'human

[2] See s. 4.3 below.

authors . . . who used sources, syntax, and words to convey their message' (p. 46), and yet ultimately he is interested in the point that the divine message was not corrupted through the human choice of expression. Barr (1977: 286–99) regards theories of double authorship as typically fundamentalist and as less consistent than sixteenth- and seventeenth-century dictation theories. Double-authorship theories, he argues, move some way towards a modern recognition that the biblical writers were 'people with diverse consciousnesses and experiences'. Yet if it is suggested, for example, that 'the writer of the fourth gospel, a man of lively individual consciousness, had thought up out of that consciousness some of the terms and images in which he describes Jesus . . . fundamentalists are back in a moment with an inspiration that excludes these ideas' (p. 291).[3]

Even more incriminating, in the light of Barr's critique, is Stott's supposition that the alternative to an evangelical attitude towards scripture is one which finds scripture erroneous. He writes: 'it is not dishonest in the face of apparent discrepancies, to suspend judgement and continue looking for harmony rather than declare Scripture to be erroneous. On the contrary it is an expression of our Christian integrity' (p. 46). Stott thus displays two further fundamentalist assumptions: that non-evangelicals think in terms of uncovering error in scripture, i.e. that they are rationalistic in this sense; and that the most important defence one can state for the Bible is that it contains no errors.

The strongest claim made against Barr is that he has not been sufficiently attentive to developments within evangelicalism. Evangelicals were tackling problems Barr identifies in *Fundamentalism* long before Barr exposed them. In particular, there has been awareness of the weakness of evangelical scholarship for several decades and a stock of self-criticism far outweighing Barr's attack. Henry (1978*a*: 24) asserts that 'American evangelicals have for a generation distinguished between what is desirable and what is undesirable in fundamentalism', and have not had to wait for Barr's critique in order to realize their shortcomings. He had himself warned evangelicals in 1965 of the 'need to overcome any impression that they are merely retooling the past and repeating cliches'.[4]

[3] Problems with a dual authorship theory are discussed at s. 4.5.3 below.

[4] Henry, 'American Evangelicals and Theological Dialogue', *Christianity Today*, 15 Jan. 1965, p. 29, quoted in Noll 1986: 119–20.

Barr could have paid more attention to advances in evangelical thought and to debates and divisions within the evangelical fold, as shall become increasingly apparent throughout this study. However, Barr's work is not a polemic that is easily silenced by evangelical self-criticism. The problems it discusses are often not sufficiently recognized even in evangelicalism's most painfully honest moments. In the same year that *Fundamentalism* was published, John Stott addressed the second National Evangelical Anglican Congress (NEAC '77). There he encouraged evangelicals to confess that they are 'sometimes slovenly, sometimes simplistic, sometimes highly selective and sometimes downright dishonest' in their treatment of scripture (Stott 1977*a*: 21). Yet we have seen that Stott displays at a more basic level the fundamentalist tendencies which are the real object of Barr's critique.

2.2.2. *Concessions over Scholarship*

Evangelicals are concerned to raise the integrity and academic quality of their research. It is actually in the area of conservative scholarship, where Barr is most critical, that they most agree with him. John Goldingay (1977*b*: 302) finds Barr's criticisms of conservative biblical and theological study to be 'generally justified'; William Wells (1978: 32–4) acknowledges the inconsistency between the dogmatic and the maximal-conservative approach; and Russ Bush (1978: 101) accepts that evangelicals are involved in hypocrisy. Clark Pinnock (1979: 31) admits to 'devious reasoning' on the part of evangelicals. He finds Barr's case 'so convincing that . . . any open-minded evangelical reader will be driven to conclude that inerrancy language needs to be discarded or at least qualified and nuanced so as not to require such acrobatics'. Stott (1978: 45) summarizes three areas where evangelicals should learn from Barr's attack: 'We do sometimes use our venerable evangelical tradition to shelter us from the radical challenges of the Word of God'; 'we cannot resist his stricture that we produce more biblical scholars than creative theological thinkers'; and 'Dogmatic assertions about infallibility and inerrancy are no substitute for conscientious, painstaking studies'.

At the same time, evangelicals feel that Barr has not dealt justly with differing positions and standards in conservative scholarship and has not given credit to good evangelical scholars such as F. F.

Bruce, James D. G. Dunn, and I. Howard Marshall (Stott 1978: 44; Pinnock 1979: 33; France 1991: 52–5). Again, they have to an extent misunderstood the nature of Barr's criticisms. Their distinction between good and bad evangelical scholarship will not cause Barr to alter his critique so long as the good scholarship is primarily concerned to be conservative.

Barr welcomes scholarship whose emphasis is upon sound enquiry rather than upon conservative conclusions. Bruce and Dunn are not considered fundamentalist by Barr, however well respected they may be in conservative evangelical circles, because they do not put conservatism before scholarship. Marshall, on the other hand, is judged to be fundamentalist because, 'typically of conservative interpretation, [he] abandons the literal sense as soon as it would imply error or disagreement in the Bible' (1977: 57).[5] Conservative scholarship is worthy of respect 'in proportion as it *fails* to be partisanly conservative', Barr (1977: 127–8) writes:

> it may be accepted and admired, but only in such measure as it does *not* do what conservative apologists insist that it must do and has done. In so far as it is seen as committed to a purely conservative line, it is discounted and unrespected. Thus the deservedly high reputation of some conservative scholarship rests to a large extent on the degree to which it *fails* to be conservative in the sense that the conservative evangelical public desiderate.

Evangelicals concede that there are poor elements in evangelical scholarship but point out that in other ways evangelical scholarship is improving. They know they are not innovative in the field of biblical scholarship. Their major contributions are in textual or lower criticism (Noll 1986: 117–19), and they tend to be several years behind in their acceptance of new methods. Yet, though Barr (1977: 154) suggests otherwise, they do engage in form and also redaction criticism.[6] Debating this point, however, brings them either to stalemate or to a renewed preoccupation with the

[5] Marshall's position is not as clear-cut as Barr suggests. In the year that *Fundamentalism* was published Marshall also published an article in which he was willing to accept that there 'may be a stage at which difficulties involved in explaining away an apparent historical error are greater than those caused by accepting the existence of the error' (Marshall 1977: 135). See s. 4.5.1 below.

[6] Much evangelical attention to these and other critical methods arose after *Fundamentalism* was written. Marshall's volume, *New Testament Interpretation* (1977*b*), contains two early articles on form and redaction criticism by Travis and Smalley respectively.

distinction between evangelical and fundamentalist. So again we can appreciate their frustration in wrestling with Barr's critique. Robert H. Gundry's removal from the Evangelical Theological Society (ETS) in 1983 was due to his employment of redaction criticism in *Matthew: A Commentary on His Literary and Theological Art* (1982). In citing this incident (e.g. France 1991: 60), evangelicals score an own-goal. Barr regards the case as shedding 'a worse light on evangelical scholarship than the arguments of my own book did'. Gundry's dismissal manifests the 'fundamentalism' of ETS in refusing to tolerate 'diversely-minded, creative, non-fundamentalist, evangelical thinkers' (1991*a*: 145).

At best evangelical scholars succeed in forcing a question mark over Barr's terminology, as is partly their purpose. Gundry's continued affirmation of inerrancy leads one to suspect that Barr would regard Gundry as himself a fundamentalist. Gundry is in the curious position of retaining a fundamentalist doctrine of scripture as inerrant, while letting go of the assumption that apparently historical narratives correspond to factual states of affairs. Evangelicals who go this way keep one foot within fundamentalism.[7] They do so because evangelicalism has no distinctive theory of scripture besides that inherited from fundamentalism (Barr 1980*a*: 67; 1991*a*: 146). Gundry adopts a different critical attitude from that endorsed by ETS.[8] Evangelical scholars, if they pressed this point, could demand that Barr clarify his terms. Barr could either state that Gundry is fundamentalist because of his commitment to inerrancy, in which case Barr would have to concede that redaction criticism has made inroads into fundamentalism, or that Gundry is not fundamentalist, in which case Barr has allowed at least one inerrantist evangelical to escape the fundamentalist label. Evangelical scholars may feel that this is a trifling gain, won only at the cost of highlighting the fundamentalist tendencies of one of their largest organizations. Furthermore, it is a gain which places them in a self-contradiction, for even the *evangelical*

[7] See s. 4.5.2 below.

[8] Noll characterizes ETS's position as 'critical anti-criticism' and Gundry's as 'believing criticism' (1986: 156–73, esp. 167–9). Critical anti-criticism performs biblical study in order to protect biblical infallibility from the conclusions of faulty criticism. Believing criticism, which has recently gained a foothold among American evangelicals, allows research to overturn traditional evangelical conclusions about the Bible without necessarily undermining beliefs in the Bible's inspiration and inerrancy (see s. 4.2 below). Barr's critique implicates both kinds of conservative scholarship.

identity of Gundry was thrown into dispute by his departure from ETS.

2.2.3. *Catch-22*

The overriding feeling among evangelicals is that Barr has given them a no-win situation. Stott (1978: 45) complains that Barr characterizes evangelicals as hostile to modern criticism, and yet accuses evangelicals who do attend to historical and literary origins of being inconsistent with their own principles: 'It is hardly just to condemn us for both doing and not doing the same thing'. Carl Henry (1978*a*: 25) objects that fundamentalists are criticized for not reading non-conservative work and also criticized when they quote non-conservatives who defer to conservative positions: 'Fundamentalists are apparently damned if they do and damned if they don't, because in Barr's views they are damned fundamentalists'.

However, that Barr (1991*a*: 141–2) does not consider Bruce and Dunn fundamentalist is evidence that he has not given evangelicals a no-win situation. Barr is cornering those evangelicals who both use the tools of critical scholarship and predetermine that they will only accept conservative results. He is further riled by fundamentalists who claim the support of critical scholarship which happens to produce conservative results. This practice weds them to methods based upon presuppositions more usually denounced by fundamentalists. Such opportunism, Barr (1977: 152) argues, reveals that fundamentalists are prepared to overlook ideological failings for the sake of securing historical conservatism.

R. T. France (1991) challenges the fairness of Barr's stance in the recently formed Anglican evangelical journal, *Anvil.* France (ibid. 52–3) clearly feels implicated by Barr's work on fundamentalism and yet finds it 'unfair' that he and others like him, who are evangelical scholars and accept the conservative evangelical label, are also described as fundamentalist. France's claim is that there is 'an "evangelicalism" which is neither "fundamentalist" nor "liberal", and it is that sort of evangelicalism which is most typically to be found involved in academic biblical and theological studies. It is this strand of genuinely evangelical scholarship which is most difficult to recognise in terms of the model set up in Barr's *Fundamentalism*' (p. 54).

France accuses Barr of producing a catch-22 argument: 'The moment a strain of creativity appears the work concerned must be denied the label "conservative". The possibility of creative conservative scholarship is ruled out by definition' (1991: 56, cf. 61). France (pp. 62–3, 54–5) suggests that evangelical scholarship benefits by being distanced from the kind of inerrancy position advocated by B. B. Warfield, and by developing a more sophisticated hermeneutical position. In these ways, he proposes, evangelicals move away from fundamentalism. It was openness to such new approaches in biblical interpretation and theology that led to the founding of *Anvil* in 1984, a journal whose position France locates as mid-way between 'fundamentalism' and 'liberalism' (ibid. 54–5; 1993: 55–6).

As already noted, Barr does allow that a scholar may be truly evangelical and not fundamentalist, but anyone who makes conservatism towards scripture a criterion of evangelicalism is not such a scholar. In his response to France, Barr (1991*a*: 146–7) objects to the way in which 'conservative' is defined 'by the standard of approximation to the fundamentalist position', so that one who is closer to the fundamentalist position is more clearly a 'conservative' evangelical. This problem is exacerbated, Barr says, because the fundamentalist view of scripture is the only one that is distinctively evangelical. It is an identity badge for evangelicals (p. 146). No other position has been worked out or accepted. Therefore, when evangelicals reject a particular critical position because it is 'inconsistent with evangelical theology', as France (1991: 60) does, they are implicitly endorsing fundamentalism.

This explains how France is implicated. Although he encourages greater toleration among evangelical scholars he adopts the very attitude Barr abhors—that the evangelical tradition provides the standard of what is acceptable in scholarship. He continues to think in terms of a 'boundary line between those results of critical study of the Bible which are felt to be compatible with an evangelical doctrine of its inspiration and those which are not', even while accommodating ideas which would be unacceptable to the non-scholarly evangelical (ibid. 63). Barr does not explicitly inculpate France in these ways, but he does suggest that France displays allegiance to fundamentalist standards by expressing pleasure at Robinson's early dating of the New Testament. France (ibid. 59) writes: 'John Robinson has shown us that views of the date and authorship of New Testament books which have been thought to be distinctively "evangelical" can be argued for with even greater vigour by a scholar whose espousal of these views in no way moderated his radical theology!' Barr's objection is to France endorsing a work by a scholar of whom evangelicals would normally disapprove, on the grounds that it 'constitutes an approximation to the fundamentalist position' (Barr 1991*a*: 147).

What seems like a catch to France is really a reflection of the multifaceted nature of the fundamentalist mentality. Barr's critique has more horns than France realizes. Openness and creativity are not enough if one continues to give priority to evangelical doctrine over good scholarship, and if one's acceptance of new ideas is determined by fundamentalist standards. However, France (1991: 62) also suggests that conservative scholars do accept an alternative, non-fundamentalist doctrine of scripture by moving 'over to Orr rather than Warfield'. The debate over evangelical allegiance to James Orr reveals a certain amount of confusion on both sides.

Barr has mixed reactions to an evangelical appropriation of James Orr's position. He does not explain his ambivalence, but we can infer its reasons. In *Revelation and Inspiration* (1910), James Orr posited two different arguments against Warfield's concept of inerrancy, only one of which would be acceptable to Barr. He insisted that scripture is 'free from demonstrable error' so that on innumerable occasions objectors to inerrancy have been shown to be wrong (1910: 215–16). He denied the complete factual inerrancy of scripture because he suspected that the Bible contained instances of minor error. According to Barr (1991*a*: 147), Orr 'assumed something like ninety nine per cent factual inerrancy, while grounding biblical inspiration in a different way'. This renders him too similar to Warfield for Barr's liking. However, Orr (1910: 199, 213–14) also argued that inspiration neither entails nor is proved by inerrancy, and that the 'proof of the inspiration of the Bible . . . is to be found in the life-giving effects' of its message (p. 217). This second argument is compatible with Barr's own statements against fundamentalism.

On the one hand, Barr (1977: 269) implies that Orr provides only an alternative fundamentalist position. Hence, when France claims that evangelicals have in fact moved closer to Orr, Barr plays down the significance of such a move: 'Fussing over the minor points of Orr's differences from Warfield is only a search for a way to remain within fundamentalism but with greater comfort' (1991*a*: 147–8). On the other hand, he argues that Orr was an early advocate of views which later became labelled neo-orthodox, and thought it unlikely that fundamentalists would make a substantial move in Orr's direction. Among other things, 'fundamentalists would have to give up their mode of arguing that the Bible is inerrant and infallible because Christ and the apostles said so' (p. 270). Barr predicts that fundamentalists 'will stay with Warfield because they think like Warfield' (ibid.). His judgement is somewhat justified by the tale behind France's endorsement of Orr. France follows James Dunn's argument in 'The Authority of Scripture According to Scripture' (1982), but Dunn's article was largely responsible for the rift among evangelicals which occasioned the *Churchman* split and the birth of *Anvil*. Evangelicals were reacting to Dunn's criticism of Warfield. The fracture of the *Churchman* suggests that Barr was right about evangelical discomfort with Orr, but the creation of *Anvil* suggests that he overestimated the breadth of evangelical commitment to Warfield.

The France–Barr exchange raises one further issue which we will consider more thoroughly in Chapter 8. France (1991: 53–4) suggests that evangelicals move away from a fundamentalist approach to scripture by engaging in philosophical hermeneutics. Barr (1991*a*: 149–52) finds evangelical promotion of hermeneutics inconsistent, for evangelicals remain concerned over the historical accuracy of the biblical reports. They adopt philosophical assumptions which are alien to the fundamentalist heritage and yet remain tied to a fundamentalist ideal. That is to say, they appeal to hermeneutics as a means of avoiding difficult historical issues so that a biblical conservatism can be maintained: 'All hermeneutical suggestions are welcome—except for those that lead towards historical criticism . . . But why should the historical arguments seem so dangerous? Only because of the heritage of fundamentalism, for which historical criticism appeared as the most serious threat. So, fundamentalism is not so far away after all' (1991*a*: 150). Barr's suspicions might be further fuelled by a follow-up article in which France (1993: 53) remarks that 'hermeneutical debate allowed traditional questions to be seen in a new light' so that 'what had hitherto been seen as a simple issue of evangelical versus non-evangelical views came to be seen as areas on which evangelicals might legitimately differ'. The logic of this argument is that evangelicals have been liberated to accept what were once rejected as non-evangelical views, because they can now do so while remaining evangelical. So long as evangelical scholars are primarily concerned with their conservative evangelical identity, Barr will not consider that any of their innovations save them from fundamentalism.

Barr denies that a true scholar can have a prior commitment to evangelical or conservative interpretations of scripture. Evangelicals feel that this sort of commitment manifests a correct confessional stance towards scripture as God's revelation in writing. They regard such a stance as central to their identity and as essential to a true study of scripture. Curiously in their response to Barr they do not defend this fundamental commitment. They prefer to imply that they abide by the same critical presuppositions as anyone else. As we shall see, in other contexts evangelicals attack the presuppositions of non-evangelical biblical critics. Yet, when seeking recognition for their scholarship, evangelicals do not usually draw attention to their own presuppositions. Rather, they ask that evangelical scholarship, be judged by the same criteria as biblical scholarship, which does not bear this commitment. It is against these criteria, however, that their scholarship is judged to be insufficiently critical.

2.3. Changes and Variations

2.3.1. *'Pentecostalism and the like'*

One area in which Barr anticipates change within fundamentalism is in its relationship to pentecostalism and the charismatic movement:

> It is possible that, just at a time when the intellectual leadership of conservatism, especially in literature and biblical scholarship, becomes more prominent, it may at the same time become more irrelevant, because the actual popular interest may be attracted away into another direction, more concerned with experience and emotion than with

doctrine and apologetics. It is, on the other hand, also possible that movements that are at present fairly fluid and doctrinally relaxed may move towards an intellectual rationalism of the normal fundamentalist type. (1977: 208–9)

Barr's criticism of conservative evangelical scholars may be understood in the light of his sadness that the experiential emphasis of conservative evangelical people is undermined by 'their official doctrinal polemicists' (p. 261). He wonders whether official conservative evangelical doctrine will also temper the pentecostal and charismatic movements.

Pentecostal and charismatic religion provide extreme illustrations of the tension that exists for evangelicals between their personal apprehension of faith and a fundamentalist mentality. Evangelicals have always sought God's 'guidance'. Paradoxically, this becomes for them a 'second channel of divine influence' after scripture (Barr 1986*a*: 31). Evangelicals have a very personal and experiential understanding of their faith which, as shall be argued in Chapter 5, sits awkwardly with the direction in which they have taken their apologetics and particularly their view of scripture. They are not entirely at ease with the incongruity between personal guidance and biblical authority, which has been exacerbated by charismatic influences.

When the charismatic movement began in the 1960s, its relations with evangelicals were strained. Charismatics accused evangelicals of being lifeless, powerless, and empty in experience. Evangelicals berated the charismatic movement for starting with experience rather than basing itself on the sound foundation of the Word of God (Cowdell 1992: 58–60; Tidball 1994: 27–30). Martyn Lloyd-Jones felt that charismatics stressed the experience of the Spirit, while 'virtually proclaiming that doctrine does not matter at all' ([1971] 1992: 28). However, since the late 1970s there has been closer co-operation between charismatics and the wider evangelical body (Pawson 1993: 55–61), as evidenced by the recognition of charismatics at NEAC '77, charismatic membership in the Evangelical Alliance (Calver *et al.* n.d. 9, 11), and such joint ventures as the Spring Harvest interdenominational teaching weeks which began in 1979. John Wimber's 'signs and wonders' movement, very influential in the 1980s, became known as the 'third wave' of the movement of the Holy Spirit this century after pentecostalism and charismatic renewal.[9] Since January 1994 another wave of charismatic fervour has emanated from Wimber's Vineyard Ministry, originating in the Vineyard church at Toronto Airport. This wave has been dubbed the 'Toronto Blessing' in Britain.[10]

Charismatics challenge traditional fundamentalist thinking about God's supernatural activity. Traditionally fundamentalists confine miracles to the Bible and regard them as violent divine interventions (Barr 1984: 86). In John Wimber's words: 'Christians unconsciously consign the supernatural to an impenetrable upper tier (except for the resurrection, early church miracles, and transcendent moral standards), excluding God's power from their theology and practice' (1985: 88). However, increasingly in fundamentalist circles God is regarded as ever-present and active, providing such mundane services as finding parking spaces in the centre of town on a Saturday morning. As Nancy Ammerman (1987: 48–9) found, having spent a year studying a fundamentalist church in New England,

> Almost anything good or bad can be explained as God's doing. God keeps the dishes from breaking, locates things that are lost. He supplies friends and offspring. He makes sure cars get fixed at affordable prices. He arranges convenient overtime work schedules and makes hiring and firing more pleasant, He provides clothes and food when they are needed, as well as less essential items like tickets for a rodeo or a pet dog for the children.[11]

Charismatics have not so far developed a systematic theological understanding of the relation between biblical authority and spiritual guidance, though they insist that the Spirit never contradicts

[9] Wimber's Vineyard Ministry is based in California. His theory of signs and wonders, propagated through the books *Power Evangelism* (1985) and *Power Healing* (1987), received endorsement from Fuller Seminary when Wimber joined C. Peter Wagner in 1982 to create a course on 'Signs, Wonders, and Church Growth'. Martyn Percy (1996) provides the most comprehensive treatment of Wimber's work and writings. From his study of Wimber's movement he interprets the wider phenomenon of fundamentalism as a form of religion more committed to a God of power than to a God of love.

[10] Seemingly related phenomena have been affecting British churches, beginning with Holy Trinity, Brompton, and the South-West London Vineyard. For an early account of the 'Toronto Blessing' by a member of the Toronto Vineyard see Guy Chevreau's *Catch the Fire* (1994).

[11] Similarly, Kathleen Boone (1989: 93–4) and Alan Peshkin (1986: 20) encountered beliefs that God provides guidance over such specific matters as the purchasing of cars and houses.

scripture and that where scripture is clear no further, spiritual, revelation is needed (e.g. Pawson 1988: 12–13). However, the older pentecostal movement, which dates back to the start of the century, has become more theologically reflective over the last two decades.[12] The pentecostal attitude to scripture largely resembles that of fundamentalists, but its assumptions are often precritical. Now pentecostals are undecided as to whether they should actively adopt 'evangelical/fundamentalist hermeneutic principles' (McLean 1984: 37). Evangelical theologian R. K. Johnston (1984) and pentecostal theologian Gordon Fee (1976) both feel that this would be appropriate. Mark McLean (1984: 50) on the other hand feels that 'the Pentecostal understanding of the mode of God's presence among his people in conjunction with our use of Scripture in the common life of the Church results in a distinctive pentecostal hermeneutic and theology', which would be undermined by such a move.[13]

Those who are concerned to develop distinctive, pentecostal, hermeneutic principles emphasize a 'pneumatic epistemology'. Clark and Lederle (1989: 30) propose a 'pneumatic epistemology' over and against an epistemology which recognizes only two ways of knowing, reason and sensory experience. The pentecostal emphasis, they argue, is that 'the reader of Scripture can identify with the writer by virtue of common spiritual experience'. In this framework, the Bible 'is not used primarily as a source-book of Christian doctrine' but is associated with activity and experience (ibid. 101). They quote Howard Ervin, who advocates a 'truly existential' understanding of the way in which a believer relates to the biblical witness:

> A pneumatic epistemology posits an awareness that the Scriptures are the product of an experience with the Holy Spirit which the biblical writers describe in phenomenological language . . . When one encounters the Holy Spirit in the same apostolic experience, with the same charismatic phenomenology accompanying it, one is then in a better

[12] Several journals and publications manifest the concern to develop a distinctive pentecostal theology, including Duffield and Van Cleave (1983); M. S. Clark *et al.* (1989); and Parker (1996). The American periodical *Pneuma: The Journal for Pentecostal Studies* (from 1978) now has a British counterpart in the *Journal of Pentecostal Theology* (from 1992). Sheffield Academic Press is in the process of publishing pentecostal commentaries on every book of the Bible. For theological reflection within the charismatic movement see Smail, Wright, and Walker (1993).

[13] For further discussion see *Pneuma*, 1 and 2 (1984), and Clark and Lederle (1989: 25–34).

position to come to terms with the apostolic witness in a truly existential manner.[11]

Through emphasizing the role of spiritual experience in a person's acceptance and understanding of biblical authority, pentecostals challenge what they see as 'the rationalism of twentieth-century evangelical Christianity' (Johns and Johns 1992: 110). They have found this rationalism to be 'an inadequate vehicle for passing on a faith which honors the active presence of the Holy Spirit in the contemporary world' (ibid.).

By contrast, other pentecostals have appropriated a militant defence of the Bible's inerrancy in scientific and historical matters. Duffield and Van Cleave (1983: 15) accept inerrancy as 'the position of all the confessions of the great evangelical churches down through the years', and denounce 'atheists, agnostics and liberal theologians' for declaring 'the Bible to be full of errors'. This suggests that within some pentecostal groups fundamentalism has succeeded, as Barr predicted it might, 'in disciplining and overcoming the newer religious impulses that have their origin in the modern world' (1977: 209).

2.3.2. *British and American 'Fundamentalism'*

Barr acknowledges the difficulty that 'American and British terms seem not to agree precisely'. He suggests that the fundamentalism he depicts 'might fall into the more extreme segment of Evangelicalism and the less extreme of Fundamentalism, as the terms are used in the States' (1977: 6). Thus he decides upon a usage of the term which causes confusion in America. 'American readers will have to adjust their vocabulary somewhat', one critic warns: 'As [Barr] uses the term, fundamentalist designates a position somewhat to the left of American fundamentalism; he does not at all intend to limit his discussion to the theological and social perspectives associated with Bob Jones or Carl McIntire . . . So American readers can and probably should substitute conservative evangelical wherever Barr uses fundamentalist' (Wells 1978: 30).[15]

[11] Ervin, 'Hermeneutics: A Pentecostal Option' (1985); p. 33, quoted in Clark and Lederle (1989: 31).

[15] Other American reviews which make a similar point include those by Bush (1978), Dockery (1981), and Hinson (1978).

What American reviewers did not seem to realize at the time is that, whereas to Americans such as Bob Jones and Carl McIntire 'fundamentalism' is a label of pride, it is not an acceptable term to most British evangelicals. George Marsden inferred from the British fundamentalism debates of the 1950s and from Barr's critique that fundamentalism is common parlance in Britain for conservative evangelicalism (1977: 221 n. 17; 1979*b*: 520). 'Fundamentalism', however, is not simply a way of referring to conservative evangelicals but a way of criticizing them. Evangelicals have appropriated the label only in order to respond to their critics, 'because, whether the critics know it or not, it is Evangelicalism that they are attacking under this name' (Packer 1958*a*: 24).

Barr is describing a broad group of non-militant, reflective, self-critical and so widely diverging evangelicals. He has not in fact restricted himself to the British scene but attacks many American evangelical scholars including R. K. Harrison, Bernard Ramm, and Cornelius Van Til. Ironically all these scholars have themselves rejected aspects of fundamentalism: Van Til as one of Dutch descent,[16] and Harrison and Ramm as new evangelicals.[17] Barr (1977: 187) makes fleeting reference to Bob Jones and Carl McIntire, while not emphasizing their militant separatist nature which in the States is generally understood to differentiate them from evangelicals.

Although he distinguishes dispensationalism from '"orthodox" fundamentalism' (ibid. 198), Barr suggests that the Scofield Reference Bible is 'perhaps the most important single document in all fundamentalist literature' (p. 45). This seems an inappropriate remark in relation to those evangelicals who are his main focus. The Scofield Bible is a King James Bible with notes bearing dispensationalist interpretations. Its use by the families of those students with whom Barr was at university (p. 191) may reflect the limited choice of reference Bibles and of Bible translations

[16] See Ch. 7.

[17] Ramm wrote a book entitled *After Fundamentalism* (1983), in which he sets out a supposedly non-fundamentalist evangelical approach based on the theology of Karl Barth. He regards Barth's theology as 'the best paradigm we have for theology in our times', but says 'we do not need to defend Barth at every point' (p. 48). In his own theology Ramm has said that biblical revelation is given in too many diverse forms to be called propositional, but he retains the language of inerrancy. He insists that the Word of God is to be brought to new hearing in each generation but rejects the suggestion that revelation only occurs in an existential encounter.

acceptable to conservatives at the time. Its dispensationalist interpretation was probably not endorsed by the majority of its British readers. Dispensationalism in Britain had declined even among the Brethren by the 1960s (Bebbington 1994: 373). In America, new evangelicals drifted away from dispensationalism, and the Scofield Bible is used only by dispensationalists who are 'fundamentalist' in a sense more extreme than Barr intends.

Barr seems to find new evangelicalism refreshing (1977: 222–34) yet most of the American scholars discussed in *Fundamentalism* identify with the new-evangelical movement. Carl Henry felt strongly implicated by Barr's attack in *Fundamentalism*, despite being personally praised by Barr (pp. 222, 223) as one of the new evangelicals who has introduced a spirit of self-criticism into fundamentalist circles. Henry (1978*a*: 26) correctly perceived that Barr's critique of fundamentalism was broad enough to include principles shared by new evangelicals: '[Barr's] elastic use of "fundamentalism" to include at times not only what is biblically deplorable but also what is evangelically commendable forces the conservative scholar who seeks to refute Barr to identify himself on crucial matters with the fundamentalist cause, even where he would prefer to detach himself from much of the so-called fundamentalist mentality.'

By the 1970s new-evangelical scholarship had diversified beyond its original commitment to Princeton theology. Barr is sympathetic to some of the directions taken by new-evangelical scholars, particularly those influenced by neo-orthodoxy who reject a purely propositional and cognitive notion of biblical truth.[18] However, an attack on inerrancy and infallibility, as well as on such traditional evangelical doctrines as substitutionary atonement, will be felt by new evangelicals as much as by any 'fundamentalist'. Moreover, criticism of the maximal-conservative argument is especially pertinent to new evangelicals since they have most keenly addressed the possibility of combining new trends in biblical scholarship with a belief in inerrancy. Barr (1986*a*: 27) later changes his verdict on the movement: 'Sometimes in recent years people who accept all the fundamentalist tenets have identified themselves as "Evangelicals" simply or as "Neo-Evangelicals". This does not mean that they think any differently

[18] However, Barr shows no particular regard for Bernard Ramm in this respect.

from fundamentalists but rather that they seek by their use of terminology to take over the "Evangelical" name and deny that any other kind of evangelicalism exists.'

American evangelicalism, particularly the new-evangelical variety, has been far more affected by the fundamentalist episode than has its British cousin. The current divergent strands in American evangelicalism are to be understood partly as differing reactions to its fundamentalist heritage, particularly its inheritance of the problem of inerrancy. American evangelicalism is riddled with debates over inerrancy, a topic little represented in British evangelical discussion. New-evangelical institutions, notably Fuller Seminary and the ETS, have suffered serious divisions over maintaining the doctrine. Fuller suffered rifts throughout the 1960s when Daniel Fuller, son of the Seminary's founder, challenged the doctrine of full inerrancy. The Seminary finally removed inerrancy from its statement of faith in the 1970s (Marsden 1987: 200–19). ETS has retained the doctrine.

By contrast, evangelical organizations in Britain seem barely conscious of inerrancy. The Evangelical Alliance's Basis of Faith upholds 'The divine inspiration of the Holy Scripture and its consequent entire trustworthiness and supreme authority in all matters of faith and conduct' (*Evangelical Alliance*, n.d.: 15). UCCF (formerly IVF), whom Barr cites as 'an excellent point of reference' for his research (1977: 21), affirms: 'The divine inspiration and infallibility of Holy Scripture as originally given, and its supreme authority in all matters of faith and conduct' (*Evangelical Belief*, 1988: 11).[19]

This is not to suggest that British evangelicals are concerned only with scripture's faultless guidance and not with its accurate reporting. Their attempts to preserve the maximum amount of factual truthfulness in scripture renders their concept of infallibility very close to that of inerrancy. Moreover, periodically inerrancy has been represented in the writings of British evangelicals, among Anglicans more than Nonconformists. James Packer defended a version of the inerrancy doctrine in *'Fundamentalism' and the Word of God* (1958*a*: 94–101), as did John Wenham in *Christ and the Bible* ([1972] 1993: 52, 169–95, 204 n. 19). Packer and

[19] When CICCU split from SCM it defended 'inerrancy of faith and practice', and so was already qualifying the term 'inerrancy' in ways which have led evangelicals to drop it altogether.

Wenham both participated in the International Conference on Biblical Inerrancy in Chicago in 1978, Packer playing a large part in drawing up the Chicago Statement on Biblical Inerrancy.[20]

Nevertheless, British evangelicals manifest a greater flexibility in their approach to inerrancy. John Wenham looks for 'adequate evidence' rather than 'absolute proofs' that 'the text is precisely as God gave it'. He even suggests that an 'uncertainty fringe of text or Canon may be a positive blessing, if it forces us to focus our attention upon the central truths of revelation' (ibid. 192, 193). While American formulations vary in their insistence upon scientific and historical inerrancy, they generally reflect a greater anxiety over factual accuracy than has ever been present in the British evangelical heritage. Most arguments for inerrancy in the States are intended as inductive arguments and require that biblical statements be proved correct and consistent. Some arguments are deductive, beginning with the premisses that God inspired scripture and God cannot err, and usually even the inductive arguments assume this deductive element. Scripture is bound to be inerrant, either by force of logic or by the need to preserve an empirical defence. Attempts to maintain the doctrine empirically put the greatest burden on factual accuracy. British evangelicals usually begin with Jesus, our trust in him, and his witness to the authority of the scriptures (e.g. Manley 1926; Packer 1958*a*: 54–62; Wenham [1972] 1993).[21] This line of reasoning is present in American evangelical apologetics (e.g. Pinnock 1974) but more dominant are arguments beginning from scripture's own claims to be inspired.

Barr denies any significant distinction: 'The Bible is inerrant because the Bible says it is inerrant, or because Jesus, Paul and Peter, as represented in the Bible, say that it is inerrant, which is the same thing' (1977: 72–3).[22] However, doctrines of scripture

[20] For fuller discussion of this Conference and Statement see Ch. 8.

[21] Ian Rennie notes this more Christocentric approach in the British evangelical view of verbal inspiration, which he illustrates by reference to C. H. Waller's *The Authoritative Inspiration of Holy Scripture (As Distinct From the Inspiration of Its Human Authors) Acknowledged by Our Lord and Saviour Jesus Christ* (1885; 1887), and to Waller's influence within Anglican evangelicalism. However, Rennie (1994: 337–8) argues that despite the British emphasis on Jesus' validation of scripture, 'there is little or no difference from the Princeton position'.

[22] Barr dismantles arguments which start from Jesus' sayings by showing that Jesus was not a submissive follower of scripture and that his attitude was not the fundamentalist one of insisting on the historical accuracy of the Old Testament. See 1984: 8–19.

which start with Jesus have a different centre of gravity. They seem not to demand such rigorous standards of precision, perhaps because the focus is on Christ, whose authority more clearly does not depend on rational or empirical proof. So Daniel H. C. Bartlett, who stood against evangelical liberalism in the first half of the century, was concerned to defend the historical accuracy of the Bible in general rather than in detail (Bromiley 1959: 40–2). The conviction by which he did so was that 'the historical and spiritual are closely interwoven', so that one could not 'question or reconstruct most of the history of Israel or even of Jesus and still expect to preach the same Gospel' (p. 41).

Logically Barr is right that an argument that begins with the biblical record of what Jesus says about scripture does not have a significantly different structure from an argument that begins with what the Bible says about itself. Yet an argument that has Jesus as its primary referent has an additional quality. One's acceptance of biblical authority becomes intimately connected to one's acceptance of Christ's authority: 'The question, "What think ye of the Old Testament?" resolves into the question, "What think ye of Christ?"' (Packer 1958*a*: 59). Despite the coercive nature of this connection, which links non-fundamentalist views of scripture with disloyalty to Christ, it makes possible an acknowledgement that one's experience of God in Christ is relevant to one's view of scripture. This consequence may be unintended since evangelical apologetics is dominated by the concern to provide a less personal and more objectively reasoned defence of scripture. Nevertheless, outside their apologetics evangelicals are keen to affirm that their regard for scripture grows with their love for Christ. Their very experience of the mediating role of scripture in their personal relationship to God undergirds their beliefs about the Bible. Barr recognizes this: '[the fundamentalist] believes in the truth of the entire Bible because every portion of it in his experience seems to speak to him of God and to bring to him a living experience of God in Jesus Christ' (1977: 76).

Arguments from experience are not logically connected to arguments from Jesus' sayings but in practice they are related. Evangelical acceptance of scripture is grounded in evangelical experience of God in Christ. Hence, if Christ is brought into the formal argument for inerrancy, this does seem to have two significant effects. One is that a rigid insistence on inerrancy in every detail is tempered and does not acquire central significance. The other is that the personal element in evangelical religion is more successfully accommodated, as illustrated by John Goldingay (1977*b*: 301):

> My conviction about the inspiration of scripture derives experientially from the impression it has made and makes on me. This experience meshes with what I discover to be the attitude of Jesus to the Old Testament scriptures, which (because it is his) ought to commend itself also even to those who have not (yet) been grasped experientially by scripture in this way.

The experiential aspect is manifested in the work of such British evangelical stalwarts as G. T. Manley and John Wenham:

> The Bible often presents a dull exterior . . . But one day there comes a conversion of soul, and the Bible is now approached in a new spirit, and as if by a magic key the door is opened to illimitable spiritual treasure. (Manley 1926: 4–5)
>
> Theology is a fallible human attempt to co-ordinate the data of revelation. The human intellect, even when renewed by the Holy Spirit, cannot know with absolute certainty. In his inmost being the Christian believer has an absolute assurance (that is, an assurance which comes from God's direct witness within him) that he has heard the voice of God and that he is a child of God. (Wenham [1972] 1993: 192)

2.3.3. *Philosophical Presuppositions*

A common evangelical response to unsympathetic biblical critics is to attack the presuppositions by which they operate. Barr recognizes this to be an increasing tendency among conservative polemicists (1981: p. xvii; 1977: 145–9, 152, 235). He rejects demands, made also by the biblical theology movement, that presuppositions be taken into account in matters of biblical exegesis and interpretation: 'who, really, would be favourably impressed by a book that openly confessed from the beginning that it was written to satisfy certain partisan ends and that all selection of material had been motivated by this aim?' (1988: 13). He dismisses conservative 'criticism of the supposed philosophical preconceptions behind biblical criticism' as 'irresponsible carping' (1977: 149), for he finds that conservatives offer no theories regarding the influence that philosophical trends should have on biblical scholarship.

In fact, criticisms of non-conservative presuppositions reflect three major and conflicting philosophical influences upon evangelicals, which shall be described in the following chapters. Fundamentalists and their evangelical heirs have traditionally been suspicious of philosophy, associating it with a love of human wisdom and a vain exaltation of the human powers to discover truth. 'Philosophy', says Martyn Lloyd-Jones, 'has always been the cause of the church going astray, for philosophy means, ultimately, a trusting to human reason and human understanding' ([1971] 1992: 45). An article on 'Modern Philosophy' in *The Fundamentals* expressed this sentiment thus:

> Prominent among the elements of the world and of human tradition is the principle that the world reflects the grandeur of *man*, and that human reason is the highest and mightiest factor in it . . .
>
> It follows of necessity that philosophy and divine revelation are utterly irreconcilable . . . The pursuit of truth to be *philosophical*, must be conducted in directions in which truth *cannot possibly be found*.
>
> (Mauro n.d.: ii. 88–9)

Such anti-philosophy itself constitutes a philosophical stance. Lloyd-Jones declares that 'the evangelical *distrusts reason and particularly reason in the form of philosophy*' (Lloyd-Jones [1971] 1992: 44–5). The suspicion of reason and philosophy was a feature of Reformation thought and of post-Reformed scholasticism, where they were given ministerial rather than magisterial functions. The role of reason was to draw legitimate theological conclusions from the explicit statements in scripture, while philosophy was to prepare the way for the higher discipline of theology (Muller 1987: 236–49). These attitudes were maintained in some quarters even in the intellectual climate of the eighteenth century, when the light of reason was brought to bear on the claims of revelation. The Scottish Common Sense philosophers reflected both the old and new ways of thinking. They defended common sense against fanciful philosophical reasoning, and encouraged the acquiescence of reason to divine mysteries. Yet they also used reason to test the evidences of scripture.

Evangelicals have inherited this dual approach. On one level they continue to think of reason as a servant of scripture: 'We may not look to reason to tell us whether Scripture is right in what it says (reason is not in any case competent to pass such a judgement); instead, we must look to Scripture to tell us whether reason is right in what it thinks on the subjects with which Scripture deals' (Packer 1958*a*: 48). On another level they suggest that their belief in the authority of scripture is justified when the truth of biblical propositions is verified by proper textual criticism and extra-biblical inquiry. They further maintain 'that biblical truth is both objective and absolute', and that 'the meaning expressed in each biblical text is single, definite and fixed', and is to this extent open to unbiased cognition (Chicago Statement on Biblical Hermeneutics, Arts. 6 and 7).

Within this context, presuppositions are generally regarded as negative elements which hinder true science and harbour 'un- and anti-biblical principles' (Chicago Statement on Biblical Inerrancy, Exposition). This attitude was particularly prevalent among evangelicals in the early twentieth century, prior to developments in the philosophy of science which drew attention to subjective aspects in scientific research. Evangelicals did not pretend that they were without presuppositions (e.g. Manley 1926: 9, 22), but they regarded as more harmful the naturalistic principles behind modern criticism. They attributed to higher critics a bias against the supernatural fed by a materialist philosophy. Some evangelicals rejected biological and social evolution as fanciful hypotheses. Evangelical apologists called for 'an objective study of the evidence' which would not postulate that 'every story of the miraculous or evidence of the supernatural' be accounted for on naturalistic grounds (Manley 1926: 25, 21–2).

Since the beginnings of fundamentalism, evangelicals informed by Dutch Reformed thought have developed their own distinct philosophical position. They have rejected the assumption that a wholly objective approach to scripture is possible. Cornelius Van Til, in particular, has written extensively on the role of legitimate and illegitimate philosophical presuppositions in biblical apologetics. In the mid-twentieth century a rift developed in evangelical circles in the United States between so-called 'presuppositionalists' and 'evidentialists', the latter insisting that study of the biblical evidence could be objective. Herman Dooyeweerd reflects the same Dutch tradition as Van Til. Barr (1977: 276) notes evangelical interest in Dooyeweerd's 'Christian philosophy'. A Christian philosophy as opposed to other kinds of philosophy is alien to the Common Sense outlook, which assumes that all people basically think alike. Dooyeweerd and Van Til insist that presuppositions underlie all forms of reasoning, and they distinguish Christian from non-Christian presuppositions. Evangelicals of this persuasion consider their presuppositions to be superior in that they offer the most coherent account of the data at hand. This position is discussed in Chapter 7.

The recent interest in philosophical hermeneutics, described in Chapter 8, has encouraged evangelicals to acknowledge the influence of cultural presuppositions. Barr notices that increasingly evangelicals are defending their position on the grounds that their presuppositions are as good as anyone else's (1981: p. xvii; 1991*a*: 151). This development is unfavourable to both the Common Sense and the Dutch heritage. Those who attempt to provide objectively valid arguments would not celebrate the '*anti-objectivist* tendency of modern hermeneutics' (Barr 1991*a*: 151), and those who follow the Dutch line in advancing a Christian philosophy are not content to receive equal recognition alongside other viewpoints.

Many evangelicals reflect aspects of more than one of these philosophical strands, although the first strand has remained the most dominant. Common Sense assumptions among evangelicals have been the least self-conscious and the most intuitive.[23] Influence from Dutch and hermeneutical philosophy has been more consciously appropriated. However, these other philosophies have not been widely successful in overcoming the empirical rationalist characteristics that mark the fundamentalist mentality.

The next chapter goes back to the eighteenth century to discover the philosophical origins of these characteristics, and suggests features of the Scottish Common Sense philosophy which find their parallel in fundamentalism. Chapter 4 traces the influence of Common Sense assumptions upon fundamentalist thought via the theology of Old Princeton and early fundamentalism. These provided alien contexts for the philosophy, which was employed to serve a conservative, biblical apologetic. The appropriation of an empirical rationalist framework contributed to the fundamentalist apprehension of the apologetic task. A

[23] Some fundamentalists have preserved Common Sense thought more consciously than others. Mark Noll (1985: 233) gives examples of those who made a point of reaffirming a Common Sense alignment, including J. Oliver Buswell and Henry Thiessen of Wheaton College and Lewis Sperry Chafer of Dallas Theological Seminary.

fundamentalist style of apologetic continues to pervade much contemporary evangelical thought, thus substantiating Barr's main point that evangelicalism is 'spoiled by the rationalistic mind-set into which it is led by its own doctrine of scripture' (1980*a*: 79).

3

The Fundamentalist Mentality: Its Philosophical Roots

> A particular philosophical pattern, born in the eighteenth century, has through a set of unusual circumstances been able to survive and to give remarkable stability to the fundamentalist religious pattern.
>
> (Barr 1977: 276)

3.1. Empirical Rationalism

James Barr regards rationalism as one of the factors differentiating fundamentalism from earlier, similarly closed forms of Christianity (1977: 116, 171–4), and as the key feature in rendering contemporary conservative evangelicalism fundamentalistic in character. He illustrates fundamentalist rationalism by reference to the Princeton theologians Charles Hodge and Benjamin Warfield. He attributes to them a 'pre-Kantian eighteenth-century empirical rationalism' (ibid. 272), in that they display great confidence in reason and the authority of facts, and assume ultimate unity between science and religion. He finds affinities between these Princetonian ways of thinking and contemporary fundamentalism. More specifically he regards Hodge and Warfield as 'leading figures in the [fundamentalist] movement', and attributes to Warfield the 'most influential traditional fundamentalist view' of scripture (ibid.; 1984: 141).

Barr makes no specific mention of Scottish Common Sense Realism, which was the dominant philosophy at Princeton throughout the nineteenth century. Since George Marsden wrote his history of fundamentalism (1980), the role of Common Sense philosophy in shaping fundamentalist thought has been heavily emphasized.[1] The historical process by which the Scottish philosophers came to influence American clergymen and theologians has been researched by various religious historians (Ahlstrom 1955; Bozeman 1977; Holifield 1978; Sloan 1971; Noll 1989; Gauvreau 1985; 1994). Marsden (1980) traces the influence of Common Sense Realism not only through Princeton theology but also through dispensationalism and revivalism, and finds it the most formative philosophy for early twentieth-century fundamentalism. He further notes its continuing influence upon evangelicalism (1983; 1989), as do Mark Noll (1985) and Mark Ellingsen (1985). John Gerstner (1974) and D. Clair Davis (1984) represent evangelical recognition of the influence of Common Sense philosophy upon Princeton theology and their own evangelical tradition.

Common Sense philosophy has been little expounded by those who note its impact on fundamentalism and evangelicalism. This is partly because the effects of the philosophy have been general rather than precise. Noll (1985: 219–21, 225 incl. n. 29) warns that historians who look for a specific influence will be disappointed, and he criticizes those who make a simple equation between Common Sense themes and evangelical thought. This is an important point, but may be more readily heeded if historians possessed greater knowledge of the philosophy itself. Recent claims about its effects have been excessive. Mark Ellingsen (1985: 197) suggests that Common Sense Realism is 'the cutting edge of Conservative Evangelical identity', and Martin Marty (1992: 6) states that 'Baconian inductivism and Scottish common sense realism represent fundamentalist *creencias*, ideas which are so close that one does not know one holds them'. Common Sense Realism is now so frequently associated with fundamentalism and evangelicalism that an examination of the philosophy and a proper assessment of its influence seem long overdue. The following account

[1] Theodore Dwight Bozeman (1977: pp. xiv, 171–3) previously noted its influence on fundamentalism, which he saw as coming via Princeton. John C. Vander Stelt (1978) traced its influence from Princeton to Westminster Seminary. Vander Stelt's study reflects the Dutch tradition of Abraham Kuyper, shared by G. C. Berkouwer and Herman Dooyeweerd, which has been critical of the rationalistic effects of Common Sense philosophy upon Princeton and Westminster theology. Others, like Barr, attribute fundamentalist assumptions and evangelical attitudes to Enlightenment influences more generally (e.g. Bebbington 1989: 50–69), or to the philosophy of Locke (Sandeen 1970*b*: 115–17; Schouls 1990). See s. 4.1 below.

should enable us to evaluate its contribution to the fundamentalist mentality.

3.2. Scottish Common Sense Philosophy

3.2.1. *Introduction*

Common Sense Realism is best exemplified in the works of Thomas Reid (1710–96). It received popular expression in James Beattie's writings (1735–1802), and was brought into disrepute by James Oswald (d. 1793). Reid's *Inquiry* was published in 1764, followed two years later by the first volume of Oswald's *An Appeal to Common Sense in Behalf of Religion*, and six years later by Beattie's *An Essay on the Nature and Immutability of Truth in Opposition to Sophistry and Scepticism.* Beattie's and Oswald's use of the phrase 'common sense' and their dependence upon Reid invited their association with him as the Common Sense philosophers. The three received collective denunciation from Priestley (1775: 5), who referred to them as 'a set of pretended philosophers', and from Kant ([1783] 1953: 8), who charged them with appealing to common sense 'like an oracle when one cannot produce anything sensible with which to justify oneself'. After the success of the *Essay*, Beattie wrote a common sense defence of Christianity called *Evidences of the Christian Religion Briefly and Plainly Stated* (1786). Both he and Oswald employed the methods of Reid's philosophy of the human mind for a Common Sense defence of religion.

Reid presented a fuller definition of common sense in the *Essays on the Intellectual Powers of Man* (1785). He then turned from mental to moral enquiry in the *Essays on the Active Powers of Man* (1788), where he posited a moral sense which recognizes objective moral truth. Dugald Stewart (1753–1828) systematized Reid's philosophy and widened its reception in academic circles. He dedicated his *Elements of the Philosophy of the Human Mind* to Reid, who was his tutor, and wrote a *Life of Reid* ([1802] 1863) which includes a critical analysis of his philosophy. Stewart's *Elements* came to three volumes (1792; 1814; 1827), the first of which was supplemented by a collection of *Philosophical Essays* (1810). Like Reid, he applied the principles of his philosophy of mind to ethics, and wrote a two-volume *Philosophy of the Active and Moral Powers of Man* (1828).

Although Stewart exchanged the term 'common sense' for a less ambiguous phrase, 'the fundamental laws of belief', it is appropriate to regard him as a Common Sense philosopher, indeed as the last of the philosophers in this particular school (Grave 1960: 5–6). Later in the nineteenth century Sir William Hamilton revived an interest in Reid and greatly influenced James McCosh. McCosh became president of Princeton College and a key figure in sustaining the Scottish philosophy at that institution and in America more generally. His explicit contribution to the development and impact of Common Sense Realism was a thorough and incisive account of *The Scottish Philosophy from Hutcheson to Hamilton* (1875).

The main preoccupation of the Common Sense philosophers was to combat the 'ideal' theory, which Reid attributed to Locke and ultimately to Aristotle. Their prime target was Hume's scepticism, which grew out of Locke's doctrine of ideas and which, they believed, manifested its unsound nature. Locke posited that the direct objects of our perceptions are not external realities but ideas in the mind which represent these realities in some way. He drew upon Descartes's distinction between primary and secondary qualities of matter.[2] According to this distinction, primary qualities, namely extension and motion, are essential to matter, whereas secondary qualities, such as colour, smell, and taste, reside not in the external object as such, but in the mind as it perceives the object (Descartes 1984: 88–90, 284–5; 1985: 29–31). Locke ([1689] 1979: 135) defined secondary qualities as 'nothing in the objects themselves, but Powers to produce various Sensations in us by their *primary Qualities*'.

Berkeley interpreted Locke as distinguishing (arbitrarily) between qualities which exist materially and qualities which exist only mentally. He brought both primary and secondary qualities into the mind, and thus extinguished matter as a substance distinct from ideas.[3] He regarded ideas and the minds perceiving them as the only realities. In order to avoid any gap between ideas and the real world, through which scepticism might enter, he defined the real world in terms of ideas and denied the existence of a mind-

[2] René Descartes, *The World*, Ch. 5; *Principles of Philosophy*, Part Four, sect. 198 (both in Descartes (1984)); *Meditations on First Philosophy*, Third Meditation (in Descartes 1985); Locke ([1689] 1979: 134–43, 301–2, 544–8).

[3] Berkeley ([1734] 1975), Introduction and Part I.

independent material world ([1734] 1975: 88). Hume attributed our idea of external existence directly to ideas and impressions rather than to external objects themselves. He further rejected the notion of minds as substances with continued existence and identity.[4] The way to scepticism which Berkeley tried to close was thus held open. When Reid realized this, he ended his endorsement of the Berkeleian system and criticized the ideal doctrine in its entirety. He traced its inception to Cartesian thought and devoted most intellectual effort to the refutation of Hume's sceptical conclusions (Reid 1863: 206–8, 283).

In the exposition offered below, I indicate areas where it is fruitful to postulate a relation between Common Sense Realism and fundamentalist and evangelical thought. These may be introduced briefly here.

3.2.1.1. *Realism*

Reid posited a direct realism in place of the doctrine of ideas. He defended the common-sense belief that we perceive objects rather than ideas of objects, and hence that we perceive the outside world directly. He further argued that memory puts us in relation with the object remembered rather than with our idea of that object, so that our memory reliably informs us about past events in our own experience. Similarly, he held that, with certain qualifications, testimony can be trusted to tell us of actual events in the experience of others and not simply of the reporter's point of view. Language corresponds to states of affairs external to the mind and so puts us in touch with reality. His philosophy was based on the assumption that God would not give us one set of faculties—the senses—to deceive us, and another faculty—reason—to unearth the deception. Against Hume's claim that our experiences are mediated by copies of impressions in the mind, Reid insisted that our experiences are immediate.

Evangelicals prefer Reid's directly realist solution to scepticism, over Kant's solution. Their differences with non-evangelicals may be understood on a philosophical level in terms of the distinction between the Common Sense faith in the ability to know things in themselves and the Kantian denial that this is possible.[5] Kant

[4] Hume ([1739–40] 1978), I. 2. 6; I. 4. 6; ([1777] 1975), 12.

[5] Ellingsen (1985: 201, 202) draws this distinction which is helpful, though he overestimates the role of Common Sense Realism in creating the conservative evangelical identity.

distinguished between (phenomenal) mental impressions and (noumenal) things in themselves. He denied that our senses give us access to the truth of things in themselves since we always process our information. Kant thus accorded a significant role to human consciousness in constructing truth: the world as we know it is perceived in accordance with concepts we have imposed upon it. Evangelicals are wary of the subjectivism entailed by Kant's proposal. As Mark Noll (1986: 146) explains:

> Evangelicals are 'realists' in the sense that they believe that the world enjoys an independent existence apart from its perception by humans, that essence precedes existence, and that the mind is capable of perceiving existence beyond itself with at least some accuracy . . .
>
> [They are] almost always pre-, anti-, or (in selected cases) post-Kantian. A few evangelicals may study Kant with profit, but almost none accept the Kantian conclusion that the human mind is the determining element of ontology and ethics.

They are particularly unhappy with the Kantian influence on biblical interpretation, which has undermined confidence in the factual nature of the biblical reports and encouraged critics to focus on the way in which the human authors understood and presented their message.

Reid was a Doctor of Divinity and a Presbyterian clergyman, but within the Moderate rather than the Evangelical wing of the Church of Scotland. He said little in his philosophical works and lectures about the Bible, and gave greater consideration to natural religion. However, his realism and his thoughts on language and testimony provided philosophical support for the conviction that in scripture we have records not of ideas of events but of events themselves. This aspect of his philosophy is pleasing to evangelicals, who above all guard the objective nature of biblical truth and who detect subjectivizing trends in most modern theology.

3.2.1.2. *Common Sense*

In order to combat scepticism, Reid posited the existence and reliability of principles of common sense which are inherent in our constitution and which act as the first principles of knowledge. Though he did not argue from God to the reliability of these principles, he did believe that our Creator has endowed us with principles which we are obliged to take for granted. Reid claimed that the principles of common sense are self-evident, their contraries absurd, and their denial impossible in practice. In attempting to reject such foundational principles, he argued, one implicitly presupposes them. He held that there are certain truths evident to all human beings except those who are of unsound mind, or affected by unsound philosophy. The Common Sense school, particularly the populists James Beattie and James Oswald, held in suspicion any philosopher who employed reason to furnish conclusions which are contrary to common sense.

Evangelicals borrowed arguments from Common Sense philosophy to defend the perspicuity of scripture. They found in Reid's disapproval of sophistry and fanciful reasoning a way to counteract the influence of false principles of biblical interpretation coming from Germany. In the mid-nineteenth century, Alexander Carson (1863: 223–4), an Ulster Baptist, suggested that:

> He [Reid] has shown the danger of admitting, as the foundation of reasoning, any principle that is not self-evident, and the equal danger of endeavouring to prove by reasoning that which is evident in itself.
>
> Of all human studies the interpretation of the Scriptures is the most important, yet of all subjects this has afforded the greatest and most numerous discrepancies . . . It is a self-evident truth, that if the Scriptures are the Word of God, their phraseology cannot give just ground for this extravagance.

As new interpretative methods emerged, evangelicals protected the beliefs of the common man against the learned judgements of the scholar and biblical critic: 'In ninety-nine out of a hundred cases the meaning that the plain man gets out of the Bible is the correct one.'[6] It became a principle of fundamentalist interpretation that: 'When the plain sense of Scripture makes common sense, seek no other sense.'[7]

3.2.1.3. *Baconianism*

The method of enquiry adopted by the Common Sense philosophers was the inductive method of Francis Bacon. Reid (1863: 271–2) described 'the true method of philosophising' thus: 'From real facts, ascertained by observation and experiment, to collect by

[6] Reuben A. Torrey (1906), source unclear, quoted in McLoughlin (1959: 372).

[7] Lindsey (1970: 50), and quoting David L. Cooper, *When Gog's Armies Meet the Almighty in the Land of Israel* (Los Angeles: Biblical Research Society, 1940).

just induction the laws of Nature, and to apply the laws so discovered, to account for the phaenomena of Nature'.[8] Reasoning which strayed from these rules was discredited as hypothesizing, and was considered the vice of philosophers. Hypotheses were rejected as systems 'built partly on facts, and much upon conjecture' (p. 249). They were said to occur when reason proceeded beyond the facts presented to it by the senses and enquired into 'the secret operations of nature' (p. 234).

Since the nineteenth century biblical conservatives have applied the inductive method to the task of theology, which they describe as the collecting and classifying of biblical facts. 'Baconianism', as the commitment to Bacon's method was known, gave plain thinking a further boost over the vain philosophy and hypothetical fancies of so-called experts.

3.2.1.4. *Evidentialist Apologetics*

Revelation itself became an area for inductive enquiry. The testimony of the Holy Spirit to the authority of scripture was undermined by a demand for reason and evidences. Among the Common Sense philosophers this was especially apparent in J. Beattie's *Evidences of the Christian Religion* and Reid's *Lectures on Natural Philosophy*. The idea that scripture 'evidence[d] itself to be the Word of God' (Westminster Confession, 1.5) was not new, but evidences had previously been regarded as supportive of, rather than foundational to, claims to the Bible's truth and authority. A fundamentalist biblical apologetic is based upon evidences, such as the harmonizing of apparent contradictions within scripture, or the matching of biblical statements to archaeological, historical, and scientific discoveries. To someone of a fundamentalist way of thinking, a problem with the evidence on this level would deprive the Christian faith of solid ground by undermining the truth and authority of scripture.

3.2.2. *Exposition*

3.2.2.1. *Reid's Realism and the Doctrine of Ideas*

Although Reid was not the founder of Common Sense Realism he is regarded as its 'fit representative' (McCosh 1875: 192).[9] His main

[8] To assess the great extent to which these principles accord with Bacon's own thought see *Novum Organum* (1889), and Fowler's Introduction, pp. 126–31.

[9] Predecessors in this philosophical strain included Lord Shaftesbury (1671–1713), who believed in the power of nature to educate humankind and would not go so far as Locke in

contribution to philosophy is the refutation of the ideal theory which he replaced with the doctrine of common sense. Reid rejects the ideal theory as a hypothesis for which he can find no evidence, 'excepting the authority of philosophers' (Reid 1863: 127–8, 140, 283). The 'vulgar' are not aware of strange ideal objects in the mind. They know of only one object, 'which in perception, is something external that exists; in memory, something that did exist; and in conception, may be something that never existed' (p. 369).

That perception puts us in contact with the outside world is a belief to which, by the constitution of our nature, we are compelled to assent. In perceiving an object, 'we have, as it were by inspiration, a certain knowledge of its existence' (p. 260). Reid employs natural instinct against a sceptical conclusion: 'Nature intended the visible figure as a sign of the tangible figure and situation of bodies, and hath taught us, by a kind of instinct, to put it always to this use' (p. 146). A radical empiricism which refuses assistance from other mental powers will result in a total scepticism which refuses to make any connection between visible and tangible figures.

In a section entitled 'The Geometry of Visibles' (pp. 147–52), Reid presents a technical mathematical argument to defend the claim that visible figure and extension are the signs of tangible figure and extension. The geometrician 'does not consider that the visible figure presented to his eye, is only the representative of a tangible figure', nor that 'these two figures have really different properties' (p. 147). According to the ideal theory, the mind knows only some copy of the impression that a tangible object makes on the sense organs. Reid uses the example of a right-lined triangle to make the point that a tangible figure is projected on to the bottom of the eye as a spherical triangle, but is seen as the rectilinear triangle that it is (p. 148). If we knew only copies of impressions, he argues, we would have developed a spherical rather than Euclidean geometry to match these spherical perceptions.

denying innate ideas, and Francis Hutcheson (1694–1746), who expounded Shaftesbury's views and exported them to Scotland. Hutcheson believed in the existence of cognitive powers which he called senses and which are a part of our very nature and constitution. McCosh therefore considered him to be the founder of the Scottish school (1875: 68–9), though Sir William Hamilton gave this title to Hutcheson's teacher, Gershom Carmichael (in Reid 1863: 30 n.).

Perception is an active process and is directed immediately to external objects. Ideas are, then, thoughts about objects, rather than objects of thought (p. 373). Similarly with regard to memory, the objects of remembrance are distinct from the act of remembrance (p. 340). Like perception, memory is an unanalysable 'original faculty, given us by the Author of our being' (ibid.). Reid can find no necessary connection between remembering an act and the act having happened, and can say only that the belief which we have of what we remember 'is the result of our constitution' (p. 341). Reid's point is partly that our inability to explain the operation of memory does not affect our belief that it yields 'knowledge . . . of things past' (p. 341). Memory is an original faculty which inexplicably yields immediate knowledge of things remembered.

The task of philosophy is not to explain the secret causes of nature, but to investigate the facts of physical and mental behaviour and to infer laws. The laws of mental philosophy do not explain why our minds work as they do, any more than the discovery of the law of gravity explains the falling apple. Only nature can explain why the apple falls, and only our constitution holds the explanation for why we trust our senses and our memory. Reid does not indulge in metaphysical speculation about unseen causes, but vindicates belief itself as an ultimate category: 'It is a dictate of common sense, that the causes we assign of appearances ought to be real, and not fictions of human imagination' (p. 261). He finds comfort in the fact that the 'vulgar are satisfied' with the testimony of their senses while 'Men of speculation' are impatient to account for that testimony (p. 260).

3.2.2.2. *The Principles of Common Sense*

Common sense is Reid's antidote to the scepticism engendered by the ideal doctrine. Principles of common sense are a priori principles which bear immediate, irresistible, and unanalysable conviction. They are discovered through self-conscious reflection and have their being in our very constitution. They are also referred to as first principles, axioms, common notions, self-evident truths, natural knowledge, and fundamental reason (p. 434). Reid is primarily interested in the principles of contingent truths. These yield conviction of the reality of the objects of our perceptions. They also furnish conceptions of the self and other minds, the actions and testimonies of fellow human beings, and the laws of nature (pp. 441–52). They are self-evident and cannot be defended by reason: 'No man seeks a reason for believing what he sees or feels; and, if he did, it would be difficult to find one. But, though he can give no reason for believing his senses, his belief remains as firm as if it were grounded on demonstration' (p. 328). Reid trusts inference as much as he does deduction, and accords the highest degree of probable reasoning the status of 'certainty' (p. 482; cf. Stewart 1814: 240).

Reid by no means attempts exhaustive treatment of the principles of common sense. He does not fully enumerate them, nor does he state systematically the criteria for determining them. This reflects his conviction that they are not at all mysterious. Everyone recognizes common-sense principles. They are fundamental to our functioning and survival, and their criteria are pragmatic: 'we are under a necessity to take [them] for granted in the common concerns of life' (p. 108). However, Reid does characterize the principles of common sense according to their self-evidence and absurdity of the contraries. Hence, reason plays a discerning role in the recognition of these principles although not a discursive role in establishing them: 'To reason against any of these kinds of evidence, is absurd; nay, to reason for them is absurd. They are first principles; and such fall not within the province of reason, but of common sense' (ibid.). A further test of their legitimacy is that they are held by the bulk of mankind. Not that mass judgement must necessarily be right, but the fact that so many people rely upon them indicates their inherent place in human nature. This provides their ultimate justification. We cannot sustain a scepticism which does violence to our constitution (p. 448).

Reid cites the general trustworthiness of our faculties in justification of our reliance upon them. He does not, like Descartes, found his defence of our faculties upon a theistic argument. Nevertheless, his faith in the reliability of the human mind ultimately rests upon faith in 'the Author of our nature', who 'wisely fitted' our intellectual powers 'for the discovery of truth' (p. 468). The belief in our senses is 'the immediate effect of our constitution, which is the work of the Almighty' (p. 329). One need not believe in God in order to trust one's senses, for one trusts them anyway by nature. Still, if justification for our trust is required, then the explanation must end with God: 'If the power of perceiving external objects in certain circumstances, be a part of the original constitution of the human mind, all attempts to account for it will be vain. No other account can be given of the constitution of things, but the will of Him that made them' (p. 260). Common sense is 'purely the gift of Heaven' (p. 425). Reid is not preaching but merely indicating an end to all further enquiry.

3.2.2.3. *Philosophy and Reason*

Reid sets the 'wisdom of *philosophy* . . . in opposition to the *common sense* of mankind' (p. 127). He has in mind Humean scepticism, which 'pretends to demonstrate, a priori, that there can be no such thing as a material world; that sun, moon, stars, and earth, vegetable and animal bodies, are, and can be nothing else, but sensations in the mind'. Common sense regards this 'as a kind of metaphysical lunacy, and concludes that too much learning is apt to make men mad' (p. 127).

In his first work, *The Inquiry*, Reid sets the principles of common sense over reason, and represents the intuitions of the plain man against the vain speculations of philosophers. He gives a passionate disclaimer of philosophy which has rendered his writings suspect in the eyes of many philosophers: 'I despise Philosophy, and renounce its guidance—let my soul dwell with Common Sense' (1863: 101). He denounces in particular the modern philosopher whom the plain man thinks either merry or mad for his claim that 'there is no smell in plants, nor in anything but in the mind' (p. 112). Philosophy, it seems, 'puts men into a new world, and gives them different faculties from common men' and thus is 'set at variance' from common sense (ibid.). Reid sides with the vulgar, who are 'unpractised in philosophical researches, and guided by the uncorrupted primary instincts of nature' (p. 302, cf. 254, 292).

In the *Intellectual Powers*, Reid is obliged to respond to criticism and formulate more thoroughly what he means by common sense. Here he describes common sense both as 'the first-born of Reason' and the first function of reason:

> We ascribe to reason two offices, or two degrees. The first is to judge of things self-evident; the second to draw conclusions that are not self-evident from those that are. The first of these is the province, and the sole province, of common sense; and, therefore, it coincides with reason in its whole extent, and is only another name for one branch or one degree of reason. (1863: 425, cf. 476 and *Active Powers*; ibid. 558)

None of the Common Sense philosophers, with the possible exception of Beattie, wishes to sustain antagonism between reason and common sense, though all remain ambivalent towards philosophy.[10] Their ambiguity in seeing reason and common sense as both opposed and complementary should be understood in the light of a distinction between true and false philosophy—a distinction which Oswald, for all his faults,[11] makes more explicit than do the others (e.g. 1768: 91–3, 168). Oswald (ibid. 93) accuses the learned of indulging a 'licentiousness in reasoning', and of not preserving 'that harmony and good understanding which ought always to subsist between philosophy and common sense'. False, speculative philosophy makes it appear that the dictates of reason are at odds with those of common sense, while true philosophy must be grounded in common sense. It is impossible that the two should be opposed. As Reid (1863: 425) argues, a 'conclusion drawn by a train of just reasoning from true principles cannot possibly contradict any decision of common sense, because truth will always be consistent with itself'. The new sceptical philosophy is a false philosophy.

Dugald Stewart, a pupil of Reid's, is less tolerant of vulgar reasoning than is his tutor, and more tolerant of philosophical speculation (e.g. 1792: 233, 354, 360–1). He therefore denies that it is 'vulgar prejudice that [Reid] wishes to oppose to philosophical speculation', or that it is philosophy *per se* that he refutes, despite Reid's bold denunciation of philosophy in the *Inquiry*. Instead he

[10] Beattie, whose *Essay* was in its day read more widely than Reid's *Inquiry*, remains insistent that reason should be distinguished from common sense (1771: 40–51). However, he confuses reason and reasoning: 'who will assure me that my reason is less liable to mistake than my common sense? And if reason be mistaken, what shall we say? Is this mistake to be rectified by a second reasoning, as liable to mistake as the first?' (ibid. 50). Such suspicion of reasoning is in much the same vein as the rest of the school. Beattie (ibid. 397–403) allows that reasoning is in its proper sphere only when it is based on common sense.

[11] James Oswald barely limits the scope of common sense, enumerating as many principles of common sense as suit his purpose, particularly in establishing the primary truths of religion and morality (1768: 206–29). Anything he cannot explain is called a first principle, as though our inability to explain a truth were an indicator that the truth is primary. His extravagances, for example claiming that monotheistic as opposed to polytheistic belief flows from a principle in our constitution (1772: 75–7), have caused some to set him apart from the Common Sense school (Grave 1960: 5; Beanblossom and Lehrer 1983: p. xxxix). His influence has been minimal compared to that of Reid and Stewart, and of Beattie in his lifetime. His work, nevertheless, provides a useful illustration of how the philosophy can be dogmatically manipulated.

presents Reid as opposing the 'essential principles of the human understanding to the gratuitous assumptions of metaphysical theorists' (1810: 60).

Though he can go to great lengths to defend Reid's use of the phrase 'common sense' (e.g. ibid. 59–61), Stewart rejects the nomenclature himself. He finds the phrase 'common sense' too lax for the precision with which the Common Sense philosophers want to use it. He objects that 'common sense' is generally understood as nearly synonymous with 'Mother-wit' ([1802] 1863: 28). The term does not do justice to such weighty laws of belief as the '*constituent elements of human reason*' (1814: 64), which Stewart suggests be called the 'Fundamental Laws of Belief' (1814: 57, 58, 60; [1802] 1863: 27–8). This phrase receives approval from McCosh (1875: 290) because it avoids the ambiguity in the term 'common sense'.

3.2.2.4. *Induction and Hypotheses*

The Common Sense philosophers were impressed by Isaac Newton's use of the inductive method in the realm of natural philosophy. They applied the same method to their enquiries into the mind. Reid (1863: 97) accords the method itself the status of common sense:

> By our constitution, we have a strong propensity to trace particular facts and observations to general rules, and to apply such general rules to account for other effects, or to direct us in the production of them . . . [Newton's] *regulae philosophandi* are maxims of common sense, and are practised every day in common life; and he who philosophizes by other rules, either concerning the material system or concerning the mind, mistakes his aim.

The inductive method keeps philosophy in its place, investigating the available empirical phenomena rather than enquiring into their secret causes. The 'object of physical science', Stewart (1814: 308) writes, is '*not* to investigate the nature of these efficient causes on which the phenomena of the universe ultimately depend, but to examine with accuracy what the phenomena are, and what the general laws by which they are regulated'.

Philosophy which oversteps its boundaries, such as Berkeleian Idealism, is condemned as hypothetical. Reid (1863: 293) warns philosophers 'to beware of hypotheses, especially when they lead to conclusions which contradict the principles upon which all men of common sense must act in common life'. Thus common sense is a judge of true philosophy. Reid accuses Berkeley of arguing from a 'hypothesis against fact', the fact being 'that all mankind have a fixed belief of an external material world' (ibid. 132). Similarly, Stewart regards it as 'a simple and literal statement of *the fact*' resolved in a law of our constitution that qualities 'have an existence *independent* of our perceptions' (Stewart 1810: 80, 81).

However, Stewart criticizes Reid for going further than was necessary in his 'indiscriminate zeal against every speculation to which the epithet *hypothetical* can in any degree, be applied' (1814: 424). He argues that a qualified acceptance of hypotheses reflects the precepts of Bacon and of some of his most enlightened followers (ibid. 407). He remarks that the theory of gravitation and the Copernican system were developed from hypotheses (ibid. 403). Stewart even suggests that our judgements of common sense may be hypotheses awaiting further information. For example, the 'conclusions of one individual with respect to the springs of action in the breast of another, can never, on the most favourable supposition, amount to more than to a Hypothesis supported by strong analogies' (ibid. 418). He is less sure than are the other Common Sense philosophers that we can know when we have reached the limit of enquiry, that is, when we have arrived 'at the simple and original laws of our constitution' (1792: 384). Stewart warns against multiplying original principles unnecessarily. He probably has in mind Oswald and Beattie, who affirmed principles of common sense as final explanations for a vast number of mysteries.[12]

3.2.2.5. *Language and Testimony*

Reid draws an analogy between perception and human testimony based upon the way in which language operates. In language 'things are signified to us by signs', and the mind, 'either by original principles or by custom, passes from the sign to the conception and belief of the things signified' (1863: 194). Reid (p. 117) distinguishes 'natural language', an innately understood sys-

[12] Reid for his part was critical of Stewart's endeavour to develop a theory of mind to the extent that Stewart's theory was 'grounded upon the Hypothesis of hidden trains of thinking'. He reminded Stewart that his own work was an 'Inquiry' into the human mind, not an attempt at a comprehensive 'System' (Aberdeen University Library MS 2131/1/II/3, fos. 6, 11, quoted in Robinson 1989: 413, 414).

tem of signs, from 'artificial language', which acquires its meaning from convention and agreement. The signs of natural language are modulations of voice, gestures, and features, and we know their interpretation innately. The signs of artificial language are articulate sounds, and the connection with the things signified is established by men and learnt through experience. The development of artificial language is dependent on natural language, which establishes the very possibility of meaning. In both forms of language, once the connection is discovered the sign 'always suggests the thing signified, and creates the belief of it' (p. 195). However, as artificial language expands and becomes more abstract it loses its natural grounding. Meanings of given words and phrases become less widely shared across time and cultures, and confusion and ambiguity arise. Reid believes it is possible to establish firm connections between artificial signs of language and the things signified. He finds 'no greater impediment to the advancement of knowledge than the ambiguity of words' (p. 220).

Reid arrives at our faith in human testimony through a consideration of how we learn language. We believe that 'men, who have it in their power to do otherwise, will continue to use the same words when they think of the same things' (p. 196). This belief is not derived from experience, from reason, or from any compact or promise. It arises from two principles implanted in our natures by the Author of our Being, who intended that 'we should receive the greatest and most important part of our knowledge by the information of others' (ibid.). The first of these principles is a propensity to speak truth, which is there even in a lie because it is a yielding to a natural impulse. The second is the principle of credulity—of believing what one is told—which is unlimited until one encounters instances of deceit (pp. 196–7).

The major difference between human testimony and the testimony of the senses (perception) is that as we get older 'the credit given to human testimony is restrained and weakened, by the experience we have of deceit', while the credit we give to our senses is confirmed by the uniformity and constancy of the laws of nature (p. 184). The language of nature never lies, although we are, as Lord Bacon showed, apt to misinterpret it (pp. 199–201). Still, the bulk of human knowledge is built upon human testimony (p. 482). Acknowledging Reid's principle of credulity, Stewart (1814: 235–6, 239–40) asserts that if our instinct to trust testimony is regulated by lessons of experience, testimony can yield certain knowledge. Although 'philosophers are accustomed to speak of the event as only *probable* . . . our confidence in its happening is not less complete, than if it rested on the basis of mathematical demonstration' (ibid. 240).

Beattie grounds his *Evidences of the Christian Religion* in a defence of the apostolic witness. In the *Essay* (1771: 137) he describes our reliance upon the testimony of our fellow-creatures as 'agreeable to nature, to reason, and to sound philosophy'. He roots our trust in testimony partly in the universality of human sense-experience:

> When we believe the declaration of an honest man, in regard to facts of which he hath had experience, we suppose, that by the view of those facts, his senses have been affected in the same manner as ours would have been if we had been in his place. Faith in testimony, therefore, is in part resolvible [*sic*] into that conviction which is produced by the evidence of sense. (ibid.)

Hence, faith in testimony terminates in common sense, being 'itself instinctive, and such as cannot be resolved into any higher principle' (ibid. 143).

3.2.2.6. *The Problem of Diversity*

The Common Sense philosophers want to find the underlying presuppositions of all human experience. They think these are universal, but that unsound philosophy denies them. Reid recognizes that his work on the human mind constitutes only a provisional enquiry, but he considers those who dispute the principles of common sense to be unsound, fools (1863: 104), in a delirium (p. 107), or, at best, immoral or misguided due to some defect in educational and cultural nurturing (pp. 98, 468–75). Deviation from the judgement of common sense arises 'from a disorder in the constitution', and is called '*lunacy*' (p. 209). A man who 'suffers himself to be reasoned out of the principles of common sense' experiences '*metaphysical lunacy*' (ibid.), such as the 'philosophical delirium' Hume displays as he tries to discredit reason by reason (p. 485). This is the result of ingenious philosophizing, and is only intermittent: 'it is apt to seize the patient in solitary and speculative moments; but, when he enters into society, Common Sense recovers her authority' (p. 209). A sound constitution represents the standard by which to gauge permanently or temporarily affected reasoning.

Oswald enumerates common-sense beliefs beyond those which Reid observes humanity taking for granted. He alone among the Common Sense philosophers puts theistic belief on a par with the principles of common sense, and posits 'primary truths' of religion. He attributes religious scepticism not simply to folly or madness but to corrupt, bad or dishonest hearts (1772: 46, 98–103, 353). Beattie more closely resembles Reid, in that he grounds his religious apologetic upon 'evidences'. He holds the heart and affections as well as the understanding responsible for unbelief (1786: ii. 59). He berates 'Light minds, from inattention or ignorance; profligate minds, from a dislike to its purity; and vain minds, out of ostentation, and from the love of singularity' for refusing the 'evidence of our faith' (ibid. ii. 10).

3.2.2.7. *Religious Apologetics*

For the most part the Scottish philosophers do not regard belief in God as part of our constitution, such that it cannot be defended rationally. Reid (1863: 196, cf. 329, 341) does not cite theistic propositions as principles of common sense, although he attributes the authorship of the principles of common sense to the 'wise and beneficent Author of Nature'. He suggests that belief in God follows almost inevitably from something that is a principle of common sense, namely that 'from certain signs or indications in the effect, we may infer that there must have been intelligence, wisdom, or other intellectual or moral qualities in the cause' (p. 460). He then summarizes the argument from final causes (the teleological argument):

> *First*, That design and intelligence in the cause, may, with certainty, be inferred from marks or signs in the effect. This is the principle we have been considering . . . [*second*], That there are in fact the clearest marks of design and wisdom in the works of nature; and the *conclusion* is, That the works of nature are the effects of a wise and intelligent Cause.
>
> (pp. 460–1)

The inference that God exists is not itself a first principle according to Reid, for he considers the possibility that one can reject one or other of the premisses in the argument from final causes (p. 461). Moreover, he thinks that the argument 'gathers strength as human knowledge advances', so that the knowledge of nature in his day makes the argument more convincing than it was some centuries before (pp. 460, 461). Reid is therefore aware of steps taken in a process of reasoning, as one argues for the 'existence and perfections of the Deity' (p. 460). Even the belief that God is the author of our common notions is not itself a common notion according to Reid. Reid regards it 'good sense' to believe that the Almighty has built into our constitution a principle by which we trust the testimony of our senses. However, he acknowledges that 'a man would believe his senses though he had no notion of a Deity' (p. 329). It follows that while belief in one's senses is a common-sense principle, belief in God is not.

By contrast, Oswald's main concern in the *Appeal* is to claim common sense for the truths of religion, which he understands to be as evident to the plain understanding as are the primary truths of nature.

> For a man in his senses can as little doubt of the reality of vegetation, as he can doubt the reality of the tree or shrub which he sees with his eyes, and feels with his hand. However philosophers may amuse themselves with questions upon these subjects, a man of plain understanding will reckon him delirious who entertains the least doubt of the primary truths of nature. And we hope to make appear, that whoever doubts the primary truths of religion is liable to the same charge. (1768: 205–6)

The very being of God is considered '*too obvious and sacred a truth to be subjected to the reasonings of men*' (1772: 50). Anyone '*above the level of an idiot, may see the invisible perfections of God from the visible harmony of the universe*' (ibid. 68), and to dispute the attributes of God '*betrays great stupidity, or gross prevarication*' (ibid. 80). Oswald (1768: 6) argues that were belief in the truths of religion dependent upon reasoning, it would be unattainable by the multitudes, 'who have neither leisure, nor capacity, nor inclination to pursue the same course'. Accordingly, 'the primary truths of religion ought to be proposed to sceptics, not as points to be disputed, but as first principles' (ibid. 333).

Like Oswald, Beattie is interested in applying the principles of common sense to a religious apologetic. Oswald's *Appeal* is on behalf of natural religion. Beattie's *Evidences* (1786: ii. 49) is a defence of Gospel truth in the form of biblical evidence: 'We are commanded to search the Scriptures, and told that in them we shall find evidence of their truth'. He is the only member of the school to offer an apologetic for the Bible. In so far as Reid and Stewart write on religious matters their subject is natural religion. Reid gives no philosophical consideration of biblical authority in his major works. However, in his lectures on natural theology delivered in 1780,[13] he argues that to be justified in accepting the Scriptures as revelation one must use reason to establish that they come from God:

> It is no doubt true that Revelation exhibits all the truths of Natural Religion, but it is no less true that reason must be employed to judge of that revelation; whether it comes from God. Both are great lights and we ought not to put out the one in order to use the other . . . We acknowledge then that men are indebted to revelation in the matter of Natural Religion but this is no reason why we should not also use our reason here . . . Tis by reason that we must judge whether that Revelation be really so . . . [T]hat man is best prepared for the study and practice of the revealed Religion who has previously acquired just Sentiments of the Natural.[14]

Beattie shows a greater deference for scripture than does Reid, but he also manifests some ambiguity about the relation of reason to revelation. He argues that reason should acquiesce to the mysteries of religion, but he also believes that evidences make such acquiescence possible.

3.2.2.8. *Beattie's* Evidences of the Christian Religion

Of all the Common Sense literature, only in Beattie's *Evidences* is the Common Sense philosophy made to serve a biblical apologetic. Beattie's aim is to defend the Gospel history as true. His method is principally to maintain the reliability of human testimony and the trustworthiness of the apostles. Discrepancies between the Gospels are said to exist only in so far as the writers 'could not have stood all in the same place, nor consequently taken notice of the very same particulars without variation' (1786: ii. 100). Indeed, a 'perfect co-incidence, where testimonies consist of many particulars, would breed suspicion of a pre-concerted

[13] The substance of these lectures has been derived from student notes and published (*Lectures on Natural Theology*, ed. Elmer H. Duncan, Lanham, Md.: University Press of America, 1981).

[14] Ibid. 1 2, quoted in Wolterstorff (1983: 63).

plan' (ibid. i. 151). The Gospels differ in such details as one would expect from reports of four different witnesses: 'If in this manner we judge of the veracity of one another, and if the common sense of mankind warrants the judgement, and their experience after long trial finds no flaw in it; why should we argue from different principles, in judging of the veracity of the evangelists?' (i. 151–2).

Allowing that some inaccuracies may have entered scripture through transcribers (ii. 83–4), Beattie claims that supposed 'obscurities' have been 'both multiplied and magnified far beyond the truth' (ii. 82). He judges it 'the intention of Providence that we shall have difficulties to encounter', but denies that these pose considerable difficulties for the religion of the New Testament. When 'fairly stated, they will be found rather to add to its evidence' (ii. 88, 90).

Beattie (i. 89) defends the unbiased nature of the apostles' testimony: 'all is fair, candid, and simple: the historians make no reflections of their own, but confine themselves to matter of fact, that is, to what they heard and saw'. Their reports of miracles and prophecies are to be accepted as 'facts, in regard to which they could not be mistaken, though they had been the most credulous of mankind' (i. 164–5). Such was the nature of the miracles, 'that, to make an attentive spectator a competent judge of them, neither learning nor genius was necessary; nor any other talent or accomplishment, but a sound mind, an honest heart, and the right use of one's senses' (i. 160).

Beattie combines a Common Sense defence of vulgar understanding with a theological justification for the simplicity of scripture. Since 'the common people have neither time nor capacity for deep reasoning', and as a divine revelation must be intended for 'the vulgar as well as the learned', the evidence of such a revelation should 'command general attention, and convince men of all ranks and characters, and should therefore be level to every capacity' (i. 59). Acceptance of the evidence is hindered only by sophisticated reasoning and false philosophy: 'Minute cavillers may grow more sceptical, the greater dexterity they acquire in misrepresenting facts, and misapplying language. But I know not whether a single instance can be mentioned of a truly philosophick mind, who both understood Christianity, and disbelieved it' (ii. 155).

The 'essential doctrines of our religion' are 'within the reach of every mind, who is willing to be instructed' (ii. 92–3). Doctrines which 'may at present transcend our reason' (ii. 52) are not more difficult to accept than many of our everyday beliefs (ii. 52–5). So the incarnation 'is not to us more unintelligible, than the union of a human body with a human soul', and atonement for the sin of others 'may be as possible to a superior being . . . as, among inferiour [*sic*] beings, for one man gratuitously to pay another's debts' (ii. 54). Beattie thus presents doctrines which are beyond our understanding as appropriate for our acquiescence. Though too mysterious to fathom, they demand simple consent:

> While one too anxiously endeavours to *explain* these, and some of the other mysterious doctrines of our religion, one may no doubt say unwarrantable things. But if we take them as they are delivered in Holy Writ, our only infallible standard of faith, we shall not find that they contain any thing, in which a man of the soundest and fairest mind, who has studied the gospel and its evidences, may not without difficulty acquiesce. (ii. 55–6)

The 'essentials of religion are intelligible to all capacities' (ii. 82). However, because of the nature of that being defended, the evidences are not straightforward (ii. 58–9). A particular moral and spiritual posture is required for one to accept and understand them (ii. 10, 60, 139–40, 154–5). While the evidences 'are indeed so powerful, that nothing but ignorance, or hardness of heart, can prevent their making a deep impression . . . their full effect is felt by those minds only, who, together with lowliness, docility, and candour, entertain a predilection for [the] gospel' (ii. 60–1).

Christianity is thus presented as supported by the strongest evidence and acceptable to the soundest reason. Its rejection cannot be endured without the mental and moral health of its objectors being impugned. The Christian faith is rational but may not appear to be so to those who take reason beyond the true limits of philosophy and attempt to explain that to which reason should simply assent. Beattie's views on reason and evidences, and his appeal to the evangelists as reliable eyewitnesses, backed by harmonizations of the Gospel records and a defence of their general consistency, all find their parallels in fundamentalist apologetics.

3.2.3. *Common Sense Philosophy and Fundamentalist Apologetics*

Certain 'habits of mind' associated with the Scottish philosophy affected evangelical thought in a formative period and became apparent in fundamentalist apologetics.[15] Common Sense intuitions receive their parallels in fundamentalist convictions about the nature of revealed truth and our access to it. Both are attributed the same source—a providential God who supplies us with what is required to recognize our true needs and to behave accordingly. The influence of Common Sense philosophy upon fundamentalist apologists is usually, though not always, unconscious. However, the articulation of certain positions—for example, in defence of plain thinking especially regarding the factual nature of the Bible's historical narratives, and against inappropriate uses of reason—is consciously fashioned.

3.2.3.1. *Realist Truth*

Part of the appeal of Common Sense philosophy for fundamentalists is its philosophical support for the conviction that the biblical records inform us not of ideas or interpretations of events but of events themselves—a welcome antidote to the German Idealist influence upon higher criticism. J. Gresham Machen maintained that the 'Bible is quite useless unless it is a record of facts' (1936: 65). His philosophical differences with modernists became intensely relevant in debates over the nature of Jesus' resurrection. Machen decried the modernist concern with 'the belief of the disciples in the resurrection' which refused to deal with 'whether the events really took place'.[16] He insisted that the biblical narratives are factual accounts of real events from the past. Fundamentalists and evangelicals persist in this belief, as far as it is possible for them to do so without imparting error to scripture. (Among themselves they operate with different thresholds beyond which scientific or historical evidence or textual dissonance render a factual reading problematic.) In the words of one recent English evangelical writer, evangelicals read 'narratives which give the

[15] Grave (1960: 1–10) and Noll (1985: 220) helpfully distinguish between any influence that Reid's specific philosophical arguments may have had, and the habits of mind engendered by Common Sense philosophy more generally.

[16] 'The Relation of Religion to Science and Philosophy', *Princeton Theological Review*, 24 (Jan. 1926), 38–66, quoted in Marsden (1980: 216–17).

impression of being fact, rather than fiction . . . as historical events' (Tidball 1994: 79). They are uncomfortable with the concept of myth and wary of the suggestion that the biblical writings manifest an authorial bias.

The Common Sense philosophers accepted the verdict of 'all mankind' that truth is 'fixed, unchangeable and eternal' (Beattie 1771: 25), and 'has no dependence on our belief or disbelief of it' (Stewart 1792: 311). This verdict was protected by an epistemological dualism which separates subject from object, the self from the external world, the perceiver from the facts to be perceived. While Kant regarded our minds as instrumental in constructing our world, Reid (1863: 649) insisted that 'the truth of a proposition' has no dependence 'upon our believing it to be true'. Contemporary fundamentalist thought endorses a strongly realist understanding of truth, as is apparent in the definition from a book on Christian education at Fig. 3.1.

Such an understanding of truth contributes to two assumptions in the fundamentalist view of scripture: that the biblical text gives us objective, factual accounts of real states of affairs; and that the 'plain sense' of scripture is available wherever the reader does not obscure the text with subjective interpretation.

3.2.3.2. *Harmony of Science and Religion*

Although it cannot be demonstrated that truth exists independently of, and in conformity with, our constitution, the Common Sense philosophers posited a harmonious relation between our constitution and God's wider creation. Any theory which

TRUTH
An Eternal
Unchanging
Statement or
Principle
That Is In
Agreement
With Reality
Unaffected by the consciousness of the perceiver,
'TRUTH IS OBJECTIVELY COMPREHENSIBLE BY MAN'

FIG. 3.1 Definition of truth (Cunningham and Fortosis 1987: 67, 71)

undermined this harmony was rejected as false philosophy. Biblical conservatives include scripture within this harmonious whole. Charles Hodge (1871: 15) reasons: 'All truth must be consistent. God cannot contradict himself. He cannot force us by the constitution of the nature which He has given us to believe one thing, and in his Word command us to believe the opposite.' When the author of our world and of our constitution is believed also to be the author of scripture there is reason to deny that any statement in scripture could contradict either common sense or the discoveries of science.

3.2.3.3. *Suspicion of Hypotheses*

Reid pitched fact against hypothesis. In his day the term 'hypothesis' was used reproachfully by those who defended the inductive method against Cartesian a priori reasoning. Reid (1863: 249–50) himself employed Newton's celebrated dictum, *Hypothesis non fingo.* Theories which he found contrary to common sense he rejected as hypothetical and unphilosophical contraventions of facts, for 'to argue from a hypothesis against facts, is contrary to the rules of true philosophy' (ibid. 132).

Fundamentalist approaches to scripture tend to take as fact matters which are interpretative, and reject as hypothetical theories which contradict the facts of the Bible. At the dawn of fundamentalism advocates of higher criticism and evolution were commonly accused of indulging in mere hypothetical speculation or guesswork. Dyson Hague (n.d.: i. 90) in *The Fundamentals* accused 'learned German thinkers' who failed to heed Newton's words 'I do not frame hypotheses' of lacking 'in a singular degree the faculty of common sense and knowledge of human nature'.[17]

3.2.3.4. *The Inductive Method*

We have no indication from any of the Common Sense philosophers that they would have regarded biblical theology as a suitable subject for the Baconian method. They applied Bacon's method

[17] Cf. F. Johnson (n.d.: ii), also in *The Fundamentals*. William Jennings Bryan thought 'hypothesis' too good a word to describe Darwinism: 'the word "hypothesis", though euphonious, dignified and high-sounding, is merely a scientific synonym for the old-fashioned word "guess"' (*New York Times*, 26 Feb. 1922, repr. in Vanderlaan 1925: 251).

to mental philosophy. The Princeton theologians, however, applied it to theology, a science based on biblical data:

If natural science be concerned with the facts and laws of nature, theology is concerned with the facts and the principles of the Bible. If the object of the one be to arrange and systematize the facts of the external world, and to ascertain the laws by which they are determined; the object of the other is to systematize the facts of the Bible, and ascertain the principles or general rules which those facts involve.

(Hodge 1871: 18)

Fundamentalists followed suit: '[Theology is the] collecting, scientifically arranging, comparing, exhibiting, and defending of all facts from any and every source concerning God and his works.'[18] Hence the Bible came to be called the textbook of theology (e.g. Packer 1958*a*: 112; Stott 1982: 188; Wenham [1972] 1993: 11).

The inductive method keeps philosophical enquiry within strict confines, permitting it only to observe phenomena and not to speculate on their hidden causes. A parallel structure of argument provides a refuge for the defenders of verbal inspiration, who provide evidence for the effects of inspiration while rejecting attempts to explain its process. Thomas Chalmers (1780–1847), whom McCosh (1875: 393) credits as reconciling the Scottish philosophy with the Scottish theology, takes this approach in *The Evidences and Authority of the Christian Revelation* (1814).[19] Chalmers (iv. 353) criticizes the 'senseless and unphilosophical speculation . . . on the modes and degrees of inspiration' in which scholastics of the last and present century have indulged, and which attempts to 'lift that veil, which screens from our discernment the arcana of a hidden operation'. It is, he says, 'enough for us to know the result', and so to 'the imaginations of men as to the *modus operandi*' he 'infinitely prefer(s) the palpable testimonies of Christ and his apostles as to the qualities of the *opus operatum*' (ibid.). Early in the twentieth century one of the few British evangelicals to defend inerrancy, W. E. Vine, argued that the result of inspiration is clear but the 'process is undefinable', for the 'supernatural acts

[18] Lewis Sperry Chafer, *Systematic Theology* (1947), i. 5, quoted in Noll 1985: 223–4.

[19] The full title of this work is *On the Miraculous and Internal Evidences of the Christian Revelation, and the Authority of its Records*. Quotations are from *The Works of Thomas Chalmers* (25 vols.) (Glasgow: William Collins, 1836–42), where the *Evidences* is found in vols. iii and iv.

of God do not admit of human analysis' and the 'operations of the Spirit can be registered only by their effects' (1923: 10, 11).[20]

3.2.3.5. *Faith in Testimony*

Ironically, the defence of verbal inspiration intensified amidst a growing tendency to defend Gospel truth by means which suit the verification of human testimony. The doctrine of verbal inspiration protects scripture from human contamination, but the evidences used to support the doctrine came increasingly to be of a kind applicable to the defence of eyewitness reporting. Chalmers (iv. 363–4) insisted that there exists in the Bible 'but one ingredient of pure unmixed divinity, utterly separated and free from the contamination of all that is human'. Yet at the same time he rested 'the question of the truth of the christian religion' on 'the credibility of its messengers' (iii. 151), reasoning that since the 'bearers of this message were beings like ourselves . . . we can apply our safe and certain experience of man to their conduct and their testimony' (iii. 150).

The factual nature of testimony was regarded, by apologists such as Beattie and Chalmers, as little affected by the witness's point of view. Combined with the conviction that language adequately describes the world, such faith in testimony supported a belief that scripture reliably informs us of actual states of affairs, even regarding the miraculous. Beattie (i. 61) argued in the *Evidences* that 'every event admits of proof from human testimony, which it is possible for a sufficient number of competent witnesses to see and to hear'.

Reid's principle of credulity does not itself warrant a reading of the Gospels as direct factual reports. The principle is unlimited in children (Reid 1863: 196), but it is restrained as we learn to regulate our responses to testimony. It might therefore lead us to read the biblical narratives as something other than straight eyewitness accounts—although recognition of this possibility is not apparent in fundamentalist apologetic. The fundamentalist emphasis upon testimony raises two issues: whether testimony can be regarded as straight statement of fact, and whether any parts of scripture comprise testimonies in the sense of eyewitness reports. One crea-

[20] Barr notes that fundamentalists resist describing the mode of inspiration, but he traces the source of their reluctance no further back than Princeton (1977: 289–90).

tion scientist defends his claims even about the origin and age of the earth by an appeal to testimony: 'All that is required for scientific proof of a once-only historical event . . . is that we have a credible witness of the event, and an intelligible report or personal testimony of what he saw' (Jansma 1985: 54).

3.2.3.6. *Intolerance*

Beattie (1771: 136) argued that one who refused to trust testimony 'would be called obstinate, whimsical, narrow-minded, and a fool'. The Common Sense position that all human beings share the same rational nature renders diversity problematic. Enlightenment philosophies generally share the Scottish school's faith in the universality of human consciousness. Yet the Common Sense philosophy is capable of engendering greater intolerance precisely because it is a philosophy of common sense. Such intolerance is carried over into fundamentalist exclusivism. George Marsden (1980: 115–16) explains that 'if Christian and non-Christian reason are essentially part of one human consciousness', then wrong conclusions reached in human enquiry are explained in terms of 'moral error, faulty reasoning, speculative hypotheses, metaphysical fancies, and the prejudices of unbelief or false religions'.

3.2.3.7. *Reason and Evidences*

The Common Sense school's restriction of reason and philosophy, especially in Beattie's *Evidences*, resembles the fundamentalist attitude that 'Reason's part is to act as the servant of the written Word' (Packer 1958*a*: 48). Beattie's view that a study of the Gospel and its evidences renders the acquiescence of reason easy reveals a tension present in fundamentalist apologetics: scripture is defended rationally even while reason is to submit to it. Basing the authority of scripture upon reason has theologically been the most unhelpful aspect of an evidential apologetic for evangelical religion. It has undermined the inner testimony of the Holy Spirit and has contributed to the fundamentalist preoccupation with a factually inerrant Bible. As one apologist proclaims: 'Precisely because of this primacy of reason to faith, Scripture must first be authenticated to provide a rational basis for its acceptance' (Gerstner 1974: 123). This ordering of priorities is characteristic of a fundamentalist mentality.

3.3. Verbal Inspiration and Common Sense

The philosophy of Common Sense belongs to a later age than the one which nurtured the doctrine of verbal inspiration. Nevertheless, it provided a congenial intellectual context for the furtherance of the doctrine. That verbal inspiration came to be supported within a Common Sense framework affords us insight into the transition from dogmatic to empirical methods in biblical apologetics—a transition which remains incomplete in many conservative works. The doctrine of verbal inspiration, which received elaborate formulations in the Protestant scholastic era, is an essential component of the doctrine of inerrancy. Deductive arguments for inerrancy rely on the premisses that the very words of scripture are inspired by a God who would not deceive us. The doctrine of inerrancy is itself a later development. It retains deductive elements, but the strictness of the doctrine reflects an anxiety to defend the inspiration of scripture by inductive means, that is, by appeal to evidences. This awkward combination of deductive and inductive proof is manifest in fundamentalist apologetic wherever it is determined that the evidence will support the (necessary) conclusion that inspired scripture can contain no errors.

A belief in the plenary inspiration of scripture was standard evangelical orthodoxy in nineteenth-century Britain, but was not everywhere taken to mean that the very words of scripture were God's own words. The defence of verbal inspiration and an error-free Bible was a minority position. It was expounded in 1816 by Robert Haldane.[21] Haldane had left the Presbyterian Church in Scotland, and was at this time in Geneva, where he held Bible studies and took communion with a small group outside the Established Church. He blamed the state of religion in Geneva on Romantic notions that scripture was inspired in the same way as poetry (Bebbington 1989: 87). This is the context in which he developed his doctrine of scripture. He presented his case in *The Evidence and Authority of Divine Revelation* (1816) and more comprehensively in *The Books of the Old and New Testaments Proved to Be Canonical* (1830). The quotations below are from this second vol-

[21] A small but growing number of evangelicals, Anglican, Brethren, and Baptist, supported Haldane. They were known as the Recordites after their journal *The Record*, which was founded in 1828 by Robert's nephew, Alexander Haldane.

ume, which was written as a complementary work to Alexander Carson's *The Inspiration of the Scriptures* (1830).

Both Haldane and Carson defended their doctrine of scripture in terms borrowed from the Scottish philosophy. Haldane presented verbal inspiration as a self-evident truth:

> That inspiration extends to words as well as to matter, is so obvious, that it never could have been questioned, if those who deny it had not misled themselves by their vain reasonings on the subject, or taken the contrary for granted without inquiry, on the authority of others. A writing inspired by God self-evidently implies, in the very expression, that the words are the words of God; and the common impression of mankind coincides with this most entirely. (Haldane [1830] 1853: pp. xvi–xvii)

Carson (1847: 402, 401) drew upon Reid's attack on the 'vain pretensions' of sceptical philosophers to warn theologians against 'subjecting the contents of the Word of God to the control and determinations of reason'. He also used Reid's position that 'the greater part of knowledge, even of philosophers, rests upon foundations of which no account can be given', to berate those who would not receive 'the testimony of the divine word, like that of any plain, honest man' (ibid. 402, 404).

These were distortions of Reid's concepts and arguments. The doctrine of verbal inspiration was not self-evident, and little resembled Reid's principles of common sense. Reid had not even defended the existence of God as a truth for which no reason could be given or which humankind of necessity took for granted. Furthermore, although Reid observed a natural reliance on testimony, he nowhere advocated unquestioned acceptance of particular testimonies. He did not privilege biblical testimony, but taught that scripture must be tested by reason.

Haldane intended something of an inductive apologetic. He argued that the inspiration of the scriptures was attested 'both by the nature and value of their contents, and by the evidence of their truth' ([1830] 1853: 90). He insisted that our knowledge of the inspiration of the Bible 'must be collected from itself', and he accepted the credentials of the authors of scripture as authorizing them to make that truth known (ibid.).

Nevertheless, his argument was essentially deductive, based on the claim that 'testimony is a first principle' (ibid. 77). It is 'by testimony', he argued, that 'Christians in their successive generations receive the canon of Scripture as a matter of revelation' (p. 82). Thus, scripture is 'authenticated by a first principle, to which God has bound us by the constitution of our nature to submit' (p. 87). Haldane allowed that internal evidence 'may confirm the authenticity of a book sanctioned by the canon', but not that a book approved as part of the sacred canon could 'contain any internal marks of imposture'. His central point was that we cannot posit the 'clashing of two first principles' (pp. 86–7). However, his concept of first principles was confused. It seemed to include both the content of that which is accepted by testimony, and the true Christian response to biblical evidence: 'when a book is substantially approved, by testimony, as belonging to the canon, no evidence can, by a Christian, be legitimately supposed possible in opposition to its inspiration' (p. 86).

This apologetic was particularly demanding on the evidence, because Haldane took verbal inspiration to imply a claim 'of infallibility and of perfection' (p. 90).

> By presenting themselves as *inspired*, they bring the truth of their contents to the most decisive test. They occupy ground which nothing but *truth* and *perfection* can enable them to maintain. Could there be found in them any thing absurd, or false, or erroneous; could the smallest flaw in the character or doctrine of the Author of Salvation; any degree of weakness, of want of wisdom; or any contradiction be detected, they must immediately be compelled to relinquish this ground. (pp. 152–3)

He suggested that the claim of inspiration, if false, could be 'easily disproved' by the detection of some flaw in the scriptures. Yet the structure of his apologetic ruled out the possibility of there being any genuine contrary evidence. He reasoned that if 'in a book recognised by the canon . . . we find a matter which to our wisdom does not appear to be worthy of inspiration, we may be assured that we mistake' (p. 87). The force of his argument led him to conclude that 'all the light of science, throughout all the ages of the world, has not been able to discover one single error in the Bible' (p. 153).

Louis Gaussen in Switzerland also produced a defence of verbal inspiration. His work *Theopneustia* was written in French and translated immediately into English in 1841. Gaussen was a convert of Haldane's in Geneva and later a professor of theology there.[22] His apologetic resembled Haldane's in many ways. Like Haldane, he insisted that inspiration extends to the words of scripture and not only to the subject matter (Gaussen 1841: 210–24; cf. Haldane [1830] 1853: p. xvi). He was more explicit than Haldane in concluding that the scriptures can therefore 'contain no error' (Gaussen 1841: 36). He denied errors of reasoning, contradictions in fact, or errors contrary to the laws of nature (ibid. 122–204).

Gaussen accepted science as true only in so far as it 'is the friend of faith', and regarded it as false if, 'instead of standing in its character as an inquirer, it takes the place of judgement' (p. 269). The same criterion held for 'Sacred criticism', whose task was 'to collect facts connected with the Scriptures' (p. 277). Sacred criticism is science 'only as long as it continues true, and preserves its own place' (p. 269). Otherwise it degenerates into 'senseless guess-work', and 'vain hypotheses' which 'would contain nought but our own conceits, to dazzle the eye of our faith' (pp. 269, 271, 302).

Thus, like Haldane, Gaussen developed a structure which enabled him to reject as false any evidence that would threaten the 'pre-established harmony' between faith and science (p. 269). This was less problematic in Gaussen's apologetic where the scriptural proof of *theopneustia* was the last matter to be considered (pp. 370–431). For Gaussen the 'effects' of scripture in bringing 'health, life, heat, and light' were more powerful than biblical 'assertions' as to its own inspiration. He made use of 'Evidences which result from feelings' in order to dispose his readers to a readier acceptance of the scriptural proofs he would later present (p. 300). Neither he nor Haldane ultimately based their apologetic on textual evidence. Haldane began from first principles, and by rational argument denied the possibility of error. Gaussen took a more experiential route, whereby the assurance of faith would itself override any difficulties in the text.[23]

It is unlikely that Haldane, Carson, or Gaussen conceived of so strict a doctrine as that stated by A. A. Hodge and B. B. Warfield

[22] He was part of the small group influenced by Haldane's work in Geneva in 1816 (Broadbent 1931: 302–3). He hailed Haldane as 'the second father of the Geneva Church' (Haldane 1852: 445). He also read Thomas Chalmers, whom he mentions in *Theopneustia* (1841: 290).

[23] See s. 4.1 below.

in 1881. The doctrine of inerrancy as formulated by Hodge and Warfield demanded a greater standard of precision. Two factors are especially significant in contributing to its stringency. First, Warfield bravely insisted that a full inductive proof of inspiration was possible, and he encouraged the hesitant Hodge and others within the Old Princeton tradition to accept his apologetic technique (Letis 1991: 185–6).[24] Second, the evidence that Warfield had in mind was that being unearthed by the new methods of text criticism coming from Germany; methods which Warfield adopted via Westcott and Hort. Since Warfield's time, a very high expectation of factual accuracy has come to distinguish American from British accounts of inerrancy.

3.4. The Scottish Philosophy Brought to America

Historically it is possible to speak of 'a general appropriation' of Common Sense philosophy by American evangelicals between the Revolution and the Civil War (Noll 1985: 219). Common Sense philosophy was brought to America principally by two Scottish presidents of Princeton College, John Witherspoon (1723–94) in the eighteenth century and James McCosh (1811–94) in the nineteenth.[25] Witherspoon claimed to have expounded a philosophy of Common Sense before Reid (Collins 1925: i. 41; Vander Stelt 1978: 65–75). He was invited to Princeton in order to combat the prevalent Berkeleian Idealism. Through his influence and that of his students, the Scottish philosophy came to bear upon the political, educational, and clerical structures of American society. Leaders in the post-Revolutionary period welcomed the idea that all humanity shared principles upon which public morality could be established, and by which metaphysical and religious scepticism could be challenged (Noll 1985). Reid's writings were most influential in scholarly circles, Stewart's in political. Beattie's work received acceptance among the clergy. Witherspoon had a formative influence on James Madison's thought, as had Dugald Stewart on the thought of Thomas Jefferson. Witherspoon drafted

[24] See s. 4.1 below.

[25] Although before Witherspoon's arrival, Frances Alison had imported Hutcheson's moral philosophy.

the Federalist Papers, together with Madison and Alexander Hamilton, and was the sole clerical signatory of the Declaration of Independence.[26]

Samuel Stanhope Smith (1751–1819) was Witherspoon's pupil and son-in-law, and his successor as president of Princeton College. He drew from Common Sense principles an educational model which came to dominate American college curricula (Noll 1989; Vander Stelt 1978: 75–82). By 1825 this model had been extended to the University of Pennsylvania, Harvard, Yale, Brown, and Columbia. At its base lay the inductive method, which supplied a vision for the integration of all knowledge. The method was applied across all disciplines from moral philosophy to the social sciences (Sloan 1971: 243–4). Theodore Dwight Bozeman (1977: 23–30) has discovered veneration for Bacon in such areas as poetry, medicine, law, and agriculture, as well as in theology.

Most relevant to our study is the way in which Baconianism and the Bible were brought together in America (Bozeman 1977: 132–59). The Bible was conceived as a factual resource, essential to any comprehensive understanding of the world: 'The very genius of the inductive philosophy forbids the exclusion of a single pertinent fact from its generalizations . . . The philosophy . . . which will ignore the Bible . . . has apostatized from the fundamental articles of the Baconian creed.'[27] The method of 'Lord Bacon' was praised as able to show that 'the Scriptures admit of being studied and expounded upon the principles of the inductive method; and that, when thus interpreted, they speak to us in a voice as certain and unmistakable as the language of nature heard in the experiments and observations of science'.[28] Newton was regarded as the best-equipped student of scripture in that he had 'a mind tutored by the philosophy of facts' and 'saw that the religion of the Gospel is a religion of facts'.[29]

One early influential figure in promoting such a scientific conception of biblical and theological study was James W. Alexander,

[26] Another signatory to the Constitution was James Wilson, a native Scot and a Reidian, and Associate Justice on the first US Supreme Court.

[27] Benjamin M. Palmer, 'Baconianism and the Bible', *Southern Presbyterian Review*, 6 (1852), 226–53, quoted in Bozeman: 110.

[28] Lamar, *The Organon of Scripture Or, the Inductive Method of Biblical Interpretation* (1860), quoted in Bozeman 1977: 144–5.

[29] Anon., 'A Series of Discourses on the Christian Revelation' (1817), quoted ibid. 142.

son of Archibald Alexander, the first professor of Princeton Seminary. He depicted theologians as arriving at truth by investigating the propositions of scripture as one would the phenomena of science: 'by careful examination of these data, from which result generalization, cautious induction, and the position of ultimate principles'.[30] When Charles Hodge came to write his *Systematic Theology* for use at Princeton, he presented the same basic theological method.[31]

Advocates of a variety of theological positions found in the Scottish philosophy ways of reconciling religion and the modern spirit. Common Sense Realism rejected scepticism and atheism, affirmed the reality of the material world, supported evidences for a divine Creator, and maintained its position according to the dictates of reason and the rules of science. We should not assume that it was thereby an obvious or inevitable ally to evangelical religion. It had the potential to dispense with the supernatural and with the Bible. As we have seen, Reid, Stewart, and Oswald defended *natural* religion: God could be known through nature, and his will known through conscience or the moral sense. Everybody was capable of making moral judgements. Such was the conclusion of the ethical philosophy of the Scottish school. Hutcheson had denied the need for supernatural revelation, and declared the nature of man sufficient for theology. His philosophy was influential among the Unitarians at Harvard and the New Divinity men at Yale (Ahlstrom 1955; Holifield 1978: 63, 111; Hoeveler 1981: 313–14). The New Divinity thinkers softened Calvinist anthropology with something of an Enlightenment appeal to moral sense. They accepted natural religion but denied its adequacy. Common Sense philosophy lent itself to this position: the principles of common sense made knowledge possible but were not the sources of truth. Yet inherent within the philosophy was a potential to make human consciousness itself the arbiter of truth.

Witherspoon and McCosh imported the philosophy to America in an evangelical form. Both had opposed the Moderates in the Church of Scotland, Witherspoon as an organizer of the Evangelical party and McCosh as a founder of the Free Church. In the anonymously published *Ecclesiastical Characteristics*, Witherspoon

[30] 'On the Use and Abuse of Systematic Theology' (1832), 171–80, quoted ibid. 151.

[31] See s. 3.2.3.4 above.

satirized the cultured, intellectual, doctrinally innovative stance of the Moderate clergy. His caricature of moderate maxims included being '*very unacceptable to the common people*' ([1753] 1763: 27, 32–4). He also wrote a satire on the creed of the moderate, which he called the Athenian Creed and in which he parodied Hutcheson's moral philosophy: 'I believe in the beauty and comely proportions of Dame Nature, and in almighty Fate, her only parent and guardian; for it hath been most graciously obliged (blessed be its name) to make us all very good' ([1753] 1763: 40).

McCosh's attack on moderatism in *The Scottish Philosophy* resembled that of Witherspoon. He criticized the apologetic air of the preachers of the new school:

> The manner and spirit were highly pleasing to many in the upper and refined classes; were acceptable to those who disliked earnest religion, as they had nothing of 'the offence of the cross;' . . . But all this was powerless on the great body of the people, who were perfectly prepared to believe the preacher when he told them that they were sinners, and that God had provided a Saviour, but felt little interest in refined apologies on behalf of God and Christ and duty. (1875: 14, cf. 18)

Being jointly influenced by William Hamilton and Thomas Chalmers, McCosh was aware of tensions between Common Sense philosophy and evangelical religion. He attempted to add to the philosophy's conception of human nature a sense of sin and of the need for grace. 'The philosophers were laudably engaged when they were unfolding man's intellectual, esthetic [*sic*], and moral nature; but they missed the deepest properties of human nature, when, in the fear of the ghosts of fanaticism, they took no notice of man's feelings of want, his sense of sin, and his longing after God and immortality' (ibid. 87). He lamented that the Scottish metaphysicians, with the exception of Chalmers, 'never identified themselves very deeply with the more earnest spiritual life of the country'. However, he approved of their co-ordinating the facts of consciousness which, he said, 'can never be antagonistic to a true theology' and may even establish some vital truths of religion (ibid. 21–2). He considered philosophy to be a handmaid to religion, and wherever he modified the Common Sense philosophy it was to the service of evangelicalism.[32]

[32] e.g. for theological reasons he wanted to avoid Hamilton's concessions to Kant's philosophy. To this end he used religious reasoning to validate his philosophy of mind and defend knowledge of external reality (Hoeveler 1981: 123, 127–8, 133).

Common Sense Realism remained the dominant philosophy in America until after the Civil War when almost all thinkers, except conservatives in the evangelical tradition, replaced it with a materialism or idealism. Originally a philosophy against scepticism, by the end of the nineteenth century it was used as an antidote to subjectivism and Romantic theories of development. McCosh's adversary was not Berkeleian but German Idealism. Evangelicals and early fundamentalists continued to hope that common sense would prevail against German philosophy, which they held largely responsible for the development of higher criticism. The *Record*, a newspaper representing the most conservative evangelical opinion in Britain, invoked 'the good sense of LOCKE, the analogies of BUTLER, and the "Common Sense" of REID', against 'the vagaries of Prussian or German Rationalists'.[33] In *The Fundamentals*, Dyson Hague (n.d.: i. 90) condemned the lengths to which 'the German fancy can go in the direction of the subjective and of the conjectural', and Franklin Johnson (n.d.: ii. 49) suggested that the results of higher criticism were less radical in America and England than in Germany, 'owing to the brighter light of Christianity in these countries'.

In this chapter we have looked in some detail at the Common Sense philosophy, which has been identified by historians as a formative influence on fundamentalism. The philosophy of Reid, a moderate Presbyterian clergyman, does not lend itself to a fundamentalist apologetic as readily as some scholars imply. Nevertheless, biblical conservatives took from Common Sense philosophy an empirical-rationalist framework for their biblical apologetics, and this has been a significant factor in the formation of the fundamentalist understanding of scripture. We turn now to a fuller consideration of the development of fundamentalist apologetics, beginning with the contribution of Princeton Theological Seminary. We then consider ways in which contemporary evangelicals continue to operate with a fundamentalist conception of the Bible.

[33] 2 Jan. 1863, p. 2, quoted in Bebbington (1989: 143).

4
The Fundamentalist Mentality Among Evangelicals

4.1. Old Princeton

> In the history of American theology no nobler chapter on the inspiration of the Bible has been written than that by 'Old Princeton.' Among the Old Princetonians none has contributed more than the big three of Charles Hodge, B. B. Warfield, and J. Gresham Machen, with Warfield being the unequalled leader.
>
> (Gerstner 1984: 347)

This verdict of the evangelical church historian, John H. Gerstner, would receive endorsement from many of America's fundamentalists and evangelicals who continue to draw heavily upon the work of Old Princeton. In particular, Warfield's writings on the inspiration and authority of the Bible still provide the starting-point for much evangelical teaching in that area (D. Clair Davis 1984: 359–60). George Marsden (1989: 26) regards the Princetonians as 'more influential in twentieth-century evangelicalism than they were among their nineteenth-century contemporaries' due to the centrality of their theology for a surviving and flourishing, 'Bible-believing, evangelicalism'.

Princeton Theological Seminary, although separated from the main College since 1812, bore the mark of its philosophy. Archibald Alexander, first professor of the Seminary, was familiar with Witherspoon's writings and read Reid, Beattie, Stewart, and even Oswald. In his lecture on the 'Nature and Evidence of Truth' he stated that the 'greatest possible assurance which we can have of any truth is that the constitution of our nature obliges us to assent to it' (1812*b*: 65). He went on to argue that 'I am so constituted that I find it utterly impossible to doubt the reality of what I perceive by my senses', and 'that I am under a necessity of believing what I remember, as well as what I perceive or am conscious of' (ibid. 68–9).

Subsequent Princeton professors wrote in the same philosophical vein. Charles Hodge's indebtedness to Common Sense Realism is evident in his *Systematic Theology* (1871–3) which became the basic text for theological teaching at the Seminary. In his opening section, entitled 'The Knowledge of God is Innate' (1871: i. 191–9), he describes sense perceptions and moral truths as intuitive, and as 'axioms' which are 'assumed in all reasoning' (ibid. 193). Hodge claimed that knowledge of God is 'innate and intuitive', 'founded on the very constitution of our nature' (ibid. 199, 197). He thus went beyond any affirmation made by Reid. At the same time, he qualified his statement by a reference to the noetic effects of sin, which is also absent in Reid's philosophical writings: 'as men are ignorant of the nature and extent of sin' they need instruction by the Word of God and by his Spirit 'to give them any adequate knowledge of the nature of God, and of their relations to Him' (ibid. 199).

Sandeen (1977*b*: 115–17 incl. n. 24) regarded Locke as bearing the greater influence at Princeton, because he found no evidence of the Common Sense dualism there after Archibald Alexander. However, the Princetonians' belief in original principles as opposed to an endorsement of Lockian empiricism discredits Sandeen's interpretation: 'our conviction that God is what He has revealed Himself to be, rests on the same foundation as our conviction that the external world is what we take it to be. That foundation is the veracity of consciousness, or the trustworthiness of the laws of belief which God has impressed upon our nature' (Hodge 1871: i. 340). The Scottish philosophers rejected thoroughgoing empiricism, and advocated inductive enquiry which accepted the fundamental nature of common-sense beliefs. Such a middle way was walked at Princeton.

From its inception, Princeton Seminary steered a path between excess in reason and in emotion. These extremes were later termed rationalism and mysticism. Both were considered to be forms of subjectivism. Rationalism, wrote Warfield ([1895]: 589), substitutes 'purely human reason' for '"external authority" in religion'. Mysticism 'differs from technical Rationalism only in a matter of temperature' (ibid. 590). It appeals 'to the feelings as the sole, or at least as the normative, source of knowledge of divine things' ([1917]: 651).

Barr (1977: 272) contends that the Princeton theologians 'rejected the "mystical" tendency completely, while against the "rationalists" they contested only the *misuse* of reason', in the belief that a correct use of reason would defeat deistic arguments. They accorded reason 'a free rein in deciding what was meaningful, what was credible (!), what was evidence, and in what direction that evidence led' (ibid. 274). It is to this emphasis upon reason that Barr ascribes the rationalistic tendency in Princeton and subsequent fundamentalist thought.

Yet the main burden of the Princeton theologians was not to celebrate reason but to combat subjectivism, which they thought arose whenever the source of authority was located within humanity, 'whether it is the rational, emotional, or volitional element in the activities of the human spirit to which appeal is chiefly made' (Warfield [1917]: 650). This throws light on the paradox in subsequent fundamentalist thought, that it opposes rationalism while itself seeming strongly rationalistic. Rationalism was rejected because it 'assumes that the human intelligence is the measure of all truth' (Hodge 1871: i. 41). Hodge did not regard 'reason, rational demonstration, or philosophical proof' as 'the ground of faith' (ibid. 42). However, in repudiating rationalism he did not 'reject the service of reason in matters of religion' (p. 49). On the contrary, 'it is the prerogative of reason to judge of the credibility of a revelation' (p. 50).

Nevertheless, Hodge kept reason strictly within its servant role, lest it assume to be the judge of truth. Like James Beattie, he did not think it necessary 'to the rational exercise of faith that we should understand the truth believed' (p. 40). He acknowledged that the mysteries are 'incomprehensible', but did not regard their incomprehensibility an obstacle to their acceptance: 'Unless a man is willing to believe the incomprehensible, he can believe nothing' (p. 50). Hodge advocated obedient acquiescence. He asked, as had Alexander Carson, why, since we are prepared to believe things on the testimony of our senses and on the testimony of men, 'may we not believe on the testimony of God?' (p. 40).

The Princetonians did not regard reason as sufficient for faith. They acknowledged the role of religious experience in bringing a person to conviction. Archibald Alexander was influenced by revivalist experience and has been described as something of a Romantic (Nelson 1935: 223–65; Hoffecker 1981: 16–19). He argued that the mind may at times be 'rather perplexed, than relieved, by mere human reasoning', and only sees clearly when 'a lively impression made by the Spirit of truth banishes all doubt and hesitation' ([1812*a*]: 86).[1] Charles Hodge (1817: i. 15) found 'the controlling power over our beliefs exercised by the inward teachings of the Spirit, or, in other words, by our religious experience' to be 'perfectly consistent . . . with the admission of intuitive truths' and with the application of the inductive method to the Word of God. Even Warfield, who retained little of the earlier Romantic strain at Princeton and who significantly advanced the evidentialist nature of biblical apologetics, declared in *The Fundamentals* (n.d.: i. 27–8), 'The supreme proof to every Christian of the deity of his Lord is . . . his own inner experience of the transforming power of his Lord upon the heart and life'.

It is therefore misleading to accuse the Princeton theologians of rationalism, if by that one means that they failed to acknowledge the importance of religious experience. They regarded inner testimony as crucial for arriving at faith. However, in their apologetics they had difficulty in saying so, because they allowed religious experience to affect only one's acceptance rather than one's understanding of faith.[2] It is their insistence on the rational apprehension of faith, even the reasonableness of faith, that invites the charge of rationalism. They maintained that feelings did not guide our understanding but were tested by it. Charles Hodge ([1805]: 192) insisted that 'feelings demand truth in their object; and no utterance is natural or effective as the language of emotion which does not satisfy the understanding'. Internal and external testimony were ordered accordingly: 'the inward teaching of the Spirit, or religious experience, is no substitute for an external

[1] At the same time, Alexander ([1808]: 53) was wary of 'enthusiasm', which in his day had connotations later associated with mysticism. He regarded enthusiasm as 'proceeding . . . from the exuberance of the imagination', and as discarding 'the authority of the scriptures of truth' no less than does rationalism.

[2] W. Andrew Hoffecker, in his work *Piety and the Princeton Theologians* (1981), attempts to reverse the standard verdict on the rationalism of Princeton by arguing that the Princetonians practised an active Christian piety. Much of Hoffecker's data comes from religious journals, personal correspondence, sermons, and some works specifically about religious experience. The Princetonians were not lacking in personal piety, but they did not adequately incorporate this side of their faith into their apologetics.

revelation, and is no part of the rule of faith', but 'is, nevertheless, an invaluable guide in determining what the rule of faith teaches' (Hodge 1871: i. 16). Machen (1923: 72) echoed this position: 'Christian experience is rightly used when it confirms the documentary evidence. But it can never possibly provide a substitute for the documentary evidence'. Warfield (1903*b*: 25) argued that the Holy Spirit supplies us with 'just a new ability of the heart to respond to the grounds of faith, sufficient in themselves, already present to the understanding'.

At Princeton, faith was conceived primarily as 'assent to the truth', or 'the persuasion' or 'affirmation of the mind that a thing is true or trustworthy' (Hodge 1873: iii. 42, 85). Though a gift of God, faith 'is yet formally conviction passing into confidence; and . . . all forms of convictions must rest on evidence as their ground, and it is not faith but reason which investigates the nature and validity of this ground' (Warfield [1908]: 15). Knowledge was described as 'the measure' of faith: 'What lies beyond the sphere of knowledge, lies beyond the sphere of faith' (Hodge 1873: iii. 85). Faith was said to differ from knowledge only in that knowledge is based on perception and faith on testimony, so that faith involves a greater element of trust; 'they rest equally on evidence and are equally the product of evidence' (Warfield [1911*b*]: 330).

This evidence-based conception of faith was an important factor in the development of the doctrine of inerrancy. Belief in inerrancy involves an assumption that only scriptures which are free from factual inaccuracies can satisfactorily convey the truths necessary for faith. The doctrine of inerrancy is the most characteristic product of the union of evangelical biblical apologetics and empirical rationalism.[3]

[3] It is debated how innovative Princeton's doctrine of inerrancy was. Sandeen (1970*b*: 125–31), Abraham (1981: 15–16, 28–9) and Letis (1991) argue that Warfield's doctrine contained much innovation. Balmer and Woodbridge, by contrast, cite works from 16th-c. Puritan writers and other 19th-c. orthodox theologies, including Baptist, Methodist, Congregationalist, and Lutheran, to argue that 'the concept of complete biblical infallibility, what we today call biblical inerrancy, was no new creation of the late nineteenth century' (Woodbridge and Balmer 1983: 254, cf. Balmer 1982). Their case is dependent upon their conflating the doctrines of infallibility, plenary inspiration, and verbal inspiration of the original autographs, with that of inerrancy as it came to be defined at Princeton. Hannah's volume *Inerrancy and the Church* (1984) contains articles written by evangelicals attributing early inerrancy doctrines to Wesleyans and Baptists, and even to Calvin and the Westminster Confession. The Princeton doctrine did contain elements from earlier traditions, but the intellectual climate in the late 19th c. encouraged Warfield to seek a higher

Barr does not explicitly relate the doctrine of inerrancy to Princeton's philosophical outlook. However, he follows Sandeen in arguing that Princeton apologetics had moved a long way from the Westminster Confession's appeal to the witness of the Holy Spirit 'by and with the Word in our hearts' (Barr 1977: 261–70; Sandeen 1962; 1970*b*: 118–21).[4] He distinguishes the way in which the authority of scripture is experienced by conservative evangelicals from the defence of its authority by their 'official doctrinal polemicists' (1977: 261). He attributes the divergence between the two to the theology of Old Princeton which reduced the many reasons why scripture is authoritative to one point, namely its inspiration, which, in Warfield's apologetics, was verified by the absence of error in scripture (ibid. 261–9).[5]

Whereas the Westminster Confession attributes our full persuasion of the infallibility of scripture to 'the inward work of the Holy

standard of scientific accuracy than was demanded by previous apologists of an error-free Bible (see s. 3.2.3.5–3.3 above). For further disagreement among evangelicals on this issue see Bloesch 1994: 126–40, and n. 5 below.

[4] Gerstner (1974), and Woodbridge and Balmer (1983) question Sandeen's proposal. Nevertheless, Harold Lindsell's explicit rejection of the argument 'that the Holy Spirit bears witness with our spirits that this is the Word of God that can be trusted' as an apologetic tool (1976: 183) strongly suggests that somewhere within the heritage of American fundamentalism a departure from the Confession occurred. Reluctance to perceive a shift may be due to a fundamentalist and evangelical tendency to read the Reformers through Puritan and orthodox theology. However, those evangelicals who posit some post-Reformation turn towards rationalism disagree over whether this shift occurred between the Reformers and Protestant orthodoxy, as Rogers and McKim (1979) propose and as would be supported by R. T. Kendall's (1976) work on Calvin and Calvinism, or between Protestant orthodoxy and contemporary fundamentalism, as Muller's (1987) and Phillips' (1986) non-rationalist accounts of Calvinist orthodoxy imply.

[5] Some evangelicals, disaffected with the Princeton legacy, also question its loyalty to the Westminster Confession, notably Jack Rogers and Donald McKim in *The Authority and Interpretation of the Bible* (1979). Rogers and McKim have been influenced by the Dutch Reformed position which has challenged the rationalistic assumptions of American evangelicalism. They judge Princeton theology to be scholastic and the Dutch position to follow the Augustinian tradition of the Reformation (Rogers 1977; McKim 1985). In *Confessions of a Conservative Evangelical*, a book approved by Barr, Rogers describes his surprise at finding that the Westminster Divines did not argue for the truth of scripture from external evidence (1974: 97). Significantly, evangelicals who defend Princeton's Reformed heritage against Rogers and McKim do so not by highlighting the role that Princeton gives to the Spirit, but by emphasizing elements in Calvin and the Confession which they take to imply inerrancy (e.g. Woodbridge 1982; Gerstner 1979; Packer 1984*a*). Inerrantists believe the doctrine of inerrancy to have 'been integral to the Church's faith throughout its history' and deny that it was 'invented by Scholastic Protestantism, or is a reactionary position postulated in response to negative higher criticism' (Chicago Statement on Biblical Inerrancy, Art. 16).

Spirit', Charles Hodge attempts to defend infallibility by appeal to the doctrine of inspiration. His view of scripture was informed by the theory of verbal inspiration of Francis Turrettin of Geneva, the seventeenth-century champion of Calvinist orthodoxy.[6] Turrettin had regarded even the vowel points of the Hebrew manuscripts as inspired. Hodge (1817: i. 153) argues that the 'infallibility and divine authority of the Scriptures are due to the fact that they are the word of God; and they are the word of God because they were given by the inspiration of the Holy Ghost'.

Hodge's doctrine of inspiration was more rigid than Archibald Alexander's had been. Alexander felt that 'there existed no necessity that every word should be inspired' so long as there was 'a directing and superintending influence, as in regard to the things themselves'.[7] Sandeen considers him to be rather liberal on this point. Charles Hodge, by contrast, defended the claim that '*The Inspiration of the Scriptures extends to the Words*' (1871: i. 164–5), such that 'the words uttered were the words of God' (p. 165). The Holy Spirit rendered the biblical writers 'the organs of God for the infallible communication of his mind and will', such that, 'what they said God said' (ibid. 154). This distinctive formula, oft repeated in the subsequent evangelical tradition, is echoed in the well-known title of an article by Warfield (1899*a*): '"It says:" "Scripture says:" "God says"'. In another article, 'The Divine and Human in the Bible', Warfield ([1894*a*]: 278–9) used the Lutheran orthodox concept of *concursus* to describe the principle of human and divine speaking: 'the Scriptures are the joint product of divine and human activities, both of which penetrate them at every point, working harmoniously together to the production of a writing which is not divine here and human there, but at once divine and human in every part, every word and every particular'.

The scope of inspiration was significant in determining the scope of inerrancy, but it was not the sole contributory factor to a total inerrancy position. Charles Hodge (1871: 163) regarded inspiration as extending to 'everything which any sacred writer asserts to be true', including 'statements of facts, whether scientific, historical, or geographical'. He declared the Bible 'free from all error

[6] Before Hodge wrote his *Systematic Theology*, Turrettin's *Institutio theologiae elencticae* (Geneva 1688–9) was employed as the theological text at Princeton.

[7] *Evidences of the Authenticity, Inspiration and Canonical Authority*: 226–7, quoted in Sandeen 1970*b*: 123–4 n. 36.

whether of doctrine, fact, or precept' (ibid. 152). However, he dismissed minor errors as bearing 'no proportion to the whole'.

No sane man would deny that the Parthenon was built of marble, even if here and there a speck of sandstone should be detected in its structure. Not less unreasonable is to deny the inspiration of such a book as the Bible, because one sacred writer says that on a given occasion twenty-four, and another says that twenty-three thousand, men were slain. Surely a Christian may be allowed to tread such objections under his feet. (ibid. 170)

Later inerrantists have been upset by this passage. Gerstner (1984: 351) finds 'Hodge napping as far as *inerrancy* is concerned'. However, this is to judge Hodge by standards which did not apply until Warfield attempted to defend inerrancy in conjunction with an empirical historical method, thereby significantly altering the structure of conservative apologetics.

Charles Hodge grounded the doctrine of infallibility in the doctrine of inspiration. Warfield ([1893]: 212) insisted that we must prove the 'trustworthiness of the New Testament writings before we prove their inspiration'. In his essay 'The Real Problem of Inspiration', he inverted Hodge's position:

Inspiration is not the most fundamental of Christian doctrines, nor even the first thing we prove about the Scriptures. It is the last and crowning fact as to the Scriptures. These we first prove authentic, historically credible, generally trustworthy, before we prove them inspired. And the proof of their authenticity, credibility, general trustworthiness would give us a firm basis for Christianity prior to any knowledge on our part of their inspiration, and apart indeed from the existence of inspiration. ([1893] 1948: 210)[8]

Thus, sometimes in Warfield's writings evidences played a foundational rather than supporting role. It was therefore less easy for Warfield than it had been for Charles Hodge to dismiss inconsistencies and minor factual errors as insignificant.

Warfield's apologetic was more evidentialist than any previously presented at Princeton or elsewhere, yet it bore the same tension between inductive and deductive proof inherent in other inerrancy doctrines. He formulated his doctrine of inerrancy in an article for

[8] Later in the same essay he expressed a preference for a method which begins with the doctrine of inspiration as taught by scripture and then tests it by the facts, although allowing that one can start with the facts and infer inspiration ([1893]: 223–4).

Presbyterian Review, entitled 'Inspiration' (1881), which he co-authored with Charles Hodge's son, A. A. Hodge. Warfield was professor of New Testament at Western Seminary at the time. In this article the full inerrancy of scripture was inferred from the doctrine of verbal inspiration. Hodge and Warfield asserted that 'the scriptures not only contain, but ARE THE WORD OF GOD, and hence that all their elements and all their affirmations are absolutely errorless' (p. 237). They treated 'apparent affirmations presumably inconsistent with the present teachings of science, with facts of history, or with other statements of the sacred books themselves', on the presumption that actual error was impossible. They suggested that 'the original reading may have been lost, or . . . we may fail to realize the point of view of the author, or . . . we are destitute of the circumstantial knowledge which would fill up and harmonize the record' (ibid.). 'With these presumptions, and in this spirit' three important demands were made which, being impossible to meet, served to protect scripture from charges of errancy. These were: let the alleged error be proved to have existed in the original autographs; let the interpretation which occasions the apparent discrepancy be proved to be the 'one which the passage was evidently intended to bear'; and 'Let it be proved that the true sense of some part of the original autograph is directly and necessarily inconsistent with some certainly known fact of history, or truth of science, or some other statement of Scripture certainly ascertained and interpreted' (ibid. 242).

Theirs was a dogmatic apologetic, but one for which Warfield and Hodge sought empirical support: 'The critical investigation must be made, and we must abide by the result when it is unquestionably reached' (ibid.). While not basing claims to inspiration on an inerrant Bible, they contended that a 'proved error in Scripture contradicts not only our doctrine, but the Scripture claims and, therefore, its inspiration in making those claims' (ibid. 245). As Hodge realized, Warfield's critical method made scripture vulnerable. In a letter to Warfield, Hodge expressed concern that Warfield was 'putting *authenticity* and *genuineness* as essential prerequisites to inspiration' rather than saying 'that any criticism which denies the truth of any testimony of Christ . . . is inconsistent with inspiration'.[9]

[9] A. A. Hodge to B. B. Warfield, 3–4 Jan. 1881, quoted in Letis (1991: 186).

Warfield persisted with his procedure because, influenced by Westcott and Hort, he thought that sound textual criticism was bringing critics close to unearthing the original manuscripts (Letis 1991: 180–3). He attempted to repristinate the autographs, which, he reasoned, would be inerrant because verbally inspired. He used Charles Hodge's Parthenon passage to contend that difficulties adduced by disbelievers in plenary inspiration are '"for the most part trivial," "only apparent," and marvellously few "of any real importance"', but he significantly altered Hodge's meaning. Warfield argued not that there are few errors, but that seeming errors need 'only to be fairly understood in order to void them', and that correct exegesis and criticism shows them to be 'a progressively vanishing quantity' ([1893]: 220–1). He shifted the emphasis away from a recognition of insignificant errors towards an expectation that seeming errors will in time be proved true.

This bifurcation between a priori and a posteriori proofs for inspiration reflects not only a difference of opinion between Hodge and Warfield, but a tension within Warfield's own thought. Some of Warfield's evangelical heirs have interpreted his arguments as deductive and others as inductive. The British evangelical scholars David Wright (1980) and Nigel M. de S. Cameron (1984) attribute to Warfield a dogmatic, a priori, defence of inspiration of a kind typical of nineteenth-century evangelical thought. They are correct to the extent that Warfield does employ theological arguments for inspiration. In his article 'The Church Doctrine of Inspiration' ([1894*b*] 1948), he posits two distinct but mutually dependent arguments: that the Church experiences the Bible as a holy or numinous object; and that the Bible itself teaches inspiration. The American evangelical apologists Dan Fuller and Clark Pinnock, however, are anxious to establish the genuinely empirical nature of Warfield's apologetic.[10] David H. Kelsey suggests an interpretation of Warfield's position which helps to make sense of these two quite different readings. He finds an implicit distinction in Warfield's writings between 'scripture', which on theological grounds Warfield takes to be inspired, and 'texts', which on critical grounds may be tested for their authenticity, credibility, and general trustworthiness. The rule that scripture is inspired in-

[10] See s. 4.5.2 below.

structs us a priori to treat seeming errors as merely apparent. Kelsey (1975: 22) interprets Warfield as having inerrancy follow inspiration and not the other way round.

Whether Warfield should be interpreted as putting inerrancy or inspiration first, his critical testing of inerrancy exposed the sacred texts to risks from which they had previously been protected. In this respect it is illuminating to contrast Warfield's arguments with Louis Gaussen's defence of an error-free Bible earlier in the century. Warfield knew Gaussen's work. An American edition of the immensely influential *Theopneustia* appeared in 1842, and received Warfield's approval (Warfield 1948: 419–42, esp. 421 n. 4). Gaussen gave apologetic primacy to an experiential argument. Before turning to the proofs of *Theopneustia*, he counselled the reader that only by hearing the voice of scripture and feeling it to be 'powerful and efficacious' will he be persuaded of its inspiration (Gaussen 1841: 290, 291). He warned that the life which flows from scripture is too often quashed by 'a prolonged study of the outworks of the sacred book—of its history, manuscripts, versions, language, &c.' (p. 286). Accordingly, he put strictures on biblical criticism of a kind which Warfield was not prepared to impose. He cautioned the critic, 'if, from this Scripture . . . you dare to retrench aught . . . [t]hen is science an enormity, to be condemned as much by reason as it is by faith' (p. 271).

Warfield ([1894*b*] 1948: 110) felt that scientific study of scripture enhanced rather than diminished one's appreciation of its spiritual treasures, and quoted Westcott to that effect. He dared to propose that the resurrection account in our copies of Mark's Gospel is 'no part of the word of God', confident that scientific criticism would reveal the contents of the inerrant, inspired original manuscripts.[11]

[11] Letis (1991: 181) draws attention to this argument, from an article by Warfield entitled 'The Genuineness of Mark 16: 9–20'. Abraham (1981: 28) notes the 'gap that divides Gaussen from the tradition that stems from Warfield'. Gaussen made no mention of the original autographs as did Warfield, and he identified inspiration with dictation whereas Warfield resisted this identification (ibid. 28–38). Warfield himself did not perceive this distance. He defended Gaussen against those who attributed to him a mechanical theory of inspiration. Gaussen, wrote Warfield, 'explicitly declares that the human element is never absent' (1948: 421 n. 4). However, Warfield's own rejection of dictation terminology was a concession to the sentiments of scientific critics which Gaussen had not felt obliged to make. Moreover, his employment of an original autographs theory was a response to the problems presented by historical criticism of the extant autographs. Gaussen had scoffed at such problems forty years earlier.

Whereas Gaussen (1841: 277) had insisted that the 'safeguard of a believer . . . is still in the doctrine of inspiration', Warfield was prepared to test the inspiration of the texts as we know them. Warfield significantly raised the stakes for conservative apologetics by combining an inerrancy doctrine with the new textual-critical methods.

The Princeton theology was shaped by a dual commitment to a fully inspired Bible and an evidentialist apologetic. Mark Noll describes the legacy it left as 'a clash between two traditional loyalties, to scientific scholarship as a neutral, objective inquiry, and to the Bible as the factually accurate Word of God' (1986: 25). As proof of biblical accuracy by scientific enquiry became increasingly problematic, defenders of inerrancy devised methods of harmonizing scientific discoveries (both textual and extra-textual) with their doctrine of scripture. They either rejected problematic conclusions as unscientific, or they forsook factual interpretations of biblical narratives. The motivation behind each of these solutions was to present their biblical apologetic as though it were scientific while preserving the Bible from the charge that it contains any errors.

4.2. British Evangelicalism

In the first half of the nineteenth century, Robert Haldane and Louis Gaussen had some influence among British evangelicals in their advocacy of an error-free Bible. They did not require the level of scientific precision demanded by those who attempted later to substantiate biblical inerrancy by purely inductive means. Their approaches have been described as deductive (Abraham 1981: 18–24; Bebbington 1989: 90), although they were not entirely so.[12] Bebbington (ibid. 87–90) records how the circles of Gaussen and Haldane suspected a flaw in attempts to provide inductive validation, for it was by employing Baconian reasoning that Pye Smith in the 1820s had reasoned that Song of Songs and Esther should be excluded from the canon.

Later in the century, Hodge and Warfield's doctrine was largely rejected in Britain. While Warfield could not see how, if inspired

[12] See s. 3.3 above.

by God, scripture could contain any error, most British evangelicals regarded it as inappropriate to expect that inspiration guarantee inerrancy in minor matters. They were, like Warfield, influenced by the work of Westcott and Hort, and believed that true criticism would verify the truth of scripture (Glover 1954: 98–107; D. F. Wright 1980). However, few made recourse to an original autographs theory as a means of explaining away discrepancies, and most thought it flying in the face of facts and contrary to common sense to assert inerrancy. Henry Wace, professor of ecclesiastical history at King's College, London, 1875–9, and dean of Canterbury from 1903 until his death in 1924, regarded the minute exactitude of scripture as 'a matter partly for common sense, but chiefly for determination by the facts'.[13] He believed the Bible to be free from error in history as well as doctrine, but allowed that there might be trivial mistakes of the text. Bebbington (1989: 189–90) attributes the British restraint partly to Wace's influence as vice-president of the Bible League.

The Brethren leader W. E. Vine (1923: 25–9, 108) did argue for the inerrancy of the autograph originals. He, together with Alfred H. Burton, also of the Brethren, and David M. McIntyre, who later became principal of the Bible Training Institute, Glasgow, were among the few in Britain in the early decades of the twentieth century to defend a totally error-free Bible.[14] McIntyre (1902: 34–6) argued that error had been eliminated even from the transcriptions of the Holy Writings; this was a rare stance, and one which McIntyre himself came to rescind. In his book *The Spirit is the Word* (1908), he chose not to employ the term 'inerrancy' because it 'can apply only to the original documents, concerning which we are in fact altogether ignorant' (ibid. 4–5). Others were more reticent still. W. H. Griffith Thomas, principal of Wycliffe Hall, gave no explicit endorsement to the inerrancy doctrine. In the 1925 symposium *Evangelicalism*, G. T. Manley (1925: 136, 137) would not press for 'verbal inerrancy in detail', although believing that 'as a fact' the Bible contains 'no scientific error', and T. C. Hammond (1925: 182) would argue only for 'substantial accuracy'.

[13] *Record*, 5 Oct. 1922, p. 605, quoted in Bebbington (1989: 190).

[14] Burton wrote an article called 'The Inerrancy of the Bible' for *Advent Witness*, Apr. 1921.

Whereas in America inerrantist convictions generated biblical scholarship and apologetics among evangelicals, in Britain a method of 'believing criticism' was more influential. Believing criticism developed especially in Scotland. It admitted trifling errors in Scripture while retaining confidence in its infallibility. James Orr epitomized this position. In an article for *The Fundamentals* (n.d.: ix. 34), he explained that he did not object to criticism *per se*, but to criticism which 'starts from the wrong basis . . . proceeds by arbitrary methods, and . . . arrives at results which I think are demonstrably false'. In an SCM publication of 1930, entitled *Letters to a Fundamentalist*, Percy Austin denied fundamentalists the right to claim James Orr for their side, on the grounds that Orr 'wrote *as a critic*', albeit a 'conservative critic', and 'would not have felt complimented if he had heard himself described as an opponent of Biblical criticism' (p. 58).

Orr was a critic of the Princeton doctrine. In *Revelation and Inspiration* (1910: 213 n. 1) he described his method partly in contradistinction from Warfield's. Orr approached 'the subject of inspiration through that of *revelation*', rather than proving 'first the inspiration (by historical evidence, miracles, claims of writers), then through that establish the revelation' (ibid. 197). He regarded it a 'most suicidal position' to claim that unless inerrancy can be proved down to the 'minutest details, the whole edifice of belief in revealed religion falls to the ground' (pp. 197–8). He believed that the Bible, because inspired, was an 'infallible guide in the great matters for which it was given' (p. 217), but that inspiration did not entail exclusion of 'all, even the least, error or discrepancy in statement' (p. 213). Inerrancy 'is a violent assumption which there is nothing in the Bible really to support' (p. 214).

That fundamentalism did not develop in Britain as it did in the United States is attributed partly to such qualified acceptance of modern criticism. Today some British evangelicals regard this as a positive feature of their heritage. I. Howard Marshall (1977*a*: 132) accepts historical criticism practised 'in the light of the doctrine of biblical inspiration', by which he means criticism which does not stop at the discovery of historical difficulties, but attempts to harmonize apparent discrepancies. Alister McGrath and David Wenham (1993: 31) commend evangelicals for 'welcoming the critical method in principle, yet denying that its implementation necessarily undermines, in theory or practice, the historic Christian conviction concerning the divine authority of Scripture'.

Others, significantly for Barr's thesis, concur with Carl Henry's (1976*b*: 48) negative interpretation that the 'emphasis on biblical inerrancy did not conspicuously dominate the evangelical scene in Britain' because there 'critical theory took a larger toll'. Cameron (1984) believes that British evangelicalism was weakened by its quest for a 'better' and 'truer' criticism because, once admitting the principle that infallibility be tested by historical-criticism, evangelicals opened the way for conservative defeat. Similarly, D. F. Wright (1980) prefers an approach which he associates with Old Princeton, in which the nature of scripture is established dogmatically (with the recognition of possible historical-critical rebuttals) rather than in dialogue with biblical criticism.[15] Cameron and Wright are therefore grateful in their different ways for the influence of Old Princeton theology upon British evangelicalism in the 1950s. It was around this time, according to Barr (e.g. 1980*a*: 82–3), that British evangelical thought began to be restrained by rationalism.

4.3. Proof-Texting in the Holiness and Dispensationalist Movements

Biblical conservatives in America who were less scholarly than the Princetonians nevertheless shared the Princeton rhetoric of theological science. However, they had a more naïve grasp of the inductive method.

Reuben A. Torrey, a teacher at the Moody Bible Institute and the Bible Institute of Los Angeles, likened his theological method to that 'pursued in the study of nature; first, careful analysis and ascertainment of facts; second, classification of facts' (1920: 12). He described his book, *What the Bible Teaches*, as an 'unbiased, systematic, thoroughgoing, *inductive* study and statement of Bible truth' ([1898] 1957: 1). It was a 500-page compilation of biblical propositions supported by proof-texts. Torrey's

[15] Our discussion of Warfield above would suggest that they assume too great a similarity between Warfield and earlier 19th-c. thinkers such as Gaussen (see D. F. Wright 1980: 102; Cameron 1984: 159), and too great a dissimilarity between Warfield and the advocates of 'better' criticism who were together influenced by Westcott.

favoured technique, advocated in *How to Study the Bible For Greatest Profit* (1920: 34, 26, 35), involved '*verse by verse analysis*', examination of 'parallel passages', and classification into 'numerous subdivisions'.

Warfield considered the inductive method to have been improved by the discipline of 'Biblical Theology', which encouraged a more holistic approach to scripture. He regarded Torrey's method as 'altogether alien to this truly inductive process': 'He [Torrey] begins with isolated passages, collected under a purely formal *schema* already present explicitly or implicitly in his mind: and this is not made induction merely by arranging the texts first and the propositions which they support second, on the printed page' ([1899*b*]: 300). Warfield (ibid.) denied that Torrey's procedure had any right to the name 'inductive' since it was 'indistinguishable from the ordinary method of the exercise known as "Bible-readings"'.

Torrey was a regular Keswick speaker and an evangelist.[16] His technique, as described and attacked by Warfield, was that used in the holiness movement and in the Bible conferences. James H. Brookes sets out the procedure thus: 'select some word . . . and with the aid of a good Concordance, mark down . . . the references to the subject under discussion . . . thus presenting all that the Holy Ghost has been pleased to reveal on the topic' (*Truth* (1879), quoted by Weber 1982: 110). 'Proof-texting' was employed on the grounds that all of the Bible is equally inspired, and so equally accurate. Dyson Hague (1909?: 110–11) noted that before the sting of higher criticism, 'any text from any part of the Bible was accepted as a proof-text for the establishment of any truth of Christian teaching, and a statement from the Bible was considered an end of controversy'. An emphasis upon the divine character of scripture warranted proof-texting by encouraging a disregard for historical study. Ironically, this emphasis also 'provided the point of contact with conservative scholars', so that the Princeton conservatives 'entered into an uneasy alliance' with holiness advocates

[16] He presided over the Welsh revivals, and had a greater following in Britain than did Moody a decade before him. I am grateful to Ian Rennie for pointing out that Torrey had a singular influence in England through E. J. H. Nash, the missioner to public schools, who regarded Torrey as his theological mentor. Nash introduced Torrey's theology to his 'Bash' camp disciples, including John Stott, Michael Green, Dick Lucas, and David Watson.

and dispensationalists whose method and theology they decried (Noll 1986: 59).

Dispensationalists regarded their elaborate method of 'rightly dividing the word of truth' (2 Tim. 2: 15, KJV) as the only scientific procedure.[17] In his work of that title Scofield (1896) decreed: 'The Word of Truth, then, has right divisions . . . *so any study* of that Word which ignores those divisions must be in large measure profitless and confusing' (quoted in Marsden 1980: 59). Scofield (1909: Introduction) defended the consistency of scripture by employing the principle, 'Distinguish the ages, and the Scriptures harmonize', quoting Augustine. The ages of scripture were discovered through rigorous division and classification of the text, based upon painstaking attention to variations in the written word. Scofield, for example, discerned Seven Judgments made upon God's creatures (ibid. 1351 n. 1), and distinguished the Kingdom of heaven from the Kingdom of God, regarding the former as 'the earthly sphere' of the latter (ibid. 1003 n. 1, 996 n. 1).

Dispensationalism demands greater precision from the biblical text than do most other fundamentalist systems. Numbers have to refer to exact periods of time, and prophecies to predict actual events. The extensive attempts by dispensationalists to provide empirical interpretations of scripture passages are equalled today only by creation scientists.[18] The comparatively moderate 'fundamentalists' whom Barr describes make more concessions to figurative language in scripture. Nevertheless, in so far as they operate on the principle that a factual reading is to be taken wherever possible, and 'wherever possible' means without attributing error to scripture, they differ from dispensationalists more in degree than in kind. They are more concerned with the factual nature of historical narratives than of apparent prophetic or scientific passages, and so disagree with dispensationalists and creation scientists principally over the number and type of passages for which factual interpretations are to be pressed.

[17] For the influence of Baconianism upon dispensationalists see Marsden (1980: 55–62). Others influenced by the general common-sense outlook included the premillennialist Millerites (Weber 1991: 7–8), and the post-millennialist Alexander Campbell, who believed that an emphasis upon biblical 'facts' and exercise of Baconian induction would bring agreement among Christians (Hughes 1991: 115–17).

[18] See s. 4.5.7 below.

4.4. Early Fundamentalism

Early fundamentalists shared many Enlightenment assumptions with their modernist liberal opponents.[19] Both valued the standards of science and the application of reason. They bypassed tradition and went back to the primitive sources in order to unearth the historical facts and the essential truths of Christianity. In doing so, each side claimed to represent the truly scientific and open-minded approach, regarding the other as closed-minded and dogmatic.

On the fundamentalist side, it was argued that modern criticism was not based on a sound philosophy acceptable to Christians, but on Idealism, which fostered an 'evolutionary theory of all history' and minimized divine intervention in the affairs of the people of Israel (W. H. G. Thomas n.d.: 14–15). Fundamentalists did not approach the biblical writings as texts conditioned by the understanding of the religious communities by and for whom they were written. They read historical and miracle narratives as straightforward pieces of factual reporting and accused critics who attempted to rationalize supernatural elements of failing to work 'in the spirit of scientific and Christian scholarship' (Hague 1909?: 89). In his debate with modernists, J. Gresham Machen insisted that 'the *Christian* religion is most emphatically dependent upon facts—facts in the external world, facts with which "science" in the true sense of the word certainly has a right to deal' (1936: 62). 'What good does it do to tell me', he asked, 'that I have a fine pattern of religion in the account of Jesus in the Gospels, whether that account is history or an inspiring ideal?' (Machen 1936: 64).

Modernists were influenced by both Kantian and Romantic thought. They accepted the Kantian dualism between science and religion, and so regarded faith and scientific enquiry as separate and compatible. Consequently, fundamentalists (or, at least, their intellectual spokesmen) regarded the modernist religion as void of reason. Warfield lamented that 'faith . . . after Kant, can no longer be looked upon as a matter of reasoning and does not rest on rational grounds' ([1908]: 14). Machen, who abhorred the 'false and disastrous opposition' between faith and knowledge, de-

[19] William R. Hutchison's practice of portraying modernism as one form of Protestant liberalism is followed here ([1976] 1992: 1–9).

scribed modernism as a 'retrograde, anti-intellectual movement' which 'degrades the intellect by excluding it from the sphere of religion' (1925: 26, 18). He argued that 'Modern liberalism' was a totally different religion from Christianity and, moreover, was 'unscientific' (1923: 7). Shailer Mathews responded with a defence of *The Faith of Modernism* (1924). He contended that only modernists are 'open-minded in regard to scientific discovery' because they 'rely on scientific method' as opposed to 'church authority' (reprinted in Smith, Handy, and Loetscher 1963: 241–2, 240).

Underlying the modernist conception of Christianity was an assumption that ideas and beliefs do not directly correspond to external reality but are mental constructions which develop as a culture evolves. Hence religion was thought not to reflect objective knowledge of God, but progressive human understanding. Mathews argued that religious experience provided the data for modernist studies of religion: 'Christian religion develops as a group-possession when men's experience and knowledge grow' (ibid. 242). For fundamentalists the hard facts of the Bible constituted scientific data from which doctrine was constructed. Doctrine was understood to be 'any presentation of the facts which lie at the basis of the Christian religion with the true meaning of the facts' (Machen 1923: 45). Fundamentalists believed that the best defence for Christianity was a reassertion of the facts recorded in scripture. They neither revised their notion of fact nor questioned the historicity of the biblical narratives in the light of emerging philosophical emphases upon historical conditioning:[20]

> when the gospels tell us that Jesus Christ was conceived by the Holy Ghost and born of the Virgin Mary, that He died a sin-offering, that He rose from the grave with the marks of His passion in His body, and that He walked on the sea and stilled the tempest, and fed a multitude of people with a few loaves and fishes, they are telling us what is fact.[21]

Conscious interpretation of scripture was kept to a minimum by fundamentalists. James Gray, Dean of Moody Bible Institute, advised: 'The facts must come first and interpretation afterwards.

[20] George Marsden and Grant Wacker illustrate this lack of historical consciousness by contrasting Machen's view of reality with that of Carl Becker and Walter Lippmann respectively. Machen's perception was ahistorical. He insisted that truth was absolute, not relative, that Christian doctrine was true for all generations and independent of cultural variation and the flux of history (Marsden 1979*a*; Wacker 1985: 21–4).

[21] Macartney, letter in *Presbyterian* (1923), repr. in Vanderlaan (1925: 187–8).

To a great extent, if we get the facts, the interpretation will take care of itself.'[22] William Jennings Bryan resisted the suggestion made at the Scopes Trial that he had interpreted passages of scripture:

Bryan I would not say interpretations, Mr. Darrow, but comments on the lesson.
Darrow If you comment to any extent these comments have been interpretations?
Bryan I presume that any discussion might be to some extent interpretations; but they have not been primarily intended as interpretations.
Darrow Do you claim that everything in the Bible should be literally interpreted?
Bryan I believe everything in the Bible should be accepted as it is given there . . .

(Scopes Trial Transcript, pp. 734–5)

Suspicion of interpretation lay behind the increasing 'creedalism' of conservatives in the denominations, who attempted to fend off 'loophole' interpretations of the traditional Confessions or Statements of Faith. This was especially striking among the Baptists, whose commitment to soul liberty had always deterred them from establishing creeds. As numbers in their ranks seemed to move towards more moderate views of scripture they came to regard their statements of faith as insufficient. 'Who could have imagined', asked one member of the Southern Baptist Convention, looking back over developments this century, 'that "truth without any mixture of error" would one day be taken by some to mean that the Bible contains both truth and error, but that they are not mixed?' (Draper 1988: 125).

Fundamentalists developed a biblical apologetic which they described as 'scientific' and which reflected early modern thought. Their methodology, they claimed, was inductive. They drew selectively on the results of scientific study of the biblical text, and on the discoveries of archaeological and natural science, and they demanded from the text a standard of scientific accuracy which would not have been expected in a previous age. Their outlook was not simply modern, it was early modern because it assumed the neutrality of the facts with which it dealt. The apologetic was ultimately inconsistent because motivated by a belief that a divinely inspired scripture cannot contain error, and

[22] Gray, *Synthetic Bible Studies* (1923), quoted in Weber (1982: 113).

this was a dogmatic stance reflecting a pre-modern form of reasoning.

4.5. The Fundamentalist Mentality in Recent Decades

4.5.1. *The Nature of Truth*

James Barr observes that the sort of truth important to fundamentalists is 'correspondence to external reality' to the extent that veracity 'as correspondence with empirical actuality has precedence over veracity as significance' (1977: 49). Fundamentalists want to affirm in the first instance that the Bible gets its facts right. We should not thereby think that fundamentalists do not value scripture as a source of vision, motivation, and correction. Barr is right, however, in that fundamentalist apologetics focus primarily on the factual accuracy of scripture, and regard factual truth as underpinning any other sort of truth which the Bible might be said to contain.

Mark Noll makes the same point more sympathetically. He describes as a 'distinct group' within the Christian and theological world evangelicals 'who affirm that the Bible is uniquely true with respect to divine–human relationships and either substantially or entirely true with respect to matters of fact'. Such evangelicals 'set themselves apart from those who deny that the Bible conveys cognitive truth', or 'who argue that the Bible is uniquely true, but only as a record of religious experience or of divine–human encounter' (Noll 1986: 144). Noll's description allows for what I see as varying degrees of fundamentalist thinking among evangelicals.

The fundamentalist mentality at its most crude operates under the anxiety that unless we have fully accurate reports, we cannot know that the biblical stories have any anchor in real events. It opposes truth to myth, and a Bible which tells us about factual reality to a Bible which bears no relevance for our world. As a member of the Council on Biblical Inerrancy explains, 'one would want biblical statements to correspond to reality, for few, if any, would rest their eternal destiny on notions that have nothing to do with the world and universe in which they live' (J. S. Feinberg 1984: 40, 41). Evangelicals vary in the severity with which they manifest this either/or way of thinking. They have different ways of acknowledging and explaining variant readings in scripture, as will be apparent from the discussion of inerrancy below. Noll himself mentions I. Howard Marshall, who acknowledges the possibility of a 'genuine historical mistake' in the chronology of Acts 5: 33–9. Marshall urges that 'our understanding of the truth of the Bible' allow for such mistakes.[23] Evangelicals respond in different ways to Marshall's work. Some resist his conclusion that the Acts passage contains error (Noll 1986: 244–5 n. 3). Others happily present Marshall as a counter-example to Barr's critique (e.g. France 1991: 52–3).

This study enquires into fundamentalist ways of thinking among evangelicals. The fundamentalist mentality goes beyond an insistence that the concepts of 'religious truth' or 'religious significance' be grounded in historical events, to a conviction that historical grounding is not available unless our biblical accounts of the relevant events can be trusted as factually accurate. Marshall's position is that some factual inaccuracy in the biblical writings will not disturb the essential historicity of the Christian faith. In 1977, Barr judged Marshall to be fundamentalist for abandoning the literal sense of the text in order to preserve the Bible from error. In that same year, Marshall was accepting the possibility that the biblical text contains error.[24] We should expect that on Barr's analysis, Marshall would still qualify as basically fundamentalist in the same way that James Orr qualifies as basically proto-fundamentalist—in that he acknowledges only minor or unimportant errors in scripture.[25] As we have noted, Barr's attitude to Orr is somewhat inconsistent, in that he also suggests that Orr provides an alternative to fundamentalism. One could envisage a parallel inconsistency creeping into a discussion of Marshall, which would be further complicated by the fact that Marshall's own position is a developing one. Marshall is increasingly ready to revise the notion of biblical truth, and to allow his biblical scholarship to inform his revision. If we think of the fundamentalist mentality existing among evangelicals in varying degrees, we might say that the degree of fundamentalist thinking in Marshall's work has diminished or even disappeared.

[23] *Biblical Inspiration* (Grand Rapids, Mich.: Eerdmans, 1982), quoted in Noll (1986: 144).

[24] See s. 2.2.2 above.

[25] See s. 2.2.3 above.

The following survey identifies characteristics of the fundamentalist mentality by means of its starker manifestations in recent fundamentalist and evangelical apologetics.

To the fundamentalist-minded, there is a sense in which the possibility of error in scripture is less threatening than the category of myth. To ask whether scripture is in error is to remain within a discussion about 'objective cognitive validity', to use a phrase of Carl Henry's (1976*a*: 44). Henry (ibid. 45) regards myth as essentially incompatible with 'rational truth and historical events':

> The basic issues reduce really to two alternatives: either man himself projects upon the world and its history a supernatural reality and activity that disallows objectively valid cognitive statements on the basis of divine disclosure, or a transcendent divine reality through intelligible revelation establishes the fact that God is actually at work in the sphere of nature and human affairs.

Less sophisticated evangelicals tend to regard '"mythical" as simply synonymous with "untrue"', as is noted in the Preface to *The Truth of God Incarnate* (M. Green 1977*a*: 14).[26] Harold Lindsell (1976: 80) takes this view. He equates the belief that Adam and Eve are mythical with the verdict that scripture is erroneous. More commonly, evangelicals view 'myth' as a woolly and evasive concept. Michael Green implies, in effect, that biblical critics appeal to myth when they will not commit themselves to the Bible's 'real meaning': 'when the New Testament writers ascribe deity to Jesus they did not mean it in any attenuated, mythical or poetic sense. They meant what they said: that God had visited and redeemed his people, and that he had done so in and through Jesus' (1977*a*: 36).

Principally, for the sake of apologetics, evangelicals present the Bible as providing the reader with facts. From these facts, writers such as J. N. D. Anderson in *The Fact of Christ: Some of the Evidence* (1979) and Josh McDowell in *Evidence that Demands a Verdict: Historical Evidence for the Christian Faith* (1972) compile a case for the truth of Christianity. They value facticity because they believe it furnishes objective proof and minimizes the interpretative element both in the writing and the reading of the biblical records. They understand facts to exist prior to judgement and independently of

[26] This book is an evangelical response to John Hick (ed.), *The Myth of God Incarnate* (London: SCM, 1977).

their being known. That the Bible is true means that its statements correspond to these entities. The Chicago Statement on Biblical Hermeneutics (1982) affirms that 'the Bible expresses God's truth in propositional statements, and . . . that a statement is true if it represents matters as they actually are, but is an error if it misrepresents the facts' (Art. 6).

The sorts of facts which evangelicals are most concerned to preserve are historical facts. The same Chicago Statement denies emphatically that 'generic categories which negate historicity may rightly be imposed on biblical narratives which present themselves as factual' (Art. 13). The bottom line, as expressed in *The Truth of God Incarnate*, is 'the fact of the resurrection of Jesus of Nazareth . . . [which] stands behind every page of the New Testament', and without which 'there would have been no New Testament, no Christianity' (Butler 1977: 89).

A factual reading is associated with the 'plain sense' of the text, if the text is thought to present itself as factual. In defending the plain sense of scripture, evangelicals wish to protect scripture from misinterpretation, and to maintain its accessibility to its most unlearned readers. Their heartfelt plea is that scripture 'should be allowed to speak for itself, and . . . we should be allowed to hear what it really does say' (Neill 1977: 69). However, they can too readily attribute the status of fact to matters which others would regard as interpretative. Packer (1958*a*: 144) contends that 'Evangelicals face facts which the exponents of "critical orthodoxy" overlook: namely, that the Bible teaches a positive doctrine of its origin and nature, which Christ incorporated in His own teaching'.

Most open to distortion are attempts to establish a correspondence between supposedly scientific or prophetic (in the sense of predictive) passages in scripture, and empirical actuality. Some such instances can clearly override more natural interpretations of biblical verses. Wallie Criswell (1982: 120), an ultra-conservative in the Southern Baptist convention, finds the 'finest statement of the atomic theory you will ever read in your life . . . in Hebrews 11: 3. God made this world out of things that are not seen'. Harold Lindsell (1976: 38), in his infamous polemic *The Battle for the Bible*, rejects the suggestion that 'Job 38: 7 [where] the morning stars are said to sing together' should be taken as figurative, since 'scientists now tell us that in the air there is music that comes from the stars'.

The camera crew in Pat Robertson's Christian Broadcasting Network discussed the possibility of situating TV cameras in Jerusalem in order to televise the Second Coming. They even took into consideration how to avoid the glare of Christ's radiance (Straub 1986: 161).[27] A plainer, and indeed more matter-of-fact, reading of passages about the Second Coming would suggest it capable of public viewing without televisual aid.

4.5.2. *Inerrancy and Inductive Validation*

It is one thing to believe that a narrative points to historical reality, and another to insist that unless the text is free from error we cannot know about that reality. The inerrantist argues that since no historical event is open to our personal and individual confirmation, we must depend on the reliability and sufficiency of our sources, which will be discredited if found to contain error. A 'necessary relation' is assumed to exist 'between accuracy of the words and authority of the message'.[28] The tenacity of commitment to an inerrantist view of scripture derives from the conviction that in defending inerrancy, one is defending the authority of the Bible and thereby one's basis for faith.

Inerrancy has become a loose concept and can no longer by itself be taken as a reliable indicator of extreme biblical conservatism. Evangelicals argue among themselves over its meaning and scope. There exists a multitude of formulations and modifications of the inerrancy doctrine, and many versions concede various kinds of error (S. T. Davis 1977: 24–5; James 1987: 177–84). Most versions admit error in grammar and form, and imperfections in presently existing Bibles. Some insist that only the author's intended meaning is inerrant. The qualification is normally added that supposed mistakes or contradictions must be indisputably false or contradictory. When too many qualifications are added the doctrine is over-protected and becomes unfalsifiable (S. T. Davis 1977: 28). Some recent definitions of inerrancy have been given 'in terms of truth and falsity rather than in terms of error', as is the case in Elwell's *Concise Evangelical Dictionary of Theology*

[27] Gerard Straub, having once worked for CBN, gave a critical, insider's view of the organization in *Salvation for Sale* (1986).

[28] Charles C. Ryrie, *What You Should Know About Inerrancy* (Chicago: Moody Press, 1981), 16, quoted in McKim (1985: 57).

(P. D. Feinberg 1993: 63). The Chicago Statement on Biblical Inerrancy makes a similar move. This means that the Bible can be said to be 'entirely true in all it affirms' (ibid.), or 'entirely true and trustworthy in all its assertions' (Chicago Statement on Biblical Inerrancy, Exposition), allowing for leeway in matters which the Bible, it could be said, does not expressly affirm. This leaves inerrancy rather open-ended, for the Bible could be said not to affirm a six-day creation or the Pauline authorship of the pastoral epistles, or other convictions which traditionally inerrantists have wanted to protect.

Due to the confusion surrounding the term 'inerrancy', British evangelicals are usually happy to abandon it (e.g. Goldingay 1977*b*: 301; Stott in Edwards and Stott 1988: 95). James Packer ([1965] 1979: 110) is prepared to sacrifice both the terms 'inerrancy' and 'infallibility', since they have 'turned into noses of wax, malleable and often misshapen in recent discussion'. Many evangelicals in America, by contrast, retain inerrancy as a badge even while significantly altering its implications. Their affirmations of inerrancy should not always be equated with an insistence on factual accuracy. Daniel Fuller caused rupture in Fuller Seminary's faculty by proclaiming inerrancy only in revelational matters.[29] He persisted with the term 'inerrancy', but Pinnock (1973: 334; 1971*a*: 79) ridiculed his approach as one of 'limited inerrancy'.

Limited inerrancy presents evangelicals with a new 'domino theory', to use Barr's phrase. Traditional inerrantists have reasoned that if any part of scripture is regarded as uncertain, then other parts are open to doubt and one is thereby in danger of losing one's grounds for faith. Limited inerrancy poses the problem of how to determine 'which biblical material is revelational and which is not' (Pinnock 1973: 334), the worry being that there is no clear place to draw the line and the dominos can go on falling. Donald Bloesch affirms inerrancy in Berkouwer's sense of undeceiving rather than impeccable (1978: 67; 1983: p. ix). In effect, Robert H. Gundry (1982: 623–40) means by inerrancy that the Bible is the sufficient and authoritative resource for theology even where it is unhistorical. He applies redaction criticism to

[29] Daniel Fuller publicly aired his views at the annual meeting of the Evangelical Theological Society in Toronto, 1967, and in the subsequent paper 'Benjamin B. Warfield's View of Faith and History' (1968). See also Fuller (1972).

Matthew's Gospel, finding a 'change of a historical report . . . into a theological tale' where Matthew edits his material (ibid. 20). Consequently, Gundry does not demand historical accuracy from the text: 'Matthew's subtractions, additions, and revisions of order and phraseology . . . represent developments of the dominical tradition that result in different meanings and departures from the actuality of events' (ibid. 623).[30]

Inerrancy debates among American evangelicals turn partly on who is most truly following the inductive method advocated by Warfield. Fuller claimed that in following Warfield's empirical historical method 'to the bitter end', he was 'facing squarely' biblical errors in non-revelational matters.[31] In his understanding, Warfield 'let induction control from beginning to end' (Fuller 1973: 332). Pinnock likewise believes himself to be no less empirical than Warfield. Pinnock, however, more faithfully reflects Warfield's deductive premisses when he claims that scripture can only be approached 'from within a standpoint of faith' (1971*a*: 135). Fuller (1973: 331) rightly argues that if Pinnock begins with faith, he cannot 'talk very meaningfully about induction'. The radical critical aspect of Warfield's work is picked up by Fuller, but with a crucial difference. Whereas Fuller distinguishes revelational from non-revelational matters in scripture, Warfield distinguished the extant manuscripts from the autographs. He then protected the autographs from any empirical findings which threatened their total inerrancy.

No amount of empirical investigation detracts from the fact that the doctrine of inerrancy is initially established dogmatically. This is why evangelicals such as Fuller, who claim to be thoroughgoing inductivists and who have opened a gap between theological and empirical truth, remain committed to the notion of inerrancy. The doctrine is based upon the premiss, which is sometimes stated explicitly, that: 'All Scripture is the direct product of the omnipotent and omniscient God who is not subject to error' (J. J. Davis

[30] Gundry (1982: 13–19) begins by attributing theological rather than historical significance to the genealogy of Jesus. He regards Matthew's treatment of OT prophecy as manipulations or embellishments of the tradition, albeit ones which rest on historical data and foreshadow genuinely historical events such as the vindication of Jesus as God's Son in the resurrection (pp. 35, 37). He sees Matthew's hand in the telling of Jesus' sayings and works, and in the account of his resurrection (pp. 585–91).

[31] Fuller in debate with faculty members of Fuller Seminary, Dec. 1962, quoted in Marsden (1987*a*: 212).

1985: 17 n. 20). Packer ([1965] 1979: 27) can conceive of no reason for asserting inspiration except to proclaim freedom from error: 'what is the cash-value of saying Scripture "inspires" and "mediates the Word of God", when we have constantly to allow for undetectable possibilities of error on the part of each biblical author?'

Verbal inspiration is essential to a defence of inerrancy and is not itself established inductively. In a form of argument which at times is crudely circular, the words of the Bible are said to provide evidence and explication of its inspiration:

> The book is either what God says it is or God is not true. God is true. His Word is true. When Scripture claims it is the Word of God, that claim is also true. Therefore, the inspiration concerns the words. The Bible defines its inspiration as verbal. If the inspiration of the Bible is not verbal then God has absolutely no right to call it 'The Word of God.' Since this is the name He used, the matter should be settled.
>
> (Zimmerman 1984: 193)

The Bible, it is thought, 'evidences itself to be the Word of God' (Packer [1965] 1979: 122). The verses most commonly employed to 'prove' inspiration from scripture are 2 Timothy 3: 16 and 2 Peter 1: 20–1. The Lutheran dogmaticians, who defended their doctrine of verbal inspiration also from these verses, regarded the circularity involved in this reasoning as entirely appropriate: one proves God from God, the sun from the sun, colour from colour, and the divine origin of scripture from scripture itself (Preus 1970: 282–4; 1955: 41–2). Fundamentalists and evangelicals likewise appeal to the *sola scriptura* principle, but do not reflect the same rich circularity. They either feel negatively constrained by the circle of logic and expect that the content of a particular verse will enable them to move beyond it; or they introduce inductive validation in order to justify trusting the Bible's own arguments about itself by demonstrating that scripture can be established as reliable and authoritative on other grounds. Both paths lead them into inconsistency.

Charles Ryrie's (1983: 4) argument for inerrancy illustrates the first tendency. He attempts to use the force of 2 Peter 1: 21 as conclusive, when in fact on the basis of his two premisses there is no reason why the verse in 2 Peter should be considered trustworthy:

A standard deductive argument for inerrancy is this: God is true (Rom. 3: 4); the Scriptures were breathed out by God (2 Tim. 3: 16); therefore the Scriptures are true (since they came from the breath of God, who is true). This is not to imply that those who deny or adjust the meaning of inerrancy deny that God is true; rather they point out that because God used fallible men, it is to be expected that what those men produced (the Bible) contains errors.

Logic alone could lead to either conclusion, but the Scriptures in 2 Peter 1: 21 indicate which is correct.

Evangelicals who function according to the second tendency anticipate that inductive study will yield results compatible with the authority they have attributed to scripture. The quest for inductive support increases the demands for scientific accuracy and historical precision. Warfield believed he was on the edge of uncovering the original revelation. Evangelicals today defend inerrancy with no such prospect in sight. Some move away from scientific and historical inerrancy and promote a limited inerrancy doctrine. Others, such as Harold Lindsell, persist in attempting to provide validation through a textual criticism of sorts. Lindsell (1976: 175–6) notoriously harmonizes the passion narratives to conclude that Peter denied Jesus six times. Those looking for extra-biblical evidence share Wallie Criswell's (1982: 116) expectation that 'every spade of dirt turned over by the archaeologist confirms the Word of God'. Creation scientists, in particular, collect biological and geological data in defence of inerrancy. Most evangelicals do not go so far as creation scientists and few demand as much factual precision from scripture as does Lindsell. However, many evangelicals, especially in the States, want to be seen to endorse an inductive approach.

Those British evangelicals who uphold a version of either inerrancy or infallibility are more ambivalent than their American counterparts towards inductive validation. They prefer an '*ex hypothesi* infallibilism' to 'infallibilism-on-the-merits' (Cameron 1984) and insist that the 'authority of the Scriptures is a matter of faith and not of argument' (Lloyd-Jones 1958: 38). Acceptance of scripture, James Packer (1958*b*: 44) argues, is more a matter of submission than of scientific proof: 'if we call Scripture *inerrant*, we mean, not that we think we can demonstrate its accuracy in stating facts, but that we receive its statements as true on the credit of its divine Author'. John Wenham ([1972] 1993: 191), quoting from

Theopneustia, notes with pleasure Gaussen's ridicule of the 'immense toil' to prove the integrity of the New Testament, which ends in a result 'wonderful in its insignificance' and 'imposing by its nullity'. Wenham dismisses attempts to discover the ideal New Testament, as though this would prove its integrity (ibid.), and rests content with 'essential infallibility' of the 'scriptures once inerrant but now slightly corrupt' (ibid. 194).

Nevertheless, the majority of evangelicals, whether British or American, retain a hope that biblical truth will be empirically verified. When empirical support is available they are generally pleased to accept it. If the Bible appears to be right, even about relatively minor matters, their enjoyment of scripture is increased. Moreover, their convictions about the appropriate, humble and submissive attitudes towards scripture are enhanced. So R. T. France gladly appropriates John Robinson's early dating of the New Testament.[32] It is a comprehensible and not inconsistent move to accept validation when it is forthcoming. However, non-scholarly literature can be mercurial in this practice. According to British creation scientist David C. C. Watson ([1975] 1989: 21), the appropriate attitude towards the Genesis account of creation is one of faith, where faith is 'exercised in regard to matters of which the believer [has] no previous experience'. So 'faith in creation means a simple acceptance of the statement: "God made two great lights . . . and the evening and the morning were the fourth day."' Watson believes that the 'historical record of God's creating the universe in six days was written by the finger of God on tables of stone, the accuracy of the whole book being vouched for by Christ himself' (ibid. 34). In support of his literal interpretation of Genesis, he quotes Barr's words: 'In fact the only natural exegesis is the literal one, in the sense that this is what the author meant . . . he was deeply interested in chronology and calendar' (Barr 1977: 42, quoted in Watson, ibid. 4). Thus Barr himself has become someone whose conservative verdicts are used to fundamentalist advantage; the fundamentalist tactic being to preserve the doctrine of scripture from hostile evidence by basing it on faith tenets, but to validate it inductively if evidence even from seemingly hostile camps appears friendly.

[32] See s. 2.2.3 above.

It is surprising that evangelicals should ever present their biblical scholarship as primarily inductive, since they are not ashamed but proud of their commitment to vindicate the truth of scripture. However, they are caught in the conflict between a commitment to scientific method and a belief in a fully inspired Bible, with all the assumptions that their belief in inspiration entails. They combine dogmatic and empirical approaches, favouring historical enquiry which accepts 'in advance that what Scripture says is true' (Packer 1958*a*: 154). This is why the 'maximally-conservative' argument identified by James Barr (1977: 85–9, 124–8) is in bad faith.

Evangelicals are not always conscious of the strains incurred by merging deductive premisses with an inductive method, although some have acknowledged Barr's criticism.[33] Generally they operate under the belief that certain premisses are necessary if the study of scripture is to be true to the nature of scripture. In past decades they spoke in terms of their scholarship being truly scientific: ' "scientific", "objective" study of anything is simply study of it in terms of itself, and . . . Scripture is studied "scientifically" and "objectively" when—and only when—it is studied in full recognition of its character as Scripture, the infallible Word of God, (Packer 1958*a*: 157). Nowadays they are pleased that faith has been identified as an aspect of scientific enquiry, and so they refer more readily to their faith-assumptions or 'presuppositions'.[34] Yet they believe that their presuppositions alone recognize scripture for what it is. Herein lies a possible explanation for why evangelicals, so conscious of the presuppositions of non-evangelical biblical scholars, rarely direct critical attention to the presuppositions at work in their own scholarship.[35] They regard their presuppositions as the true and correct presuppositions, and barely recognize any bias in them at all.

4.5.3. *Dictation?*

W. J. Abraham and Kern Robert Trembath are evangelicals who reject the predominant evangelical method of locating inspiration in the words of scripture, and instead locate it in the present

[33] See s. 2.2.2 above.

[34] See Ch. 8.

[35] As noted at s. 2.3.1 above.

among religious believers.[36] They both argue that since fundamentalists begin with God and the fact of his speaking, their reasoning is never genuinely inductive (Abraham 1981: 15–32; Trembath 1987: 8–46). They attribute the problem of inerrancy to the link assumed between divine inspiration and divine speaking, so that the very words of scripture are thought to be inspired (Abraham 1981: 30–8; Trembath 1987: 87–103). Furthermore, they claim that the conservative evangelical understanding of inspiration is no different from dictation (Abraham 1981: 34–5; Trembath 1987: 91).

Defenders of inerrancy explicitly state that the doctrine is necessarily implied by inspiration (e.g. Montgomery 1965; Nicole 1983). However, they reject theories of dictation, which they regard as straw-men used by liberals to discredit fundamentalists (Packer 1958*a*: 78–9; Criswell 1982: 99).[37] Lindsell (1976: 33) claims not to know 'any scholar who believes in biblical inerrancy who holds that the Scriptures were received by dictation'. Abraham (1981: 34–5) and Trembath (1987: 91) are not convinced by these disclaimers; they argue that such evangelicals reject dictation only by name, for without it their commitment to inerrancy would be inexplicable.

It is still common for fundamentalists and evangelicals to tread the fine line between endorsing a doctrine of plenary verbal inspiration and renouncing dictation. They attempt to maintain a balance between the divinity and the humanity of scripture while avoiding the implication that the human contribution is 'subjective': 'It is the words that are inspired, not just the thoughts of a man who is attempting to write down a subjective experience' (Criswell 1982: 101). Derek Prince (1986: 34–5), an ex-Cambridge philosopher and now a charismatic leader living between Jerusalem and Florida, draws an analogy with man's control over satellites in space to explain how 'every message' in scripture 'has its origin with God': 'If men can achieve such results as these, then only blind prejudice—and that of a most unscientific character—

[36] They are evangelicals who do not manifest a fundamentalist mentality. Abraham, like Barr, expresses dissatisfaction with 'the orthodoxy of the recent past in Evangelical circles', and cites the development of the Princeton doctrine of inspiration as the point at which continuity with the 'Evangelical tradition' was broken (1981: 111, 112–13).

[37] e.g. as used by Alan Richardson in his article on fundamentalism for *Chambers' Encyclopedia* (1950), to which Packer (1958*a*: 178–81) objects, and David Edwards in dialogue with John Stott (1988: 41).

would deny the possibility that God could create human beings with mental and spiritual faculties such that He could control or direct them, maintain communication with them, and receive communication from them.'

Some even accept dictation, and object only to mechanical dictation: 'Each writer was guided so that his choice of words was also the choice of the Holy Spirit, thus making the product the Word of God as well as the work of man. This definition disavows mechanical dictation, although some parts of revelation were given by direct dictation' (S. E. Anderson 1955: 13). An incident involving Bob Jones University and Dr John R. Rice illustrates the precariousness of this position. In 1971 the university lost Rice from its faculty, having feared that in his publication *Our God-Breathed Book: The Bible* (1969) he advocated 'not verbal inspiration but actually "*mechanical*" inspiration'.[38] 'Face it honestly,' Rice wrote, 'if God gave the very words and men wrote them down, that is dictation'. He argued that a rejection of dictation was a reflection of 'the carnal attitude of the unbelieving world that always wants to give man credit instead of God'. All those who are unable to discover differences between a book which is fully inspired and one which is dictated may feel that Rice was at least being upfront. Yet Rice insisted that scripture was not given by '*mechanical* dictation' (Rice, ibid. 286, 287).[39] Mechanical dictation seems to be universally rejected by fundamentalists and evangelicals, even though some evangelicals have suggested that fundamentalists might define inspiration 'in very mechanical terms' (Stott 1956: 5–6).

It is difficult to imagine how plenary verbal inspiration, dictation, and mechanical dictation would differ from one another in practice. Fundamentalists and evangelicals offer little clarification of what the processes would entail. The early British inerrantists, W. E. Vine and David M. McIntyre, justified this silence by arguing that the operations of the Spirit are beyond our understanding. Vine (1923: 10) maintained that the 'fact of Inspiration may be proved by evidence', but 'the mode of Inspiration lies outside the range of discovery'. McIntyre (1902: 156) warned, 'we must be careful lest, in determining the *extent* of inspiration, we

[38] *A Statement from the Chancellor of Bob Jones University*, n.d., Fundamentalism File document 657, Bob Jones University archives, p. 1.

[39] Quoted in McKim (1985: 57).

should—unconsciously—define the *manner* of the "God-breathing"', for that 'will always elude our grasp'. More importantly, the Bible refuses to enlighten us on this matter. It must remain mysterious, for, as John Stott (1996: 25) says, 'Scripture nowhere describes it mechanics'. Therefore, evangelicals elaborate less on the means and more on the effects of inspiration, and devote most space to scripture's 'claims' to be inspired.

Despite this reticence to describe how the words of scripture were inspired, one can appreciate why plenary verbal inspiration rather than mechanical dictation is the preferred theory. It conveys that the biblical writers were inspired to select certain words, not that they took down dictation in a way that suspended their own mental activity. Dictation theories threaten to undermine the human aspect of the biblical witness for they imply that the human authors were mere passive receivers. Evangelicals frequently employ analogies with the doctrine of Christ—that Christ is both fully human and fully divine—in order to hold together their concept of inspiration with the freedom and integrity of the biblical writers. The 'humanity of the Scriptures', writes John Wenham, 'is no more destroyed by inspiration than is the humanity of Christ by incarnation' ([1972] 1993: 204 n. 19; cf. Packer 1958*a*: 82–4).[40]

Moreover, it is crucial to most evangelical apologetics that the text be a historical document which can be acknowledged as empirically and factually true. Evangelicals trust in the reliability of eyewitness evidence and human testimony—appeals to which would be redundant if dictation were mechanical. Machen (1936: 59, 58) insisted 'that the Biblical writers used ordinary sources of historical information', and urged the importance of the evangelists' eyewitness connections 'because they give the Bible such evidential force'. Evangelicals perform harmonistic exegesis not only on the basis that God is the sole author of scripture, but also on the assumption that the Gospels are apostolic in origin and stem from 'witnesses who worked together for a good many years

[40] For a history of this analogy combined with evangelical reservations about its usefulness see Cameron 1985. Barr (1973: 22) finds the analogy wanting, for there is 'no good reason why the relationship between God and man in the person of Christ should be supposed to hold good also for the relationship of divine and human in the Bible'. However, in *Escaping from Fundamentalism* (1984: 125–6), he suggests that this analogy provides an alternative, non-fundamentalist way for thinking about inspiration.

and who in many cases participated in the same events' (Wenham [1984] 1992: 127–8). Discrepancies between the Gospels are commonly accounted for on the grounds that they exhibit 'well-known characteristics of accurate and independent reporting' (ibid. 11).

Evangelicals assume a common humanity with the biblical writers which a belief in dictation would undermine. They attempt to identify with the human author by transporting themselves back to his cultural context until they 'begin to think what he thought and feel what he felt' (Stott 1982: 185). These days, evangelicals typically look for the meaning of a passage by reflecting on the intention of the human author and attempting to place the passage in its historical setting.[41] This marks a departure from the traditional evangelical assumption that the meaning of a passage resided in the divine author's intention and was to be discerned through a canonical reading of a text. Gaussen (1841: 330–4) had maintained in the mid-nineteenth century that 'it is with the book we have to do, and not with the writers'. He had demanded to know: 'If the words of the book are dictated by God, of what consequence to me are the thoughts of the writer?'

This mixture of attitudes reveals an ambivalence towards the human in evangelical and fundamentalist writings. On the one hand, apologetics which conceive of the biblical narratives as comprising eyewitness reports are fashioned as though scripture were principally a human rather than a divine testimony. The main effort is spent on justifying the biblical narratives as reliable human reports. Frank Morison, in his bestseller *Who Moved the Stone?* (1930), scrutinizes the biblical evidence as he would testimony in a court of law. Josh McDowell takes the same basic approach in *Evidence that Demands a Verdict* (1972). The use of human faculties is crucial to such an apologetic, even while these faculties are understood to be directed by God so as to communicate a divine message.

On the other hand, the humanity of the scriptures may be acknowledged only in so far as it contains expressions of different personalities and the marks of the authors' cultural milieu. These personalities are said to be 'fully employed' by God to his

[41] See Ch. 8.

'deliberate purpose' (Stott 1956: 6, 5); the culture and conventions to be 'utilized' and 'control[led] in His sovereign purpose' (Chicago Statement on Biblical Inerrancy, Exposition). This divine control implies the overruling of much that is part of human mental activity. Derek Prince (1986: 34) states most uncompromisingly that 'the men associated with [the Bible] were in every case merely instruments or channels'. He attributes 'the complete accuracy of the divine message in the Scriptures . . . to the perfect operation of the Holy Spirit, overruling all the frailty of human clay, and purging all the dross of human error from the flawless silver of God's message to man' (ibid. 36–7).

Sometimes an interpretative role is accorded to the human writers in recording and editing. Indeed, recently John Stott (1996: 21) has expressed the importance of the authors being eyewitnesses in terms of their interpreting for us the significance of God's mighty acts whose 'meaning was not self-evident'. Stott has further said that the human authors 'made their own theological emphases' (ibid. 25). Nevertheless, he continues to portray their work as essentially separate from but parallel to the Spirit's guidance, and as largely oblivious of it: 'even while they were researching and reflecting, and writing in a manner that was appropriate to them, the Holy Spirit was carrying them forward to express what was intended by him' (ibid.). Stott's position reflects the notion of concursus or double authorship, which he has inherited via Warfield and Packer (1996: 24–5). Strangely, this concept barely permits the Holy Spirit to illumine the authors' meditative reflections. Instead, inspiration is portrayed as a logically problematic and slightly deceptive process. It had, at one and the same time, to be fully dominating and yet to be an operation of which the biblical authors were unaware.

4.5.4. *The Foundation of Faith*

Evangelicals are frequently perceived as allowing the Bible to usurp the proper place of Christ. John Barton argues that to view biblical inspiration as a 'supernatural injection of revealed knowledge' can result in making 'everything apart from [the Bible] unnecessary in the economy of salvation' (Barton 1988: 37). Even Jesus need not really have existed for such a theology and such a faith, Barton suggests, for it is the text that reveals the truth about

God (ibid.). Evangelicals are not without a reply. They do not worship the Bible (Edwards and Stott 1988: 45). Formally they recognize Christ to be the foundation of their faith, and the Word of God. Had Jesus not existed we would not have the Bible in its present form. They describe the Bible as the written Word of God, and attribute to it such importance because it bears witness to Christ.

At the same time, they regard the Bible as a correlate of Christ: 'The Bible is the Word of God, and Christ is the Word of God. Each alike is a divine, authoritative, perfect revelation of God. Each agrees perfectly with the other. The Bible perfectly reveals Christ; Christ perfectly fulfils the Bible' (Prince 1986: 25). Since the Bible is the more accessible reality, to use James Barr's phrase (1977: 36), it is that by which their faith is articulated and justified. If scripture is not trustworthy, they say, 'we have no assurance that our Christian faith is founded upon Truth' (E. J. Young: 30). The emphasis in evangelical theology tends to fall on biblical propositions as the standard of truth for what is said about Christ, rather than on Christ as forever challenging our understanding of scripture. In this sense, Barton is right that the text has come to be viewed as that which almost exclusively reveals the truth about God.

For the last 150 years evangelicals and fundamentalists have been preoccupied with defending scripture, and this has resulted in distorted presentations of Christian belief. One fundamentalist preacher has even suggested that the authority of scripture is the current scandal of our faith: 'The offense of Christianity has shifted with the changing times from the cross to the Bible . . . The offense that true Christians must bear today is caused by their belief in Holy Scripture' (Zimmerman 1984: 187). Within the ETS inerrancy has been proclaimed the 'traditional evangelical cornerstone' and 'foundational truth', 'a stone of stumbling and a rock of offense' for those who do not believe (Oss 1989: 181). It will be argued in the next chapter that in so far as evangelicals develop fundamentalist arguments, they misrepresent even their own way of believing. Evangelicals come to accept the authority of scripture within the context of their life-relation to Christ, and yet if they accept a fundamentalist apologetic, they reason that they cannot recognize that relation unless they first know that what scripture says is fully true.

4.5.5. *The Inductive Method in Theology*

Methodologically, the doctrine about the Bible precedes all other doctrines, and is one of the first items in most evangelical systematics. With the doctrine of scripture in place, further doctrines are derived from the biblical text. One infers doctrine from scripture by 'biblical induction'. John Stott (1982: 183) refers to this practice as 'the only safe way to begin theology, moving, that is, from a wide variety of particular texts to general conclusions'. The method is considered safe because it avoids personal bias and speculation. An emphasis upon induction encourages the view that theology can be studied in the same way as any other subject. Jerry Falwell regards theology as 'an exact science' which brings everyone to the same objective knowledge of God: 'You come to exact, simplistic answers if you follow the proper equations, and the proper processes . . . God is God. The Bible is the inspired [inerrant] word of God. And if everyone accepts the same theses and the same equations, they will arrive at the same answer.'[42] Similarly, Wallie Criswell (1982: 24–5) believes that: 'As we take a look at our text, we learn the truth of God just as we learn anything else.' 'All of us learn alike', he writes, 'beginning with fundamentals and then adding more and more . . . we learn in those repetitious ways, and finally come into the full knowledge of the truth.'

Biblical induction 'presupposes a thorough knowledge of the diverse particularities of Scripture' (Stott 1982: 183). A study-aid from Gordon-Conwell Theological Seminary, aptly named *Let the Bible Teach You Christian Doctrine* (J. J. Davis 1985), assists students of scripture by listing for them references already gathered and classified under various themes. The book consists entirely of biblical verses quoted in full and supplemented only by 'explanatory annotations' (ibid. 11). It sets out the texts on inerrancy as at Fig. 4.1.

This method of collecting biblical verses on a theme resembles the practice of proof-texting which was so disliked by Warfield. Proof-texts have been used throughout the Christian tradition with varying degrees of sophistication. Warfield's objection to their use in the holiness and dispensationalist traditions was that they were 'isolated from their contexts' and so did not enhance 'insight into the doctrinal whole' of scripture ([1899*b*]: 300).

[42] Jerry Falwell interview, *Penthouse*, Mar. 1981, quoted in Noll (1985: 225).

Inerrancy[1]

Ps 12: 6 And the words of the Lord are flawless, like silver refined in a furnace of clay, purified seven times.

Ps 18: 30 As for God, his way is perfect; the word of the Lord is flawless.[2]

Ps 19: 7 The law of the Lord is perfect, reviving the soul.

Ps 19: 9 The ordinances of the Lord are sure and altogether righteous.

Ps 119: 89 Your word, O Lord is eternal; it stands firm in the heavens.[3]

Ps 119: 151 Yet you are near, O Lord, and all your commands are true.

Ps 119: 160 All your words are true; all your righteous laws are eternal.

Ps 119: 172 May my tongue sing of your word, for all your commands are righteous.

Pr 30: 5–6 'Every word of God is flawless; he is a shield to those who take refuge in him. Do not add to his words or he will rebuke you and prove you a liar.'

Mt 4: 4 Jesus answered, "it is written: "Man does not live on bread alone, but on every word that comes from the mouth of God." '[4]

Lk 24: 25 He [Jesus] said to them [disciples on Emmaus road], 'How foolish you are, and how slow of heart to believe all that the prophets have spoken!'

Jn 10: 35 '. . . the Scripture cannot be broken.'[5]

Jn 17: 17 'Sanctify them by the truth; your word is truth.'

Ac 24: 14 'I [Paul] believe everything that agrees with the Law and that is written in the Prophets.'[6]

[1] All the texts cited in this section in relation to *verbal inspiration* are directly relevant to *inerrancy*. All Scripture is the direct product of the omnipotent and omniscient God who is not subject to error.

[2] The word translated here as 'flawless' is a participial form of the verb *tsaraph*, used in reference to purging gold or silver by fire, and to separate from dross, Ps 12: 6[7], Isa 1: 25. The implication is that God's word is free from all dross and impurities.

[3] Cf. the words of Christ in Mt 24: 35: 'Heaven and earth will pass away, but my words will never pass away.' The word of God is more enduring than the physical universe itself.

[4] For Jesus and the NT writers, the entire canonical OT came from the mouth of God.

[5] *ou dunatai luthēai hē graphē*: from *luō*; here, 'annul, subvert, do away with, deprive of authority' (Thayer, *Greek-English Lexicon of the NT*). Notice how Christ here defends his claim to equality with God (10: 30) by appealing to a *single word* (*theoi*, gods) from a non-Davidic psalm, Ps 82: 6—thus demonstrating his sublime confidence in the unshakable authority of Scripture.

[6] 'The Law and the prophets' was a term used to designate the OT as a whole: cf. Mt 5: 17, 'Do not think that I have come to abolish the Law or the Prophets; I have not come to abolish them but to fulfil them.'

FIG. 4.1 Inerrancy (J. J. Davis 1985: 17–18). Copyright © John Davis 1985. Published by Paternoster Press, Carlisle, UK.

Developments in biblical criticism over the last 150 years present a different sort of challenge, by throwing into question the very unity of scripture. Generally there is no longer the confidence that verses from different parts of the Bible can simply be ranged alongside one another as conveying a single theological perspective.

Evangelicals who retain the practice of proof-texting do so partly out of commitment to a canonical approach to scripture. They still regard the practice as part of the inductive process. Some seem to bring to it the intention of presenting God's word without human admixture, whereas others reject the 'mere listing of proof texts' as 'of no value unless each verse is underwritten by sound exegetical work' (Ramm 1956: 158). Evangelicals reveal differing levels of sensitivity to the literary and historical context of the verses they cite. The least sensitive often come from premillennialist traditions, where proof-texts are cited in support of prophetic interpretations. Hal Lindsey, in his bestseller *The Late Great Planet Earth* (1971: 119), defends the seeming 'Biblical hopscotch' of turning from one prophet to another, by arguing that it 'is the complete agreement of all parts of Biblical prophecy which makes its study so absorbing'. A tract entitled 'Perhaps To-day!', distributed by the Independent Baptists in Britain, so arranges the following verses on the Bible's teaching about the return of Christ:

The Bible Declares Christ Will Return

'This same Jesus . . . shall so come in like manner as ye have seen him go into heaven.' Acts 1: 11.

'He shall send Jesus Christ.' Acts 3: 20.

'Waiting for the coming of our Lord Jesus Christ.' 1 Cor. 1: 7.

'When Christ who is our life shall appear.' Col. 3: 4.

'He shall appear the second time.' Heb. 9: 28.

'Behold, He cometh . . . every eye shall see Him.' Rev. 1: 7.

'Looking for that blessed hope and the glorious appearing of the great God and our Saviour Jesus Christ.' Titus 2: 13.

Biblical quotations are taken from a variety of contexts and combined, without commentary, to make a particular point.

Evangelistic tracts also employ a similar technique, supplying scriptural references to describe the human predicament and God's solution, as at Fig. 4.2.

1 YOU HAVE A PROBLEM

If we claim to be without sin, we deceive ourselves and the truth is not in us. 1 John 1: 8.
The wages of sin is death. Romans 6: 23.
We will all stand before God's judgement seat. It is written: As I live, says the Lord, every knee will bow before me; every tongue will confess to God. So then, each of us will give an account of himself to God. Romans 14: 10–12.
Whoever puts his faith in the Son has eternal life, but whoever rejects the Son will not see that life, for God's wrath remains on him. John 3: 36.
The wrath of God is being revealed from heaven against all the godlessness and wickedness of men. Romans 1: 18.

2 YOU CANNOT SOLVE THE PROBLEM

A man is not justified by observing the law, but by faith in Jesus Christ. If righteousness could be gained through the law, Christ died for nothing! Galatians 2: 16, 21.
God demonstrates his own love for us in this: While we were still sinners, Christ died for us. Romans 5: 8.
Jesus said: I am the way . . . no-one comes to the Father except through me. John 14: 6.
Salvation is found in no-one else; for there is no other name under heaven given to men by which we must be saved. Acts 4: 12.
It is by grace you have been saved. through faith—and this not from yourselves, it is the gift of God—not by works, so that no-one can boast. Ephesians 2: 8–9.

3 GOD HAS SOLVED YOUR PROBLEM

God so loved the world that he gave his one and only Son, that whoever believes in him shall not perish but have everlasting life. For God did not send his Son into the world to condemn the world, but to save the world through him. John 3: 16–17.
This is love: not that we loved God, but that he loved us and sent his Son as an atoning sacrifice for our sins. 1 John 4: 10.
When the kindness and love of God our Saviour appeared, he saved us, not because of righteous things we had done, but because of his mercy. Titus 3: 4–5.
Christ died for your sins once for all, the righteous for the unrighteous, to bring you to God. 1 Peter 3: 18.
The gift of God is eternal life through Christ Jesus our Lord. Romans 6: 23.

4 YOUR PROBLEM IS SOLVED FOR EVER

Jesus said: Whoever hears my word and believes him who sent me has eternal life and will not be condemned; he has crossed over from death to life. John 5: 24.
In Christ we have redemption through his blood, the forgiveness of sins. Ephesians 1: 7.
Jesus lives for ever . . . therefore he is able to save completely those who come to God through him, because he always lives to intercede for them. Hebrews 7: 24–25.
If anyone is in Christ, he is a new creation; the old has gone, the new has come. 2 Corinthians 5: 17.
He is able to keep you from falling and to present you before his glorious presence without fault and with great joy. Jude 24.

FIG. 4.2 Four steps to life (from a tract by Scripture Gift Mission). Copyright © SGM International, London. Scripture quotations taken from the Holy Bible, New International Version. Copyright © 1973, 1978, 1984 by International Bible Society. (UK trademark number 1448790)

Proof-texting relies upon the belief that biblical verses have some obvious or plain sense so that time and space are not required for their interpretation. Fundamentalist and evangelical sermons often contain only a string of references for the congregation to write down and look up at home. The Baptist fundamentalist, Wendell Zimmerman, preached a sermon on 'The Inerrant Infallible Word of the Living God' (1984) which contained over seventy-five scripture citations. He used the phrase 'And God said' in Genesis 1, and other verses of equally nebulous relevance, as evidence that the Bible is verbally inspired (193–4). The sense ascribed to proof-texts is often far from obvious. As Kathleen Boone (1989: 40) remarks, 'my commonsensical reading of a biblical passage might strike someone else as obtuse, nonsensical, heretical or any combination of these adjectives'. Bob Jones University employs, among other verses, Revelation 11: 15 and 21: 24 to argue 'in regard to the races that the Bible in its entirety clearly indicates that God has separated people for His own purposes'.[43] Verses can be chosen in such a way as to fashion biblical pronouncements on almost any topic.

4.5.6. *The Bible as Encyclopedia*

The Bible as textbook has been a favourite metaphor among fundamentalists and evangelicals, but it is a metaphor restricted to the theological application of scripture (e.g. Lindsell 1976: 31; Manley 1925: 137; Stott 1956: 17). At the same time, some evangelicals have come to view the Bible as almost encyclopedic in nature, believing that it gives 'affirmations about that in which science has an interest' (Schaeffer 1975: 25), or that 'when the writers of Scripture spoke of matters embraced in these disciplines [of history, science, and mathematics], they did not indite error' (Lindsell 1976: 31).

Roy Clouser (1991) considers the 'encyclopedic assumption' to be an essential characteristic of fundamentalism. This is the assumption that 'sacred Scripture contains inspired and thus infallible statements about virtually every conceivable subject matter', even in its 'inferences and suggestions'. Thus 'Scripture is seen as *able to provide at least some truths for almost every sort of theory-making*

[43] Bob Jones University statement on racial segregation, untitled (n.d.).

enterprise' (ibid. 94). This assumption underlies fundamentalist challenges to secular education. The American Association of Christian Schools makes the Bible 'the central subject in the school's curriculum', because 'God is central in the universe and is the source of all truth', and therefore 'all subject matter is related to God'. They do not 'imply that the Bible is a textbook on anything and everything', but see it as 'the point of reference from which we can evaluate all areas and sources of knowledge' (quoted in Peshkin 1986: 39). The fundamentalist school featured in Alan Peshkin's study operates on the principle that 'the Word of God is central to the curriculum of a Christian school'. It instructs its pupils to 'bring [their] Bible to every class . . . with the exception of physical education', because 'a teacher in any one of his classes might want the Word of Scripture about some point or another' (ibid. 49).

David Beck, professor of philosophy at Jerry Falwell's Liberty University, considers it the duty of Christian education to incorporate the facts of scripture into its teaching: 'what gives a Christian institution its distinctiveness is the inclusion of the propositions of Scripture within the hard data of its instructional content' (1991*a*: 15–16). He edited a symposium compiled by the Liberty faculty entitled *Opening The American Mind: The Integration of Biblical Truth in the Curriculum of the University* (1991*b*). The volume instructs university teachers on how to incorporate the 'data of Scripture' (p. 11) into the teaching of philosophy, literature, social and natural sciences, and even health and sports.

4.5.7. *Faith Justified by Science, Science Determined by Faith*

The practice of combining biblical and non-biblical 'data' is most evident in the interface between science and religion, where natural and theological science are conceived of as part of one great scientific enterprise. It relies upon the conviction that nature and scripture cannot contradict one another because God is the author of both:

> Any time you set out to prove a scientific error in the Bible, you are going to have a difficult time. Any time a person stands up to asseverate or avow that all true science corroborates the Word of God and that God's Word will always corroborate all true science, that person has an easy time. The hand that wrote the Book up there in the sky and in the earth

is the same omnipotent hand that wrote the Book we hold in our hands. (Criswell 1982: 116)

Apparent conflicts are said not to be between religion and science, but 'between religion and irreligion' (Bryan, Scopes Trial Transcript, p. 434), or between true science and false science. True science accepts scripture as authoritative. Martyn Lloyd-Jones explains that 'whatever is asserted in the Scripture about creation, about the whole cosmos, is true because God has said it'. He encourages evangelicals not to be shaken by dogmatic scientific pronouncements, because 'though Scripture may appear to conflict with certain discoveries of science at the present time . . . ultimately the scientists will discover that they have been in error at some point or other, and will eventually come to see that the statements of Scripture are true' (Lloyd-Jones [1971] 1992: 78).

A position was taken earlier in the century that the biblical authors, while not ahead of their time regarding any scientific expertise, were preserved from writing anything that would conflict with later scientific discoveries. W. H. Griffith Thomas considered it 'marvellous that although, naturally, not setting down scientific truths in scientific phraseology, the writer of Genesis was prevented from setting down anything inconsistent with scientific results'. In this way the 'oldest book in the possession of man has wonderfully anticipated some of the latest discoveries of science'.[44]

Creation scientists at the end of the twentieth century make stronger claims.[45] They argue not only that scripture coheres with

[44] 'What About Evolution? Some Thoughts in the Relation of Evolution to the Bible and Christianity' (1918), repr. in Vanderlaan 1925: 243.

[45] The present interest in creation science began in the 1960s with the publication of *The Genesis Flood* (Whitcomb and Morris 1961). The Creation Research Society was founded in 1963 in San Diego by disaffected members of the new-evangelical American Scientific Affiliation (founded 1951). After a split the Institute for Creation Research (ICR) was organized in 1972, with Morris and also Duane Gish, author of the best-selling *Evolution: The Fossils Say No!* (1972). ICR has been the main intellectual force behind drafting creation science laws in Arkansas, Louisiana, and other states. The British Evolution Protest Movement (founded in 1932) changed its name to the Creation Science Movement (CSM) in 1980. CSM is based in Portsmouth and a Creation Resources Trust is based in Somerset. Both are members of the Evangelical Alliance. They promote ideas from both British and American creationists. For a history and commentary on scientific creationism, and details of further organizations see Montagu (1984) and Numbers (1992). Christians in Science (CiS), a branch of UCCF, has recently expressed alarm at the promotion of creation science views, 'which are claimed to be biblical but unfortunately can have the effect of encouraging a false view of scripture', News Sheet, 7 (1994), 4.

scientific discovery, but that it positively contributes to and confirms it. Werner Gitt (1986: 31), a German creation scientist, argues that the 'biblical creation narrative is an indispensable and irreplaceable source of information when we are looking for the origin and purpose of this world and life itself'. Sidney Jansma (1985: 53), an oil producer whose book *Six Days* receives endorsement from the Institute for Creation Research, insists that 'the Biblical record . . . is a scientific exhibit that must be reckoned with'. According to James L. Hall (n.d. *a*), from the Museum of Earth and Life History at Liberty University: 'One of the most significant evidences for the inspiration of the Bible is the great number of scientific truths that have lain hidden over the past centuries only to be discovered by recent scientific advancement'.

To unearth these truths, creation scientists attribute factual content to passages of scripture which in many cases would more naturally be interpreted as figurative. Hall (n.d. *b*) takes the phrase 'My substance, being yet unformed' in Psalm 139: 16 to describe 'perfectly' the way in which each of us 'begins life as a single cell'. He also believes that the mention of 'springs of the sea' in Job 38: 16 is ratified by photographs taken by the research submarine Alpha in 1976. Jansma (1985: 14) suggests that Isaiah 10: 23 and 27: 1, which predict the destruction of the godless at the day of judgement, demonstrate 'the second law of thermodynamics and the entropy principle' according to which 'any ordered system tends to disintegrate and become more and more disordered in time'. David C. C. Watson ([1975] 1989: 11–12), a member of the English Creation Science Movement, is more careful to distinguish fact from poetry in scripture. He takes Psalm 33 to be poetry because 'each idea is repeated in different words', and Genesis 1 to be history because it contains 'No parallelism, no repetition'.

Once scripture is thought to provide insights on science, science has the potential to verify scripture. As James Hall (n.d. *a*) argues: 'If the Bible claims to be inspired by an eternal, omnipotent God then science should not threaten but reveal the authenticity of the scripture'. Roy Clouser (1991: 97–8) suggests that fundamentalists treat religious belief 'as though it were itself a theory, or at least to be evaluated as theories are', a trait he finds typical of their 'rationalism'. They frequently attempt to show that biblical presentations of facts or events deliver more successful explanations than alternative hypotheses. Such success is then viewed as 'confirming the truth of Scripture' (ibid. 98).

Creation scientists are undecided over whether to present their approach as primarily deductive or primarily inductive. In their creation–evolution debates they waver between arguing that evolution is no less a religion than Christianity, and proposing that creation science is no less scientific than evolution. In the context of the Arkansas creation–evolution trial in 1981, Norman Geisler (1982: 20) claimed that 'creationism is science and not religion': 'Teaching scientific creation is no more or less teaching religion than is teaching evolution from a scientific perspective. Both are consistent with certain religious worldviews, but neither is the essence of religion' (ibid. 19). Duane Gish, on the other hand, defends creationists against the 'accusation' that they claim to posit a scientific theory: 'Creationists have repeatedly stated that neither creation nor evolution is a scientific theory (and each is equally religious)' (quoted in Montagu 1984: 355).

Inductive considerations are in fact tailored to deductive premisses and are rarely admitted to discredit the fundamentalist view of scripture. When James Hall writes, 'I am sure that as new scientific discoveries are made in the future we will continue to see more examples of correlation between the Bible and modern science' (Hall n.d. *a*), he can be sure that his expectations will be met. Only those discoveries which do correlate with scripture will be recognized as part of true science. Creation scientists typically question the scientific nature of any empirical research which challenges their reading of scripture. Sidney Jansma (1985: 18) describes evolution as 'rooted in a materialistic, naturalistic philosophy or world view that has been adorned with a scientific facade'. The notion of science is redefined to include only that which is in accordance with scripture: 'Any explanation we give has to be "scientific" in that it has to agree with all the observed facts as well as be consistent with what the Bible implies or says' (Pimenta 1984: 204).

Gitt provides a diagram (Fig. 4.3) to support his position that only science 'which is followed according to biblical principles is realistic and takes into account all reliable observation of the natural world' (1986: 23). The diagram is intended to illustrate the relation of the Bible to research, and to show the extent of the overlap between biblically revealed knowledge and the natural sciences.

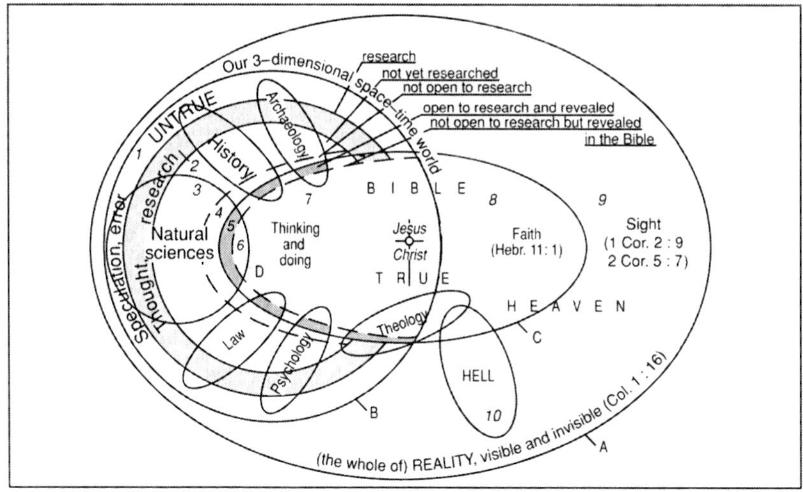

FIG. 4.3 The relation of the Bible to science (Gitt 1986: 17). Reproduced by kind permission of Evangelical Press, Durham.

According to Gitt, of those items of knowledge revealed in the Bible, some are open to further investigation and others are not. Some items must simply be accepted on scripture's authority, such as the length of days of creation, about which all argument 'is pointless' (ibid. 28). For other items there is 'complementary evidence' from both scientific research and scripture, which means that 'both sources of knowledge must arrive at the same conclusion' (ibid. 25–6). Much of natural science does not overlap with scripture at all in Gitt's diagram. At the same time, he insists that science will 'correspond with reality' only if it accepts the biblical account of creation, which 'contains basic scientific facts which make up an indispensable framework for any research' (ibid. 36).

4.5.8. *Summary*

Creation scientists are more extreme in their emphasis upon the factual nature of scripture than are most evangelicals, though Walter Kaiser probably reflects the majority evangelical opinion when he says, 'I feel that they are my brothers and they are my kind' (1988: 208). The sorts of fundamentalists Barr describes revise their interpretations of scripture to fit scientific discoveries more readily than do creation scientists. Barr (1977: 40, 42) notes that 'most conservative evangelical opinion today does not pursue a literal interpretation of the creation story in Genesis', an interpretation which Barr himself regards as the most natural reading of the text. The scientific evidence 'has become too strong to withstand', says Barr. A literal interpretation would require 'pitting the Bible against scientific truths' thus forcing the 'admission that the Bible in this respect had been wrong'.

We should not necessarily conclude that those evangelicals who surrender a six-day creation are applying the rules of induction more consistently than are creation scientists. If their reason for relinquishing a literal interpretation is to preserve the Bible from error, they share the same basic motivation as creation scientists. They differ from creation scientists principally over the number of biblical passages for which a factual interpretation is to be pressed. As we saw above, advocates of inerrancy disagree over this issue irrespective of the creation science movement. The assumption prevails within evangelicalism that the Bible's authority is best maintained by finding a direct correspondence between biblical statements and empirical actuality. This is why inerrancy remains an ideal for so many evangelicals.

We have considered the influence of fundamentalism within evangelicalism primarily by investigating how the fundamentalist mentality operates in biblical apologetics. The ideal which remains in the consciousness of fundamentalist-minded evangelicals is of a Bible which is wholly true with respect to facts. The degree to which they move away from this ideal varies. They would rejoice to see the factual truth of scripture confirmed, but they also feel obliged to depart from factual interpretations in order to protect the integrity of scripture. We found inerrancy itself to be a loose concept. Evangelicals highlight variations in their views of scripture in response to such critics as James Barr whom they feel paint in unjustly broad brush-strokes. Nevertheless, they are not themselves entirely comfortable with the diverse developments in evangelical theology. There remains a strong level of suspicion among evangelicals that those who question the 'facts' of the Bible are failing to submit to its authority. Even some avowed inerrantists have been accused of conceding too much ground to modern scholarship. In Chapter 5, we will find that evangelicals typically divide the Christian world between those who submit to the authority of scripture, and those who judge scripture by some subjective principle such as human reason.

5

Fundamentalist Apologetics and Evangelical Experience

Evangelicals tend to set themselves apart from others in their view of the Bible, and to regard modern theology as essentially subjective for its refusal to submit to the authority of scripture. This assessment of the theological world lends a sense of identity to the many and varied groups within their ranks. They feel that they allow scripture to speak for itself, but that others subject God's Word to human judgement and interpret it selectively to suit their particular sensibilities.

5.1. The Letter and the Spirit

Fundamentalists and evangelicals are deeply suspicious of the subjective. The early fundamentalist opposition to modernism was not opposition to learning. Rather, the fundamentalists believed that their position would be redeemed through the correct use of the intellect—one which did not indulge the subjective feelings and judgements of individuals. They in turn were depicted by modernists as defending a static as opposed to a dynamic religion, as killing the Spirit by the letter. Harold Emerson Fosdick contrasted fundamentalism, with 'its i's all dotted and its t's all crossed', with modernism, which is 'like a tree whose roots are deep in the spirit of Jesus'.[1] Fundamentalists were accused of holding attitudes that were directly contrary to the teaching of Christ and Paul. As one Presbyterian modernist minister argued: 'Christ attacked the literalism of the Pharisees who taught the inspired authority of every word of the law and the prophets. Saint Paul declared that the letter killeth—the spirit giveth life.'[2]

[1] Fosdick, 'Progressive Christianity' Sermon (1921), repr. in Vanderlaan 1925: 42.

[2] Revd Murray Shipley Howland, from statements collected in *Homiletic Review*, Sept. 1923, quoted in Vanderlaan 1925: 30.

However, the real distinction between fundamentalists and their modernist critics lay not in who was quenching the Spirit, but how each considered the Spirit to speak: in the very words of scripture, believed to be the words of God and so a challenge to our human precepts; or as a voice transcendent above the words, which are only temporal and imperfect human expressions of the movement of the Spirit. The conflict remains the same today. Episcopal bishop of Newark, John Shelby Spong (1991: 184), in his populist polemic, *Rescuing the Bible from Fundamentalism*, seeks a place where 'in the fullness of humanity the presence of God can still be experienced'. Since a 'literal view of Holy Scripture will never lead one to this vision', he urges his readers to 'discern the hand of a transcendent deity underneath these literal words' (ibid. 74–5), and to 'travel behind and beneath the words of Scripture . . . to seek entry into the experience that created the words' (ibid. 241–2). Evangelicals fear that liberals thus confuse the challenge of the Spirit with their own subjective experiences. For them, the words of scripture are the richest lifeline to the Spirit, but the experience of truth is secondary to its cognitive presentation.

The deep-rooted differences between evangelical and non-evangelical conceptions of the appropriate attitude towards scripture shall be elaborated in the following dialogue on biblical authority. Evangelicals denounce as subjectivist biblical scholars who bring scripture before the bar of reason. Meanwhile, their critics view evangelical approaches to scripture as rationalistic and lacking in spirituality. This paradox increases in the light of the intensely personal way in which evangelicals conceive of their own relationship to the Bible. They believe that God speaks to them personally through scripture. The second half of this chapter considers the tension that evangelicals experience in accommodating this implicit subjectivism.

5.2. A Dialogue on Biblical Authority

At the outset it is worth noting a significant asymmetry in the debate between evangelicals and their critics over biblical authority. On the evangelical side, the debate is taken up more keenly by theologians than by biblical scholars, whereas the most significant non-evangelical critiques come from biblical scholars rather than from theologians. This may have some bearing on the different styles of approach. The evangelicals concerned locate the debate within the context of apologetic theology. Their arguments on authority and on the true nature of biblical scholarship are theologically loaded. Biblical studies is not usually their area of expertise. Their critics, meanwhile, revise notions of authority according to the biblical scholarship that they perform. They deconstruct the evangelical doctrine of scripture by arguing that although it purports to be biblical, it in fact distorts the process of biblical interpretation.

5.2.1. *Submission and Subjectivism*

'Evangelicals' are, according to James Packer (1958*a*: 176), 'bound, as servants of God and disciples of Christ, to oppose Subjectivism wherever they find it'. Packer has been the leading British evangelical theologian from the 1950s to the present, and he shall provide the evangelical voice for much of this dialogue. He contrasts subjectivism with submission to the Word of God. Subjectivism can take various rationalistic or mystical forms, he argues, but 'all its many varieties spring from a single principle, namely, that the final authority for my faith and life is the verdict of my reason, conscience or religious sentiment (subjectivists vary in the way they put this)' (ibid. 50). This principle clashes with the evangelical acceptance of the written scriptures as 'finally authoritative', and the accompanying 'readiness to take God's word and accept what He asserts in the Bible' (ibid. 47, 49).

Packer regards liberalism as a modern form of subjectivism (ibid. 45–6, 153).[3] This assessment is perpetuated in the 'liberal-evangelical' dialogues that have taken place in Britain between David Edwards and John Stott (1988) and in North America between Delvin Brown and Clark Pinnock (1990). Pinnock regards disagreement over 'whether Christianity is tied to the truth content of Scripture or rests on a subjectivist principle' as a 'crux in the liberal–evangelical dialogue' (Pinnock and Brown 1990: 45). Stott describes 'the fundamental difference' between evangelicals

[3] Although Packer recognizes that liberalism is a specific 19th-c. movement which has declined in the 20th c., he continues to apply the label to his opponents, for in comparing early liberals and their 20th-c. disciples, 'the differences seem to be superficial, while the subjectivist principle which underlay original Liberalism remains unchanged' (1958*a*: 146).

and liberals in terms of the 'submissive spirit' of evangelicals as opposed to the 'biblical selectivity' practised by liberals. Evangelicals have an 'a priori resolve to believe and obey whatever Scripture may be shown to teach', whereas such an 'open, unconditional commitment to Scripture would not be acceptable to liberals' (Edwards and Stott 1988: 104).

Evangelicals perceive their differences from liberals in terms of their own obedient submission to the Word of God. They accept criticism more readily from those whom they believe share their deference for scripture, than from those whom they regard as lacking an appropriate attitude of humility. 'The real issue in fundamentalism', William Wells (1978: 30) writes in response to Barr's critique, 'is an attitude toward the Bible . . . The fundamentalist reads the Bible as God's Word. Consequently he tries to listen humbly and obediently'. The 'evangelical community', he continues, 'must of necessity be skeptical of speakers and writers who set themselves up as judges of God's Word. The opinion of those who lack the humility to place themselves in subjection to God's Word is inherently suspect' (ibid. 31).

That the theological world is divided along the lines of those who do, and those who do not submit to scripture is a thesis peculiar to evangelicals. In claiming that their critics fail to understand what is at issue, evangelicals are exemplifying how the division is perceived from their own side.

> Our critics say that the way in which we deal with the Bible is fundamentally dishonest. We reply that they think so only because the way in which they deal with the Bible is fundamentally un-Christian. They hold that what needs revision is our doctrine of biblical authority; but it seems that what really needs revision is their method of biblical scholarship. Instead of subjecting their own judgement wholly to Scripture, they subject Scripture in part to their own judgement. (Packer 1958*a*: 140)

5.2.2. *Authority and Interpretation*

Evangelicals reject their critics' methods of biblical interpretation on grounds of authority. Their critics attack the fundamentalist view of biblical authority on interpretative grounds. According to Barr, the imposition of a conservative ideology upon scripture prevents fundamentalists from reading scripture as it ought to be read. He argues, 'not . . . that the Bible is unreliable as an authority for faith but that, if it is taken as reliable authority, it points in many places in directions quite different from the evangelical tradition of interpretation which fundamentalism adopts and seeks to uphold' (1984: 149). Similarly, John Barton (1988: 2) in his Bampton Lectures, *People of the Book?*, accuses fundamentalists of using 'biblical material with extreme selectivity, under tight constraints of a doctrinal system that owes little to the biblical text itself'. Barr and Barton argue, essentially, that since fundamentalists claim to take the Bible so seriously, they ought to be more scrupulous in their attention to what it actually says and means.

Yet evangelicals believe that only those who have a proper respect for the Bible's authority correctly interpret what scripture is saying. They believe that the only true approach to scripture is provided by the 'exercise of reasoning faith', for only then is scripture appreciated '*as what it is*—God's truth in writing' (Packer 1958*a*: 130). They argue that a process which treats scripture 'as something other than it is', by subjecting it 'to a scientific critical technique designed to help us to tell true from false among fallible human records would be an act of unbelief that was both unscientific and uncritical' (ibid.). They reject historical criticism as 'rationalistic' when it accepts only those parts of the Bible that are 'intellectually acceptable', and views the rest as 'error' (Barclay 1977: 52–3). They oppose 'the supposition that Scripture errs' on the basis that 'Scripture claims not to err', and 'regard as mistaken those who believe themselves to acknowledge the authority of the Bible while adopting principles of biblical criticism which Scripture repudiates' (Packer 1958*a*: 74).

They are themselves regarded as rationalistic for thinking in this way, as though it were appropriate to ask of biblical statements only whether they are true or in error. Packer (1971: 152), in answering this criticism, shows it to be justified: '[Inerrancy] represents not so much a lapse into rationalism as a bulwark against rationalism . . . What it expresses is not an irreligious interest in "proving the Bible" but a retention of reverence for the sacred text which some were irreverently expounding as if it were in places self-contradictory and false.'

The desire of evangelicals is to defend that doctrine of scripture which scripture itself promotes. They believe that their defence of biblical authority is in accordance with what scripture teaches about itself. Barr (1973: 23) contests this belief. He regards their notion of biblical truth as innovative and misleading. He argues that the concept of biblical authority neither implies nor demands biblical 'accuracy, inerrancy, and infallibility', but rather moves the emphasis away from these questions. In Barr's opinion, if critical scholars accepted conservative conclusions they would not thereby have a conservative evangelical view of the Bible: 'For the essence [of such a view] is, not that this date or that should be earlier or later, but that the understanding of truth and meaning as applied to the Bible has become thoroughly different' (1977: 159).

Barr's position is a direct challenge to what Mark Noll (1986: 143) describes as the 'most important conviction of evangelical scholars . . . that the Bible is true not just as religion but also as fact'. Barr (1973: 24) locates 'the real ground for the authority of the Bible . . . not . . . within the nature of the Bible itself', but 'beyond the Bible, in the authority of God'. The Bible derives its authority from the events of salvation which it relates. Barr (ibid. 24–5) suggests that this view is liberating to those worried about the historicity of the saving events, for 'it permits their exact historical nature, and the relation between them and the biblical narratives, to be left somewhat vague'. He explains how the Bible's authority remains independent of its factual accuracy:

> The Bible has emerged from these past events as an interpretation of them in faith; it does not offer an exact transcript of them, and may indeed be confused, contradictory or in error about the historical facts. The events nevertheless, whatever their historical character, are the centre of salvation; and the authority of the Bible derives from the saving content of these events and the faith that responded to it, and not from the accuracy of its historical reporting.

Authority can therefore be applied to the Bible without implying perfection (ibid. 25).

5.2.3. *Historicity and Spirituality*

Barr (1984: 66–90; 1986*b*) does not abandon the need for a historically grounded faith, but he loosens the connections between the historical accuracy of the biblical records and the actual occurrence of events, and between historical fact and theological significance. Evangelicals reason that if the record of the events is questioned then the events themselves can be doubted, and if the events are doubted there is nothing to justify their religious significance: 'Conservatives . . . would argue that it is foolish to talk of the significance of the resurrection of Christ, for example, if that event did not in fact occur' (W. W. Wells 1978: 32).[4]

There is a very close link for evangelicals between feeling confirmed in their faith and having their belief in the factual reliability of scripture justified. Barr (1980*a*: 87) contends that it is not spiritually enriching to be told that Paul did after all write the letters to Timothy and Titus. Yet indirectly evangelicals may be spiritually enriched by the verdict that Paul wrote these epistles, for it enhances simple trust in scripture. Any evidence for this trust is evidence also for the religious life they experience. They will not be comforted by Barr's reassurance that 'On the day of judgement you will not be asked what view of scripture you have held' (1984: 162). Evangelicals do not think that their standing before God hinges directly on their view of scripture, but they do believe that their submission to scripture—the Word of God—manifests the correct attitude towards God himself. Moreover, they perceive a connection between submitting to the authority of scripture and experiencing a conviction of its truth, as this testimony from Billy Graham indicates:

> I was waging the intellectual battle of my life . . . Finally in desperation, I surrendered my will to the living God revealed in Scripture. I knelt before the open Bible and said: '. . . Here and now, by faith, I accept the Bible as Thy word. I take it all. I take it without reservations. Where there are things I cannot understand, I will reserve judgement until I receive more light . . .' . . . I discovered the secret that changed my ministry. I stopped trying to prove that the Bible was true. I had settled in my own mind that it was . . . Over and over again I found myself saying 'The Bible says'. (*Christianity Today*, 1, 15 Oct. 1956, p. 6)

The motivation behind their biblical conservatism derives, to some extent, from a concern to maintain that spirit which enables them to get life from the scripture. That spirit, which they might describe as a spirit of humility or submission, they feel is sapped by research which calls into question what 'the Bible says'. They

[4] Barr (1980*c*: 21; 1986*b*: 35–6) himself makes a similar point when attacking canonical criticism and Barthian approaches to scripture.

suspect that the fundamental problem with such research is that it promotes human reason over and above biblical authority.

Evangelicals believe that the Bible makes claims. Whenever its statements are questioned, they feel that its authority is being eroded. They ask how, if some parts of scripture are doubted, any of it can be trusted. They regard as dangerous any development which would undermine the Bible's authority in providing the epistemological foundation for the Christian faith: 'persons denying the full truth of Scripture . . . have moved away from the evangelical principle of knowledge to an unstable subjectivism, and will find it hard not to move further' (Chicago Statement on Biblical Inerrancy, Exposition).

John Barton (1988: 12) recognizes that so long as the question remains that of 'what *residual* authority Scripture can be held to possess, how far we can still *even so* believe in the Bible at least to some respectable extent', one remains on conservative territory. He therefore wants to redefine the questions that should be asked about scriptural authority. He does this by going back to Jesus and Paul, to the source, which, like Barr, he claims to take at least as seriously as do fundamentalists themselves. What he finds there is not 'the high and absolute biblicism favoured by conservatives', but 'an overwhelming sense that God has just done (or is just doing or is just about to do) something so new that Scripture cannot contain it, and could never have led anyone to foresee it' (ibid.).

In Barton's reconstruction, the Bible offers historical evidence not only 'for events or "facts"', but also 'for the beliefs of the first Christians and for their reaction to the events on which Christian faith rests' (ibid. 41). Besides providing evidence, the Bible is also a source of theological insight for faith (pp. 48–58) and a channel whereby the God of the Bible is still encountered in the present (pp. 58–63, 66–7). Whereas Packer (1958*a*: 117) regards the first manifestation of faith to be cognitive, and depicts evangelicals as 'teaching . . . God's own textbook' (1983: 44; cf. Stott 1982: 188), Barton (1988: 45, 48) discourages an overly cognitive rendering of biblical authority and an overemphasis on the Bible as a textbook. The gospel 'is not about . . . conceptual certainty . . . [but] about the encounter with a gracious God' (ibid. 86). Packer (1958*a*: 42) insists that 'faith in Jesus Christ is possible only where the truth concerning Him is known'. Barton (1988: 59), by contrast, accepts the position that faith preceded the Bible and could in principle survive without it.

5.2.4. *Knowledge and Encounter*

Clark Pinnock's recent position resembles Barton's in certain respects. Pinnock avoids identifying the Bible with revelation, but rather regards revelation as 'that to which the Bible bears testimony' (Pinnock and Brown 1990: 40; cf. Barton 1988: 55–7). Like Barton, he suggests that evangelicals have often overemphasized the divine element in scripture and treated the Bible as Muslims treat the Koran (Pinnock and Brown 1990: 41; cf. Barton 1988: 1). He himself is concerned 'with the gospel, not with the Bible per se', and defines an evangelical as one who is 'committed to the gospel as it is biblically defined' (Pinnock 1984: p. xi; cf. Barton 1988: 84–7, 89).

Yet however close evangelicals come to agreement with non-evangelical scholars, they retain a separate identity. The similarities that exist between Pinnock and Barton do not eradicate their fundamental differences. Pinnock maintains the distinctive evangelical perception that he differs from liberals on the grounds that he submits to the authority of scripture, whereas they submit to some subjective principle (Pinnock and Brown 1990: 45).

Most significantly, despite his recognition that God speaks through the Bible (Pinnock and Brown 1990: 41), and that the Bible introduces a 'saving transforming knowledge of Christ' (Pinnock 1984: p. xix), Pinnock understands biblical authority primarily in cognitive terms. If it were understood functionally rather than cognitively, he argues, 'the locus of authority in theology would automatically shift from divine revelation coming to us from God over to human reason and religious experience already resident in us' (Pinnock and Brown 1990: 47). Evangelicals assume that the authority of the Bible involves 'commitment to the cognitive truth of the information the Bible delivers' (ibid. 53). Barton (1988: 57) accepts the Anglo-Saxon emphasis upon the Bible as giving us access to events and ideas, and upon *knowledge* as the aim of our biblical study, but supplements it with something from the Germanic tradition: 'what our study of the Bible ultimately presents us with is not a body of knowledge or a corpus of doctrine which we have to assimilate, but a divine challenge to which we have to respond . . . The biblical text mediates not information or opinion but encounter.'

Some evangelicals have advanced in an existentialist direction through becoming acquainted with the thought of Kierkegaard and Barth, and are themselves willing to talk about experiences of encounter. Notable among these are E. J. Carnell (1957: 73; 1965), Bernard Ramm (1983), and Donald Bloesch (1983; 1985; 1992). However, they have been tentative in their existential ventures and do not allow 'propositional or conceptual truth' to be 'sacrificed for existential and emotive truth' (Bloesch 1992: 19). They speak as though biblical truth is somehow realized at the point of impact upon the reader, and yet they protect its objective status from any re-evaluation: 'Biblical propositions are truth only (so far as the *receiver* is concerned; I do not refer to the objective state of the text) when they transform'.[5]

A bifurcation exists in the minds of evangelicals, in so far as they reflect fundamentalist modes of thought, between the objective account of the faith given in scripture, and the Holy Spirit's ministry through scripture. The objectivity of the text is held over and against the subjective means by which the Spirit makes possible an individual's acceptance of the faith. Evangelicals see the Bible as giving facts against which one is to judge experience: 'We contend that the Biblical view of truth requires subjective (existential, if you will) truth to be grounded in objective, empirical facticity, for only then can existential truth be distinguished from existential error' (Montgomery 1965: 83). They depict the scriptures more as describing the facts that make possible one's life in Christ, and less as themselves manifesting that life. Their

[5] Carnell to Clark, 23 Feb. 1953, quoted in Nelson 1987: 153. For an account of Carnell's existentialist leanings see ibid. esp. pp. 151–78, and Marsden (1987: 183–4). Carnell, one of the most challenging new-evangelical critics of fundamentalism, experienced acutely the tension between acknowledging the personal apprehension of biblical truth and upholding the inerrancy of scripture. He was accused of surrendering to subjectivism and neo-orthodoxy, suffered a nervous breakdown, and was possibly driven to suicide. Barr finds Carnell's self-critical approach refreshing (1977: 222), but Carnell did not finally remove himself from the fundamentalist mentality. For insisting that the scriptures 'witness to a body of redemptive events that are as much a part of history as the voyage of Columbus' (Carnell 1960: 143), Nelson (1987: 142) accuses him of sharing the same 'cultic credulity' he had himself attributed to fundamentalism, and the same Common Sense assumptions (ibid. 222–3). Carnell remained an inerrantist, and Lindsell dedicated *The Battle for the Bible* in part to him.

conception of encounter barely takes them beyond the traditional evangelical position that: 'Our God-given textbook is a closed book till our God-given Teacher opens it to us' (Packer 1958*a*: 112).

In effect, a fundamentalist-style apologetic reduces the inspiration of scripture to the getting right of facts and the relating of accurate information. In their religious life, evangelicals find inspired scripture to be a source of vision, motivation, correction, and discovery, but this richness can be sadly lacking in their apologetics. Their devotion to the Bible derives from their experience of reading it. They feel their spirit quickened by the Spirit who speaks through scripture. It would be consistent with this experience to describe the biblical writings as inspired renderings of faithful believers who were moved by the Spirit as they themselves are today. This view is taken by some pentecostal theologians.[6] Yet evangelicals for the most part suspect that such an account of inspiration makes the Bible too human a book. Instead, they portray inspiration as a process of which the biblical writers were unaware. Ironically, they imply that a straightforward factual report would have more marks of the divine than would meditative writings whose authors truly knew what it was to be conveying words of life. They fear that an emphasis upon the experience of God's truth undermines the importance of cognitive apprehension, and leads one down the slippery slope to abandoning an authoritative Bible—a process they have come to equate with losing an evangelical identity. Were they to loosen the relation between biblical authority and factual accuracy, they would not so much cease to be evangelical as cease to be fundamentalist-minded. One does not stop being fundamentalist by sliding down a slope, but by changing one's thinking more radically and in such a way that the slippery-slope argument (what Barr refers to as the 'domino theory') is no longer relevant.

5.3. Retaining a Personal Religion

Evangelicals recognize one another not only by their 'high' view of scripture, but by reference to their 'personal relationship' with Christ. They have inherited the tension between external and

[6] See s. 2.3.1 above.

internal authority that is manifest in Princeton apologetics. The Princetonians acknowledged the role of the Holy Spirit in bringing us to conviction, but they required that the understanding be already satisfied. Similarly, evangelicals do not consider their faith to be purely cognitive. A personal experience of God through scripture is crucial to their faith and may be temporally prior to their conviction that scripture has authority. However, in their apologetics, evangelicals have given logical priority to the claims that scripture is said to make about itself and about Christ, which they regard as providing the necessary objective grounding for their subjective experiences.

We should note that charismatics do not share the usual evangelical unease over arguments from experience. Martyn Percy (1996: 44–5, 106–7) ascribes an 'inductive strategy' to charismatics, by which he means that they reason primarily from their religious experience. First-hand religious experience confirms and supplements their analysis of the biblical text and subsequent Christian history. The effectiveness of scripture as able to change lives bolsters their belief in its inerrancy. The power of the Holy Spirit and the immediacy of God's presence are believed to bring people to a point of conversion. Tales of the efficacy of such experience encourage other believers in their evangelistic tasks. Percy records a story used by John Wimber to advocate 'power evangelism'. The story is of a Buddhist who was converted on the basis of his experience when two Vineyard members prayed 'on him':

> they laid hands on him and asked the Holy Spirit to come upon him. He immediately began to weep and they asked, 'Do you feel that?' 'Yes, oh yes,' he replied. 'That's Jesus,' they said. 'Would you like to know him?' He said, 'yes,' and was converted. Only after he had received the touch of God and responded to him did they tell of the claims of Christ. (Wimber, *Signs and Wonders and Church Growth*, conference manual (1984), s. 1, p. 10, quoted in Percy 1996: 106–7)

The inductive method which we have previously considered uses biblical texts and involves a naïve attitude towards human testimony. The charismatic approach that Percy (ibid. 106) describes entails a similarly naïve attitude towards accounts of human experience. The accounts must be read uncritically, taken at 'face value' as 'proof' of the power and truth of God. The presentation of Christ's claims, and uncritical readings of the biblical text, can then follow.

Charismatics are less anxious than most evangelicals about religious experience being subjective, unverifiable, or open to unsound interpretation. They expect frequent and indisputable displays of divine power. They treat both the biblical records and their experience in the present as raw data, and believe that the two directly parallel one another. Therefore they happily argue from religious experience prior to arguing from scripture. Most of the evangelicals featured in this study regard the Bible as objective, and experience as subjective. Consequently they have difficulty relating their experiential insights to their 'objective' biblical apologetic. Experience and understanding interact in the biblical narratives and in the lives of believers today in ways which neither these charismatic nor non-charismatic evangelicals have appreciated.

5.3.1. *Evangelical Faith, Fundamentalist Apologetics*

It is easier to see how one is attracted to evangelicalism than it is to see how one comes to believe the accompanying apologetics. People are attracted by the offer and feeling of forgiveness, not because they have been taught to harmonize the passion narratives or have been convinced of the historicity of Adam and Eve. Usually they enter the faith through what they understand to be some personal experience of God. By their own testimonies, this initial experience may be mediated through the Bible, and interest is first awakened often through meeting evangelical Christians. Converts may stress the impression that the love and happiness of Christians made upon them: 'I couldn't understand it—no one had ever treated me like that before'; 'There was something clean and nice about them. They were so different . . . They joked and laughed' (D. Hall 1986: 39, 132). Yet, sadly, the evangelical faith often appears to be unloving and restricting. Once in the fold, evangelicals learn the arguments that are used to defend the faith, and all too often they pass on the good news within a framework of rationalism and its practical counterpart, legalism.

Children of evangelicals sometimes miss the warmth that first brought their parents to the faith. Randall Balmer (1993: 106), raised a fundamentalist but now ambivalent towards American evangelicalism, realized this about his own upbringing:

> the 'gospel' presented to me was really an adumbration of the New Testament 'good news'. Much of the news I heard was bad—that I deserved damnation for my sinfulness and that if I didn't do something about it quickly I would certainly receive my just deserts . . . [T]he way of salvation seemed to lay [*sic*] in subscribing to a set of doctrines and then hewing to strict standards of morality, usually expressed in negative terms: Don't dance, drink, smoke, swear, or attend movies.
>
> That differed, I suspect, from the message that brought my parents into the evangelical fold. They heard about their sinfulness, yes, but the complementary element of the law is God's grace, which saves us in spite of ourselves . . . In time, first-generation evangelical converts learn the canon of evangelical taboos, but only *after* their experience of grace. For their children, however, the sequence is often reversed.

Douglas Frank (1986: pp. viii–ix) calls himself an 'evangelical by coercion'. In his experience, the Gospel was hidden 'behind a wall of doctrinal certainties, theological catchwords, devotional prescriptions, and obvious self-justifications, all of which informed the reader of exactly what he or she would find in the pages of the Bible before the book was even opened, making it much less probable that the Word might be a surprise'.

Critics of fundamentalism have assumed that its appeal lies in its plain and unambiguous stance, its black-and-white rules, and its offer of certainty (e.g. Boone 1989: 107–8). Spong (1991: 133) finds fundamentalists appealing 'to the need for emotional security by trafficking in religious certainty':

> A major function of fundamentalist religion is to bolster deeply insecure and fearful people. This is done by justifying a way of life with all of its defining prejudices. It thereby provides an appropriate and legitimate outlet for one's anger. The authority of an inerrant Bible that can be readily quoted to buttress this point of view becomes an essential ingredient to such a life. When that Bible is challenged, or relativized, the resulting anger proves the point categorically. (ibid. 5)

Such an explanation is insufficient, for it cannot account for one coming to accept a fundamentalist outlook in the first place. It seems, from the experiences of Balmer and Frank, that the certainties are not terribly appealing. Most probably people are attracted by other factors, and the fundamentalist mentality follows later. Barr (1980*a*: 69) suggests that 'the doctrine produces the psychology, not the psychology the doctrine':

> Young evangelical Christians, open, free and delightful, are often quickly reduced through the life of their society and the pressure of their doctrine to a strained, suspicious and exclusivist frame of mind . . . These are not people who were inherently bigoted or who had from the beginning a pathological personality structure. They did not begin this way: it was fundamentalism that made them this way.

The hard exterior of fundamentalism engenders the perception that those who manifest a fundamentalist mentality are rationalistic through and through. For example Boone (1989: 73), well into her appraisal of fundamentalism, justifies having said 'almost nothing about *faith*, an ingredient usually found in religions, because fundamentalism itself so thoroughly emphasizes the virtues of rationality and objectivity'. She continues: 'When apologists are backed into a corner, however, they do appeal to faith, the connotation of which is far better understood as a political attitude rather than as a spiritual condition.' Boone (ibid. 73–4) attributes the substitution of 'attitude' for 'faith' to the influence of Common Sense philosophy on fundamentalist thought. Common Sense epistemology asserts that basic truths are common to all persons, and cannot accommodate differences of belief that result from anything so fundamental or subjective as faith.

Boone is right in that, to the extent to which this epistemology has been influential for fundamentalism, faith is considered too subjective a factor to be given prominence in apologetics. However, she has failed to appreciate that when not offering apologetics, evangelicals talk of faith much of the time. Indeed, when they are the least defensive they are brave enough to mention this personal element. This is particularly so when they are evangelizing or are in fellowship with one another, sharing testimonies, insights from scripture, and experiences of answers to prayer. To mention faith in an apologetic context takes particular courage, for it is to remove any common ground upon which to base their arguments and so to risk charges of fideism. Faith is invoked when evangelicals feel confident, rather than when under severe attack. Usually they attempt to present their religion rationally, though the experiential side more effectively portrays its appeal.

5.3.2. *Evangelism*

The tension between the experiential and the evidential is most clearly seen in the ambiguous methods of evangelism. Evangelicals learn to present a rational defence of Christianity while praying for the salvation of those they evangelize. Evangelistic meetings are considered to be vain labours unless preceded by prayer that God will give the speakers the right words for the night, that he will cause those ripe for the Gospel to attend, that he will 'prepare their hearts' and 'touch' them with his word. Arguments are presented clearly and systematically, but are believed to be futile unless God convicts people in their hearts. Campus Crusade (1986: 2) insists on the one hand that:

> A fundamental principle in dealing with questions is to point out that Christian faith is based on facts. It is not a leap into the dark, or an irrational optimism, but a well thought out step based on the evidence of history and scripture focused on Jesus Christ. Challenge people to face the force of that evidence and take that step.

On the other hand, they warn that 'No one is won into the Kingdom of God by being beaten in an argument' (ibid. 1). Even though someone may look personally and with an open mind into the evidence for Christianity, 'he will never be convinced until he has made the final "experiment", coming to God in repentance and faith to accept Jesus Christ' (ibid. 29).

Much energy is expended on learning evangelism technique, which has assumed vast importance under the influence of Campus Crusade and of such training schemes as James D. Kennedy's Evangelism Explosion and C. Peter Wagner's Church Growth programme.[7] Trainees are encouraged to memorize certain scripture passages and arguments, with the aim that the evangelist become 'completely familiar and conversant with the outline' (Chapman 1981: 122). Salvation is often depicted as operating according to laws. This is the impression that Bill Bright (1965: 2), founder of Campus Crusade, creates in his tracts: 'Just as there are physical laws that govern the physical universe, so are there spiritual laws which govern your relationship with God.' Training

[7] Evangelism Explosion was first practised in Kennedy's Coral Ridge Presbyterian Church, Fort Lauderdale, Florida, in the 1960s; Wagner founded the Evangelistic Association's Department of Church Growth at Fuller Seminary in 1976 (Quebedeaux 1978: 61–4; Tidball 1994: 124).

The 2 Ways to Live

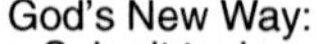

Our Way:
- Reject the ruler-God
- Try to run life our own way

Result:
- Condemned by God
- Facing death and punishment

God's New Way:
- Submit to Jesus as our ruler
- Rely on Jesus' death and resurrection

Result:
- Forgiven by God
- Given eternal life

'Whoever believes in the Son has eternal life, but whoever rejects the Son will not see life, for God's wrath remains on him. (John 3: 36)

Which of these best repnesents the way you want to live?

FIG. 5.1 The two ways to live (from Chapman 1981: 126)

for evangelism often involves learning diagrams to illustrate these laws and to set out the steps that the would-be convert needs to follow. John Chapman, who has conducted both CICCU and OICCU missions in recent years, outlines a training session in his book *Know and Tell the Gospel* (1981). He gives several pages of simple diagrams, made up of stickmen in varying relations to God and the world (ibid. 123–6). The hearer should deduce that one way of life is preferable to the other (see Fig. 5.1).

One man, Paul, converted through this method describes such a diagram thus: 'there's God on this side of a ravine: you're on the other side. There is nothing that you can do to bridge that gap . . . God knew about that gap and sent Jesus to die on the cross to bridge it' (D. Hall 1986: 117). The method is therefore not unsuccessful, though the account goes on to say, 'Something clicked in Paul's mind and heart' (ibid.). The element of personal encounter is crucial, yet evangelicals are fearful of crediting it.

5.3.3. *Testimonies*

That evangelicals memorize arguments in this way for the sake of converting others is all the more curious, considering that such arguments play a relatively little role in their own conversion experiences. Personal testimonies, whether of conversion or of some incident within one's Christian life, provide a rich resource of experiential claims. Testimonies are used both in evangelism and in the encouraging of fellow Christians. Conversion testimonies provide good evidence that the way in which a person understands his or her entrance into the faith is primarily experiential rather than intellectual. One might question the extent to which testimonies can be taken at face value, especially since they betray a tendency to exaggerate the unhappy nature of life prior to conversion. However, since we might expect converts to offer objective and public evidence where possible, the intensely personal nature of their testimonies is revealing for our purposes.

John Chapman (1981: 62) explains in his own testimony that the arguments used in his conversion had 'before seemed ridiculous and totally unimportant', but that they 'suddenly took on new meaning and significance' when 'God's Holy Spirit . . . opened my eyes and gave me the ability to repent and trust God's word'. Some converts testify to being brought to faith despite having opposing rational and scientific expectations. *Real Science, Real Faith* (Berry 1991) comprises essays by professional scientists who testify to how they relate their scientific studies to their faith. Most of the contributors are conservative evangelicals who had connections with UCCF as students. They describe a personal faith and express surprise at having come to belief through means which are not wholly scientific.

I had all week been trying, through the normal processes of intellectualism, to establish God's existence or otherwise—the otherwise was preferred! . . .

[My wife's] transformation, for such it was, brought me to the realisation that God was there, even if I'd never discovered him. That discovery took place at about 2.30 a.m. the following morning. It was awesome for it transcended any analytical scientific appraisal I could make.

I saw a vision—I didn't believe in visions; I heard a voice—I certainly didn't believe in voices, and the words, 'The harvest is past, the summer is ended, and we are not saved' (Jer 8: 20), thundered audibly about me. (Prof. Roy Peacock, Berry 1991: 33)

I realised the key to my belief was the resurrection of Jesus. The historical evidence alone is not the basis of that belief. As a scientist, however strong that evidence seems to be, it cannot on its own compensate for the scepticism I am bound to feel about dead bodies coming to life. But there is other evidence too. There is the testimony of millions of Christians over the centuries, from the first disciples who carefully recorded their experiences in the books of the New Testament, to that of Margaret, still very vivid in my memory. And there is the personal experience I have of Jesus as one who is alive in my experience today. The Jesus I meet in the pages of the Gospels is the One I meet as I attempt to communicate with God in prayer and the One I meet through the lives and conversations of others in the Christian community. (Dr John Houghton, ibid. 51)

In the academic world it seems that more scientists espouse a conservative evangelical faith than do people working in the arts. Biblical interpretation is at a further remove from their own area of expertise and they may be more sceptical about incorporating the role of the interpreter in constructing meaning. Eta Linnemann, however, provides an interesting example of a biblical scholar who converted to conservative evangelicalism. She was a professor of New Testament at Marburg and had studied under Bultmann, Fuchs, Gogarten, and Ebeling. She underwent a conversion to evangelical Christianity and turned her back on her previous scholarship, even throwing away her academic publications and asking that her readers do the same (Linnemann 1990: 20). She now teaches for a Bible College in Indonesia, and her subsequent writings have been translated into English by a professor from Wheaton College. She describes her movement from historical-critical theology to evangelical religion thus:

Intellectually comfortable with historical-critical theology, I was deeply convinced that I was rendering a service to God with my theological work and contributing to the proclamation of the gospel. Then, however, on the basis of various observations, discoveries, and a resulting self-awareness, I was forced to concede two things I did not wish: (1) no 'truth' could emerge from this 'scientific work on the biblical text,' and (2) such labor does not serve the proclamation of the gospel. (ibid. 17)

According to Linnemann's own testimony: 'God led me to vibrant Christians who knew Jesus personally as their Lord and Savior. I heard their testimonies as they reported what God had done in their lives. Finally God spoke to my heart by means of a Christian brother's words' (ibid. 18). It is after she had taken the step of conversion that she became convinced of Jesus' deity and changed her attitude towards scripture: 'About a month after entrusting my life to Jesus, God convinced me that his promises are a reality' (ibid.). She heard a testimony which she matched to a passage of scripture, and all that she had heard in recent months 'fell into place at that moment'. She arrived at a point of momentous decision: 'Would I continue to control the Bible by my intellect, or would I allow my thinking to be transformed by the Holy Spirit?' (ibid. 19). Having chosen the latter option, because she had 'recently experienced the truth' of John 3: 16, she was 'permitted to realize that Jesus *is* God's Son, born of a virgin. He *is* the Messiah and the Son of Man . . . I recognized, first mentally, but then in a vital, experiential way, that Holy Scripture is inspired' (ibid. 19–20).

5.3.4. *Bible Study or 'Quiet Times'*

The practice of quiet times indicates a devotional attitude towards scripture rather than the dry biblical exegesis one might logically expect from fundamentalists. Quiet times are times set aside each day for reading the Bible and praying. While they are intended partly for the acquisition of biblical knowledge, and Bible dictionaries and commentaries are generally considered to be helpful aids, their primary aim is that the believer develops his or her relationship with God. It is expected that through one's prayerful meditation on the scriptures, God will speak some personal truth or bring guidance for one's present circumstances. Several evangelical bodies produce daily Bible reading notes. Scripture Union, in an introductory booklet to its Bible reading notes, *Daily Bread*, expresses the hope that the Bible will 'become your "*Daily Mirror*", where you see yourself; and your "*Daily Mail*", through which God speaks to you about Himself' (Eddison 1975: 2–3).

Quiet times are considered crucial for one's growth in faith. They are understood to be not an intellectual but a spiritual discipline. 'Your object in the Quiet Time', wrote G. T. Manley in his IVF Bible Study Course, 'is not so much to gather information as inspiration . . . and [to] use the Word to light and feed the fire of devotion' ([1934] 1949: p. ix). Hence the work of the quickening Spirit in one's reading of the written Word is crucial: 'First, in a quiet act of worship, look to God to give and renew the workings of the Spirit within you; then, in a quiet act of faith, yield yourself

G Go to God in prayer daily (John 15: 7).
R Read God's Word daily (Acts 17: 11)—begin with the Gospel of John.
O Obey God moment by moment (John 14: 21).
W Witness for Christ by your life and words (Matthew 4: 19; John 15: 8).
T Trust God for every detail of your life (1 Peter 5: 7).
H Holy Spirit—allow Him to control and empower your daily life and witness (Galatians 5: 16, 17; Acts 1: 8).

FIG. 5.2 Steps to growth (Bright 1965: 14)

to the power that dwells in you, and wait on Him, that not the mind alone, but the life in you, may be opened to receive the Word.'[8] Through this regular discipline, the believer comes to realize 'the need of the Bible for *spiritual life and power*' (ibid. p. ix).

Kern Trembath (1987: 98) reasons, logically but mistakenly, that a position of inerrancy 'makes the maturing of faith dependent on a purely intellectual concept: the evaluation of truth claims'. He concludes that for 'the conscientious inerrantist . . . growth in salvation must always be postponed until all of the relevant factors in the truth claim may be adjudicated'. This, however, is not how inerrantists actually function. Bill Bright (1965: 14) believes that 'Spiritual growth results from trusting in Jesus Christ', living a life of faith, and practising the steps described in Fig. 5.2.

Although evangelicals refer to the Bible as their textbook, their experience of learning from scripture is not like textbook learning. Jeffery and Milton (1981: 6), writing for the Evangelical Press of Wales, maintain the necessity of a personal relationship with God in order for one to understand scripture. While claiming that the Bible 'does not merely contain the Word of God, it *is* the Word of God', and 'the unique source of information about God', they insist that one '*come to the Scriptures prayerfully*, seeking the illumination of the Holy Spirit without whose help you will never understand the truths that God would have us believe'.

Often the meaning that evangelicals derive from the Bible is very specific to the particular reader. As Kathleen Boone notes, popular fundamentalist literature abounds with accounts of the

[8] Andrew Murray, quoted in Manley [1934] 1949: p. x.

unchurched and biblically uneducated happening upon a Bible and being converted through some passage. Boone (1989: 17) comments: 'Although conversion on this basis may seem improbable (what if the reader haplessly turns to Leviticus or Ecclesiastes?), it is a commonplace of fundamentalism that any reader, unaided by clergy or even long-suppressed Sunday School training, can read successfully by him or her self'. However, she misses the point in thinking that these testimonies are about the authority of the individual interpreter. They are about the providence and grace of God: that the person should happen upon a Bible which should fall open on a particular page, and that the reader's attention be drawn to a particular verse. Despite claiming to move beyond reading the text of fundamentalism to reading the text with fundamentalism Boone (ibid. 13) has not entered into the spirit of fundamentalist testimony when she suggests that the unconverted might have come across some Old Testament text less enlightening and liberating than a piece of New Testament good news. From the point of view of those whom she calls fundamentalist, if one had fallen upon Leviticus or Ecclesiastes it would be so that God could reveal something to the reader through these texts. Jeremiah 8: 20 might not generally be regarded as a helpful text to aid conversion, yet Professor Roy Peacock found it powerful in his transformation.[9]

Furthermore, it is not simply a plain interpretation of a passage that is understood to strike the reader, as though anyone reading it at any time would be so struck. Rather, it is some timely personal revelation, in which something beyond mere intellectual recognition occurs. Howard Marshall (1977: 16–17) explains that, while the significance of the doctrine of inspiration is that the message of the New Testament rings true for every generation, certain situations 'may enable us to feel its impact in a more telling manner'. He tells of how, having 'long had a theoretical knowledge of 1 Thessalonians 3 . . . something happened to that chapter for me on 24th January, 1969', when Paul's situation was powerfully conveyed by a Czechoslovakian preacher 'prevented by Satan from visiting his friends in the west' (1977: 16–17). Bilquis Sheikh, a Muslim woman from the Pakistani upper classes,

[9] See s. 5.3.3 above.

converted to evangelical Christianity after a series of dreams and encounters with the Bible. Her story, *I Dared to Call Him Father* (1978), is immensely popular in evangelical circles. She writes of her first encounter:

> Lightheartedly, I opened the little Bible and looked down at the pages.
>
> Then a mysterious thing happened. It was as if my attention were being drawn to a verse on the lower right hand corner of the right page. I bent close to read it:
>
> > *I will call that my people, which was not my people; and her beloved, which was not beloved. And it shall be, that in the place where it was said unto them, Ye are not my people, there shall they be called sons of the living God.*
> >
> > Romans 9: 25–26
>
> I caught my breath and a tremor passed through me. Why was this verse affecting me so!
>
> . . . the words burned in my heart like glowing embers. (ibid. 22)

She recounts further incidents of being struck by biblical verses, and of God speaking to her through scripture, through other Christians, and in dreams, until she was brought to a point of conversion.

So convinced are evangelicals of this method of personal revelation that individuals sometimes try to effect it themselves by allowing their Bibles to fall open and then pin-pointing a verse.[10] Evangelical leaders specifically discourage this practice, which is parodied in *The Sacred Diary of Adrian Plass*: 'Opened my Bible at random and put my finger on the page. It said, "The dogs licked up the blood". Went to bed. I don't understand God sometimes . . .' (Plass 1987: 6).

On a purely intellectualist understanding of scripture, persons who 'knew' all of the Bible would have nothing more revealed to them. However, in seeking fresh guidance evangelicals are not usually looking for a verse that they have never read before, as though God could say something new to them only by their discovering a new piece of text. They are expecting to be struck by something they have never realized before, or to have some truth

[10] This practice predates evangelical religion. Keith Thomas, in *Religion and the Decline of Magic* (1971), finds evidence of such biblical divination in the medieval church and in the 16th and 17th c. (pp. 45–6, 118).

revealed to them again with fresh impact. This may well happen through an old, familiar verse.

Fundamentalist logic allows no room for such dynamic interaction with scripture, and therefore fails to do justice to evangelical experience. James Dunn (1982: 214) views the 'logic of the inerrancy school' as a muzzle around scripture, for it requires that scripture 'say precisely the same thing in every historical context'. As a result, he argues, evangelicals perform a process which 'filters out much that God would say to particular situations, and lets through a message which soon becomes predictably repetitive, whatever the Scripture consulted'. Inerrantists do experience frustration when attempting to describe their personal apprehension of biblical truth within the constraints of the inerrancy position. This sense of confinement led Edward Carnell to criticize the implication of Gordon Clark's reasoning:

> On your view a person can have the infallible assurance that the chronologies in the Old Testament or the dimensions of the temple or the endless Levitical laws are true, and then yawn and go to sleep; on my view this truth must be probed until it blesses the heart, moves, and convicts: *then* inspired truth has been found. Our consolation in the Bible is more than that which comes from a rational assurance that it is infallibly true; it is a spiritual response based upon a source of life.[11]

Evangelicals do not believe that a person can exhaust all that the Bible has to reveal, since God by his Spirit continues to speak anew through scripture. However, their fundamentalist-style apologetics are more concerned with the Bible's factual truthfulness than with its life-giving effects. The testimony of the Holy Spirit plays a greater role in evangelicals' submission to biblical authority than such apologetics imply. The following chapters investigate philosophical influences upon evangelicalism which could in principle accommodate the Spirit's testimony more successfully. In the final chapter, we shall see how evangelicals appropriate hermeneutical philosophy to describe a process of interaction between a text and its reader. They introduce the Holy Spirit into this process, as the agent who transforms the thinking of the reader and makes it biblical. First, we shall consider neo-Calvinist thought. Neo-Calvinism denies the theoretical possibility

[11] Letter, 5 Jan. 1953, quoted in Nelson (1987: 153).

that a person who is untouched by the Holy Spirit could be persuaded by arguments for the truth of Christianity and the authority of scripture. It thus presents a challenging alternative to the assumptions which underlie a fundamentalist apologetic.

6

The Dutch Influence

6.1. Neo-Calvinism

Much that has been said in this study regarding the empirical rationalism of the fundamentalist mentality is not news to evangelicals themselves. There are those within evangelical circles who attempt to undo what they see as the harmful legacy of Enlightenment philosophy in evangelical thought. Particular among them are those who emphasize their Reformed over and above their evangelical status, and whose thinking has been shaped by Abraham Kuyper, the leading Dutch theologian of the turn of the century.

Abraham Kuyper (1837–1920), together with Herman Bavinck (1854–1921), led the Dutch neo-Calvinist revival at the end of the nineteenth century. His thought was described as 'neo-Calvinist' by his opponents. He accepted the designation in recognition that he was reformulating some of Calvin's ideas. He argued that world-view and presuppositions are more basic than facts and propositions, and that one's presuppositions are affected by the presence or absence of the regenerating work of the Holy Spirit.[1] Whereas the Princeton theologians emphasized the Spirit's role in the ultimate decision to come to faith, Kuyper believed that regeneration affects one's entire understanding. He questioned the extent and type of common knowledge between believer and non-believer, and denied the existence of unvarnished data in anything but the most basic exercises of weighing and measuring in natural science.

Kuyper's system of thought challenges the rational empiricism of the Princeton tradition. It has been suggested that Cornelius

[1] Like some other theologians of his time, Kuyper appropriated the German concept 'world-view' (*Weltanschauung*). He mentioned James Orr's lectures, *The Christian View of God and the World* (1897), in this respect. Kuyper's preferred English rendering of *Weltanschauung* was '*life and world view*', though he was encouraged to use the phrase '*life system*' in America (Kuyper [1898] 1932: 29 n. 1). For an account of the influence of Orr and others upon Kuyper's notion of world-view see Heslam 1993: 126–35.

Van Til (1895–1987), a key exponent of Kuyperian ideas among fundamentalists and evangelicals, pre-empted Barr's critique of fundamentalist rationalism (Edgar 1977: 156). Van Til presents an apologetic in which presuppositions rather than evidences and rational argument are basic to the defence of the faith. His method is commonly labelled 'presuppositionalist'. All Kuyperians reject evidentialist apologetics. They also criticize what they regard as evangelical 'pietism': the retreat from 'worldly' activities to the 'sacred' pursuits of soul-saving, personal piety, and theological study. In particular, the Dutch philosopher Herman Dooyeweerd (1894–1977) challenged evangelicals to relate their faith to every sphere of activity. Dooyeweerd's followers have inherited the neo-Calvinist label. Neo-Calvinists have contributed significantly to a widening of the evangelical vision to all areas of life, so reflecting Kuyper's desire to see culture in its entirety reformed upon Christian principles.[2]

In the Preface to his *Encyclopedia*, Kuyper ([1898] 1968: p. viii) explains how he turned away from the theological liberalism and indeterministic philosophy he had known at Leiden. He was impressed by the stability of thought and unity of comprehensive insight of some descendants of 'the ancient Calvinists' whom he had met. They possessed 'a world-view based on principles which needed but a scientific treatment and interpretation to give them a place of equal significance over against the dominant views of the age'. Kuyper was not only a theologian but also a minister, journalist, politician, and educational reformer. His active concern in politics and education was the outworking of his conviction that Christian, and more specifically Calvinist, principles should be brought to bear in every department of life. He founded the Free University of Amsterdam in 1880. Bavinck succeeded him there when, as leader of the Anti-Revolutionary Party, Kuyper served as prime minister of the Netherlands from 1901 to 1905.

Writings particularly relevant to Kuyper's construction of a Calvinist world-view, and the corresponding rejection of evidentialist apologetics, are his three-volume *Encyclopedia of Sacred Theology* (*Encyclopaedie der Heilige Godgeleerdheid* 1894), and his Stone Lectures on *Calvinism* delivered at Princeton Theological Seminary in October 1898 (page numbers are from the 1932 edition).

[2] The thought of Van Til, Dooyeweerd, and those whom they influenced will be examined in the next chapter.

The *Encyclopedia* was abridged and translated into English with Kuyper's co-operation by J. Hendrik de Vries as *Principles of Sacred Theology*, 1898 (page numbers are from the 1968 edition).[3]

Kuyper and his American contemporary, Benjamin Warfield, were united in their opposition to liberalism. Kuyper fought it on many fronts; Warfield concentrated on theological polemic. The two differed markedly in their defence of scripture and in their responses to the historical-critical method. However, their only formal theological disagreement was over apologetics, a subject which highlights the essential differences between Kuyper's system of thought and the Common Sense views of Old Princeton.

Scottish Common Sense philosophy arose in a Calvinist context, yet its optimistic anthropology was inhospitable to Calvinist emphases on the degenerate character of human nature.[4] Common Sense Realism endorsed a view of the human constitution as basically moral, basically rational, and universally the same. It lessened the requirement of moral and spiritual preconditions in the seeker after truth, although it recognized the value of educational and cultural nurturing. It conceded a doctrine of natural reason, or what Herman Dooyeweerd termed the dogma of the autonomy of theoretical thought.[5]

Warfield accepted the Common Sense emphasis on universal principles of knowing, and denied any significant difference in the pursuit of knowledge as performed by Christians and non-Christians. Kuyper acknowledged the logical reasoning of non-Christians, but attributed to their logic a principle different from his own. He rejected the Princetonians' central commitment to the method of induction, and did not share their faith in the ability of Christian evidences to convince unbelievers. He denied a basic tenet of Baconianism, that the same method can be transposed across the various scientific disciplines. He insisted, rather, that each science has its own method (1968: 36). To defend the

[3] A synopsis of Bavinck's *magnum opus*, the 4-vol. *Gereformeerde Dogmatiek* (1895–1901), was translated into English from the Dutch version *Magnalia Dei* (1909) by Henry Zylstra as *Our Reasonable Faith* (1956). Vol. ii of the *Dogmatiek* was edited and translated by W. Hendricksen as *The Doctrine of God* (1951). Bavinck's Stone Lectures (1908–9) were published in Dutch, English, and German simultaneously as *The Philosophy of Revelation* (1909).

[4] Paul Helm (1983) doubts that Reid was a Calvinist. He regards him as a 'moderate', who adopted 'common-sense foundationalism' not on account of his Calvinism, but because in his view it was the only alternative to Humean scepticism.

[5] Most fully explicated in his *A New Critique of Theoretical Thought* (4 vols., Eng. trans. 1953–8).

scientific character of theology by borrowing the brevet of non-theological science would be to 'cut out the heart of Theology', he argued, and transform it into a study that would fit 'the framework of naturalistic science' (ibid. 211–12; cf. Bavinck 1909*a*: 86, 206–7).[6]

Warfield grounded faith in evidence, whereas Kuyper granted faith the power to determine how one perceives evidence. While Warfield presented theology as no less scientific than other disciplines, Kuyper (1932: 203) insisted that natural science rests upon faith no less than does theology: 'Not faith and science therefore, but *two scientific systems* or if you choose, two scientific elaborations, are opposed to each other, *each having its own faith*'. This is the most significant difference for us to note, though it is neither the most basic nor the most prominent in debates between Warfield and Kuyper.

More fundamental was their disagreement over the human constitution. Whereas Warfield (1903*b*: 30) believed that 'All minds are of the same essential structure', Kuyper asserted that our constitution depends upon our state as unregenerate or regenerate beings. Kuyper drew a distinction between two types of people, based upon his view of the damage wrought by sin upon humanity. If Common Sense philosophy de-emphasized the effects of sin upon our thought, Kuyper insisted that our constitution is not as it was intended by our Creator. According to Kuyper, a process of restoration has begun in the regenerate which involves their very constitution being redirected. There is therefore no universal consensus arising out of the human constitution. Among other things, the regenerate have different presuppositions and hence a different world-view from the unregenerate. This difference is most manifest in those disciplines where the subjective element has a large role in forming our conclusions. Hence, it will be more evident in the human sciences than in the natural sciences. As for theological science, whose object is knowledge of God, this will only be found in its proper form in the circle of the regenerate. There is no common understanding to which to

[6] By 'naturalistic science', Kuyper means a system of knowing which is based upon naturalistic as opposed to Christian premisses. In this section (211–19, ch. 5, sect. 54) Kuyper seems to mean that if a theologian were to study God according to the same method as for studying natural philosophy, he would lose sight of the distinction between man and God which is essential to theology. He would forget that in theology man cannot be the thinking subject standing over against God as object. Cf. his criticism of Charles Hodge's theological method, s. 6.3.1 below.

appeal in presenting evidence or constructing arguments regarding God. Therefore Kuyper did not endorse apologetic theology. He ranged two systems or *Weltanschauung* (world-views) against one another, which are absolutely opposed by virtue of their entirely contrary assumptions. His desire was that a Christian or Calvinistic world-view underlie every sphere of life.

6.2. The Thought of Abraham Kuyper

> Without the sense of God in the heart no one shall ever attain unto a knowledge of God . . . Every effort to prove the existence of God by so-called evidences must fail and has failed . . . If thus in our sense of self there is no sense of the existence of God, and if in our spiritual existence there is no bond which draws us to God, and causes us in love to go out to him, all science is here impossible.
>
> (Kuyper 1968: 112–13)

6.2.1. *The Noetic Effects of Sin*

Kuyper's rejection of the validity of apologetics is based upon his theory of the pervasive effects of sin. The fact of sin must not be omitted from the theory of knowledge, Kuyper (1968: 114) argues, for 'Ignorance wrought by sin is the most difficult obstacle in the way of all true science'. This obstacle was conceived differently at Princeton. Charles Hodge asserted the need for supernatural revelation due to the damage incurred by sin, but his response to rationalism was to ground assent to truth in Christian evidences.

Kuyper emphasizes our subjective approach to evidence. He does not regard subjectivism as itself bad. Without sin, subjectivism would have led to a harmonious multiformity. However, sin has entered our world, and individual subjects incur disharmony in their desire to push other subjects aside (ibid. 90, 106). Thus, subjectivism has become 'a cancer to poison our science' (p. 90). At the most basic level, the weighing and measuring objectivity is possible (pp. 104, 157). Yet,

> As soon . . . as you . . . try to obtain a construction by which to discover among these scattered data a unity of thought, the process of an idea, or

the progression from a first phenomenon to a result, you have at once crossed over from the physical into the psychical, the universally compulsory certainty leaves you, and you glide back into subjective knowledge, since you are already within the domain of the spiritual sciences. (p. 104)

Hence, even in the natural sciences simple empiricism can never suffice.

Sin effects a '*darkening of our consciousness*', which Kuyper describes as loss of the bond of love between ourselves and the cosmos (p. 111). We have not lost the capacity to think logically, but we have become isolated and estranged from the object of our knowledge (pp. 110, 111). Were the process of logical reasoning itself affected by sin, the unregenerate would not be able to develop so comprehensive a system of thought required for Kuyper's antithesis. Kuyper poses a theory of two opposing world-views, one developed by those who have remained under the influence of sin, the other developed by those who have been partially restored.[7]

6.2.2. *Two Types of People, Two World-Views*

It is an assumption of evidentialist apologetics that there is a universal human consciousness and so a uniform vantage point from which evidence is assessed. According to Kuyper (1968: 152), however, regeneration 'breaks humanity in two, and repeals the unity of the human consciousness'. Palingenesis, or 'being begotten anew', begins a restoration of the faculties in the regenerate, who, being 'differently constituted . . . see a corresponding difference in the constitution of all things' (p. 155).

If this fact of 'being begotten anew,' coming in from without, establishes a radical change in *the being* of man, be it only potentially, and if this change exercises at the same time an influence upon his *consciousness*, then as far as it has or has not undergone this transformation, there is an abyss

[7] Kuyper's doctrine of common grace, meanwhile, enables him to explain the ability of human society to function and the existence of talent among the unregenerate (1932: 59, 180–92; Heslam 1993: 260–5). It is a negative and a positive doctrine, extensively formulated in *De Gemeene Gratie* (3 vols.; Amsterdam: Höveker & Wormser, 1902–5), emphasizing first the restraining of sin and then the positive achievements of sinful humanity. Cf. Bavinck, who locates the antithesis between principles rather than persons, and finds elements of truth in heathen religions and philosophy (Klapwijk 1983: 103; Bratt 1984: 31).

in the universal human consciousness across which no bridge can be laid. (p. 152)

The process of palingenesis is elaborated by an analogy with tree-grafting. Palingenesis effects a difference in kind, not only in degree: 'A tree is not one-tenth cultivated and nine-tenths wild, so that by degrees it may become entirely cultivated; it is simply grafted or not grafted, and the entire result of its future growth depends on this fundamental difference' (pp. 152–3). Yet, like grafting, palingenesis initiates a slow process, bringing about not immediate change throughout our whole being but a gradual pruning away of the old and cultivation of the new (p. 162). A tree cannot change kind by its own power. Likewise, palingenesis is wrought from outside (p. 152). However, the process causes those who are begotten anew to become 'inwardly different' from other human beings so that 'they face the cosmos from different points of view' (p. 154). Thus develop two types of being who are 'constitutionally *different*' from one another; the difference stemming from 'the *deepest impulse* of the life consciousness of each' (p. 168).

Kuyper concludes that there must be two distinct ways of seeing the world: 'Two *life systems* [*Weltanschauungen*] are wrestling with one another, in mortal combat' (1932: 29–30). Modernism, whose anti-Christian principles Kuyper traces to the French Revolution (ibid. 47), opposes the Christian heritage in Europe and America. It is a system 'bound to build a world of its own from the data of natural man, and to construct man himself from the data of nature' (ibid. 30). Modernism assails us with 'the vast energy of an all-embracing *life-system*', which can be countered effectively only by another 'life-system of equally comprehensive and far-reaching power' (ibid. 30). Kuyper posits Calvinism.

He outlines three conditions of a life system: our interpretation of our relation to God which dominates every general life-system; the fundamental interpretation of the relation of man to man; and the relation which one bears to the world (ibid. 42–59). Kuyper finds in Calvinism a sharply defined starting-point for these three fundamental relations of all human existence: (1) an immediate fellowship of man with the eternal; (2) an understanding of man as created in the divine image, and therefore an emphasis upon the human worth of each person; (3) a recognition that in the whole world the curse is restrained by grace, that the life of the world is to be honoured in its independence, and that in every domain the treasures and potencies hidden by God in nature and in human life are to be discovered and developed (ibid. 59).

Kuyper sometimes implies that there are more than two opposing life-systems or world-views. In the Stone Lectures he considers that modernism can take the form of either pantheism or agnosticism, and he mentions other examples of consistent life-systems including paganism, Islamism, Romanism, and Calvinism (ibid. 51, 58).[8] However, more often he asserts that there can be only two alternatives, and that Calvinism is the non-atheistic one: 'whosoever rejects atheism as his fundamental thought, is bound to go back to Calvinism' (ibid. 73). That there are only two is due to the fact that everyone stands either in or out of palingenesis.[9]

6.2.3. *Two Types of Science*

> And the fact that there are two kinds of *people* occasions of necessity the fact of two kinds of human *life* and *consciousness* of life, and of two kinds of *science*; for which reason the idea of the *unity of science*, taken in its absolute sense, implies the denial of the fact of palingenesis, and therefore from principle leads to the rejection of the Christian religion. (1968: 154)

Far from endeavouring to show that there is no real clash between science and religion, Kuyper reconceives the struggle as being between two kinds of science, each with its own faith. Since the whole of science proceeds from one's consciousness, the whole of science is shaped by whether or not one is under palingenesis. As Kuyper explains, by 'science' he does not mean mere empiricism but the discovery of universal law (1932: 174), or 'the scientific systematization of that which exists' (1968: 155). He uses the term

[8] In the *Encyclopedia* (1968: 172) Kuyper mentions alongside Calvinism the systems of Lutheranism and Romanism, but here he describes them as 'blended types'.

[9] The difficulty lies in alluding both to the antithesis and to the manifest plurality of world-views. Bavinck (1909*a*: 33) distinguishes three types of world-view: 'the theistic (religious, theological), the naturalist (either in its pantheistic or materialistic form), and the humanistic'. Later Kuyperians have distinguished 'biblical' from 'apostate' world-views (in the terminology of Dooyeweerd), and found the latter to exist under various forms. For example, Alvin Plantinga (1990: 31) brings a Kuyperian influence into analytical philosophy. He distinguishes those who 'enlist under Christ's banner' from those 'who fly the flag of the Earthly City'. At present, he finds the 'Earthly' category divided into three: Perennial Naturalism, Enlightenment Humanism, and Modern Subjectivism.

equivalently to the German *Wissenschaft* or the Dutch *Wetenschap* (ibid. 36–7; Heslam 1993: 249). 'Naturalistic science' is antithetical to palingenesis and to 'Christian science' (1968: 176–82).[10]

Kuyper introduces a distinction between Normalists and Abnormalists to describe the two different types of science (1932: 201–7; cf. 1968: 118). One recognizes the fact of sin and the other denies it: 'Thus what is normal to one is absolutely abnormal to the other. This establishes for each an entirely different standard' (1968: 118). Normalists 'refuse to reckon with other than natural data' (1932: 201). They believe that the present state of the cosmos is its normal condition whereas abnormalists believe that a disturbance has taken place in the past and that only by a regenerating power can its final goal be attained. Normalists do not believe in miracles but only in natural law. They reject the very idea of creation and accept only evolution, denying sin and proposing a progress from a lower to a higher moral position (ibid. 201–2). Abnormalists 'do justice to relative evolution, but adhere to primordial creation over against an *evolutio in infinitum*' (p. 202). They consider sin to have destroyed our original human nature and believe that miraculous means are necessary for the abnormal state to be restored to normality. They believe in the miracle of the scriptures, Christ, and regeneration, and 'they continue to find the norm not in the natural but in the Triune God' (ibid.).

The two sciences are absolutely opposed, earnestly 'disputing with one another *the whole domain of life*' (ibid. 203). They are like builders who are at work not on different parts of the same house, but upon two different houses (1968: 155). Their total opposition stems from the very nature of a scientific system, which must be consistent with its starting-point. Since Normalists and Abnormalists have opposed starting-points, they cannot borrow from one another and remain true scientists. Each claims the name of science for himself and withholds it from the other. This is necessarily so, 'for if one acknowledged the other to be truly scientific, he would be obliged to adopt the other man's views' (p. 156), and would thus undermine his own principles.[11]

[10] However, Kuyper also refers to sciences as separate disciplines, and defends the place of theology as queen of the sciences. See later in this section.

[11] Here Kuyper suggests that one is unscientific only when one attempts to borrow from the opposite world-view to one's own (1932: 203), so that even the Normalist can build a 'well construed science' by reasoning consistently (pp. 210–11). In the *Encyclopedia*, however,

Bare facts are accorded no significance in Kuyper's thought, for they would signal an abandonment of an overriding principle by which to interpret the world (1932: 176). Kuyper instructs the regenerate to order facts according to their own science.

Everything astronomers or geologists, physicists or chemists, zoologists or bacteriologists, historians or archaeologists bring to light has to be recorded—detached of course from the hypothesis they have slipped behind it and from the conclusions they have drawn from it,—but every fact has to be recorded by you, also, as a fact that is to be incorporated as well in your science as in theirs. (1932: 212)

Conclusions obtained from material data stand 'entirely at the foot of the ladder of scientific investigation' (1968: 157), where the two circles of investigators derive mutual benefit from the formulations and observations of the general stock of science. Such studies are menial, and should not be accredited with being the *only* strictly scientific studies: 'Science in the higher sense begins only where these higher functions operate, and then, of course, these two streams *must* separate, because the working of these higher functions, with and without palingenesis, differs' (1968: 601).

Kuyper (1968: 220) considers the normal–abnormal distinction to be most evident in the science of theology. One who has been changed by palingenesis will assume a different attitude towards the revelation of God: 'He will no longer try, as in his naturalistic period, to denounce that Revelation as a vexatious hindrance, but will feel the need of it, will live in it, and profit by it' (ibid. 171). Revelation does not simply supplement one's scientific thinking. It must rather transform it, for the scientific character of a person's knowledge would be destroyed by the incorporation of statements which conflict with one's basic principle. The revelation offered us in the Word of God is to be assimilated subjectively. Thus it will actually alter one's starting-place by effecting 'the deepest impulse and entire inner disposition' of one's being (pp. 171–2). This assimilation does not take place by the understanding only, but then no science functions without faith (pp. 131, 143, 172).[12]

he concludes that ultimately there is only one science, that of the regenerate, which the unregenerate can serve by performing the least interpretative tasks (1968: 602–3).

[12] Failure to acknowledge the aspect of faith in all science has led to a false separation of theology from the other sciences. It has further resulted in a banishment of theology from

All the other sciences are held together under the science of theology.[13] They must be 'brought under the sway of one principle by means of theory or hypothesis, and finally Systematics, as the queen of sciences, comes forth from her tent to weave all the different results into one dogmatic whole' (1932: 174; cf. 1968: 227). The unregenerate can perform the 'hod-carrier service' of scientific study, but this 'is entirely different from the higher architecture' (1968: 603). The science of the regenerate is the true science because it includes theology and 'possesses the *missing links*' (p. 602). The scientist who proceeds from naturalistic premisses either cancels the following phenomena, or else explains them naturalistically: '(1) of personal regeneration; and (2) of its corresponding inspiration; (3) of the final restoration of all things; and (4) of its corresponding manifestation of God's power in miracles (*Niphleôth*)' (p. 225). Kuyper is led to claim that ultimately there is only one scientific system, that which acknowledges palingenesis, and hence 'that the only subject of *all* science is the consciousness of regenerated or re-created humanity' (pp. 602–3).

6.2.4. *Common Sense and Faith*

How far Kuyper's thought, with its antithesis between the regenerate and unregenerate, differs from that of Reid may be discerned from Kuyper's discussion of common sense in relation to wisdom and faith (1968: 119–46). Kuyper recognizes an innate sense common to the great mass of humanity. He accounts for this 'common sense' in terms similar to those of Reid:

> It is not the fruit of early training, it is not the result of study, neither is it the effect of constant practice. Though it is granted that these three factors facilitate and strengthen the clear operations of this common sense and of this wisdom, the phenomenon itself does not find its origin in them . . . Thus we have to do with a certain capacity of the human mind, which is not introduced into it from without, but which is present in that mind as such, and abides there. (p. 122)

the universities, where the work of theologians, which by its very nature involves fewer areas where general agreement is reached, is not recognized (1968: 192).

[13] Dooyeweerd crucially rejects this aspect of Kuyper's thought ([1960] 1980), and regards philosophy instead as providing the concepts which integrate the other sciences. See s. 7.1 below.

Common sense offers a general basis for wisdom and saves the human mind 'from the clutches of scepticism' (pp. 123–4). Wisdom and common sense provide 'a relative certainty, which . . . being constantly confirmed in the fiery test of practical application in daily life, gives us a starting-point by which the conviction maintains itself in us that we are able to grasp the truth of things' (p. 123).

However, Kuyper objects that common sense cannot appropriately furnish a whole school of thought. Originally common sense meant 'a certain accuracy of tact, by which, in utter disregard of the pretensions of the schools, public opinion followed a track which turned neither too far to the right nor to the left' (pp. 121–2). It cannot itself supersede discursive thought or take the place of empiricism, 'but it has the general *universal* tendency to exclude follies from the processes of discursive thought, and in empirical investigation to promote the accuracy of our tact' (p. 124).

Innate common sense or intuitive knowledge is the same in all humanity. Kuyper regards it as of smaller consequence than faith, whose content differs between the two types of people. Faith counters scepticism more effectively than does wisdom (p. 125). Kuyper traces the origin of scepticism to the 'impression that our certainty depends upon the result of our scientific research' (ibid.). He realizes more clearly than did Reid that the result of our scientific research is governed by subjective influences. Kuyper sees it as affected also by the conflict between truth and falsehood which is the result of sin. Hence there is no defence against scepticism except in the subject itself. In order to benefit science, this defence must not bear an individual-subjective character but must be subjective in a communal sense. Faith exhibits this communal character (pp. 125–6).

Kuyper attributes to faith some of the functions Reid ascribes to the principles of common sense. Faith is a function of the soul 'by which it obtains certainty directly and immediately, without the aid of discursive demonstration' (p. 129). It is by faith that 'our *ego* believes in our senses', that one can move 'from phenomena to noumena' and believe in 'the reality of the object' (p. 133).[14] Faith

[14] Earlier in the *Encyclopedia* Kuyper (pp. 67–83) talks of the '*Organic Relation between Subject and Object*', the subject being the human consciousness, and the object all that is outside the consciousness and investigated by it. He attempts to establish an increasingly close link between the two by bringing the object in relation to human nature, then human con-

is 'the *only* source of certainty', even 'for what you prove definitely and conclusively by demonstration' (p. 129).

Thus Kuyper arrives at his claim that faith is 'the starting-point of all knowledge' (p. 130). Like Reid, Kuyper denies the Cartesian starting-point, or rather understands it to be a matter of faith and not of demonstration. Only faith can give one certainty in one's consciousness of the existence of one's ego. The *ego* proved in the *sum* is already assumed in the premiss *cogito* (1968: 131). This certainty or faith in one's ego or self-consciousness precedes every act of thought or observation (1968: 132; 1932: 200–1; cf. Bavinck 1909*a*: 56, 60–82).

Faith underlies all knowledge, but because it differs among people there is no unified basis of knowledge. Herein lies the basic distinction between Kuyper's and Reid's positions: that Reid assumes and Kuyper rejects a common foundation for knowledge. Kuyper traces the consequences of palingenesis through all realms of thought because of the different forms that faith takes in the regenerate and unregenerate. 'Every science in a certain degree starts *from faith*', which is why Kuyper does 'not speak of a conflict between faith and science' (1932: 200). Machen (1923: 5), bearing the influence more of Reid's than of Kuyper's philosophy, resists the separation of science and religion for the contrary reason, that it would relinquish 'all objective truth in the sphere of religion'.[15] Kuyper (1968: 143) denies the very possibility, fundamental to Machen's apologetics, that *science can* establish truth which is 'equally binding upon all, exclusively on the ground of observation and demonstration'. Rather, 'in the acquisition of scientific conviction, every man starts out from *faith*'.[16]

sciousness, and finally the world of thought. Yet, however close the relation there remains a gap between the ego and the non-ego. Eventually he must simply trust, as did the Common Sense philosophers, in the way in which people are created. The power that binds the subject and the object must be sought outside of each. No satisfying grounds for this correspondence, on which the possibility and development of science wholly rests, can be found 'until at the hand of Holy Scripture we confess that the Author of the cosmos created man in the cosmos as microcosmos "after his image and likeness" '.

[15] Machen's distinction between the religion of liberalism and the religion of Christianity, in *Christianity and Liberalism* (1923), may owe something to Kuyper's ideas.

[16] Nicholas Wolterstorff constructs from Reid an argument against evidentialist apologetics (1981; 1983). Like Plantinga, he is an analytical philosopher in the Dutch Reformed tradition. He is particularly interesting in that he draws on both Kuyper and Reid. He finds in Reid grounds for justifying beliefs, not on the basis of evidence or rational relations between propositions, but on one doing 'as well in one's believings as can rightly

6.2.5. *Theology*

The third volume of the *Encyclopedia* is devoted to theology. We should note that Kuyper comes to theology after his discussion of science, faith, and palingenesis, even though he will conclude that theology is the queen of the sciences. Similarly, he resolves rather than presupposes that scripture is the *principium* or starting-point of theology. We will discover in the next chapter that Van Til inverts these aspects of Kuyper's theology, beginning with scripture rather than with spiritual impulses at the depths of our being.

Van Til stands somewhere between Princeton and Kuyper, rejecting the inductive method but reinstituting apologetics upon the presupposition that scripture forms the infallible starting-point in our reasoning. Kuyper insists that an epistemology peculiar to theology is required to describe man's knowledge of God. He is therefore critical of Charles Hodge, who adopted for his *Systematic Theology* the inductive method as used in the natural and mental sciences (1968: 318–19). In theology man is passive and 'stands no longer *above*, but *beneath* the object of his investigation, and . . . in a position of entire *dependence*' (ibid. 248). 'Theology does not at first demonstrate there is a God; but it springs out of the overwhelming impression which, as the only absolutely existing One, God Himself makes upon the human consciousness, and finds its motive in the admiration which of itself powerfully quickens the thirst to know God' (p. 243).

The object of our theological investigation is not God himself, but the received ectypal knowledge of God (p. 252). Yet our given knowledge of God derives from the archetype—God's self-knowledge. That which is revealed must be 'transposed by man into subjective *knowledge* of God' (pp. 262–3), otherwise revelation will not have realized its aim. It is in the logos that man appropriates revelation to himself. The human logos reflects something of the eternal Logos. Kuyper relates humankind's knowledge of God to their innate knowledge and to the human condition preceding and following the Fall. Before the Fall, knowledge of God coin-

be demanded of a person' (1983: 46). Such a position allows that people have varying capacities to govern their belief dispositions. Wolterstorff sees this as a strand in Reid's thought which goes against Reid's emphases on common sense. His interpretation requires an altered reading of Reid on theistic belief, where, as Wolterstorff acknowledges, 'the evidence is that those adults who are justified in their theistic beliefs hold those beliefs on the basis of reason' (ibid. 62).

cided with human self-knowledge. It was just as immediate as self-knowledge, and required no further action from the human logos. Even in the present degenerate condition there is 'a background of self-knowledge and of knowledge of our own existence, which is given immediately with our self-consciousness' (p. 265). Calvin called this innate knowledge of God the seed of religion. It is an ineradicable property of human nature.

Kuyper now puts his previous account of faith into its proper context, by relating faith to the seed of religion.

> Faith indeed is in our human consciousness the deepest fundamental law that governs every form of distinction, by which alone all higher 'Differentiation' becomes established in our consciousness. It is the daring breaking of our unity into a duality; placing of another ego over against our own ego; and the courage to face that distinction because our own ego finds its point of support and of rest only in that other ego. This general better knowledge of faith renders it possible to speak of faith in every domain; and also shows that faith originates primordially from the fact that our ego places God over against itself as the eternal and infinite Being, and that it dares to do this, because in this only it finds its eternal point of support. (pp. 266–7)

Human nature contains the seeds of religion and faith (p. 268). By these means God manifests himself in our being and we perceive this manifestation. Faith in Christ and in the holy scripture is given by 'special grace'. It is found in our souls not by the natural principium of creation, but in the special principium of recreation, so that 'by one it *must* be accepted, but also by another be rejected' (p. 460).

The three constituent elements of theology are revelation, faith, and logical activity. Sin does not annihilate any of these. Regarding revelation, the fact of sin requires that the disorder in the sinner must be neutralized and the knowledge of God must be extended to include knowledge of the relation of God to the sinner. Faith belongs to human nature, but the energy operative in faith 'turns itself away from God and with all the passion at its command attaches itself *to something else*' (p. 276). Unbelief is not a lack of faith but 'the power of faith turned into its opposite' (p. 301). Palingenesis is required; a 'bending right again, from the root up' of one's psychical life (p. 281). Logical activity remains intact, but may be motivated to explain away this inworking in such a way that God is denied by the intellect (p. 277). Sin has not deprived us of the power of thought, but 'the pivot of our thought has become displaced, and thereby our activity of thought, applied to divine things, has a wrong effect' (p. 288). Divine illumination remedies this effect but does not increase the acuteness of thought: 'enlightening simply means that, according to the peculiarities of his person, according to his need and the measure of his gifts, every believer understands everything that is necessary for confession' (p. 289).

The science of theology is 'that logical action of the general subject of regenerated humanity by which, in the light of the Holy Spirit, it takes up the revealed knowledge of God into its consciousness and from thence reflects it' (p. 299). Since the development of scientific theology remains dependent upon the 'inworking and guidance of the Holy Spirit', it can only come from that 'circle in which the *divine illumination* operates' (p. 290).

> The human logos, as weakened by sin, can certainly deal with the content of this revelation, as has been the case in all ages; but as soon as this movement has reached out after something more than a mere superficiality, it has become at once antithetical, has placed itself in opposition to revelation, and has sought, and still seeks, logically to destroy it. (p. 290)

Theology being the highest science is bound to lack universal conviction, since 'it touches that which is most tender . . . and consequently has most to endure from the ruin worked by sin in our spiritual life' (p. 326). The universality of theological truth is established by appeal only to the enlightened: 'for universal validity the acceptance of all individuals is not demanded, but only of those who are receptive to the truth of a matter and are well informed of it' (ibid. cf. 339). Theology rises from the life of the Church and not vice versa.[17] 'No intellectual relation is possible in the domain of this science, between those to whom this theology is "foolishness," and the others to whom it is the "wisdom of God". They only, who by virtue of palingenesis are partakers of *spiritual illumination*, have their eyes opened to see the object to be investigated' (p. 338).

[17] Accordingly, Kuyper (1968: 616) would like the teaching of theology to be under the influence of the Church rather than the Government. The Government accepts 'the modern interpretation of Theology as "the science of religion" instead of "the science of the revealed knowledge of God," which it has always been in keeping with its own origin and principle'.

6.2.6. *The Principium*

The circle of the regenerate are those who look to the correct principium: 'These only are taken into account, just as in natural science we reckon with those alone who are men of sound sense, i.e. who live by the natural principium' (1968: 391). The principium 'is itself *ground*, and therefore allows no ground *under* itself' (p. 355). The special principium is not simply to be equated with the Bible, for its 'sphere . . . is wider than the compass of Holy Scripture', and scripture is inert without the 'ever-present work of the Holy Spirit' (pp. 397, 398). The Bible is a product of the activity of the special principium. This activity embraces the whole plan of redemption, including signs and wonders, palingenesis, illumination, as well as the inspiration and formation of scripture. Yet God has chosen the written word as the form of his special revelation, by virtue of its durability, catholicity, fixedness, and purity (p. 405). The principium was active before the first page of scripture was written, but scripture contains the data of the completed revelation from which theology must be built up (p. 347). Kuyper does finally conclude, having arrived at a doctrine of scripture via Christ and the Holy Spirit, that scripture is the principium of the regenerate (p. 562).

Special revelation, Kuyper says, is most generally conceived of as inspiration (p. 349). Hence, unlike Warfield, he distinguishes the inspiration of revelation from the inspiration of scripture (pp. 362–3). Whereas Warfield's primary conception of inspiration is the plenary, verbal inspiration of scripture, Kuyper describes inspiration as an 'inworking of the Spirit of God upon the mind and heart of the sinner, by which God makes Himself known to him, and communicates His will or His thoughts' (p. 349). The real inspiration of scripture must be distinguished from the inspiration of the revelation so as to avoid a representation of 'a Bible dictated word for word' (p. 363). The Logos of God is 'entirely different from his spoken words' and in itself 'indicates merely the psyche of thought, independent of its somatic clothing in language and sound' (p. 476). The Logos of God 'is both violated and maimed, when it is sought in the spoken words only, and when consequently one speaks of the *words* of God in Scripture' (p. 477).

At times Kuyper seems to pre-empt Barth, as when he says, 'To him who does not feel that, at the moment when he opens the

Holy Scripture, God comes by and in it and touches his very soul, the Scripture is not yet the Word of God, or has ceased to be this; or it is this in his *spiritual* moments, but *not* at other times' (p. 364). Scripture is the 'document of the central Revelation' (p. 362).[18] It is not something by itself, which 'inserts itself with a certain independence between our consciousness and God, as the principium of *revelation*' (p. 364). The error of conceiving scripture to be verbally dictated can be overcome only by keeping in mind the distinction between the content and the form of scripture, and by separately considering the inspiration that operated in the revelation itself and the inspiration that operated in the compilation of the canon.

Kuyper makes particular mention of graphic inspiration (pp. 544–52). Graphic inspiration refers to 'that guidance given by the Spirit of God to the minds of the writers, compilers and editors of the Holy Scriptures', by which the sacred writings assumed the form predestined by God to be a means of grace for his Church (p. 545). The minds of the writers were directed to good tradition and trustworthy documents. Christ gave us no theory of graphic inspiration, 'but the nature of authority, which He and His apostles after Him attributed to the Scripture of His times, admits of no other solution' (p. 550).

We accept graphic inspiration on two grounds: the 'self-witness . . . of the Scripture, which it gives of itself in the central revelation of the Christ' (ibid.), and the deeper witness of the Holy Spirit (pp. 553–63). Faith that rests upon the testimony of Christ 'is more absolute in character', but 'is obtained by inference, and not by one's own apprehension' (p. 553). The '"witness of the Holy Spirit," . . . matures more slowly', but it is 'clearer and more in keeping with the freedom of the child of God' (p. 553). A process of conviction is worked in us spiritually and has nothing in common with the learning of the schools (p. 561). It is incapable of maintaining itself theoretically. First we stand before scripture 'as

[18] Bavinck (1956: 34) likewise considers the 'inscripturation of the Word of God' to be only one way in which 'a revelation of God comes to us'. Scripture is 'not the revelation itself, but the description, the record, from which the revelation can be known', yet it is not 'an incidental and defective' record (ibid. 95). As Kuyper (1968: 412) expresses it, no 'purely accidental' relation exists between the Revelation and its written form. Bavinck (1956: 100) is not averse to human analogies for understanding the inspiration of 'the recording of revelation', such as a person being 'guided by others in his thinking', or 'the inspiration of artists'.

before a foreign object' and are hostile to it. Then by the process of palingenesis we are changed in our inner being and acquire a 'modified view of ourselves, of the things of this world, and of the unseen world'. In this struggle 'the Holy Spirit opens our eyes, that in the Holy Scripture we may see a representation of our *ego*, of the world and of the eternal things, which *agree* with what we seek to defend in the combat against the naturalistic consciousness of the world' (pp. 557–8).

For Kuyper, scripture is recognized as the principium of theology by the 'sacred circle' of those who stand in palingenesis, in whom 'the positive conviction prevails that we have a graphically inspired Scripture, on which we lean and by which we live' (p. 562). Thanks to the witness of the Holy Spirit they become firmly convinced. If they look back to the first stage of their Christian life, to personal faith in the Saviour, they realize that Christ has presented the Holy Scripture, and that the communion of saints has adopted his understanding and been assured of it by the Holy Spirit. This assurance is neither diminished nor enhanced by the critical task: 'Assurance of faith and demonstration are two entirely heterogeneous things' (p. 563). To attempt to demonstrate the principium is to fail to understand that a principium 'can be no conclusion from other premises, but is itself *the* premise, from which all other conclusions are drawn' (p. 562). Thus scripture becomes for the regenerate the principium, 'i.e. the starting point, from which proceeds all knowledge of God, i.e. all *theology*' (p. 562).

6.3. Kuyper and the Princeton Theology

> No one, able to think and to ponder, has ever come either to palingenesis, to faith in the Christ as the Son of God, or to the acceptance of the Scripture, as the result of scientific investigation. Faith is of *a different kind*, and can never be plucked as fruit from the branches of science. Faith in, as well as the rejection of, the Christ and the Scripture . . . springs from the root of our spiritual existence.
>
> (Kuyper [1898] 1968: 459–60)

> [F]aith, in all its forms, is a conviction of truth, founded as such, of course, on evidence.
>
> (Warfield 1903*a*: 146)

6.3.1. *Method*

Kuyper considers faith to be the starting-point of all knowledge. The Princetonians regard faith as assent to evidence. Crucial differences in theological method follow. Kuyper rejects a fundamental contention of the Princeton theologians; that the truth of Christianity can be established through scientific study carried out on the basis of common principles.

Of particular interest is a passage in the *Encyclopedia* where Kuyper (1968: 318) criticizes Charles Hodge for choosing the facts of the Bible as the object of his theology. By giving priority to biblical facts Hodge loses the conception of ectypal theology: 'His combination of "facts and truths" overthrow his own system. He declares that the theologian must *authenticate* these truths. But then, of course, they are no *truths*, and only become such, when I authenticate them.' Hodge's mistake lay in his succumbing 'to the temptation of placing Theology formally in a line with the other sciences' (ibid.). Consequently the 'authentication of his "facts" brought him logically back again under the power of naturalistic science', although 'as a man of faith he bravely resisted this' (p. 319). Hodge's apologetic method renders itself inconsistent by introducing into theology the alien principle of naturalistic science.

6.3.2. *Scripture*

Kuyper and the Princeton theologians saw themselves as co-defenders of scripture against liberalism and higher criticism. Their approaches to scripture differed radically, although neither party drew attention to these differences.

According to Kuyper, one comes to recognize the authority of scripture through a life-relation with Christ and the testimony of the Holy Spirit. Kuyper rejects efforts to derive, from the outward appearance of scripture, proofs for its divine character. Such 'outward proofs' as 'the "heavenly majesty of the doctrines, the marvellous completeness of the prophecies, the wonderful miracles, the consent of all its parts, the divineness of the discourse,"' will not, he contends, 'convince the reason without *enlightenment*' (1968: 558).

He only, who in palingenesis had experienced *a miracle* in his own person, ceased to react against miracles, but rather invoked them himself. He who had observed the fulfilment of several prophecies in his own spiritual life, understood the relation between prophecy and fulfilment. He who heard the music of the Divine melody of redemption in his own soul was rapt in wonder . . . in listening to the Oratorio of Salvation proceeding from the heavenly majesty of doctrine in the Holy Scripture. (p. 558)

While Kuyper does himself defend the inspiration of scripture according to the self-testimony of scripture (pp. 428–41), he dismisses as circular and inconclusive the 'naive catechetical method' of proving inspiration from 2 Timothy 3: 16 and 2 Peter 1: 20–1. He reads these verses as informing us of scripture's interpretation of inspiration (pp. 428–9). They indicate that 'the apostles held the idea of inspiration, and applied it to the Old Testament', and that they viewed the Old Testament as one codex (p. 444). Kuyper regards the study of theology as necessarily circular, but he has in mind a different type of circularity: 'the glitter of the sapphire could only be proven by the sapphire; and . . . in like manner the divine majesty of the Holy Scripture could only shine out from that Scripture' (p. 387).

Like Warfield, Kuyper provides numerous scripture citations to illustrate Jesus' attitudes regarding the inspiration of the Old Testament (pp. 429–41). However, he believes that Jesus' testimony supports the authority of scripture not because scripture is inspired (which would be an ineffective circular argument) but because of the power of a life-relation with Christ: 'they only, who stand in conscious life-contact with the life-sphere of Christ can accept the force of demonstration, which lies in the testimony concerning the Scripture by Jesus, as its highest organ' (p. 430). The accuracy of scripture does not cause one to trust Christ's testimony. Rather, one's relation to Christ shapes one's attitude to Scripture:

if by palingenesis you stand vitally related to the Christ as 'the head of the body,' the relation between your consciousness and the Holy Scripture is born from this of itself. But if that relation of the palingenesis does not bind you to the Christ of God as head of the body of the new humanity, you cannot kneel before Him in worship, neither can the Scripture be to you a Holy Scripture. (p. 459)

Kuyper rejects the argument that 'one learns to know the Christ from the Scripture, so that faith in the Saviour can follow only upon a preceding faith in the Scripture'. Reading scripture without illumination will not bring a single soul from death to life. 'The Scripture by itself is as dull as a diamond in the dark; and as the diamond glistens only when entered by a ray of light, the Scripture has power to charm the eye of the soul only when seen in the light of the Holy Spirit' (p. 551). One who confesses the Holy Scripture to be the principium of theology should be able to give account of this in order that the confession be rational. However, 'this ratiocination can neither for himself be the ground on which his confession stands, nor ever compel the opponent to come to this confession'. The witness of the Holy Spirit is 'the only power which can carry into our consciousness the certainty concerning the special principium' (p. 388).

As noted above, Kuyper does not equate the Word of God with the words of the Bible. He makes the common point that a word of Satan is not a word of God, but he also disputes that every saying of men or even of God's ambassadors which occurs in scripture is a divine saying. We need the guidance of the Holy Spirit to distinguish 'the gold from the ore' (p. 474). God uses human instruments as they are. The forms or types in scripture bear a mixed character, 'marred by want and sin' (p. 479). They are '"shadows" . . . humanly imperfect, far beneath their ideal content':

> This produces a result like what occurs in the case of many paintings of the latest French school, in which, at first sight, one sees, indeed, bubbles and daubs of paint, and even tints and lines, but not *the image*; and only after repeated attempts a view is finally obtained, so that those daubs and bubbles disappear, the tints and lines become active, and the image stands out before us. (p. 479)

Kuyper comes closest to Warfield's position in the following passage where he defends the unity of scripture:

> This unity becomes apparent when Jesus simply quotes it with an 'It is written,' and when, by His authority likewise, *the Holy Scripture* becomes the name by which it is called. In this sense *the* Scripture is *the* Word of God, and every distinction, by which we have only a Word of God *in* the Scripture, is a denial of its essentia or being. (p. 473)

He says earlier that Jesus attributes authority sometimes even '*to single words*' (p. 435), and he believes that an error on Jesus' part regarding the authority of the Old Testament would be to the detriment of his person and character (p. 457) and would entail 'a condemnation of Jesus' whole interpretation of His task' (p. 458).

However, Kuyper helpfully distinguishes two separate issues. He argues, in effect, that while Christ cannot be wrong about scripture's authority, scripture need not itself be inerrant. Biblical authority does not take such a form that errors and inconsistencies in scripture would undermine it:

> with reference to the Holy Scripture, there are . . . many remarks that have been made on logical incongruities, either in the economy of the Scripture itself, or between it and cosmic and historic reality outside of it, which, unless our confession is to lose its reasonable character, claim an answer from our side; but though these remarks might compel us to make confession in our turn of a partial agnosticism, or to subject the dogma of inspiration to revision, to us the special principium will never lose thereby its characteristic supremacy. (p. 386)

Kuyper rejects historical criticism not in order to preserve inerrancy, but so as to avoid testing scripture by the natural principium. Scripture is its own self-testimony. If a Christian theologian acknowledges in one cardinal point the assertions of historical criticism, Kuyper argues, he has lost his grasp upon the whole principium by which his theology lives (ibid.).

The sense of scripture is sought in the freedom enjoyed by the Holy Spirit, its 'primary author' (p. 450). For example, inaccurate quotations of the Old Testament in the New reflect the practice of a 'writer who quotes himself [and so] is bound to the actual content only, and not to the form of what he wrote' (p. 450). The Holy Spirit is 'entirely justified in repeating his original meaning . . . in a somewhat modified form' (ibid.). It is interesting to contrast Kuyper's solution in this respect with that of John Wenham, who, more typically of evangelical apologists, defends the authority of scripture in terms suitable for verifying human testimony. Wenham ([1972] 1993: 204 n. 19) accounts for the seeming inaccuracies in the New Testament's quotations of Old Testament passages by reference to the 'humanity of the Scriptures' with which the Spirit had to work:

> Preservation from error does not involve the destruction of normal mental processes. Interestingly, in ordinary life, freedom of quotation is often a sign of mastery of one's material. The more sure a teacher is that he understands the writer the less is he afraid of expounding his ideas in

terms that are not precisely those of the author. When he is not sure, he quotes exactly . . .

For Kuyper, that thousands have obtained full assurance and certainty despite the absence of empirical certainty in interpretation, deduction and formulation, is a 'guarantee' that the Holy Spirit has dominion (pp. 598–9). It is the work of the Spirit, not the force of Christian evidences, that leads one to certainty.

6.3.3. *Apologetics*

Although Kuyper differed from Hodge over method and from Warfield over scripture, the issue over which Warfield and Kuyper overtly disagreed was the nature and legitimacy of apologetics.

Kuyper postulates that there are two types of people each with their own world-view and body of science. Argument by means of reason and evidences cannot bridge the divide. The notion that science might settle this dispute is in vain, 'for we speak of two all-embracing representations of the object, both of which have been obtained as the result of very serious scientific study' (1968: 117–18). Little evidence is neutral except for that which is objective and, by that token, of the lowest order and the furthest removed from the fundamental principles of life. The difference wrought between people through palingenesis renders futile 'every effort to understand each other . . . in those points of the investigation in which this difference comes into play; and it will be impossible to settle the difference of insight' (p. 160). As soon as apologetics has 'allowed itself to be inveigled into details, and has undertaken to deal with things that are not palpable phenomena or logical mistakes', it has 'failed to reach results, and has weakened rather than strengthened the reasoner' (p. 160).

Rational argument cannot vindicate Christianity, but finds its true coherence only in a Christian system. The fundamental principle of one's life-system cannot be changed by argument, but only by an act of God. Human reason is insufficient but the opponent will not grant this fact. Standing outside the spiritual illumination, 'he does not perceive, and cannot perceive, the real condition of his own being nor of his reason' (pp. 384–5). He tries to force his consciousness on us 'and claims that our consciousness has to be identical with his own' (1932: 208). Kuyper did not explicitly criticize his friends at Princeton for their belief in common human consciousness, but on their home-ground he quoted scripture to reiterate his point: 'Except a man be born again, he *cannot see* the Kingdom of God' (ibid. 209). Unless, in the soul of men, God bears witness to the truth of His Word, 'men *can* no longer believe, and no apologetics, however brilliant, will ever be able to restore the blessing of faith in the Scripture' (1968: 366).

Warfield criticizes the anti-apologetical nature of Kuyper's and Bavinck's thought in two writings of 1903: a review article of Bavinck's *De Zekerheid des Geloofs* (*The Certainty of Faith*) in the *Princeton Theological Review*, and his 'Introduction' to Francis Beattie's *Apologetics*. He is bemused by their approach, and attributes their 'minifying the value of Apologetics' to 'a tendency to make the contrast between the "two kinds of science"—that of nature and that of palingenesis—too absolute' (1903*a*: 145).[19] Warfield agrees that there are two kinds of men, those under the power of sin and those under the power of palingenesis, and consequently that there are two kinds of science. However, he describes the difference between them as one of degree, not of kind. It is '"science" that is produced by the sinful object even though imperfect science' (1903*a*: 145). Thus, the science of sinful man is a substantive though less valuable part of the science produced by the general human consciousness: 'Even sinful men and sinless men are alike fundamentally men; and being both men, *they know fundamentally alike*. There is ideally but one science, the subject of which is the human spirit, and the object, all that is' (ibid., emphasis added). Superior science will eventually be recognized by the unregenerate also, since all humanity is working from the same principles: 'Just as the better science ever in the end secures its recognition, so palingenetic science, which is the better science, will certainly win its way to ultimate recognition' (ibid.

[19] Bavinck's position is less antithetical than Kuyper's. Warfield could, I think, agree with Bavinck (1956: 41–2) that '"evidences" are not enough to compel a man to believe', and appreciate with Bavinck that the appeal of evidences is not 'solely to [man's] analytical and ratiocinative mind, but also to his heart and feeling, his reason and conscience'. However, Bavinck (ibid. 42), like Kuyper, regards evidences as 'strengthening the faith', whereas Warfield regards them as furnishing rational grounds on which faith can rest.

146). Apologetics is vindicated because here too the man of stronger and purer thought will ultimately prevail:

> It is not true that he cannot soundly prove his position. It is not true that the arguments he urges are not sufficient to validate the Christian religion. It is not even true that the minds of sinful men are inaccessible to his 'evidences': though in the sense of the proverb, 'convinced against their will they remain of the same opinion still.' On the contrary, men (all of whose minds are after all of the same essential structure with his own, though less illuminated than his) will not be able to resist or gainsay his determinations. (ibid.)

Not that apologetics will cause one to embrace Christianity—only the 'Spirit of life' can do that (ibid.)—but 'apologetics supplies to Christian men the systematically organized basis on which the faith of Christian men must rest' ([1908]: 16). Warfield (1903*b*: 20) equates Kuyper's position with a mysticism which construes Christian conviction as 'the immediate creation of the Holy Spirit in his heart'. Kuyper believes that faith 'gives highest assurance' when it is immediate. He regards as absurd all faith in God and scripture 'which does not bear this immediate character, and would borrow its assurance from any course of reasoning' (1968: 366–7). Warfield espouses a chain of reasoning that would render immediacy impossible or at least improper. In this respect Warfield differs also from Charles Hodge, who argued that knowledge of God is innate and intuitive. Warfield (1903*b*: 24) insists that we must

> assure ourselves that there is knowledge of God in the Scriptures. And, before we do that, we must assure ourselves that there is a knowledge of God in the world. And, before we do that, we must assure ourselves that a knowledge of God is possible for man. And, before we do that, we must assure ourselves that there is a God to know. And in working thus back to first principles, we exhibit the indispensability of an 'Apologetical Theology'.

It will usually not take the whole 'body of evidences' to convince an individual, but surely, Warfield (1903*a*: 146) reasons, 'he does require that kind and amount of evidence which is requisite to convince him before he can really be convinced'. Faith, though a gift, still requires 'grounds in right reason'. Only the prepared heart 'can fitly respond to the "reasons"; but how can even a prepared heart respond, when there are no "reasons" to draw out its action?' (1903*b*: 25).

6.3.4. *The Significance of Kuyper's Differences with Princeton*

Disagreement between Kuyper and Warfield over the existence of a common consciousness is arguably less substantial than their different conceptions of the path to faith. Kuyper's (1968: 219, 610) absolute distinction between the two types of people and their science is undermined by his depiction of re-creation as a 'gradual' and sometimes 'a very long process'. This process entails that a person remains in some measure tied to the old life. Indeed, 'the slow process which must ensue before any activity can develop itself from what potentially is given in palingenesis' accounts for the fact that the two kinds of science have 'remained for the most part interlaced' (p. 162). Kuyper, like Warfield, rejects Perfectionism—the teaching that sanctification can be completed in this life—and believes that palingenesis is 'destined to reach completion in a higher life' (pp. 162–3). Moreover, Kuyper concludes that ultimately there is only one science, that of regenerated humanity, to which the unregenerate contribute by performing the lowlier tasks (pp. 602–3). Warfield (1903*b*: 28) agrees that the regenerate have 'the better scientific outlook, and the better scientific product'. Kuyper (1968: 272) thinks that development would have been a feature even of sinless existence. Therefore, a distinction of a kind Warfield could acknowledge, between inferior and superior science, is implicit in his system without there needing to be an absolute distinction between two types of people.

The more significant difference between Warfield and Kuyper, though one to which neither drew much attention, is their ordering of faith and evidence. For Warfield the presentation of evidence is basic to a person's arrival at faith, though the catalyst is the action of the Holy Spirit. Having arrived at faith one attempts to vindicate one's position and to think through and organize its defence by finding further evidences. Kuyper, by contrast, begins and ends with a faith for which he provides a rational form. One might say that for Warfield there is a linear process in which understanding and belief develop together, whereas for Kuyper understanding demonstrates that the circle of reasoning in which the faith of the regenerate moves is a virtuous circle.

Since Kuyper regarded faith as more basic than evidence, the influence of his thought in America has the potential to challenge what Sandeen, Barr, and Rogers regard as Princeton's inversion of the Westminster Confession, namely, a preoccupation with reason which displaced the testimony of the Holy Spirit. We shall see in the next chapter, however, that this potential is quashed wherever Kuyper's doctrine of scripture is assumed to be fundamentally the same as Warfield's.

7

Kuyperians and Warfieldians

In the middle of this century there emerged two camps of evangelical scholars with some hybrids in between. George Marsden (1983; 1989) calls these the Warfieldians and Kuyperians, although he says they 'do not necessarily identify themselves as such or follow their mentors precisely' (1989: 47). The former expect knowledge of God to be arrived at by scientific enquiry, the latter accord it the status of a first principle. The Warfieldian line has been dominant in mainstream American evangelicalism, and is prominent also in British evangelicalism. However, there has long been a Kuyperian presence in North America and a smaller but not insignificant influence in Britain.

Kuyperian thought was transported to North America in the two waves of Dutch immigration: at the end of the nineteenth century, at the time of Kuyper's greatest influence at home; and after World War II. Dutch Americans made their religious and intellectual centre at Grand Rapids, home of Calvin College and Seminary, and of the publishing houses William B. Eerdmans, Zondervan, and Baker Book House. The Dutch Reformed and American evangelical communities interacted institutionally and theologically. The Dutch publishing houses became major publishers not only of Dutch and Dutch-American theology, but also of American and British evangelical writings (Noll 1986: 100–5). Dutch Reformed thought became 'Americanized',[1] which involved among other things placing a greater emphasis upon reasoned apologetics and, for some, a Princetonian

[1] James Bratt (1984: 219–20) describes the 'Americanization' of Dutch Reformed immigrants throughout this century in terms of their contact with American evangelicalism. Generally Dutch Americans sided with the 'fundamentalists' against the 'modernists' in the first half of the century (ibid. 127–34), some even adopting premillennial ideas (pp. 94–8, 132). H. J. Kuiper earned for his camp the ascription 'Reformed Fundamentalism' by advocating loyalty to the NAE in the 1940s (p. 200), and in 1970 Lewis Smedes moved from Calvin College to Fuller Seminary (p. 216). Carl Henry made a conscious effort to form alliances between the evangelical and the Dutch Reformed communities, as illustrated by his having several members of the Christian Reformed Church on the staff of *Christianity Today* (Noll 1986: 100).

doctrine of scripture. Thus the Dutch came to share in the fundamentalist evangelical heritage: 'Faith became knowledge, and that not an intuitive grasping but a rational assent to specific propositions. Religious feeling became secondary in the sequence of salvation, and so also in value and importance' (Bratt 1984: 134). Meanwhile, American evangelicals 'Dutchified', that is, they came 'to models of theology, society, and hermeneutics that were pioneered by Dutch Calvinists . . . and that they predicted would mark the path America itself would have to take as the problems of modernity struck home' (ibid. 220). Evangelicalism acquired a recognition of presuppositions and of the plurality of world-views. Calvin College has sustained a Kuyperian influence, albeit one more moderate in tone than the strongly antithetical standpoints promoted by Herman Dooyeweerd in the Netherlands and Cornelius Van Til in the United States (Geehan 1971: p. viii; W. Young 1952: 96–7; Rushdoony 1959: 181).

7.1. Introduction to the Thought of Van Til and Dooyeweerd

Van Til's influence lies in the area of apologetical method. For a Kuyperian, Van Til had a narrow agenda: to pulverize the Kantian influence on modern theology. To this end he spoke much of presuppositions and little of world-view. He represents a conservative, defensive side of the Dutch Reformed theologians, some of whom, such as G. C. Berkouwer and more markedly H. M. Kuitert of the Free University in Amsterdam, have been conciliatory and revisionary.[2] He stood out in the middle of this century as a conservative Reformed thinker in the States who attacked what he called traditional apologetics, including those of old Princeton. Van Til reinstituted apologetics while accepting Kuyper's point that to defend the existence of God or the truth of scripture by appeal to evidence and autonomous reasoning is to

[2] Van Til reviewed Berkouwer's early work favourably, but criticized his later writing, such as *Holy Scripture* ([1966] 1975), for displaying Kantian and neo-Barthian traits and for basing its doctrine of scripture upon the idea of 'autonomous man' (1967: 133–56). Kuitert received scathing criticism from Van Til in *The New Hermeneutic* (1974). He recently wrote the Dutch religious bestseller *I Have My Doubts: How to Become a Christian Without Being a Fundamentalist* ([1992] 1993).

deny that God is all and that scripture is our ultimate authority. He is credited with developing 'Dutch convictions about the noetic effects of the Fall into a complete "presuppositional" theology' (Noll 1983: 42), and is generally regarded as the 'father of presuppositionalism' in America (Geehan 1971: p. xiii).[3]

Dooyeweerd's influence has been philosophical and social. Dooyeweerd was professor of jurisprudence at the Free University of Amsterdam from 1926 to 1965. He and his colleague D. H. Th. Vollenhoven developed the fundamental principles of Kuyper's world-view into a philosophy. They sought a theoretical framework which could serve Christian thought and action in every sphere. The philosophy came to be named after Dooyeweerd's *De wijsbegeerte der wetsidee* (1935–6), 'The Philosophy of the Law-Idea' (or Cosmonomic Idea). This work was revised and translated into English under the title *A New Critique of Theoretical Thought* (4 vols., 1953–8), a title which reflects Dooyeweerd's fundamental aim to expose the dogma of the autonomy of theoretical thought. Dooyeweerd argued that every discipline is permeated by philosophical principles which betray religious allegiances.[4] To gain an idea of how Dooyeweerd presented these ideas, it is worth looking briefly at his extension and transformation of Kuyper's concept of 'sphere sovereignty' (Dooyeweerd 1979: 40–60).

In his opening address to the Free University of Amsterdam (1880) and in his Stone Lectures on Calvinism ([1898] 1932: 125–69), Kuyper spoke of societal spheres, such as the state, the church, school, and the family. He described these spheres as each having its own identity, laws, and sovereignty, and as finding its source of authority in God, the absolute sovereign. Dooyeweerd (1979: 44) propounded a more comprehensive ontology in which he distinguished 'two types of structure within temporal reality', with sphere sovereignty pertaining to both. The first is the

[3] This is to the chagrin of Gordon H. Clark's devoted followers, who claim for Clark the truly presuppositional position. John W. Robbins (1986) promotes Clark's thought, and resents Van Til being accorded status of 'Mr. Presuppositionalist himself'. He argues that since Van Til does not reject arguments for the existence of God this 'removes him from the presuppositionalist camp'. Van Til (1963: 197; 1969: 292) accepts theistic proofs, but insists on 'formulating them in such a way as not to compromise the doctrines of Scripture'. Clark ([1973] 1977: 121) advocates 'dogmatism'—'an all-inclusive system [which] has no propositions in common with any other system', and which has as its 'axioms the propositions of Scripture' (1990: 6).

[4] The most helpful introduction to Dooyeweerd's thought is L. Kalsbeek's *Contours of a Christian Philosophy* (1975).

structure of the various 'aspects of reality' or 'modes of being' which are sovereign within 'law-spheres'. The second is the '*concrete* structure of reality' which we experience in daily life: things, events, acts, and societal relationships which function within these aspects. Fig. 7.1 sets out the law-spheres with their respective sovereign aspects, and illustrates their relation to some of the societal structures of reality.[5]

The law-spheres correspond to the various fields of modern scientific study. The highest of the law-spheres (not as a superior sphere but as that which most clearly engages the human heart) is the pistical sphere, where faith is the sovereign aspect and theology is the science. Theology 'studies divine revelation in christian and nonchristian faith' (Dooyeweerd 1979: 41). It is not queen of the sciences: it does not draw all the sciences together, but is itself studied within a theoretical framework and therefore should not be made absolute. Any attempt to reduce reality to only one aspect is idolatrous because it lacks the true knowledge that God alone is absolute (ibid.). For example, historicism reduces all of reality to the historical aspect and so views 'the truths of the christian faith [as] just as relative and transient as the ideals of the French Revolution'. Modern materialism reduces everything to particles of matter in motion. Modern naturalism sees everything in terms of the development of organic life (pp. 41, 42).

Dooyeweerd argued that 'what drives us to absolutize is not science as such but an idolatrous ground motive'. Science itself teaches us nothing about the deeper unity and origin of these aspects. Only religion, which directs us towards the absolute ground and origin of all things, can provide us with a theoretical framework for conceiving reality.[6] False religious prejudices result in false ground motives which absolutize one aspect of created reality. The true ground motive is the 'scriptural ground motive of the christian religion', which 'drives us to examine the inner

[5] For a succinct exposition and rare critical analysis of Dooyeweerd's schema with respect to the way that modal aspects determine the identity to the societal spheres see Chaplin (1995).

[6] In Dooyeweerd's system, religion rather than theology provides the theoretical framework. A major problem with this system is the extent to which Dooyeweerd's understanding of the Christian ground motive, which he calls the 'creation motive', is itself a theological interpretation. Despite Dooyeweerd's protestations to the contrary, theology is instrumental to the formation of this creation motive that '*God created everything after its own kind*' (1979: 43).

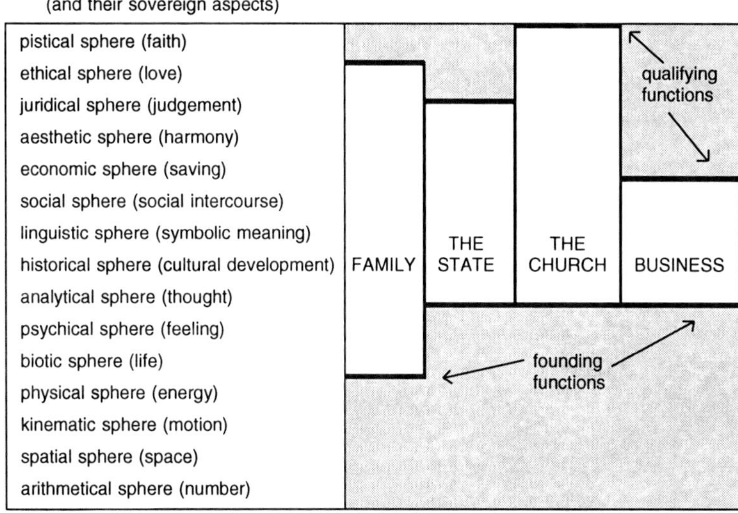

FIG. 7.1 A partial depiction of Dooyeweerd's schema (Harriet A. Harris)

nature, mutual relation, and coherence of all the aspects in God's created reality' (ibid.). When we become conscious of this motive we realize both the pluriformity of aspects in God's creation and the 'religious root unity' of these aspects (pp. 42–3). Idolatrous 'isms', such as historicism and materialism, result from failure to recognize the aspects' mutual irreducibility and proper coherence. Dooyeweerd's conviction that 'the religious ground motive of our life governs and determines our whole view of reality' (p. 47), and that different ground motives are in conflict, gives his philosophy both urgency and breadth:

> Is it not obvious that an irreconcilable antithesis is at work between the christian religion and the service of an idol? In the light of the conflict between the different ground motives, can we still maintain that the christian religion is meaningful only for our life of faith and not for our view of reality? . . . Either [the christian religion] is a leaven that permeates all our life and thought or it is nothing more than a theory, which fails to touch us inwardly. (ibid.)

Sphere sovereignty pertains not only to law-spheres but also to societal spheres such as the family, church, state, and economic enterprise. Societal spheres are not arranged hierarchically. Each has a different qualifying function or aspect, which leads the other functions and which determines the sphere's distinct identity and destination. The church's qualifying function is faith, the family's is love (the ethical sphere), and the state's is judgement (the juridical sphere). Like the law-spheres, societal spheres are both irreducible to and coherent with one another. Each has its appropriate role, and if one sphere should try to dominate the others, all become distorted. Our view of their 'inner nature, mutual relation, and coherence . . . is governed by our religious point of departure', hence our religious ground motive is of political and social importance (ibid.). Dooyeweerd developed his theory of societal sphere sovereignty in the aftermath of World War II, when his 'spiritually uprooted nation' was recovering from Nazi occupation (p. 55). Sphere sovereignty guards against totalitarianism by guaranteeing each societal sphere 'an intrinsic nature and law of life' while also attributing sovereign authority to God alone (p. 48).[7]

In reality, practice in the different societal spheres manifests a plurality of ground motives and hence of world-views. Dooyeweerd argued that with 'the christian ground motive we discover the true principles for political life and for societal life as a whole' (p. 47). Those influenced by his philosophy therefore seek to promote a Christian world-view within the different spheres. Fig. 7.2 demonstrates how one Dooyeweerdian depicts this system.

Dooyeweerd's schema resists division of the various law-spheres and societal spheres into sacred and secular realms. It depicts our religious ground motive as permeating our societal life and theoretical thought in all spheres. Dooyeweerd called for a 'staff of fellow-labourers' who would put his basic ideas 'to work in their own speciality' (1953: p. vii). His philosophy came to affect Anglo-American evangelicalism culturally, educationally, politically, and

[7] A clear defence of such a position, especially in relation to Kuyper's thought, is given in McCarthy *et al.*, *Society, State, & Schools: A Case for Structural and Confessional Pluralism* (1981). The pluralism is 'structural' in that it conceives creation as a plurality of structures, each performing its unique function in a unified operation. It is confessional in that it recognizes the plurality of faiths and philosophies in our world, and protects the religious liberty of different communities within the public order.

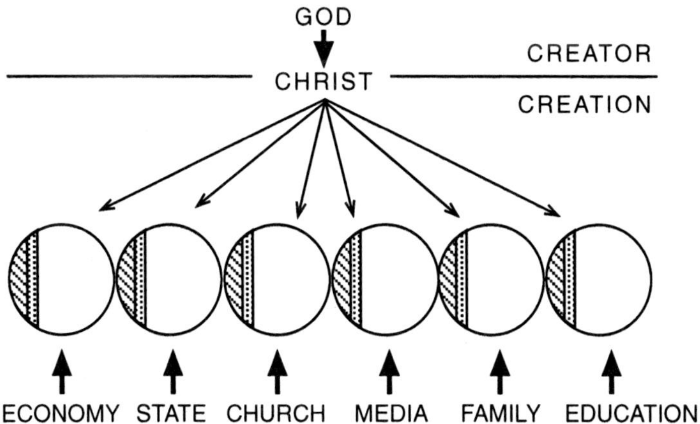

FIG. 7.2 Structural and confessional pluralism (Richard Russell)

socially, through persons who caught the breadth of his vision. To this extent the Dutch influence has provided an alternative to some fundamentalist tendencies that have dominated British and American evangelicalism this century. In particular, it challenges manifestations of sacred–secular dualism such as the withdrawal from 'worldly' involvement in politics and culture, and the preoccupation with theological and biblical studies to the neglect of other areas of scholarship.

Both Van Til and Dooyeweerd stressed the antithetical side of Kuyper's thought over that of common grace:

> it is imperative to understand that 'common grace' does not weaken or eliminate the antithesis (opposition) between the ground motive of the christian religion and the apostate ground motives.
>
> (Dooyeweerd 1979: 38)

> While . . . it is of the utmost consequence to recognize the fact of a 'common consciousness' of God as the revelational pressure of God on man, it is of no less importance to note that, in so far as men are aware

of their most basic alliances, they are wholly for or wholly against God at every point of interest to man. (Van Til 1963: 212)

Unlike the majority of evangelicals they did not regard subjectivism as their main enemy, for they acknowledged with Kuyper the necessary and potentially positive presence of subjectivity in all human activities. In Van Til's (1963: 67) words, the 'human mind as the knowing subject, makes its contribution to the knowledge it obtains'. Their fight was against the pretence to human autonomy, 'the self-sufficiency of human reason' (Dooyeweerd 1953: p. v), which they saw as epitomized in Enlightenment philosophy. 'There can be no appeasement', Van Til (1950: 19) insisted, 'between those who presuppose in all their thought the sovereign God and those who presuppose in all their thought the would-be sovereign man'. They did not deny the possibility of 'objective knowledge', so long as 'objective' was not understood to mean 'neutral': 'the world of objects was made in order that the subject of knowledge, namely man, should interpret it under God. Without the interpretation of the universe by man to the glory of God the whole world would be meaningless' (Van Til 1963: 43).

Dooyeweerd and Van Til began as allies, Van Til being the first major contact for Dooyeweerd's philosophy in America (Zylstra 1975: 28). They later came to suspect one another of undermining the antithesis and granting too much autonomy to human thought. Each found the other's critique of human thought insufficiently radical. Van Til had originally felt that Dooyeweerd's *De wijsbegeerte der wetsidee* supported his own apologetical exercise, but he questioned Dooyeweerd's later stance in the *New Critique* (Van Til 1971*b*). He criticized Dooyeweerd for raising philosophy above scripture and refusing to make Christian truth determinative for his method of transcendental criticism:

you constantly speak of creation, fall, and redemption. . . . But what you say on the subjects seems to come into the picture too late and in the way of a *Deus ex machina* into your main argument. You seem to me not to have given them their proper place at the outset of the argument, and you have *not presented them as the presupposition of the possibility of analyzing the structure of theoretical thought and experience.* (1971*b*: 98–9)

Like Kuyper, Dooyeweerd introduces scripture after he has established the need for such a starting-point. He generates an account of theory which reveals the dependence of all theory on 'ground motive' (1971: 82). Only then does he promote the proper ground motive as the biblical story-line. Dooyeweerd does not regard the biblical story, creation–fall–redemption, as knowledge which can be theologically or philosophically formulated. He sees it rather as a 'central motive power', the key to true knowledge which clenches the heart and so assumes central religious significance. By the Holy Spirit who works through scripture this power grips us and operates in the religious centre of our consciousness and existence ([1960] 1980: 143–8).

Van Til (1971*b*: 102) objects that one cannot deduce from theoretical thought a biblical ground motive. It is not possible to 'analyze theoretical thought *as such* and show that it points to the Christian story. . . . Theoretical thought is what it is only as it is seen to be operating as revelatory of the Christian story'. He presupposes from the beginning that 'Christian truth'—a concept which he merges with God as the Absolute Ideal, and with the ontological trinity, and with scripture—provides the only true starting-point: 'There is no autonomy of theoretical thought *as such*. . . . Every item that man meets in his temporal horizon *is already interpreted by God*' (ibid.: 109). Van Til combines Kuyperian thought with British Transcendental Idealism, which he studied at Calvin College and Princeton University. The British school informs his emphasis that you understand the part only in the light of the whole. Everything finds its reference point in God, the Absolute Ideal, which for Van Til must be triune.

Dooyeweerd (1971: 81), for his part, finds a 'rationalistic scholastic tendency' in Van Til's thought. According to Dooyeweerd, knowledge comes via the heart. Scripture proclaims that the heart is the 'religious root of human existence', but the Word of God is in all of creation, and it impacts the heart immediately. Theologians have no special access to the knowledge of God, and theology is not to be conceived as the queen of the sciences (Dooyeweerd [1960] 1980; Kalsbeek 1975: 66).[8] Van Til (1963: 8)

[8] Dooyeweerd attacks this Thomist conception of theology and also criticizes Christians for neglecting other disciplines. Not surprisingly, then, fewer Dooyeweerdians work in theology than in other areas. Those who do, develop their theology by reference to the framework of creation, fall, and redemption, rather than by deduction from such principles as God's omniscient, omnipotent or triune nature. This is in keeping with Dooyeweerd's rejection of the scholastic method. Gordon J. Spykman (1992: 7), from Calvin College, credits Berkouwer with liberating Reformed theology from the scholastic mould. Spykman himself attempts a comprehensive *Reformational Theology* (1992) based upon the philosophy of

regards scripture as the starting-point in a theoretical sense, 'as authoritative on everything of which it speaks', and speaking of 'everything either directly or indirectly'. In the words of one critic, he conceives it 'as a book of knowledge', commitment to which 'can solve the difficult Kantian problem of knowledge and assure that we have valid rational and objective answers to our life questions' (Rogers 1971: 164). He endorses Warfield's doctrine of scripture while rejecting an evidentialist defence of this doctrine (Van Til 1967: 20–6). This introduces an inconsistency at the heart of Van Til's method. Warfield's inerrantist doctrine cannot be embraced without an accompanying assumption that biblical truth is justified in relation to reason and evidences. That Van Til goes a significant way with Warfield blunts the challenge of his presuppositionalist critique. As a result, Van Til's success in providing an alternative to the rational empiricism encouraged by Princeton has been limited.

7.2. Cornelius Van Til

Van Til was born in the Netherlands in 1895, and his family migrated to the United States in 1905. He studied at Calvin College and Princeton University. He then became one in a line of Dutch Americans who went to Princeton Theological Seminary after Geerhardus Vos had joined the faculty there. Dutch Americans trusted Princeton as the stalwart of Presbyterian orthodoxy in the New World, and were united with them in upholding the authority of scripture. Van Til taught for a year at Princeton, resigning when the Seminary was reorganized in 1929. At Machen's request, he agreed to teach at Westminster Theological Seminary. He remained professor of apologetics there until his death.[9] Despite working with those who were at the centre of

the Law-Idea. He divides his dogmatics into parts entitled 'The Good Creation', 'Sin and Evil', 'The Way of Salvation', and 'The Consummation'. That Van Til begins with a conception of God as absolute and with such doctrines as divine immutability, eternity, and unity, fuels Dooyeweerd's charge that his theology is 'rationalistic scholastic'.

[9] Van Til was a member of the Christian Reformed Church (CRC), the more conservative of the two main Dutch denominations, the other being the Reformed Church of America (RCA). RCA was the historic Dutch church in America originating in the colonial days; CRC was founded by immigrants in the 19th c. After the schism in the Princeton faculty, the CRC contributed to Westminster Seminary both financially and academically

American fundamentalism in the 1920s and 1930s, Van Til (1963: 237) described his views as Reformed, and rejected the position of 'the "evangelical" or Arminian fundamentalist'. He objected to the emphasis upon free will in conversion, and to an over-reliance on human reasoning in evangelical apologetics (ibid. 139–46). Hence his reservations over the labels 'evangelical' and 'fundamentalist' reflect a feeling not that the movements they denote are too theologically rigid, but that they are not sufficiently strict in delimiting human autonomy.

Van Til (ibid. 208) estimates that Kuyper's *Encyclopedia* has, 'more than any other work in modern times, brought out the fact of the difference between the approach of the believer and of the unbeliever'. He develops the view that there are two totalitarian systems founded upon opposing presuppositions, which interpret the facts of the universe differently. However, he inverts Kuyper's theology. Kuyper understood faith in the truthfulness of scripture to flow from one's life-relation to Christ. Van Til's apologetical 'aim is to interpret all of life in terms of basic truths derived from the Scriptures of the Old and New Testaments as the infallible rule of faith and practice' (1969: Introd.). He takes 'the final standard of truth to be the Bible itself' (1963: 32). He overlooks Kuyper's significant distinctions between God's self-knowledge and our ectypal knowledge of God, between revelation and the graphic inspiration of scripture, and between the bare words of scripture and the Bible operating as the Word of God. Van Til's doctrine of scripture is closer to that of Warfield.[10]

However, Van Til finds that having accepted Warfield's doctrine of scripture he cannot follow him in his apologetics. Warfield's apologetics are 'based upon the idea of human autonomy' (1969: 251). The Christian faith 'is faith based on evidence' (ibid. 250), but not evidence interpreted autonomously.

with two professors: Van Til and R. B. Kuiper. Two RCA figures, Kuizenga and Samuel Zwemer, joined the new Princeton faculty to uphold the moderate conservative position (Bratt 1984: 127).

[10] Jack Rogers (1971: 162) accuses Van Til of viewing scripture as a 'system of truth yielding information', and finds him no less guilty than Old Princeton of distorting the Westminster Confession. Rogers argues that Van Til, like Warfield, believes that 'the Holy Spirit enables us to accept reasonable truth', whereas the emphasis of the Westminster divines was not rational proof but relation to the person of Christ (p. 161). Vander Stelt (1978: 264–70, esp. 267) also attributes to Van Til an 'intellectualistic . . . understanding of scripture'.

Human autonomy, Van Til explains, 'distorts the doctrine of Scripture itself by finding the ultimate exegetical tool in the subjective experience of human freedom, and by denying to Scripture and the Holy Spirit the power, authority and necessity of invading the souls of men' (1971*a*: 9). Man's assumption of his own autonomy is a manifestation of his sinfulness. It leads man to interpret the world without reference to God, the Absolute, and so to fall into inconsistency in attempting to make himself, a creature, his ideal or final reference point (1969: 21–2).

Van Til was influenced by the British Transcendental Idealists, F. H. Bradley, T. H. Green, and Bernard Bosanquet. He studied their philosophy under W. Harry Jellema at Calvin College and Archibald Alexander Bowman at Princeton University, and wrote his Ph.D. for Princeton on 'God and the Absolute' (Vander Stelt 1978: 225–30). The British Idealists' understanding of the particular in relation to the universal led Van Til to reason in the opposite direction from that of Princeton. Van Til (1955*b*: 42) worked from the system to the fact, rather than from facts to theories: 'the *whole* must be prior to the part if there is to be a fruitful methodology'. He shared the Idealist position that facts in themselves are meaningless unless interpreted in light of the whole. The only true, rational, and coherent interpretation is that which recognizes God as the timeless Absolute, and 'the Bible as the Voice of the Absolute' (ibid. 80). Truth is not determined by correspondence to facts. Rather, facts acquire their truth or coherence in relation to the Absolute.

Hence, Van Til's theory of truth is not the straightforward correspondence theory that Barr (1977: 49) finds among 'fundamentalists', but nor is it so simple a coherence theory as Pinnock (1971*b*: 421) alleges: 'that things are true if they hang together in a system'.[11] Van Til affirms the principles of coherence: that fact and interpretation cannot be separated; that facts must be set into a system of relationships in order to be intelligible; that the general precedes the particular such that to know the grounds of any one

[11] The mistake here lies less with Van Til than with Pinnock's unsophisticated conception of the coherence theory of truth, as requiring nothing more than internal consistency. F. H. Bradley (1914: 325) conceded the 'obvious view' that truth, 'to be true, must be true of something, and this something itself is not truth'. The problem, he said, was to ascertain its proper meaning. He interpreted this relation as being not between a factor in our knowing and a real fact, but between a one-sided aspect of reality and reality as a whole.

fact one must understand the general principles governing the universe upon which all facts depend. For Van Til (1963: 40), God is the 'self-complete system of coherence'. Truth is determined not by a mere consistency or 'hanging together', but by God's interpretation of the universe. God is the Absolute who contains all facts and in relation to whom all things derive their place and meaning. In Van Til's thought, the issue of autonomy becomes the issue of whether reasoning is 'from God to God-given and God-interpreted fact, or from man to man-made interpretations of brute factuality', to use the words of one of Van Til's most fervent admirers (Rushdoony 1959: 29).

The combination of British Idealism and a Kuyperian antithetical thrust promotes an outlook inimical to that of most evangelicals. Van Til presents a critique of significant aspects of the Princeton apologetic. Vander Stelt (1978: 223) interprets his stance as a rejection of Common Sense philosophy:

> In brief, what Van Til opposed in the Princeton tradition of apologetics is its incorporation of certain basic notions of CSP [Common Sense philosophy], its stress on individual facts, its predilection for the inductive methodology, its understanding of the possibility and probability of rational laws, its beginning with reason rather than with the system of truth revealed in Scripture, and its attempt to *prove* the factuality, credibility, and infallibility of the Bible, *before* talking about the Scripture's being inspired of God. By assuming that man possesses original or constitutionally inherent knowledge and that facts require human interpretation rather than mere *re*interpretation, this tradition is vulnerable to the view of human autonomy and the resultant uncertainty of subjectivism.

Van Til (1967: 26) himself argues that

> the only way in which Warfield's view of the Bible and its inspiration can be defended is by pointing out that it is and has to be presupposed in order that there be any intelligible human predication. . . . When men argue about the phenomena of Scripture as though these phenomena were intelligible in terms of themselves, apart from the revelation of God . . . then their attack or defense is nothing but a beating in the air. To assume autonomous self-interpretation is to negate the necessity of special revelation.

The following account draws particularly on two works in which Van Til advances the view that there are two opposed systems of thought. In *The Defense of the Faith* (1955, revised and abridged 1963), he is concerned with the correct mode of apologetics. He argues that only a truly Reformed position can defend Christianity consistently because it in no way presupposes human autonomy but always makes God its final reference point. He supplements these arguments in *A Christian Theory of Knowledge* (1969), in which he presents his Christian and more especially Reformed theory of knowledge.

7.2.1. *Two Theories of Knowledge*

Van Til (1969: 45) finds two senses of knowledge in scripture. Crucial for apologetics is the knowledge of fallen man who, by virtue of being created by God in his image, has knowledge of God. This provides the point of contact. Secondly, there is knowledge according to truth, which man needs in order to be what God at first made him to be. Van Til (1963: 48–9) also distinguishes three types of consciousness: the Adamic, the fallen or unregenerate, and the regenerate. It is crucial for a sound theology that the historicity of Genesis be accepted, so that we acknowledge that the Adamic consciousness no longer exists. Apologists must bear these three types of consciousness in mind and so distinguish between 'what was true for Adam, then what is true for the sinner, the natural man, and after that what is true for the saint, the regenerated man' (ibid. 210). Men do not have common notions about God by virtue of being created in his image: 'All men have a sense of deity, but there is no man who has not at the same time also something else that at once colors his sense of deity. All men are either in covenant with Satan or in covenant with God' (ibid. 211–12).

7.2.2. *Presuppositional Apologetics*

Van Til agrees with Kuyper that there is no neutral basis upon which the believer can appeal to the non-believer (1963: 151), but he does not think that apologetics is therefore redundant (ibid. 265–6; 1969: 235–54). Like Warfield, he believes that the 'natural man has the ability to understand intellectually, though not spiritually, the challenge presented to him' (1963: 266). He sees it as the Christian's duty to present such a challenge, by showing natural man the impossibility of his own principle—'that on his *principle* he would destroy all truth and meaning' (ibid.). The natural man maintains his own false theories against a better knowledge, presupposing the existence of God while verbally rejecting it (ibid. 103). The Christian must show that man necessarily presupposes God as the final reference point in predication. He can do this 'only if he shows the non-Christian that even in his virtual negation of God, he is still really presupposing God' (1969: 13).[12]

Apologetics is 'the vindication of the Christian philosophy of life against the various forms of non-Christian philosophy of life' (Westminster Theological Seminary, Apologetics Syllabus, 1971: 1). It is a comprehensive package incorporating theories on the nature of self, the universe, knowledge, and facts. There is no common area of knowledge between believer and unbeliever because there is no agreement between them as to the nature of man himself (1963: 67). It is therefore the job of Christianity to make the facts of human experience and the nature of man appear for what they really are. The issue comes down to that of one's ultimate presuppositions:

> When man became a sinner he made of himself instead of God the ultimate or final reference point. And it is precisely this presupposition, as it controls without exception all forms of non-Christian philosophy, that must be brought into question. If this presupposition is left unquestioned in any field all the facts and arguments presented to the unbeliever will be made over by him according to his pattern. (ibid. 77)

One's presuppositions affect one's entire outlook: 'The sinner has cemented colored glasses to his eyes which he cannot remove. And all is yellow to the jaundiced eye' (ibid.; cf. p. 201). Since the sinner and the regenerate see things so differently, they will not be able to reason with one another: 'There can be no intelligible reasoning unless those who reason together understand what they

[12] There is an inconsistency in Van Til's thought in his distinction between the different kinds of knowledge. On the one hand, Van Til (1971*a*: 21) argues that when 'we present the message and evidence for the Christian position as clearly as possible, knowing that because man is what the Christian says he is, the non-Christian will be able to understand in an intellectual sense the issues involved'. On the other hand, he insists that apologetics involves showing the unbeliever that his system is inconsistent because it is constructed according to the wrong reference point. How the non-Christian can have a correct intellectual understanding within an essentially inconsistent system is not resolved.

mean by their words.' Even if the natural man accepts apologetical arguments, unless his basic presupposition is questioned, the god that he finds will be something other than 'the self-contained ontological trinity of Scripture' (ibid.).

The point of contact between regenerate and unregenerate is not to be sought at the level of conscious reasoning. It lies deep down in the natural man's awareness that he is the creature of God and a covenant-breaker. This is common grace (1969: 43–4) by which man, as created in God's image, has inherent knowledge of God. We must distinguish the sense of deity which Calvin says is present in all men from the reaction to this revelation by sinful men. Every man has a knowledge of God, but every sinner seeks to suppress it (1963: 84).

If the apologist does not draw out from the sinner his knowledge of God, then he is virtually legitimating natural man's view of himself. Therefore, Van Til is at pains to posit the proper method of apologetics, which must be by presupposition. To argue by presupposition 'is to indicate what are the epistemological and metaphysical principles that underlie and control one's method' (ibid. 99). The Reformed apologist will frankly admit that his methodology presupposes the truth of Christian theism, because '*every* method, the supposedly neutral one no less than any other, presupposes either the truth or the falsity of Christian theism' (ibid. 100).

Autonomous man assumes neutrality and demands that argument be conducted by appeal to facts and reason. However, 'facts and logic which are not themselves first seen in the light of Christianity have, in the nature of the case, no power in them to challenge the unbeliever to change his position' (ibid. 229–30). Van Til (1961: pp. i–ii) addresses 'the factual question' in his course on Christian-Theistic Evidences. He takes an idealist-cum-presuppositionalist approach:

> facts and interpretation of facts cannot be separated . . . The real question about facts is, therefore, what kind of universal can give the best account of the facts . . . We hold that there is only one such universal, namely, the God of Christianity. Consequently, we hold that without the presupposition of the God of Christianity we cannot even interpret one fact correctly. Facts without God would be brute facts. They would have no intelligible relation to one another. As such they could not be known by man.

The apologist should never perform only inductive reasoning, but should challenge the a priori assumptions of the non-Christian: 'I would not talk endlessly about facts and more facts without ever challenging the non-believer's philosophy of fact. A really fruitful historical apologetic argues that every fact *is* and *must be* such as proves the truth of the Christian theistic position' (1963: 199).

Traditional 'Romanist-evangelical' apologetics of the kind practised at Princeton (1969: 19–20) makes the same assumption about neutrality and human autonomy. It is 'unwilling to challenge the natural man's basic presupposition with respect to himself as the ultimate reference point in interpretation' (1963: 79).[13] So Van Til agrees with Kuyper against Warfield over the *method* of presenting Christian truth: 'The Romanist-evangelical type of apologetics assumes that man can first know much about himself and the universe and *afterward* ask whether God exists and Christianity is true. The Reformed apologist assumes that nothing can be known by man about himself or the universe unless God exists and Christianity is true' (ibid. 223).

He accuses Charles Hodge of dropping 'to the level of evangelicalism' when he speaks of the office of reason as judge of the credibility and evidences of revelation (ibid. 80–5). Hodge means by reason, 'those laws of belief which God has implanted in our nature' (ibid. 81). He believes in 'a common sense philosophy which the natural man has and which, because intuitive or spontaneous, is, so far forth, not tainted by sin' (p. 85). He fails to distinguish between the original and fallen nature of humanity, and frequently argues as though 'that original nature can still be found as active in the "common consciousness" of men' (p. 82). Van Til (ibid.) concedes that 'the common sense of man has not strayed so far from the truth as have the sophistications of the philosophers', and 'blasphemous atheism is not usually found among the masses of men'. However, he insists that the apologist

[13] Van Til (1963: 194) describes 'Romanist-evangelical' apologetics as receiving 'its most fundamental expression in the *Summae* of Thomas Aquinas the Roman Catholic and Bishop Butler the Arminian'. He chooses C. S. Lewis as his archetypal evangelical (ibid. 58–60). American evangelicals were clearly encouraged by Lewis's defence of Christianity. Wheaton College even has a Lewis archive. However, Kelly James Clark, an advocate of Reformed epistemology, employs arguments by Lewis against evidentialist evangelicalism. For example, Lewis argues that one will not accept a miracle if one is committed to a philosophy which precludes miracles, and he defends the tenacity of the theist's belief in the face of counter-evidence (K. J. Clark: 42–3, 113–18).

'defeats his own purpose if he appeals to some form of "common consciousness of man"' (p. 84). The common notions of men are sinful.

Van Til (1969: 246) also holds Warfield at fault for attributing to 'right reason' the ability to judge revelation. Warfield would have the non-Christian decide by means of historical research whether or not there has been a supernatural revelation. He would thus arrive at the doctrine of inspiration as 'the end result' in a process of reasoning which assesses the verisimilitude of the Gospels (ibid. 246). Against this inductive approach, Van Til (ibid. 251–3) posits the self-attestation of revelation, which Warfield himself endorses. He concludes that Warfield's method of apologetics is therefore inconsistent with the foundational concepts of Warfield's own Reformed theology.

In apologetical argument an indirect route must be taken, by which the Christian puts himself in the position of his opponent for the sake of argument, and shows him that from the opponent's point of view the 'facts' are not facts. He must ask the non-Christian to assume the Christian point of view so as to see that only on that basis do the 'facts' appear intelligible (1963: 100–1). It is legitimate to start with facts or evidences, for these are the vehicle through which the Christian system is introduced. However, presuppositions must be brought to the fore to show that these facts derive their meaning from the presuppositions. To suppose, as do Aquinas and Butler, that the natural man has some correct notions about God is 'tantamount to saying that those who interpret a fact as dependent upon God and those who interpret that same fact as not dependent upon God have yet said something identical about that fact' (ibid. 203). Van Til (ibid. 197) claims to start his apologetics 'more frankly from the Bible as the source from which as an absolutely authoritative revelation I take my whole interpretation of life'.

7.2.3. *Scripture*

Van Til identifies the authority of scripture with the authority of God: 'it makes very little difference whether we begin with the notion of an absolute God or with the notion of an absolute Bible. The one is derived from the other' (1955*a*: 206). He finds in both 'the final court of appeal' (1963: 34, 35). The infallibility of scripture becomes, for Van Til, the basic presupposition of the Christian, as opposed to the principle of human autonomy upon which all others rely: 'The non-Christian's process of reasoning rests upon the presupposition that man is the final or ultimate reference point in human predication. The Christian's process of reasoning rests upon the presupposition that God, speaking through Christ by his Spirit in the infallible Word, is the final or ultimate reference point in human predication' (ibid. 180).

Scripture and God are so closely identified that 'the argument for the Scripture as the infallible revelation of God is, to all intents and purposes, the same as the argument for the existence of God'. God can be proved to exist only by presupposition, and the presupposition must be the same as that which accepts the infallibility of scripture. 'No proof for this God and for the truth of his revelation in Scripture can be offered by an appeal to anything in human experience that has not itself received its light from the God whose existence and whose revelation it is supposed to prove' (ibid. 109).

Van Til regards Kuyper, Bavinck, Warfield, and therefore himself, as sharing a common understanding of scripture (ibid. 296–7, 1967: 27). He wrote a complimentary 'Introduction' to Warfield's essays in *The Inspiration and Authority of the Bible* (1948).[14] He argues that the Bible's status as the Word of God 'pertains only to the original autographs' (1969: 27). This reflects an assumption that the Word of God is made up of words of God,[15] and an anxiety that the accuracy and reliability of our Bibles can be defended only if they are understood to be 'faithful reproductions' rather than 'exact replicas' of the autographs.

To accept Warfield's account of scripture is to inherit his preoccupation with factual evidences. Van Til accepts all the same evidences as Warfield. The novelty of his apologetic is that he

[14] This collection contains most of the essays included in the earlier volume, *Revelation and Inspiration* (1927). James Oliver Buswell, a vehement critic of presuppositionalism, suspects Van Til of being responsible for the omission of the article 'The Divine Origin of the Bible, the General Argument' (Buswell 1949: 183). In this article Warfield suggests ontological, cosmological, and design arguments for the origin of the Bible and reveals his support for Bishop Butler.

[15] He rejects mechanistic dictation theories in much the same way as do Warfield's followers, thinking like them that this distinguishes him from 'fundamentalists' (1950: 26; Vander Stelt 1978: 249–50). As Rushdoony (1959: 144) explains: 'the word "dictation" is accurate in implying God's authorship, but wholly erroneous in its inference that man's role was mechanical, rigid, and impersonal'.

places these evidences inside a presuppositional framework. In this respect, his defence of scripture is Kuyperian. It also reflects the British Idealist influence. The infallibility of scripture means, for Van Til, not that the truth of scripture will be proved by reference to the facts of science and history, but that all facts belong to God and are correctly interpreted only in relation to God and his Word. 'The Christian holds to the authority and finality of the Bible not because he can clearly, that is exhaustively, show the coherence of every fact with every other fact of Scripture. He rather holds to this doctrine of Scripture because, unless he does, there is no resting point for the search of facts anywhere' (1969: 36).

He takes scriptural infallibility to imply the historicity of Genesis (1963: 191), not because its historicity could be proved empirically but because without it 'the true meaning of the fallen and the regenerate consciousness cannot be maintained' (ibid. 211). The difference between an evidentialist and a presuppositionalist approach may be illustrated by contrasting a creation scientist's argument that 'the Bible supplies us with the only explanation perfectly congruous with all the known *facts*' (D. C. C. Watson [1975] 1989: 77) with Van Til's (1963: 211) position that it is 'only if we do take [the Genesis] narrative as historical that a sound theology can be maintained'. Van Til (1969: 35) draws Bavinck on his side: 'the orthodox believer holds to his doctrine of Scripture "in spite of appearances" ', believing that the Bible is the Word of God, not because of empirical evidence, but 'because God has said that it is his Word'.

Since the claim to infallibility does not extend beyond the original autographs, and since these are not available for inspection, Van Til (ibid.) accepts 'that there will be "discrepancies" in the Bible'. We do not know what he thinks of particular textual difficulties because he is more concerned with the form than with the content of scripture. Regarding the form, he argues the impossibility that scripture in the original autographs conflicts with the facts of history and science, since 'the God of which the Scriptures speak is the God who makes the facts to be what they are'. No fact can be 'ultimately out of accord with the system of truth set forth in Scripture' since every fact 'is what it is just because of the place that it has in this system' (ibid.). The Christian is not obliged to 'see to it that what he regards as truth revealed in Scripture is in accord with the "assured results of science"' (1969: 37). 'The question is not whether the teachings of Scripture are in accord with the facts of science as science is often understood. As often understood, science may properly interpret the facts of the Scripture without reference to the system of truth set forth in the Bible' (ibid. 36–7).

Evidences do convey the authority of scripture, but that is because scripture itself interprets them. Scripture 'presents itself as being the only light in terms of which the truth about facts and their relations can be discovered' (1963: 108), and 'claims to give men a finished system of interpretation of human life and history' (1969: 64).

As a rational being, the sinner can understand why the Reformed theologian accepts the doctrine of scripture as the infallible Word of God, but he rejects Christianity as a whole or finds it meaningless in relation to his own presuppositions of autonomy and chance (1963: 149–50). It follows that in order to persuade him with respect to scripture, as with every other issue, the Christian must reason by way of presupposition.

> That is to say, the argument must be such as to show that unless one accepts the Bible for what true Protestantism says it is, the authoritative interpretation of human life and experience as a whole, it will be impossible to find meaning in anything. It is only when this presupposition is constantly kept in mind that a fruitful discussion of problems pertaining to the phenomena of Scripture and what it teaches about God in his relation to man can be discussed. (ibid. 150)

7.3. Van Til's Challenge to Fundamentalism

In the United States divisions grew between those who followed Van Til in formulating a presuppositional apologetic and those who, in the words of Clark Pinnock (1971*b*: 421), believed that God's 'divine self-disclosure is objectively valid to all men'. The different positions were represented in the late 1940s by Van Til and J. Oliver Buswell, a defender of Old Princeton and Common Sense Realism. Buswell attacked 'presuppositionalism' in the pages of his journal, *The Bible Today*. Indeed, he claimed to have introduced the term in 1948, having got the idea from his friend Dr Allan A. MacRae (Buswell 1948*a*: 235; 1948*b*: 41). He applied it first to Carnell's work, which was influenced by Gordon Clark

(1948*a*), and soon afterwards to Van Til's position (1948*b*). Buswell's major criticism of presuppositionalism was that it denies a 'common ground of knowledge between Christian and non-Christian' (1948b: 42). He argued that in this respect Van Til was opposing not only Aquinas and Butler, but also Kuyper, Bavinck, and Old Princeton (Buswell's n. 13 to Van Til 1949: 278). Van Til (1949: 283) responded with his peculiar mixture of Calvinism, Kuyperianism, and Transcendental Idealism. He insisted that believer and non-believer 'have nothing in common'. The sinner 'looks through colored glasses' and is deceived in thinking that 'consciousness of facts is intelligible without consciousness of God'.

Allan MacRae has recently disclosed that the dominance of Van Til's method at Westminster Theological Seminary in the 1930s was a significant factor in the division of its faculty, not made prominent at the time for fear of damaging Van Til's ministry.[16] MacRae was a Princeton graduate who joined the Westminster faculty in 1929 and left with McIntire in 1937. He has written an account of that schism:

> the teaching at Westminster had completely abandoned the strong emphasis on the value of the factual evidences for Christianity that had characterized the work of Wilson and Machen and had put in its place a very strong emphasis on Presuppositional Apologetics, which denies the value of evidence. Shortly before his death Dr. Machen had been shocked to learn that this change had occurred, not only because it would undercut a large part of the work to which his life had been devoted, but also because he knew that such an anti-intellectual attitude would greatly diminish the effectiveness of the graduates in Christian thinking and evangelism. (MacRae 1991)[17]

Van Til's specific ideas have been less influential than his reputation among evangelicals would suggest, his most enthusiastic

[16] Factors made prominent in the division were disagreements over prophecy and liberty. The Dutch had a strong amillennial tradition which, it was felt, made them intolerant of the premillennialists at Westminster, and they practised a liberty which offended the non-drinking, non-smoking Americans (MacRae 1991; E. Schaeffer, 1981: 191–3).

[17] For this information from MacRae, I am indebted to Stephen and Gloria Hague who conducted interviews with MacRae on this matter. They encouraged him to write the essay 'The Antecedents of Biblical Theological Seminary', from which the above passage is quoted, for the Seminary's historical display and records. MacRae had been president of McIntire's Faith Theological Seminary, but left Faith in 1971 to found Biblical School of Theology (which later became Biblical Theological Seminary).

supporters being his ex-students from Westminster. There is little in Van Til's thought upon which to build. He offers only a single plank: an emphasis on presuppositions. Kantzer (1975: 48) and Ellingsen (1988: 214–15, 437 n. 51) see presuppositionalism as the dominant approach in contemporary evangelicalism. However, they mention evangelicals who have not endorsed Van Til's distinctive method, including Carl Henry, Francis Schaeffer, J. I. Packer, and the Council on Biblical Inerrancy.[18]

Francis Schaeffer has been one of the most effective evangelical writers in promoting what he himself called 'presuppositional apologetics' (F. Schaeffer 1968*b*: 15). His influence has been popular and evangelistic rather than scholarly. He studied at Westminster Theological Seminary under Van Til, but he never referred to his teacher. He left Westminster for Faith Theological Seminary in 1937. Schaeffer seemed to adopt much of Van Til's terminology, but he did not endorse a thoroughly presuppositional epistemology. Van Til actually associated Schaeffer with Aquinas and Butler, and denied any basic similarity between his own and Schaeffer's apologetic method.[19] Edith Schaeffer (1981: 186) describes Van Til's influence on her husband as the opening of another door, 'not so much in details, but in wider sweeps of thinking'.

In *The God Who is There* (1968*b*: 93), Schaeffer argues that finite man 'has no sufficient reference point if he begins absolutely and autonomously from himself'. He states that 'no non-Christian can be consistent to the logic of his presuppositions', and that apologetics must begin by revealing this inconsistency (ibid. 121, 125–42). However, his antithesis is less radical than Van Til's. He

[18] An influence from Gordon H. Clark is evident throughout Henry's work. Henry (1979*a*: 215) posits '*reason* [as] *the instrument for recognizing* [divine revelation]'. By 'presuppositions', he seems to mean principles of reasoning which support 'traditional logic': 'The acceptable forms of logic are not criteria which happen to be fashionable in a given era, nor are they mere human behavioristic conventions, but they are necessary presuppositions of all intelligible thought and communication' (ibid. 247). Kantzer (1975: 65 n. 46) suggests that Packer's (1958*a*: 115–29) understanding of the relation between faith and reason renders him presuppositionalist. Packer (1971: 153) sounds like Van Til when he assigns 'to all facts reported in Scripture the status of God-*interpreted* facts'. However, he does not share the radical antithesis of Van Til's position. He maintains a conviction that God's self-disclosure is 'objectively clear' and that scripture 'evidences itself to the sound mind as clearly as do light and colour to the normal eye' (1958*a*: 118).

[19] Van Til argues this in a paper written at the request of Westminster students, entitled 'The Apologetic Methodology of Francis A. Schaeffer' [n.d., n. pub.].

believes that the Christian and non-Christian know the material side to the universe in the same way. Schaeffer even insists that the 'historic Fall . . . is a *brute fact*' (1975: 44). In *Death in the City* (1969: 112–13), he depicts the Christian supplementing (rather than wholly reinterpreting) the materialist's view of reality: 'there is more to the universe than you have described . . . To understand reality in our universe properly, you have to consider both halves—both the seen and the unseen'. Schaeffer wants to say that both the Christian and the materialist know the same visible side of the universe, but that their views are mutually exclusive: 'That does not mean that the Christian cannot glean much detail from the materialist's observation. But as far as the comprehensive view of the universe is concerned, there can be no synthesis. . . . It is a total antithesis' (p. 114). Schaeffer shares with the majority of evangelicals a neutral epistemology, despite his talk of presuppositional apologetics. Van Til's assessment of him is fair in this respect. While Van Til would have rejected demands that reasons be offered for faith which 'anyone on common ground might be expected to accept' (Pinnock 1987: 54), Schaeffer would probably have endorsed them.

Van Til takes the lonely stand that commonly acceptable reasons are not available since all facts find their meaning in scripture. He makes scripture his intellectual starting-point, and practises apologetics by showing that an interpretation of the world founded upon scripture is the only rational and coherent interpretation. He thus undermines Kuyper's (1968: 366) emphasis upon God bearing witness 'in your own soul personally'. Kuyper makes reference to one's relation with Christ and to the inworking of the Holy Spirit in order to justify the way in which scripture is made the proper principium of theology. He then places theology above all other sciences as that which holds them together. Indirectly Kuyper presents scripture as that which makes sense of life, but he does not defend the infallibility of scripture on this ground. Van Til, however, does defend scripture's authority by arguing that only when it is presupposed does our world become meaningful.

Despite his unique approach, Van Til's biblical conservatism renders him vulnerable to aspects of Barr's critique. He does not share in any straightforward way the empirical rationalism that Barr identifies among fundamentalists. Yet Van Til, no less than the evidentialist, makes it impossible for scripture to err factually. He and his followers speak more of infallibility than of inerrancy, but they do not articulate a distinction between the two. They denounce those who move away from inerrancy,[20] and Westminster Theological Seminary has so far retained allegiance to inerrancy in its doctrinal statement. Since Van Til engages in little biblical commentary—a fault for which he is criticized by Berkouwer (1971)—we do not know how he would deal with particular instances of seeming errors and inconsistencies in scripture. Given that he does not divorce interpretation from fact he may not be forced to say, for example with Lindsell, that Peter denied Jesus six times. Nor would he readily go down the road of maximal-conservatism, because that road is inductivist and makes concessions to historical-criticism. His apologetic has more in common with what Barr describes as the older-style, dogmatic approach (Barr 1977: 85–9), although it is complicated by his peculiar idealist position. We can conjecture that Van Til would not simply base the Davidic authorship of Psalm 110 on the testimony of Jesus. Rather, he would protect the facts of the Bible by weaving them into a system in which every fact is said to prove the God of the Bible, and the God of the Bible is the stated reference point for every fact, such that 'If Christian theism is not true then nothing is true' (1949: 288).

Presuppositionalists believe that their defence of scripture safeguards inerrancy by denying even the possibility that scripture could err. They regard the evidentialist position as affirming only the probability that scripture does not err (Notaro 1980: 104). The difference between them is that presuppositionalists are unashamedly circular in their reasoning: 'The thinking of the consistent Christian is from God, through God-interpreted and God-given facts, and is valid though circular or spiral because it conforms to the nature of reality' (Rushdoony 1959: 140). Van Til (1963: 101) insists that 'all reasoning is, in the nature of the case, *circular reasoning*'. The starting-point, method, and conclusion are always involved in one another:

> One cannot prove the usefulness of the light of the sun for the purpose of seeing by turning to the darkness of a cave. Typically the cave must itself

[20] Thus Van Til (1967: 150) reproaches Berkouwer, and Notaro (1980: 103) criticizes Pinnock.

be lit up by the shining of the sun. When the cave is thus lit up each of the objects that are in it 'proves' the existence and character of the sun by receiving their light and intelligibility from it. (ibid. 109)

Typically evangelicals fear that this approach invites subjectivism (Montgomery 1974: 248). They prefer to consult 'objective reality' (Pinnock 1971*b*: 420), and to settle the question of inerrancy 'with careful historical, empirical investigation as well as with logical inferences' (Montgomery 1974: 249).

Since all arguments for inerrancy contain deductive premisses about the truth of scripture, so that in practice no evidence can count against its claims, there is ultimately little difference between the presuppositionalist and evidentialist positions. Presuppositionalists make this point against their evidentialist opponents. They argue that evidentialists are themselves 'sitting on a gold-mine of presuppositions' (Notaro 1980: 102). This very same point, however, undermines their own claim 'that Van Til was way ahead of his time in seeing the necessity of the presuppositional approach long before James Barr's critique' (Edgar 1977: 156). Van Til's apologetics do not counter Barr's objections to fundamentalism in so far as they conform to that disposition always to fend off challenges to conservative interpretations of scripture.

7.4. Reforming the Culture

Kuyperian thought has had less impact on the theology of mainstream evangelicals than it has had on their social awakening. An opening of the evangelical mind has occurred in ways which, though little documented and difficult to trace with precision, can be brought to light. In this respect Dooyeweerd has been an important figure. His influence has been diffuse. Relatively few evangelicals call themselves Dooyeweerdian, but those who do are scattered around Canada, Britain, the United States, South Africa, and the Netherlands. Their efforts to promote and build upon Dooyeweerd's philosophy have had a leavening effect upon evangelical activity.

Dooyeweerd (1979: 3) understood the Kuyperian antithesis not as a 'dividing line between a christian and a non-christian group', but as 'the unrelenting battle between two spiritual principles that cut through the nation and through all mankind'. The antithesis, he argued, is not limited 'to the secret regions of the human heart' or to 'a few "specifically christian areas"'. Rather, it 'penetrate[s] temporal society in science, culture, politics, and economics' (1979: 4). As one Dooyeweerdian has expressed it more recently, the sacred–secular dualism (depicted in Fig. 7.3*a*) has been substituted by a world-view according to which 'two kingdoms are two sovereigns who contend for the same territory and who lead two oppos-

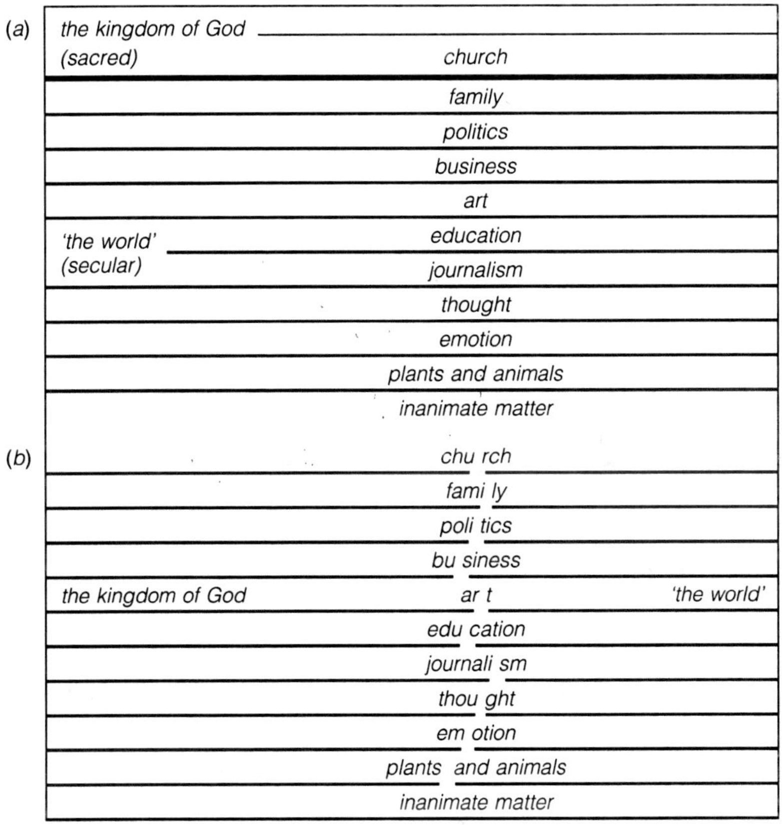

FIG. 7.3 A two-realm versus a holistic theory of creation (Wolters 1985: 68). Reproduced by kind permission of Wm. B. Eerdmans Publishing Co., Grand Rapids, Mich.

ing armies into the field' (depicted in Fig. 7.3*b*) (Wolters 1985: 69). Therefore, in order to reform a culture, Christians need to be active in every sphere.

One of the most successful evangelicals to inspire a concern with culture has been Francis Schaeffer (1912–84). His work was indirectly affected by Kuyperian thought.[21] Despite endorsing an epistemology which was more neutral than presuppositional, Schaeffer was concerned to combat the spirit of the age with Christian presuppositions. His effort was principally pre-evangelistic: he warned that our culture was in crisis, and that in our turning away from God and the truth we have lost the ability to understand our dilemma. This message was in keeping with Schaeffer's premillennial theology. Schaeffer did not fully share the Kuyperian, forward-looking drive to redirect the Christian community as a witness to the wider culture. Nor did he share Van Til's acultural outlook. In fact, Van Til criticized Schaeffer for failing 'to see that ancient and modern thought' is alike 'based on the assumption of human autonomy', so that we need to do more than simply turn back the clock (n.d.: p. iv). Schaeffer's method was to expose godless presuppositions in our culture. He gave few directives on instituting cultural reform, but his work inspired others to address secular activities through their Christian faith.

Having left Van Til's stronghold, Westminster Theological Seminary, Schaeffer became the first student to enrol at Carl McIntire's Faith Theological Seminary, and the first ordinand of the Bible Presbyterian Church (E. Schaeffer, 1981: 200). He later taught at Covenant Theological Seminary, whose founders broke from Faith Theological Seminary in 1956. Schaeffer dissociated himself from McIntire, regretting the 'harsh and ugly' nature of the schisms he incurred (E. Schaeffer 1981: 189). None the less, his work with McIntire had made for him a fortunate acquaintance. In 1948, Schaeffer attended the first meeting of McIntire's International Council of Christian Churches. This was held in Amster-

[21] Schaeffer attributed his understanding of 'the Lordship of Christ over all of life in the areas of culture, art, philosophy, and so on' (1984: 97) to the Reformation principle that God 'spoke in a true revelation concerning nature—the cosmos and man' (1968*a*: 23; cf. 1984: 22). According to that principle, 'the artist and the scientist are also under the revelation of the Scriptures' (1968*a*: 23). Schaeffer does not mention Kuyper—he rarely acknowledges any influences or sources in his writings—but he reflects Kuyperian ideas about world-views or 'philosophic thought-forms' (1968*a*: 8; cf 1968*a*: *passim*; 1968*b*: 13–91; 1984: 22, 97–8).

dam in competition with the conference of the World Council of Churches. There he met the Dutchman Hans Rookmaaker (1922–77) (L. Martin 1979: 96), who was to stimulate Schaeffer's vision for the wider culture. It has been said that the writings of Schaeffer, together with those of Rookmaaker, 'have opened the door of British evangelicalism to the possibility of taking the Kuyperian position seriously' (R. A. Russell 1973: 85).

Rookmaaker's thought had been shaped by Dooyeweerd's philosophy under the guidance of J. P. A. Mekkes in a prisoner-of-war camp in Poland (L. Martin 1979: 81–2). After the war, Rookmaaker followed Dooyeweerd's call for Christian labourers by choosing to study art history on the grounds that no other Reformed Christian specialized in that field (ibid. 91–2).[22] He was to become professor of the history of art at the Free University of Amsterdam. His book *Modern Art and the Death of a Culture* (1970), commissioned by IVP, became a key text amongst evangelicals. It provided the initial impulse for several evangelical artistic ventures, including the London Arts Centre, Edinburgh Arts Group, and Bristol Christian Arts Group which all began in 1971 (R. A. Russell 1973: 83).

The book's timing was apposite. It caught the imagination of those emerging from the hippy era. Rookmaaker linked the art of the age with the spirit of the age. He characterized this spirit as a lack of commitment due to a reversal of spiritual values. He traced the problem back to the Age of Reason, when reason or 'common sense' came to be emphasized as 'something that all men have in common'. He argued that this resulted in a 'change of emphasis from what was reasonable to what was rational'; rationalism meaning 'that there is nothing more in the world but what the senses can perceive and reason apprehend' (1970: 44). Rookmaaker interpreted art since this time, even that produced by Christians, as displaying this non-Christian view of truth (pp. 67–75). He encouraged evangelical Christians to reject the 'rationalism of the closed naturalistic "box"' (p. 224), and to take more of

[22] In his early work on aesthetics, Rookmaaker attempted a strictly Dooyeweerdian analysis. See 'Ontwerp ener aesthetica op grondslag der wijsbegeerte der wetsidee' ('An approach to aesthetics on the basis of the philosophy of the law-idea'), *Philosophia Reformata*, 11/3–4 (1946), 141–67, and 12/1 (1947), 1–35. He later found this to be too abstract and turned instead to an interpretation of art history in terms of the world-views of different eras and cultures, and to pastoral and apologetic concerns. See Seerveld (1985: 79 n. 75).

an interest in art and in culture generally (pp. 31–3, 225–50). He envisaged that as the Holy Spirit bears fruit in the lives of Christians this will lead 'to the "secondary" fruits in culture, the consensus of Christian, biblical attitudes—to work, to money, to nature, to the whole of reality—which deeply influence the whole nation'. It is these secondary fruits, he believed, 'which are reflected in the nation's art' (p. 22).

Rookmaaker's Christian dimension on the arts impressed Schaeffer. Schaeffer had founded the L'Abri Fellowship in Switzerland in 1955 as a 'shelter' for young people to live out and discuss the Christian faith. L'Abri promoted Christian thinking in art and other spheres: 'because Christianity is true it speaks to all of life and not to some narrowly religious sphere and much of the material produced by L'Abri has been aimed at helping develop a Christian perspective on the arts, politics and the social sciences' (L'Abri Fellowship n.d.). L'Abri's work extended to the Netherlands under Rookmaaker's directorship, and to Britain in 1958. An English L'Abri was established, originally in Ealing, West London, and since 1971 in Greatham, Hampshire.[23] The cultural vision appealed to those evangelicals who attended the L'Abri centres in the 1960s and 1970s, and who read Schaeffer's books, attended his lectures, and listened to his tapes. Os Guinness was one of these. Guinness's call for a 'Third Way' between the establishment and the counter-culture, in *The Dust of Death* (1973), has given its name to *Third Way* magazine, which states its intention on its inside cover to spell out 'the Christian's responsibility to relate biblical faith to secular matters'.

Evangelicals today are attempting to give a Christian angle on areas of life which earlier this century evangelicals had left well alone. They have traced a 'natural shift' in their thinking:

> it is slightly simplistic (but still valid) to see in the period from the end of World War II to the late sixties a particular emphasis on Christianity and science; from the mid-sixties to the mid-seventies, an emphasis on Christianity and the arts: [*sic*] and from the mid-seventies to the present, an emphasis on Christianity and social and political issues . . .
>
> (Dean and Porter 1984: 10)

L'Abri has been both an instance and an agent of this change.

[23] Besides the centres in Switzerland, England, and the Netherlands, there now exist L'Abri centres in Sweden, Massachusetts and Minnesota, and Korea.

The shift has been especially apparent in the work of IVF/UCCF. Douglas Johnson (1979: 248) records that, whereas in the 1930s IVF's membership mostly comprised theology and science students, in the 1960s it included increasing numbers of humanities students and was extending to the colleges of art. Oliver Barclay had started IVF's Research Scientists Christian Fellowship shortly after World War II. Another Dutchman from the Free University, the scientist R. Hooykaas, became involved with this group. Johnson remembers Hooykaas bringing new insights on science (ibid. 249). Hooykaas wanted to see the 'teaching of science and technology . . . put on a Christian basis' (Hooykaas 1960: 11). He argued that even natural science 'undergoes the influence of our philosophy and both find their roots in metaphysical "religious" preconceptions' (ibid. 6). It was Hooykaas who introduced Rookmaaker to IVF art students in the late 1960s. Rookmaaker spoke regularly at their conferences and also lectured more widely throughout Britain and America in the 1970s (D. Johnson 1979: 248–9; L. Martin 1979: 142–57; Dean and Porter 1984: 9). Other IVF/UCCF initiatives included establishing a Professional Groups Secretary to support Christians in the professions and, jointly with Scripture Union, founding an education centre at Stapleford House, Nottingham, for training Christian teachers.

Intellectually, the influence of what might be described as 'world-view thinking' among evangelicals has resulted in a range of hybrid positions, as well as in a lot of loose, untheoretical talk about world-view. In areas other than biblical apologetics, it is particularly difficult to say precisely where the Dutch presuppositionalist influence begins and ends. Hooykaas (1960: 15–19), for example, regarded Baconian science as strongly Christian in character. Therefore his ideas were agreeable to Oliver Barclay and Donald Mackay, who championed a more traditional evangelical defence of Christianity's compatibility with the discoveries of science. Hooykaas was influenced by Kuyper's theory of world-views, but he shared with Barclay a dislike of Dooyeweerd's philosophy. Barclay (1984: 22) himself promotes a 'Christian outlook that controls our life and our thinking', but resists the suggestion that a Christian 'world-and-life-view' is a complete intellectual system. He objects that Dooyeweerd's 'almost total antithesis' is 'very difficult to detect in practice in most areas of study', especially in 'mathematics and the more impersonal sciences' (ibid. 205). Packer (1988: 25), meanwhile, supports a more presuppositional view of science, which seems surprising given his promotion of Warfield's style of biblical apologetics:

World views are brought to the sciences by scientists. Christians bring a Christian understanding of this world as God's creation, and they make that the frame into which they fit their scientific knowledge. Atheists, deists, pantheists bring a different view of ultimate reality to their science. These views of God cannot be read out of science, but they do get read into science.

It is also difficult to locate exactly the social outworking of Kuyperian ideas, because the expanding vision and increased activism of evangelicals does not derive only from Kuyper's cultural mandate. The Dutch influence has converged with an increasing social conscience among evangelicals—especially since the 1960s—resulting in a more world-affirming evangelicalism. This trend is apparent in new evangelicalism in the United States, and in the evangelical 'left' in America and Britain. The left draw on Latin American liberation theology, and join voices with challenges from African, Asian, Latin American, Antillian, and Black North American evangelicals to take seriously 'the social, political and economic issues in many parts of the world that are a great stumbling block to the proclamation of the Gospel'.[24]

In England, the dominant, world-renouncing Keswick tendency has been transformed by active social concern and a positive enjoyment of culture. This was already evident in the Evangelical Anglican Congress at Keele in 1967 led by John Stott (Crowe 1967; Hennell 1988: 77–8; Bebbington 1995: 185). Stott has been a key figure in promoting and legitimizing these changes. His book *Issues Facing Christians Today* (1984) has been described as 'one of the greatest single influences on the attitude of evangelical thinking in the last twenty years' (Calver 1995: 204). Stott played a leading role at the Lausanne Congress on World Evangelicalism

[24] Statement of the Consultation on World Evangelism, Pattaya, Thailand, 1980, quoted in Costas (1983: 2). Leading figures of the evangelical left in North America include Ronald J. Sider, director of Evangelicals for Social Action and author of *Rich Christians in an Age of Hunger* ([1978] 1990); and Jim Wallis, editor of *Sojourners* magazine and author of *The Call to Conversion* (1981). In Britain, the evangelical left is represented by *Third Way* magazine, while views of like-minded evangelicals from around the world are brought together through conferences and publications organized by Vinay Samuel and Chris Sugden of the Oxford Centre for Mission Studies. Evangelical endorsement of social responsibility from this left-wing perspective is chronicled in Padilla and Sugden (1985) and Sugden (1989).

in 1974, which urged evangelicals to consider their 'Christian Social Responsibility'.[25] He also began The London Institute of Contemporary Christianity in 1982, which operates under the slogan, 'relating Biblical faith to every aspect of life'. Its building houses the Arts Centre Group, which promotes a Christian approach in art, entertainment, and communications.

Charismatic renewal has further contributed to the turnaround in evangelical social attitudes, presenting conjointly with Kuyperian thought 'a vision of the Kingdom of God with great expectations of the power of the Holy Spirit' (R. A. Russell 1973: Synopsis; cf. Bebbington 1995: 186–7).[26] In 1971, the charismatic Nationwide Festival of Light addressed the standard of morality in society. The campaigning organization CARE (Christian Action Research and Education) developed out of this initiative. A lobbying foundation similar to CARE but representing Christians and non-Christians was established by Mike Schluter and Roy Clements in Cambridge in the early 1980s. It was called the Jubilee Centre and became known through its Keep Sunday Special campaign. It changed its name in 1996 to The Relationship Foundation, to reflect its aim of preserving relationships in society, but it continues to promote biblical and specifically Old Testament societal ethics.[27]

As this variety of developments indicates, evangelicals are no longer restricting themselves to theology and biblical exegesis. They are developing theories on Christian politics and economics, opening Christian law firms and doctors' surgeries, and

[25] Lausanne Covenant, para. 5, stated in Lausanne Committee for World Evangelisation (1982: 17). The Lausanne Covenant is clearly a mainstream rather than Kuyperian initiative. It justifies social action in spite of, rather than in contravention of, the division between sacred and secular activities: 'Although reconciliation with man is not reconciliation with God, nor is social action evangelism, nor is political liberation salvation, nevertheless we affirm that evangelism and socio-political involvement are both part of our Christian duty' (para. 5).

[26] In Britain, substantial support for Kuyperian ideas has come from charismatics. They share a sense of antithesis between the Kingdom of God and the Kingdom of Darkness. Charismatic emphasis upon the reforming work of the Spirit is consistent with a Kuyperian hope for the future of the church (in contrast to a premillennial pessimism), the collapsing of the dualism between natural and supernatural realms (cf. Wimber 1985: 74–96), and the impulse to be active in society.

[27] The department which performs this biblical research has retained the name Jubilee Centre. It reasons that the New Testament provides an ethic for Christians while the Old Testament provides an ethic for the wider society. The emphasis on relationship is developed partly from a theology of the Trinity.

performing Christian music and dance. Kuyperians work alongside other evangelicals in such enterprises. Their distinctive concern to reconstruct society upon Christian principles is now often merged with the aims of less radical evangelicals, who wish to add a Christian dimension to the systems within which they operate and which they fundamentally endorse.

Some specific groups have emerged with the express intention of implementing Kuyper's vision for society, and which build consciously on the thought of Dooyeweerd and even of Van Til. The Institute for Christian Studies (ICS), founded in Toronto in 1967, is a Christian graduate school which draws on Dooyeweerd but not on Van Til. Such scholars as the late Bernard Zylstra, Hendrik Hart, C. T. McIntire, Paul Marshall, Brian Walsh, and Albert Wolters are among its past and present teachers.[28] ICS has greatly influenced the Christian schools movement in Reformed circles, and has contributed to Reformed efforts to bring a Christian world-view to bear in scholarship.[29] The Center for Public Justice has operated in Washington DC since the 1970s to develop a Christian political philosophy. It promotes a Kuyperian form of pluralism which conceives of a limited secular state granting proper autonomy to social groupings such as the family, schools, and religious institutions. Its associates include Roy Clouser, Mark Noll, James Skillen, and Nicholas Wolterstorff. In Britain, Dooyeweerdian literature is distributed by the Christian Studies

[28] H. Evan Runner is regarded as the father-figure of the Institute. He is an American Presbyterian, a graduate of Wheaton College and Westminster Seminary, who was encouraged by Van Til to study in Holland. As a professor at Calvin College he was unpopular with the faculty there for promoting Kuyper's Antithesis over common grace. However, he was influential among Calvin College's Canadian students. These were Calvinists from the Netherlands who had emigrated to Canada in the 1950s (Bratt 1984: 196). Runner played a decisive role in the early development of the Association for the Advancement of Christian Scholarship out of which ICS was established (Zylstra 1975: 28–9; *Perspective* 27/1 (1993), 2).

[29] Other moderate Kuyperians who encourage Christian scholars to perform their scholarship from a Christian viewpoint include the Reformed epistemologists, Alvin Plantinga (1985; 1990), Nicholas Wolterstorff (1976; 1987), and George I. Mavrodes (1973). They are more influential among evangelicals in the United States than is ICS. They were all colleagues at Calvin College together with George Marsden, who also confesses a Kuyperian outlook. Marsden (1973) argues within his own discipline that Christian historians will interpret the past differently from non-Christian historians. The Reformed epistemologists are analytical philosophers studying the nature of basic beliefs which shape a belief system. They do not introduce the ethical dimension that informs the thought of Van Til. Nor do they employ Dooyeweerd's (1953: p. v) image of 'the "heart" as the religious root of human existence'.

Unit in Bath, run by Anglican clergyman Richard Russell. Russell finds hope for the reformation of evangelicalism in the convergence of Dutch and charismatic influences. College House in Cambridge promotes Dooyeweerdian philosophy through evening classes and conferences. Its founders, John Peck and Steve Shaw, were inspired by the need for a Christian concept of art to undergird the Greenbelt Christian Arts Festival, first held in 1974. Both the Christian Studies Unit and College House have connections with ICS.[30]

7.4.1. *The Reconstructionists*

The reconstructionists are a highly polemical, politically and economically right-wing group who bear allegiance to Kuyper, Van Til, and to some extent Dooyeweerd. They are schismatic and in this sense might be considered a parallel to militant-separatist fundamentalism. They have rival bases in Vallecito, California, and Tyler, Texas, under the respective leadership of R. J. Rushdoony and his dissenting son-in-law Gary North. Rushdoony works primarily in the area of law. His book, *Institutes of Biblical Law* (1973), was the initiating text of the reconstructionist programme. North, who regards himself as reconstructionism's 'hard-liner' (1991: 13), writes on economics. Others associated with Reconstructionism include Greg Bahnsen, David Chilton, and Otto Scott. Reconstructionists are immensely prolific, and the amount of literature they produce is out of proportion to their small number of followers.

Their fervent 'theonomic' crusade to implement God's law in every realm has alienated reconstructionists from Van Til's followers at Westminster Theological Seminary.[31] Their dislike for what they see as the liberal interpretation of Dooyeweerd at the

[30] Other consciously Dooyeweerdian attempts to bring Christian principles to bear on social matters include the Shaftesbury Project on Christian Involvement in Society, created by Alan Storkey in 1970, which sponsored study groups on such topics as politics, business, family life, racism, and crime, and the Ilkley Group, formed in 1971 for evangelical research sociologists (R. A. Russell 1973: 82–3).

[31] The faculty of Westminster attacked reconstructionism in a symposium entitled *Theonomy: A Reformed Critique* (Barker and Godfrey (eds.) (1990)). Gary North organized an angry response, the main burden of which was captured in his *Westminster's Confession: The Abandonment of Van Til's Legacy* (1991). 'Theonomy' is a concept ranged against autonomy, but, as North (ibid. 132) acknowledges, Van Til did not accept its social and political application.

ICS in Toronto sets them apart from this major Dooyeweerdian centre. They distinguish their own capitalist, *laissez-faire* position from the supposed 'socialism' and 'feminism' of the Toronto group.[32] They reject the 'Grand Rapids–Toronto–Wheaton–Edinburgh–London–Amsterdam circuit' as tame. They place the 'battle for the mind' not between 'fundamentalism and the institutions of the Left', but between 'the Christian reconstruction movement, which alone among Protestant groups takes seriously the law of God, and everyone else' (North 1984: 71, 65–6).

Stephen C. Perks is the founder and director of Christian Reconstruction in Britain. He edits its journal *Calvinism Today*, which has 300 subscribers equally divided between Britain and the States. Perks is a minister of the Chalcedon Reformed Church for which he was ordained in the States.[33] His congregation in Whitby, North Yorkshire, currently comprises only his family members. He initially moved within wider evangelical circles but now regards evangelicals as 'not an army but a kindergarten', concerned with their 'internal condition' rather than with changing the world.[34] He promotes reform particularly in education, to which end he has written *The Christian Philosophy of Education Explained* (1992), although he also writes on law and economics. He and his wife educate their children at home, as do many families committed to the reconstructionist ideal. They can find no school, even among the growing number of private Christian schools, whose vision they trust. Perks organizes and publicizes reconstructionist conferences and speaker-meetings in Britain. Various individuals and families dotted around Britain, most of whom are members of evangelical or charismatic churches, attend these events, though not all identify with Perks.

While the fundamentalists whom Barr describes seek 'to establish a foundation in the past' (Barr 1991*b*: 37), reconstructionists are positive about their ability to change the future. They attack those conservative Christian leaders who for decades 'opposed the idea that Christians have a moral responsibility to proclaim an exclusively Christian world-and-life view for the governing of all human institutions' (North 1984: p. xii). They reject the

[32] Interview with British reconstructionist Stephen Perks, 1 Sept. 1993.

[33] In Atlanta, Ga., as a member of the Reformed Presbyterian Church in the United States, a denomination suggested to him by Rushdoony.

[34] Interview, 1 Sept. 1993.

premillennial hope of an imminent end to this world and its accompanying emphasis upon personal sanctification, which together have encouraged withdrawal from worldly affairs. Gary North has written an 'Action Manual for Christian Reconstruction' entitled *Backward, Christian Soldiers?* (1984). The book is a vehement attack against the passivism and retreat of conservative Christians, including 'old fundamentalists', in the face of secularism.

North identifies to some extent with the politically active 'new fundamentalists', whose '*vision of victory*' starkly contrasts with the 'cultural pessimism' of such books as Hal Lindsey's *Late Great Planet Earth* (North 1984: pp. 32, xi). However, reconstructionists are post-millennialists (Baxter 1991). Their vision is more long-term than that of neo-fundamentalists. They aim to influence the state from the bottom up by educating Christians at the grass-roots level, rather than from the top down by lobbying or by voting for Christian candidates:

> As godly people begin to restructure their behavior in terms of what the Bible requires, the world about them begins to change. They serve as leavening influences in the whole culture. As more converts are added to the rolls of the churches, and as these converts begin to conform their lives to the Bible's standards for external behavior, all of society is progressively sanctified. (North 1984: p. x)

More recently North, Rushdoony, and other prominent reconstructionists have affiliated with the Christian Coalition, which has taken the NCR into the 1990s and which concentrates on local politics. Under their influence Pat Robertson has modified his premillennialist views (Iannaccone 1993: 349, 363 nn. 35, 36).

The major reconstructionist criticism of fundamentalism is that it offers only 'a personal escape hatch' to those on the sinking ship of secularism, and chooses the easier, cheaper, and quicker task of producing tracts than of devising a Christian social theory to combat humanism (North 1984: 87).

7.5. Evangelism

North (1984: p. xi) describes the campus crusades from the 1950s to the 1970s as 'evangelical in the narrow sense: saving men *out of* the world, but not training redeemed men to take responsibility *over* the world'. The pietistic concern with soul-saving to the exclusion of social responsibility riles most Kuyperians, and not only their extreme reconstructionist cousins. Van Til was something of an exception in retaining a narrow apologetic and evangelistic perspective. Kuyperians generally aim to develop Christian education and culture which nurture the whole person, rather than simply to devise evangelistic arguments. 'Evangelicalism', Richard Russell argues, 'has suffered with a radically reductionistic view of EVANGELISM as if it were a technique, a few memorised words for the saving of souls, for the hereafter.'[35]

Kuyperians emphasize that fruitful evangelism comes from reflecting a Christian world-view in one's life and discourse. There are no Kuyperian equivalents to Billy Graham. 'Witnessing' is primarily a matter of the way one lives: 'the application of Scripture to Christian *character* lived before an unsaved world' (Notaro 1980: 25). Activities such as street-preaching are not rejected, but the Kuyperian is wanting to convey a whole philosophy of life and may decide that communicating on street corners or going door-to-door presents a strange image. The Christian Studies Unit in Bath has produced a booklet entitled *You Are Here*, which questions typical evangelistic methods: 'many people are, quite rightly, wary of religious fundamentalism, legalism and empty ritual, shallow or hypocritical pietism, or anyone hanging around shopping precincts with an over sincere smile on their face' (p. 42). Truth which is fundamental to the whole of human life is lived daily and in every sphere, not proclaimed from a street corner.

Tracts may be used, but these will not be concerned primarily with one's internal spiritual state or with evidences for the truth of Christianity. Rather, they will attempt to convey an entire view of life. *You Are Here* is the nearest equivalent to a tract that the Christian Studies Unit has. It provides 'an introduction to the three main themes of a Christian worldview; Creation, Fall, and Redemption' (p. 1), and it illustrates these themes with quite lengthy passages (not single proof-texts) from scripture. Its 'Good News' includes a 'route of guidance and instruction about the true contours of life and reality, and of norms that lead to peace, justice and fruitfulness in individuals and in their communal cultural practices and institutions' (p. 40).

[35] In an unpublished paper entitled 'Social Concern: Cancer or Maturity of the Evangelical Movement'.

7.6. Barr and the Dooyeweerdians

Barr (1977: 276) predicted that there would be insufficient interest in live philosophical questioning among those whom he terms 'fundamentalist' to lead to any movement based upon Dooyeweerd's 'Christian philosophy'. As we have seen, various Dooyeweerdian groups have in fact emerged. They are numerically small with a widely dispersed following. Their influence is diffuse and therefore hard to measure. By the nature of their mission they are fully acquainted with the difficulties and frustrations of encouraging evangelicals to think philosophically.[36] They offer their own critique of 'hard-headed evangelicalism', which Steve Shaw (unpub. 1994) of College House describes as a 'subculture . . . so focused on personal morality, conformity of doctrine and what happens when you die' that it is 'intellectually, artistically and politically . . . barren'.

Dooyeweerdians attempt to formulate a world-view which is shaped and tested by scripture, and which enables them to apply biblical principles to their intellectual, artistic, and political endeavours (Wolters 1985: 6). Their contribution to the substantial evangelical literature on biblical interpretation is proportionately small, but they have been prolific in relating Christian principles to non-theological disciplines. Thus, they employ scripture very differently from the fundamentalists whom Barr describes. They give biblical teaching far-reaching implications, not because it provides factual data with which to supplement one's knowledge in other areas, but because it provides a perspective which should inform all of one's thought. The Bible 'is both a message and a framework' (Vander Goot 1984: 38). It provides 'guiding presuppositions to theorizing' (Clouser 1991: 106–7). As James H. Olthuis (1987: 25) of ICS writes,

> although Scripture is not as a whole a political tract, an economic treatise or a moral homily, it does fundamentally speak to our political, economic, and moral life out of and in terms of the ultimate horizon of faith. Even though Scripture is not a theoretic discourse or a book of science, it does speak to the scientific endeavor insofar as every theoretic

[36] John Peck of College House believes that for 'many British evangelicals the very word "philosophy" . . . is threatening'. He has found it 'extraordinarily difficult' to convey the need for a Christian philosophy 'to our evangelical friends' who think of Christian truth only as something easily grasped (letter to the author, 29 June 1994).

conception and all scientific activity is grounded in and is an exposition of an ultimate commitment of faith.

Christians who are unaware of the religious root of their theoretical thought are criticized for their naïve view that an academic subject can be taught from a neutral vantage point, and for their failure to appreciate that a biblical perspective can be provided for seemingly non-religious subjects.

The difference in approach to scripture may be illustrated by contrasting Roy Clouser's deconstruction of *The Myth of Religious Neutrality* (dedicated to Herman Dooyeweerd) with David Beck's vision of Christian education for Liberty University, both published in 1991. Clouser (1991: 104) rejects attempts to 'establish religious influence' by finding 'statements in Scripture on every sort of subject matter'. He introduces the notion of the 'radically biblical position' (pp. 78–82). This is the position that '*all* knowledge depends upon religious truth' (p. 80). That is to say, 'the influence of religious beliefs is much more a matter of a presupposed perspective guiding the direction of theorizing than of Scripture supplying specific truths for theories' (p. 104).

According to Clouser, only the radically biblical position 'can do justice to the biblical claims that having the right God is basic to all truth' (p. 107). Clouser distinguishes this stance from fundamentalist 'rationalism', which expects that religious belief will be proved true by philosophy or science (pp. 97–101). David Beck can be said to display such a fundamentalist mentality. He believes 'it is not enough to incorporate the sense of Scripture into the disciplines, that is, to put forth a Christian worldview', and argues that inerrancy 'demands the full and equal incorporation of the data of Scripture: the propositions themselves' (1991*b*: 11). Clouser (1991: 97–8) regards such attempts at combining scriptural data with scientific inquiry as relegating religious belief to the status of a theory requiring validation.

The most important potential challenge that Dooyeweerdians present to fundamentalism is their rejection of the idea that the Bible's authority is known through reason and evidences. Olthuis (1987: 14) declares, 'I do not believe that we accept the authority of the Bible at bottom because of or on account of the empirical evidence of Christian experience (J. Oliver Buswell, Jr.), nor moral value evidence (E. J. Carnell), nor historical evidence (John Warwick Montgomery and Clark Pinnock), nor the rationality of Christian truth (Carl F. H. Henry and Gordon Clark).' He insists that 'scriptural authority is self-authenticating, worked in a person's heart by the testimony of the Holy Spirit' (ibid.). This challenge is largely rejected by the heirs of the Princeton tradition: 'although the faith event is certainly a mystery, God who made the human mind can surely use the evidences of his activity and existence to effect the conversion of the human heart' (Pinnock 1987: 54).[37] Dooyeweerdians are not much interested in Princeton-style apologetics. They are more concerned with the spiritually transforming effects of reading scripture. Evan Runner (1982: 42) presents a picture of 'the whole man [being] overpowered by the Holy Spirit of God through Scripture'. The reader of scripture is moved by the same Spirit which moved the characters in the Bible.

> As the reader imbibes the spirit and mind that informs the text and that is by God's decree available to man in the Bible, he is changed; the strange world of the Bible becomes his and he now goes about trying to make the world of his life relevant to the new world that he has [been] compelled to accept . . . at the deepest level of his existence. It is in this way that man is transformed and controlled by the Word of God. *The revelation of the Word of God becomes his context.*[38]

The emphasis is on biblical truth as visionary rather than as evidential. Olthuis (1987: 46) finds the Bible to be 'immediately relevant to all of life', not because it is inerrant and can be mined for apposite proof-texts, but because it is 'the story of redemption'. We are envisioned through wearing 'the "glasses" of Scripture' and 'empowered in the Spirit of God to re-envision that life-giving message in relevant specifics that make for healing and hope in our troubled times'. Thus we are 'delivered from a kind of biblicism which seeks a specific proof-text in order to live out the Gospel message in all the various areas of life' (ibid. 46, 45).

[37] Correspondence with John Peck has made me aware that some Dooyeweerdians also feel that 'talk about the witness of the Spirit' is 'obscurantist'. Peck prefers to say that 'the significance of scripture is a by-product of one's faith-encounter with Christ', which is closer to Kuyper's position (letter to the author, 16 May 1996). His point highlights the lack of Christological reference in the Dooyeweerdian writings examined here, and so their distance from Kuyper's views in this respect.

[38] See Ch. 8 for a fuller discussion of Dooyeweerdian presentation of the Bible as 'a standard against which the horizon of the reader must be normed' (Runner 1982: 47).

Similarly, Henry Vander Goot (1984: 2) of Calvin College escapes the proof-text mentality by defining the '*literal sense* of the *canon*' as the 'overall sense'. Like Olthuis, Vander Goot identifies the 'overall sense' with Dooyeweerd's apprehension of the biblical story: 'the creation–fall–redemption–consummation structure of the biblical narrative' (ibid.; cf. 3, 24–5, 67–78).

This way of thinking demands a reappraisal of the concept of inerrancy: 'The contrast in the Scriptures is between truth (as faithfulness) and lying (as instability, swerving from the truth) rather than between truth (as scientific precision), and errancy (as limited or defective information)' (Olthuis 1987: 45).

The Bible's truthfulness is preserved by moving away from an emphasis upon fact. Olthuis locates truth in non-deceiving guidance, Vander Goot in the biblical story-line, and Clouser (1991: 98) in what he terms the '*religious* point of view'. Clouser illustrates the difference between his method of biblical interpretation and that of a fundamentalist by showing how he is able to let go of the historicity of the creation account in Genesis—something which Van Til holds dear. Clouser (ibid. 99–100) interprets the creation account as 'expressing the "why" of God's creating rather than its "how"'. It conveys an 'order of *purpose*' rather than a chronological order. Hence it 'becomes ridiculous' to argue over whether the 'days' are twenty-four-hour periods or geological eras.

Does this constitute a move away from fundamentalism as Barr describes it? Barr (1977: 41–2) is aware of conservative evangelical sources which have abandoned chronological interpretations of Genesis 1. Evangelicals make these manœuvres, he argues, in order to avoid an admission that the Bible is wrong. Clouser's interpretation of Genesis is neither novel nor obviously non-fundamentalist. However, Clouser does not fit neatly into the categories in Barr's analysis. While he interprets scripture in ways which ensure that it is always on the side of truth, by biblical truth he does not mean accuracy of evidence. Therefore he does not practise the same sort of maximal-conservatism that Barr condemns in much evangelical scholarship.[39]

[39] From my discussions with Dooyeweerdians, might I suggest how their response to Barr—were they to give one—would differ from the responses of evangelical scholars noted in Ch. 2? They would not defend the genuinely critical nature of their biblical scholarship, especially since they make a virtue of not sharing the same critical criteria as historical critics. Nor would they simply state that Barr works with naturalistic presuppositions. They

One's conception of the truth of scripture is related to how one conceives the purpose of scripture, and Dooyeweerdians make this more explicit than do most defenders of (unlimited) inerrancy. Clouser (1991: 98) describes the purpose of scripture as being to record God's establishing his covenant with humankind. Wolters (1985: 6–7) and Vander Goot (1984: 42) regard its purpose as instructive: that biblical truth provides practical instruction; and that scripture draws its readers 'into its world and into its mentality' and predisposes them to 'proper doing'. None of these scholars need a doctrine of inerrancy of the kinds discussed in Chapter 4 in order to maintain their view of scripture. Rather, they need readers who identify with their sense of the immediacy and transforming efficacy with which the message embodied in scripture works in the believer's heart.

However, they renounce inerrancy by choosing soft targets, such as the inappropriateness of looking for social scientific and natural scientific data in the Bible. Clouser (1991: 98) chooses creation science, and argues that it is 'simply a colossal error to suppose that because an event is religiously important, such as the importance of the flood to the covenant with Noah, that it must therefore also be of key importance to geology or any other science'. The majority of inerrantists would agree with him. The more significant matter for investigating the difference between Dooyeweerdian and fundamentalistic approaches to scripture is that of historical accuracy. Is it important that scripture accurately record the Flood as history, rather than as science? More pertinently, is it important that the Gospels be historically accurate? Is there a relation between the truth and efficacy of the biblical story and the historical accuracy with which its main component narratives are recorded?

Vander Goot (1984: 52, 63) is interested in the possibility of a 'realistic' reading of the surface text, as suggested by Erich Auerbach and Hans Frei, by which he means taking the biblical language as 'the language of ordinary events and common sense that takes the world as we experience it for granted'. Figuration and typology are an extension of this plain reading of the text, and the only genuine framework for interpreting the Bible is a

would ask detailed methodological questions to tease out more subtle 'prejudices' in his work. So they would want to know on which scholars Barr leans. They may even suggest, as Richard Russell did to me, that he is Baconian.

canonical or theological one which gives priority to the literal and typological sense of scripture as shared by the Christian community of faith. Olthuis (1987: 44, 45) does not endorse such narrative realism. Nor does he see scripture as 'a collection of psychotherapeutic case-histories, . . . or a series of socio-political histories'. He describes scripture as inerrant on a 'depth-level' in connection 'with the ultimate questions of life', not so much as theological discourse but as encounter. Neither scholar addresses the problem of historical inconsistency directly. We do not know whether or to what extent it matters that, for example, the passion or resurrection narratives cannot be made to cohere in detail, and therefore that some and possibly all of these narratives are misleading in some way. Moreover, their bypassing of historical-criticism in favour of newer hermeneutical approaches relieves them of having to address questions of historicity that are raised by study of the sources and development of biblical writings.[40] Their evasiveness on historical issues leaves one suspecting that fundamentalist attitudes remain in this area to some degree.

7.7. Kuyperianism and Fundamentalism

Kuyperianism has suggested alternatives to a fundamentalist evangelicalism in various ways. In particular, Dooyeweerd's philosophy of the law-idea has challenged assumptions about the neutrality of theoretical thought and has encouraged greater cultural and social involvement. Van Til developed his distinctive presuppositionalism in an attempt to provide an alternative form of apologetics. In fact he produced an inconsistent Kuyperian–Idealist–Warfieldian synthesis. It is of the essence of Kuyperian thought that the fundamental principles one employs consistently underlie all of one's endeavours. Ironically, the majority of evangelicals who have had any contact with Kuyperian ideas have not consistently applied them. Many have accepted only the cultural vision alongside forms of thought and practice which reflect their fundamentalist heritage. Generally, evangelicals have not altered their apologetic or evangelistic techniques. Most have rejected whatever is threatening to their biblical conservatism,

[40] On the bypassing of historical-criticism see Ch. 8.

failing even to notice how radically Kuyper's doctrine of scripture differs from that of Warfield. Dooyeweerdian scholars have been more aware of the challenge to an evangelical understanding of scripture, but they are small in number and insufficiently explicit in addressing the major issue of historicity. Therefore, while Barr may 'not appear to be conversant with the apologetic method of Van Til, or the philosophical contributions of Dooyeweerd' (Edgar 1977: 155), these developments have not incurred major changes in the fundamentalism he describes.

8

Rescinding Fundamentalism?: Evangelicals and Hermeneutics

In responding to Barr's critique, R. T. France (1991: 53, 54–5, 62–3) suggests that evangelicals who take modern hermeneutical questions seriously do not deserve to be called 'fundamentalist'. Since the 1970s, evangelicals have made departures into phenomenological hermeneutics. Phenomenological hermeneutics operate with the philosophical conviction that in the phenomenal realm texts and other phenomena attain the meaning we attribute to them. Such hermeneutics begin with a view of readers as phenomenologically situated in a context in terms of which they interpret the text (and the whole of life). Evangelicals display varying degrees of comfort with this way of thinking. They do not themselves use the term 'phenomenological hermeneutics'—the phenomenology of Husserl is a long way from their own tradition—but they refer to these developments in the philosophy of interpretation simply as 'hermeneutics' or sometimes as the 'new hermeneutic'.

An interest in hermeneutics has added an awareness of cultural influences to evangelical talk of presuppositions. Presuppositions are no longer simply the enemies of objectivity, standing in the way of 'true science'. The scientific method has itself come to be seen as derivative of a particular way of understanding. Nor do presuppositions signify only that one has either a biblical or a non-biblical world-view. They also reflect 'our own cultural imprisonment' and the 'cultural conditioning of the biblical authors' (Stott 1992: 186).

Evangelicals now recognize it as an 'illusion that we come to the biblical text as innocent, objective, impartial, culture-free investigators' (ibid. 185). 'As a matter of fact', they argue, 'no one approaches Scripture without some preunderstanding; presuppositionless exegesis is impossible. Even Bultmann acknowledged that!' (Klooster 1984: 464). They feel gratified that the supposed objectivity of higher criticism, which they questioned since the beginning of the century, has been exposed by hermeneutical philosophy. They enjoy Gadamer's attack on the Enlightenment's prejudice against prejudice, and employ Gadamerian rhetoric against their critics: 'Let [them] not imagine that they function without presuppositions . . . they have a prejudice against presuppositions of any sort; they have a systematic aversion to systems, a dogmatic revulsion against dogma!' (Nicole 1983: 205).[1]

These developments enable evangelicals to acknowledge that no perception can be wholly objective, and so to challenge a level of *naïveté* in their earlier interpretative practices. They are worthy developments so long as they do not issue in a full-fledged constructionism which grants no separate existence to that which is construed in language. Evangelicals have a strongly realist bias which prevents them from going this far. This bias saves them from concluding that a text cannot represent reality, and it protects them from the philosophically incoherent position that all interpretation is wholly non-objective. Even a deconstruction of cultural conditioning presupposes some objectivity, in the sense of something existing in the material which is not invented by the deconstructing agent (cf. Nuttall 1983: 1–49; 1992: 201–32). At the same time, many evangelicals attempt to retain a level of objectivity which can accommodate the inerrancy doctrine. This strains their appeal to phenomenological hermeneutics and in many cases renders it implausible.

8.1. Identifying the Issues

The philosophical conviction behind phenomenological hermeneutics—that phenomena attain the meaning we attribute to them—stems from Kantian thought, and is one which evangelicals have traditionally rejected.[2] It is therefore surprising

[1] Cf. Gadamer ([1975] 1989: 270): 'The recognition that all understanding inevitably involves some prejudice gives the hermeneutical problem its real thrust . . . [The] fundamental prejudice of the Enlightenment is the prejudice against prejudice itself, which denies tradition its power'.

[2] It derives more directly from Husserl, who sought a starting-point for philosophy to overcome the 'objectivism' assumed in the inherited scientific world-view. As Gadamer ([1975] 1989: 243) points out, Husserl himself recognized his phenomenology to be a continuation of Kant's transcendental enquiry and critique of naïve objectivism.

that evangelicals are warming to interpretative principles based on this conviction. Barr (1991*a*: 151) regards their move as an opportunistic appeal to anti-objectivist trends: 'Everyone, it is thought, is working with presuppositions. Therefore evangelical presuppositions are as good as anyone else's. An evangelical bias can be slipped into interpretation without a bad conscience'. Barr (1980*a*: 73) finds it ironic that conservative evangelicals endorse such innovative and unorthodox hermeneutical theories in the hope 'that some conservative advantage could be gained from doing so'. He suspects that evangelicals seek in hermeneutics a means of circumventing the historical-critical task, so that they can continue to assert scriptural authority despite the difficult critical issues that arise for one who holds such a conservative view of the Bible. 'Ultimately', Barr (1991*a*: 150) argues, 'it is often distrust of the historical approach that is the motive . . . So long as the force of historical-critical arguments can be turned aside, any sort of reasoning is acceptable'.

Evangelicals, on their own admission, employ hermeneutical procedures which enable them to retain biblical authority:

> God's Word is unchanging, not our approach to its interpretation . . . Evangelicals need not be single-minded in their hermeneutical posture. What one overlooks, underestimates, obscures, using a particular interpretive strategy, another might uncover. It is the biblical text itself that should remain authoritative, not any particular approach to its reading. (Johnston 1988: 63)

It is because evangelicals allow nothing to challenge their view of biblical authority that critics suspect them of acting in bad faith. This unease is succinctly expressed by John Barton (1988: 65):

> Hermeneutics . . . seems to interest primarily people who combine a high view of scriptural authority with a critical awareness of the cultural gap separating us from the Bible. They thus belong to the whole movement of thought in modern theology which asks how the Bible can still be heard as authoritative and inspiring Scripture 'after all': how we can accept critical approaches *and yet still* hear the Bible as the Word of God; how we can reclaim the Scriptures for faith and for theology *despite* what the critics have done . . . Sophisticated hermeneutical moves can enable conservative biblicists to continue in their biblicism by circumventing the problems raised by critical study.

Having discovered both maximal-conservatism and an evasion of key questions about historicity in evangelical biblical scholarship, we may feel inclined to suppose that evangelicals are not being entirely straight in their use of modern hermeneutics. When we read evangelical discussions of hermeneutics we will, I think, sense some distortion. Yet uncovering precisely where the problems lie is not a straightforward matter.

Is Barr right to suspect evangelicals of combining incompatible methods of interpretation so as to avoid problems of historicity? Are evangelicals themselves making *bona fide* claims to take seriously modern hermeneutical questions—questions which demand radical changes in the way biblical truth is conceived? A factor which seems to impede Barr's interpretation is that evangelicals employ modern hermeneutical insights principally as a way of speaking about the significance of biblical statements for today. The truth or meaning of these statements is deemed to be unchanging. This should lead us to suspect the consistency with which evangelicals court phenomenological ideas. If my judgement is accurate on this matter, then Barr's suspicions are not well grounded, but equally evangelicals are not rescinding fundamentalist notions of biblical truth and authority.

Evangelicals show great caution in their acceptance of modern hermeneutical trends, and are constantly on the alert against subjectivism. The influence from phenomenological hermeneutics is confined to the point of application of a text, and is not permitted in any way to inform the meaning. The meaning of the text is still to be discovered through grammatico-historical exegesis. This method of exegesis is defined by Geisler (1984: 898) as discovering the 'meaning of the text in its grammatical forms and in the historical, cultural context in which the text is expressed', and by Packer (1984*b*: 910) as 'asking what is the linguistically natural way to understand the text in its historical setting'.

It is usual these days that evangelicals also associate the meaning of biblical passages with '*what their human writers were consciously expressing*' (Packer 1990: 48). For Packer, this principle embodies the Reformation insistence that scripture be interpreted literally rather than allegorically (p. 49). For others, it provides a response to the existence of inaccuracies in scripture along the lines that, for example, numerical or scientific precision was not the author's primary intention. However, some evangelicals feel that even the principle of authorial intention opens 'the door wide to a kind of psychological second-guessing as replacing a sober analysis of the text' (Nicole 1983: 206). They therefore prefer what Robert Johnston (1988: 60) describes as 'objective literal theories' to 'expressive theories centering on the author'.

Those evangelicals who are also aware of modern hermeneutical philosophy combine grammatico-historical exegesis and the search for authorial intention with some notion of hermeneutical dialogue. Their most common tactic is to employ E. D. Hirsch's distinction between meaning and significance, according to which meaning lies in the author's intended sense and significance lies in the present application.[3] This is reflected in Kathleen Boone's (1989) thesis that fundamentalist discourse can be likened to that of Hirsch and contrasted with that of Stanley Fish. Fish finds meaning supplied by the interpreting community.

Boone chooses as her representative fundamentalists those from the mainstream, Anglo-American, conservative evangelical tradition: James Packer, Harold Lindsell, and the Council on Biblical Inerrancy, as well as the Princeton theologians whose doctrine of scripture underlies their basic approach (ibid. 29). Her decision to use the term 'fundamentalist' is influenced by Barr's work (p. 9). According to Boone, the distinction between the 'unchanging *meaning* of the text and the text's changing *significance*' is itself cause for suspicion (p. 66). She suspects that fundamentalists might start reinterpreting biblical passages so that what was once thought to be meaning is now stated as significance, and in this way absorb evolutionary theory without ever attributing false meaning to scripture (pp. 66–7).

Barr (1977: 40–1) might point to the surrender of a literal interpretation of the Genesis creation story as a case in point. If this surrender occurs along the lines Boone suggests, then the distinction between meaning and significance is itself a tool by which evangelicals circumvent textual difficulties. My proposal that this distinction impedes Barr's interpretation of evangelical motives would then be defeated.

However, Boone's study is itself distorted in that she overlooks any evangelical discussion of hermeneutics. She discusses funda-

[3] They do not distinguish between the (unverifiable) private intention of the author and the (ascertainable) public meaning that the contemporary community placed upon the text.

mentalist discourse as though its participants are wholly ignorant of the tools she employs to analyse it, and as though they are silent within the wider theoretical debate in which she engages. She mentions that Carl Henry and Walter Kaiser specifically cite Hirsch's work (Boone 1989: 28, 122 n. 12). However, she creates the general impression that evangelicals have not consciously fashioned parallels between Hirsch's literary theory and their own interpretative practice. She seems unaware that evangelicals appeal to Hirsch's writings as a way of retaining constancy of meaning while grappling with insights from Bultmann, Heidegger, and Gadamer. She cites only the Chicago Statement on Biblical Inerrancy (1978) and not its sister document on Biblical Hermeneutics (1982), and she fails to discover Packer's (1983: 349) presentation of the interpreter as moving 'to and fro within the hermeneutical spiral'.

Having distinguished meaning from significance, evangelicals find the latter in a fusion of horizons. So John Stott (1982: 221, 186) uses both Hirsch's dictum, 'a text means what its author meant', and insights from Anthony Thiselton's work that 'understanding takes place when two sets of horizons are brought into relation to each other, namely those of the text and those of the interpreter'. Evangelicals use the term 'hermeneutics' to refer generally to the process of dialogue between text and reader, which they think of as occurring after the meaning of the text has been ascertained. That is to say, hermeneutics does not enter the discussion at the point of meaning, where the sorts of textual gymnastics distrusted by Barr and Boone might be performed, but at the later stage of transposing the biblical message across cultures.

Evangelicals value hermeneutics particularly for preaching, personal and group Bible study, and evangelism and missionary work (Thiselton 1977*a*: 328; Stott 1982; Achtemeier 1986; Conn 1984). 'Bridging the gap' across cultures, a metaphor first used by Berkouwer ([1966] 1975: 137), is a theme appearing in many recent evangelical writings (e.g. Goldingay 1977*a*: 352; Johnston 1979: 151; Stott 1982: 135–79; Noll and Wells 1988: 11; McGrath and Green 1993: 51–85). Stott (1982) seeks to make the Gospel relevant to today's youth, Johnston (1979) tackles current social issues, and Conn (1984) responds to the need for cultural relevance felt during his experiences as a missionary.

The image of the fusion of horizons is employed by evangelicals to explain how the biblical message is received in different forms. Like Kuyperian thought, it is valued largely for its cultural and social implications. A hermeneutical theory which states that the significance of a passage strikes different people in different ways enables evangelicals to relativize problematic elements in scripture. Hence, during a time of increased evangelical social awareness, socially awkward passages such as Paul's pronouncements on women are translated for the present day without biblical authority being compromised (e.g. Goldingay 1977*a*: 351; Johnston 1979: 50–76; Conn 1987: 29; Stott 1992: 202–4).[4] The reception of the text is granted no bearing on the text's meaning, which remains independent of its readers. The 'question of the inerrancy and trustworthiness of Scripture' is attached to the discovery of 'what the text *meant* when it was originally written' (Fee 1980: 182). Evangelicals are thus freed to differ over such issues as women's ministries in so far as these are regarded as questions of interpretation and not of the authority of scripture (ibid. 182–3). Their friendliness towards hermeneutics does not indicate a decline in commitment to the factual accuracy of scripture or to scripture's primacy in guiding ethical and religious practice. The Bible remains normative, its meaning unchanged.

Therefore, while Barr and Boone have identified the sorts of hermeneutical manœuvres made by evangelicals, they have located them wrongly. Evangelicals enjoy the freedom of assessing awkward texts 'hermeneutically', but they do not thereby revise the meaning or truth of biblical passages, least of all of seeming historical narratives. Instead they concentrate on the contemporary significance of prescriptive, socially problematic texts. In fact they discuss hermeneutical method more than they do its application to particular worrisome passages. Barton's (1988: 65–6) assessment seems at first to be more on target. Barton argues that the cause of biblicist anxiety is the exaggerated gap between ourselves and the text which arises because of an exaggerated view of biblical authority. Evangelicals speak frequently about the cultural gap and employ hermeneutics as, to use Barton's term, 'the solution' of this difficulty.

[4] For example, Stott (1992: 202–4) takes it as a timeless teaching that women should submit to male authority but regards its expression in women covering their heads as culturally relative. He does not simply discard this cultural expression but asks that it be transposed into appropriate contemporary symbols.

Yet on closer inspection it appears that evangelicals do not really perceive a worrisome cultural gap. Rather, they remind themselves that there is supposed to be a gap. Anthony Thiselton and others have worked hard to make them aware of one. It is not a problem that they have made their own, and they address it only half convinced of the need to do so. Therefore evangelicals would wholeheartedly agree with Barton's (ibid. 66) suggestion that the 'hermeneutical question is . . . not a question of how we can make something useful out of antique rubbish, but how we can best appropriate—and critically evaluate—literature that already speaks powerfully to us'. They do not regard scripture as ever ceasing so to speak. They are coy about saying so when providing an objective, evidence-based defence of scripture's authority, but when endorsing 'hermeneutics' evangelical scholars readily affirm the Holy Spirit's power to speak through scripture. However, in doing so they frequently undermine the need for hermeneutical theory by suggesting that the transcendent voice of the Spirit, rather than the hermeneutical process, makes transcultural understanding possible. Even then, they regard cultural similarity as more significant than cultural difference, and anyway continue to believe that biblical truth bears an objectivity that transcends all culture.

> All men and women in all cultures are made in the image of God. And when this fact is joined with a biblical concept of truth as having an objective grounding and reference point in the nature of God and in the doctrine of creation, the possibility for *adequate* (even if no one knows *comprehensively* except God) transcultural communication has been fairly provided and secured. (Kaiser 1979*b*: 32)

For these reasons their embrace of phenomenological hermeneutics is often disingenuous.

8.2. Anthony Thiselton: Introducing Evangelicals to Hermeneutics

The encouragement to evangelicals to think hermeneutically came largely from Britain, particularly through the work of Anthony Thiselton. Thiselton contributes to evangelical publications and conferences (1977*a*; 1977*b*; 1985; 1988), and his ideas are promoted by John Stott (1982; 1992), and to a lesser extent by Jim Packer (1983; 1988). His work on hermeneutics is conducted between two extremes: a 'theological conservatism' which, under 'the guise of an objectivist view of this text . . . simply assumes no difference between a "common sense" interpretive tradition and what the text itself says'; and 'supposedly progressive hermeneutics', which reduces questions about meaning 'entirely to questions about language-effect in the modern world' (1985: 80–1).

Thiselton has drawn on insights from Gadamer, Heidegger, and Bultmann, and from the distinct Wittgensteinian tradition. He weaves these strands together in the publication of his Ph.D. thesis *The Two Horizons* (1980). He critically assesses the strengths and weaknesses of the new hermeneutic of Fuchs and Ebeling, and of reader-response theories. He comes to prefer the speech-act model, which regards language-uses as acts which have effects (1970; 1974; 1980: 129, 436; 1985: 100, 107–13; 1992: 16–19 *et passim*). In this he has been influenced by J. L. Austin's writings on speech-acts (Thiselton 1970; 1974), and by Wittgenstein's emphasis upon language as forming 'part of an activity' in public interaction.

Grammatico-historical exegesis implies that individual words are the primary bearers of meaning. Speech-act theory, by contrast, puts words into the context of a speech-act. A speech-act occurs at the point of interrelation between the situation addressed by the biblical writer and the situation of the modern reader. Speech-acts lead us to take into account feelings and attitudes and not just the communication of thought. Thiselton applies speech-act theory to written texts: to the transformative function of Jesus' parables in the first instance, but also beyond the writing of oral discourse. He thus emphasizes the functional alongside the cognitive aspect of the biblical writings. '[They] embody an institutional framework of covenant in which commitments and effects become operative in acts of promise, acts of blessing, acts of forgiveness, acts of pronouncing judgment, acts of repentance, acts of worship, acts of authorization, acts of communion, and acts of love' (1992: 17–18).

Thiselton encourages one to think not in terms of a biblical message neatly packaged, but of the biblical impact in real life. However, it is not his version of speech-act theory that has been adopted by evangelicals but rather his description of the fusion of horizons derived from Gadamer's thought.

While Thiselton's work is highly technical it is trusted by evangelicals who know him to be of their general theological orientation. He wrote two articles in 1977 specifically addressing evangelicals on the subject of hermeneutics: 'The New Hermeneutic' (1977*a*) in I. Howard Marshall's collection *New Testament Interpretation*, and 'Understanding God's Word Today' (1977*b*) for the National Evangelical Anglican Congress in Nottingham in 1977 (NEAC '77). France (1991: 53) describes this Congress as 'one of the theological markers' of the year: 'All at once "hermeneutics" was on the evangelical agenda . . . Problems of interpretation and of cultural relativity which had previously been discussed mainly in academic circles now became common currency'. Packer's (1983: 325) account of NEAC '77 indicates how alien the concept of hermeneutics was to evangelical Anglicans at the time: 'many saw nothing of importance in the subject, and it became a conference joke to refer to "Herman Eutics" as the latest in a line of esoteric continental theologians'.[5]

In his NEAC article, Thiselton (1977*b*: 92) draws attention to the particular historical situations of both the biblical text and the modern reader. He warns evangelicals not to assume that the meaning of scripture is self-evident. The problem as he describes it is 'that of how the text of the Bible, written in the ancient world, can so speak to the modern hearer that it engages with his own situation and horizons without doing violence to its original purpose' (ibid.). His solution is to let the text speak (pp. 99–106). Attention to the particularity of the ancient text—its linguistic, historical, literary, and theological context—must be followed by engagement. A combination of 'distancing' and 'fusion' is required: distancing the assumptions of one's own background whilst reading the text, but allowing a fusion in which one listens to the text and allows it to speak. Failure to distance one's own assumptions will result in seeing the text 'through the spectacles' of one's own tradition (p. 104). So Thiselton warns the UCCF circle against hearing 'the text only in a "Christian Union" kind of way' (ibid.).

One brings questions to the text and reformulates these questions in the light of what the text has to say. This is the process of

[5] When Packer himself introduced Southern Baptists to hermeneutics in 1987, his talks were transcribed and the name of one Continental thinker, 'Godimer', remained mysterious (Packer 1988: *passim*).

dialogue, a key concept in Gadamerian hermeneutics. If the text is not allowed to question our questions, evangelicals will continue to ask inappropriate things of the text: 'Very seldom, if ever, can we turn Isaiah into an oracle on the subject of moving house or changing jobs, or use the Fourth Gospel for guidance about the building of a new church hall' (p. 105). Finally there is the need for response to the biblical message. Evangelicals have erred in overstressing the teaching element in scripture. The Bible 'is not simply a handbook of information, either for theological doctrine or for daily life' (ibid.), but conveys God's word as a word to be obeyed. Hence it is an authority both for faith and life.

The form in which Thiselton's presentation was accepted by the Congress can be seen in its pronouncement on 'Understanding the Bible Today' in *The Nottingham Statement* (1977: 17):

> Interpreting the Bible is a creative process which: (*a*) looks at a passage in the *ancient* theological, historical, cultural and linguistic context that forms the 'horizon' of the writer; and (*b*) allows it to come alive and arrest the *modern* hearer.
>
> The centuries of using the Bible that have passed both help and hinder the modern reader in interpreting the Bible today. The first thing he has to learn to do is to question, in the light of the text: (*i*) the assumptions with which he comes to the text; (*ii*) the assumptions made in his own culture, as these may affect his interpretation; and (*iii*) even his own church's formulations and traditions.
>
> We must beware of hearing from the text only what we expect and want to hear.

In a section on application, the Congress states that the biblical text 'must be allowed to engage with the varied "horizons" of hearers: preacher, congregation and those outside the church' (p. 18). The preacher, it advises, should be aware of the differences between these horizons, preferably through personal and emotional involvement in the cultures in which he ministers.

In the following year, the Lausanne Committee's Theology and Education Group (in which Stott, Packer, and Marshall participated) produced the Willowbank Report on Gospel and culture, which declared:

> Today's readers cannot come to the text in a personal vacuum, and should not try to. Instead, they should come with an awareness of concerns stemming from their cultural background, personal situation,

and responsibility to others. These concerns will influence the questions which are put to the Scriptures. What is received back, however, will not be answers only, but more questions. As we address Scripture, Scripture addresses us. We find that our culturally conditioned presuppositions are being challenged and our questions corrected. In fact, we are compelled to reformulate our previous questions and to ask fresh ones. So the living interaction proceeds. (Stott and Coote 1980: 317)

Thiselton's influence is slower to filter down to UCCF level. In 'Reframing the UCCF Doctrinal Basis', Vaughan Roberts (1992) considers 'the Hermeneutic Framework', but focuses entirely on the concept of 'infallibility'.

In 'The New Hermeneutic', Thiselton (1977*a*) introduces to evangelicals the thought of Fuchs and Ebeling. He modifies their work in significant ways, particularly expressing a concern for the loss of the cognitive aspect of biblical language. Thiselton attempts to balance the 'knowledge' and 'information' aspects of a text with its performative, engaging function. He de-emphasizes the cognitive aspects of scripture when addressing evangelicals and re-emphasizes them when criticizing the new hermeneutic. However, he warns evangelicals that 'at present there is more danger of neglecting the new hermeneutic than of pressing its claims too far'. The new hermeneutic '*is concerned above all with the "rights" of the text*, as over against concepts which the interpreter himself may try to bring with him and impose on it'. The traditional 'subject–object' scrutiny of the text 'tends to tame and to domesticate the word of God, so that it merely echoes back the interpreter's own perspectives' (pp. 327, 328).

The new hermeneutic poses the all-important question of how the Bible can speak to us anew. Mere repetitions of the text are rejected in favour of reformulations which better convey the original message. This involves a critique of literalism, and a move away from concentration on individual words in favour of discerning the overall 'word' (pp. 309–10). It also means a rejection of Cartesian epistemology and of the model of theology as 'the queen of the sciences'. The text is not a passive object but addresses and judges the reader (pp. 310–11, 312–13).[6] A scientific method which requires the pretence of objectivity does not suit the work of

[6] Fuchs' and Ebeling's view of language as effective or performative, and not merely informative, provides a point of contact with Thiselton's own action theory of language (Thiselton 1977*b*: 312; 1985: 108–9).

theology, which is to translate God's revelation received in one culture into language and concepts which enable it to be received with essentially the same meaning into the present culture. The hermeneutical task is to produce 'common understanding', a world of shared assumptions in which effective communication can take place (p. 311).

Fuchs and Ebeling rightly deny that the role of the Holy Spirit in communicating the word of God replaces the work of hermeneutical translation (p. 309). This is important to bear in mind when we find evangelicals suggesting that cultural confusions are eradicated by the power of the Spirit. Fuchs, Ebeling, and Thiselton are clear that the Spirit does not absolve us of our interpretative duties. As Thiselton (1977*b*: 119–20) argued at NEAC '77:

> The Holy Spirit works *through* the kind of means we have been discussing . . . in bringing man to the place where he hears in the Bible the voice of God who is beyond any one cultural form. A doctrine of the Spirit is not therefore an alternative to hermeneutics; it is an assurance that the hermeneutical endeavour is worth while.

Two central principles emerge in Thiselton's portrayal of the new hermeneutic: that of the place of the pre-understanding of the interpreter as the basis from which questions are brought to the text, and that of the text as itself a hermeneutical aid in interpreting the present experience. The latter principle prevents the subjectivity of the interpreter from becoming dominant. The two principles co-operate in Gadamer's version of the hermeneutical circle so that there is dialogue between the text and the interpreter. Once the differences between the horizons of interpreter and text have been brought to light, the interpreter is free to move beyond or enlarge his or her horizon until it fuses with that of the text (Thiselton 1977*a*: 312–18).

Thiselton's main worries about the new hermeneutic would be shared by all evangelicals who are anxious to preserve the authority of the text over the interpreter, and who wish to retain the cognitive nature of biblical language. He reaffirms the cognitive content in scripture against excessive concentration on poetry, metaphor, hymnody, and parable which results, for example, in the loss of the historicity of the resurrection (pp. 324–5). He discourages the idea that language must be either performative or descriptive and cannot be both at the same time (pp. 325–6). He is critical of the lack of concern to understand the text correctly. Evangelicals who are worried by an overemphasis upon the experience of the interpreter would agree with him that critical-historical study should be preserved (p. 323). Thiselton is sensitive to the fear that the hermeneutical circle draws one into a man-centred relativism, and refuses to allow 'what is true for me' to become the criterion of what is true (pp. 326–37). While he rejects as philosophically naïve the view that one can have access to a self-evidently true meaning of a text, he endorses Gadamer's conception of the text speaking to and moulding the questions of the interpreter. He later suggests that an image of a spiral rather than of a circle would better convey the 'ongoing movement and progressive understanding' of this process (1980: 104).

Unnoted by evangelicals, Thiselton rejects the notion that one can discern the meaning of the text independently of the process of fusion.[7] He regards one's questions and reformulated questions as having a bearing on one's interpretation of the text's meaning. He does not follow Hirsch (1967: 255) in dividing the fusion of horizons into 'two processes that are separate and distinct'. Nor would he endorse the evangelical practice of confining the fusion to the level of application of the text. For Thiselton (1977*b*: 104–5), response to the biblical message comes after the fusion or dialogue has occurred. He therefore jeopardizes a 'self-evidently "true" meaning' (1977*a*: 327) to a greater extent than most evangelicals would find comfortable. Nevertheless, evangelicals take from Thiselton the image of a fusion of horizons, and

[7] James D. G. Dunn advances a more conservative hermeneutic than Thiselton's in this respect. He presented his hermeneutical theory in the W. H. Griffith Thomas Lectures given at Wycliffe Hall in 1987, published in *The Living Word* (1987). His theory comes closer than Thiselton's to the position of the majority of evangelicals who now write on hermeneutics. He maintains that the author's intended meaning is the normative meaning (ibid. 20–1; cf. Dunn 1982), thus retaining a clear distinction between the (original and constant) meaning of a text and our present-day understanding. He endorses the image of 'the bridge of New Testament interpretation', which must not lose 'its footing in either first or twentieth centuries' (p. 24). Like Thiselton, he prefers the image of a spiral to that of a circle (pp. 7–8), though he finds the metaphor of dialogue more appropriate still (p. 8). By 'dialogue' he means that 'which allows answers to react back on the starting point, to criticize the faith which prompted the initial question, to correct or abandon presuppositions which the dialogue shows to be faulty' (p. 19). Despite his greater hermeneutical conservatism, Dunn has been less successful than Thiselton in retaining the trust of more conservative evangelicals (see s. 2.2.3 above). This is perhaps because, as a biblical critic, he works in the area where they are most sensitive.

combine it with Hirsch's claim that the meaning of the text is unchanging.[8]

8.3. Evangelical Reactions to Hermeneutics

Generally, evangelicals accept Thiselton's (1977*a*: 99) argument that understanding 'is a creative act, even a creative art, which involves the whole personality of the reader'. They now question the emphasis upon a scientific, inductive form of interpretation, and have come to regard theological interpretation as 'not only a science, but an art . . . in that the proper valuation and interaction of its sources demand a wisdom that defies a comprehensive codification' (Johnston 1979: 149–50; cf. 1987: 5). They are not totally at ease with creativity, however, and justifiably want 'protection against arbitrary interpretation made in the name of art' (Ramm *et al.* 1987: 7). Thiselton himself would do better to endorse only partial creativity, so as to avoid licensing the type of feigning which he rightly regards as inadmissible.

Thiselton's preference for a hermeneutical spiral over a hermeneutical circle is mirrored in evangelical writings. A spiral image better protects the authoritative status of the text by suggesting that our understanding is raised to the text's level. 'Evangelicals have feared', writes Harvie Conn (1987: 27), 'that to bind text and exegete into a circle is to create a relationship of mutuality where "what is true for me" becomes the criterion of "what is true"'. John Stott (1982: 186) describes scripture as 'the senior partner' so as to avoid 'the impression that the interpreter controls the meaning of the text'. In fact evangelicals can practise such caution in this respect as to create quite a distance between themselves and Thiselton, of which they may be unaware. James Packer's (1983: 348) reservations regarding the circle image reveal his assumption that only our presuppositions and not the interpretation (meaning) of the text should be challenged in the hermeneutical enterprise: 'within the circle of presuppositionally conditioned interpretation it is always possible for dialogue and critical questioning to develop between what in the text does not

[8] Hirsch (1967: 255–6) himself prefers to speak not of a fusion of horizons, but of 'a perception of the relevance assumed by the text when its meaning is related to a present situation'.

easily or naturally fit in with our presuppositions and those presuppositions themselves, and for both our interpretation and our presuppositions to be modified as a result'.

All evangelicals are apprehensive about revising their hermeneutical practice. The majority want to retain the notion of a 'plain sense' of scripture and a conception of biblical truth as objective, immutable, and universal—qualities which they associate with the meaning of the text. They feel uneasy about scholars within the evangelical community who do not utilize a distinction between meaning and significance and who are prepared to suggest that the meaning itself is not plain.[9] Their *bête noire* is what Walter Kaiser (1988: 66) describes as the 'post-Kantian relativism' of modern exegetes, in which 'meaning is personal, subjective, and constantly changing' and '[a]ll knowledge is reduced to the horizon of one's own personal prejudices and predilections'.

They fear that the authority of scripture will be compromised if its meaning cannot be readily apprehended: 'If an understanding of some biblical cultural context or some contemporary cultural form is used to contravene the plain meaning of the text, Scripture itself is no longer the authority' (McQuilkin 1984: 222). The concept of inerrancy is classically associated with a plain reading of scripture, although we saw in Chapter 4 that inerrancy is now conceived in conjunction with various sophisticated interpretative procedures, including reading the Gospels as midrash. Still, such stalwarts as Harold Lindsell (1976: 39) reject hermeneutics as destroying 'the idea of biblical infallibility neatly by providing interpretation of Scripture at variance with the plain reading of the texts'. Lindsell (ibid. 205–6) contrasts 'the new hermeneutic' with a position in which the Bible 'is taken at its face value'.

The right of the 'plain man' to interpret scripture is basic to evangelical religion and must be maintained by those who promote modern hermeneutical theory. Evangelicals commonly protest that scholars do not have a privileged understanding of scripture. Therefore any hermeneutic they adopt must be commendable to ordinary people. Stott (1982: 187) has sought to reassure evangelicals that the 'new hermeneutic' is not beyond their grasp:

[9] Harvie Conn (1987: 27; 1984: 121) is one who rejects talk of the 'plain meaning' as assuming too much cultural agreement between the worlds of the text and the reader.

[If] the new hermeneutic had really put biblical interpretation beyond the reach of all but the professionals, then we would have to condemn it as a dangerous aberration. For Scripture is intended for ordinary people like us . . . The new hermeneutic has not reversed the blessing of the Reformation, however, and taken Scripture out of the hands of the lay people again. A little patience in learning to grasp and apply its unfamiliar principles should cure us of premature pessimism.

A major worry for evangelicals is that biblical authority will be lost if meaning is made to reside in an encounter with the interpreter rather than in an objective reading of the text. They fear that interpretation will become too subjective, and they judge Fuchs and Ebeling to have lapsed 'into uncontrolled subjectivity' (Stott 1992: 188). However, the Willowbank Report has appreciated that an approach which overlooks the cultural contexts of author and interpreter is in greater danger of distorting the Bible's meaning: 'it does not seek first to understand the text in its original context; and, therefore, it runs the risk of missing the real meaning God intends and of substituting another' (Stott and Coote 1980: 316).

Increasingly evangelicals are presenting hermeneutics as able to assert the right of the text over the interpreter, so that the text is freed to set challenges and demand conformity to its norms in a way that was not possible in more traditional hermeneutics. John Stott (1992: 189) has led the way.

The old hermeneutic concentrated on the text as *object*; we stood over it, studied it, scrutinized it, applied our rules to it, and almost took control of it. The new hermeneutic, however, concentrates on the text as *subject*; it stands over us, and we sit meekly 'under it', as the Reformers used to put it. It addresses, comforts, challenges and changes us.

8.3.1. *John Stott*

Stott's presentation of the hermeneutical task reflects aspects of Thiselton's thought without the philosophical complexity. He has transmitted a much simplified version of what he calls 'the "new hermeneutic"' (1982: 185) to the wider evangelical community.

It is to the task of preaching in particular that Stott (1982) applies what he has learned through Thiselton. He employs the image of bridge-building to illustrate the obligation, urged by

Thiselton, to communicate: 'preaching is not exposition only but communication, not just the exegesis of a text but the conveying of a God-given message to living people who need to hear it' (p. 137). In doing so, he merges the concept of encounter with the problem of how scripture is to be heard in differing cultures. He speaks of the need 'to relate the given message to the existential situation, or, to use the modern jargon, to "contextualize" the Word of God' (ibid.). This task, however, should not comply with the clamant demands for relevance:

> If we acquiesce uncritically in the world's own self-understanding, we may find ourselves the servants rather of fashion than of God. So, in order to avoid the snare of being 'populist' or a modern false prophet, the type of bridge to be built must be determined more by the biblical revelation than by the *zeitgeist* or spirit of the age. (p. 139)

Stott hopes that liberals will learn from conservatives the 'necessity of conserving the fundamentals of historic biblical Christianity', while conservatives learn from liberals the 'necessity of relating these radically and relevantly to the real world' (p. 144).

It seems that Stott has learned two key principles from Thiselton: that there is a gulf that needs to be bridged and that this task requires more than mere linguistic alteration. He appreciates that a deep level of empathy is required in order to communicate across cultures: 'Incarnation (exchanging one world for another), not just translation (exchanging one language for another) is the Christian model of communication' (p. 150).

However, as Stott develops these principles, it becomes clear that his application of them falls short of the requirements of the kind of 'new hermeneutic' he has described. He conceives the gulf to be crossed as that which exists universally between humanity and God. His prescription for bridging it is to preach Christ rather than to apply some complicated hermeneutic. He recognizes 'the deep rift between the biblical world and the modern world' (p. 138), but he assumes that a common understanding links people of all ages and cultures. He focuses on questions concerning the meaning of life, freedom, and transcendence, which occupy men and women in 'every generation and every culture' (p. 151).

Stott universalizes, which is the very tendency discouraged in phenomenological hermeneutics. Fuchs employs a concept of *das Einverstandnis* (common understanding) which is more akin to 'empathy', and is more localized. He describes it by reference to a close-knit family who share the same assumptions, attitudes, and experiences, and hence speak a common language. Fuchs understands the hermeneutical task as the need to recreate the common world of understanding necessary for effective communication (Thiselton 1977*a*: 311). For Stott (1982: 154), after all his words on hermeneutics, it is through encounter with Christ that cultural transcendence is achieved. Fulfilment of 'every truly human aspiration' is found in Christ who, as our contemporary, 'now lives to meet human need in all its variety today' (pp. 151, 154). Stott therefore encourages the preacher to preach Christ, which is a commendable but not hermeneutically specific directive.

Stott introduces a different concept in order to explain how ethical teaching is made relevant to today. It is contemporized neither through hermeneutical principles nor through the person of Christ, but via a 'Christian mind' (p. 170). Here Stott reveals an influence possibly from Dooyeweerd's philosophy and certainly from Harry Blamires, a student of C. S. Lewis whose book *The Christian Mind* (1963) was popular among evangelicals in the 1960s.[10] A Christian mind 'is thinking about everything, however apparently "secular", and doing so "Christianly" or within a Christian frame of reference'. It has 'absorbed biblical truths and Christian presuppositions so thoroughly that it is able to view every issue from a Christian perspective and so reach a Christian judgement about it'. A mind may be said to be Christian when it has grasped the 'fourfold biblical scheme of creation, fall, redemption and consummation, and is able to evaluate the phenomena of life in the light of it' (Stott 1982: 170).

Stott thus merges the concept of a Christian mind with hermeneutical influences, as he did in *The Nottingham Statement* (1977: 18): 'we must not try to force the Bible to answer distinctively modern questions to which the text does not refer. The

[10] Blamires wrote independently of the Dutch influence and has had no sustained contact with Kuyperians. He espouses the nature–supernature dualism which Dooyeweerd rejects: he describes the Christian mind in terms of a supernatural orientation, and conceives of the Christian revelation as a 'breaking-in of the greater supernatural order upon our more limited finite world' (1963: 68). Stott may have caught something of a Dooyeweerdian perspective, as he did a feminist perspective, from Elaine Storkey, who succeeded Stott as Director of the Institute of Contemporary Christianity. See Storkey's (1985: 151–9) assessment of the biblical perspective on women in the light of the themes of creation, fall, and redemption.

answers to those questions come in a different way, as Christians exercise their Bible-trained minds'. The preacher as bridge-builder should be 'authoritative in expounding biblical principles, but tentative in applying them to the complex issues of the day' (1982: 178). People should be encouraged to develop Christian minds and thus enabled to make their own decisions.

Stott does not state that one develops a Christian mind through a process of dialogue between text and interpreter, though this move is open to him. Therefore, it is not clear that ultimately he conceives hermeneutical dialogue as necessary for relating biblical teaching to contemporary issues.

8.3.2. *J. I. Packer*

Packer (1983: 325) locates himself on the side of the 'theologically informed' who accepted hermeneutics as the key intellectual issue of the 1980s. He proposes that evangelical hermeneutics benefit from the 'major insight' contributed by Gadamer's teaching on the fusion of horizons (p. 338). He argues that awareness of cultural differences between our world and the world of the text, and insistence on the need for 'distancing', saves us from a *naïveté* which characterizes much popular Bible study and preaching (pp. 339–40).

Yet Packer is primarily concerned with what the text 'objectively means', which he defines thus: '"Objectively" signifies historically, permanently, and publicly and "means" is a timeless present signifying "meant at and from the time of writing"' (p. 343). The objective meaning of a scriptural passage comprises the human author's intended meaning—which Packer expresses through a reformulation of Warfield's principle, 'What he meant, God meant'—together with 'God's further meaning, as revealed when the text is exegeted in its canonical context' (p. 350). He warns evangelicals that the term 'Scripture' means something 'radically different' to 'most of today's hermeneutical pioneers' from what it means to evangelicals (p. 340). His main fear, as seen by the two questions which he puts to the new hermeneutic of Fuchs and Ebeling, is loss of an objective, authoritative standard.

His first question is this: 'Can the new hermeneutic state the relation between what, in its view, comes to each individual from the biblical text in the language-event, and what the text meant historically—that is, what grammatico-historical exegesis finds in it?' (p. 342). Packer argues that Fuchs arbitrarily chooses not to consider those aspects of the New Testament which consist of 'rational argument and systematic elucidation of theological concepts, in unambiguously subject–object terms' (pp. 343–4). Thus Fuchs develops his own account of the Christian faith, extracting from scripture the single message to cease from self-assertion and practise love instead (p. 344). The 'restraint of the text as object—i.e., as carrier of the precise meaning that its words are expressing—has been withdrawn', and an 'uncontrolled linguistic mysticism' unleashed (p. 343).

Secondly, he asks: 'Can the new hermeneutic provide any criterion of truth or value for assessing the new self-understanding(s) to which language-events give rise?' It seems not, since we have been denied the criteria of 'correspondence with apostolic teaching in general and the historical sense of the text in particular'. We cannot test the language-events that come to us, and so we are sunk in subjectivity. Packer wants to retain a 'subject-object frame of reference for knowledge of God through Scripture' (p. 344). He concludes:

> Logically, the new hermeneutic is relativism; philosophically, it is irrationalism; psychologically, it is freedom to follow unfettered religious fancy; theologically, it is unitarianism; religiously, it is uncontrolled individualistic mysticism; structurally, it is all these things not by accident but of necessity. (ibid.)

Packer applies Gadamer's method of distancing and fusing only to the task of applicatory reasoning, and even then in such a way that the mind of God as revealed in the Bible remains high above the thoughts of men: 'where Gadamer speaks of the intersecting of historically separate worlds of human thought, there evangelical application theory posits encounter with the revealed mind of the unchanging God whose thoughts and ways are never like those of fallen mankind in any era at all' (p. 346). He develops an evangelical version of the hermeneutical circle, or spiral, as 'successive approximation' in which exegesis, synthesis, and application interact (p. 348). The evangelical goes to the text of scripture to learn from it the doctrine of scripture, and takes to it his provisional presupposition. This presupposition will be 'an overall view of Christian truth and of the way to approach the Bible . . . gained from the creeds, confessions, preaching, and corporate life of the church and from his own earlier ventures in exegesis and theology'. Having discerned a doctrine of scripture, he derives 'by theological analysis' a set of hermeneutical principles. He then returns to the biblical text to expound and apply its teaching in a scientific manner. If the text challenges his pre-understanding, he allows dialogue to develop so that his understanding can be brought in line with biblical teaching (p. 349).

Though not made explicit by Packer, the key difference between his evangelical spiral and the hermeneutic which he modifies is that in his evangelical version the interpreter will always *defend* evangelical assumptions against challenges from the text. Moreover, the ultimate form of defence is scriptural exegesis, so that the supposedly historical and objective meaning of scripture is used to answer questions thrown up by scripture:

> If his exegetical procedure is challenged, he defends it from his hermeneutic; if his hermeneutic is challenged, he defends it from his doctrine of biblical authority; if his doctrine of biblical authority is challenged, he defends it from biblical texts by exegesis, synthesis, and application. At no point does he decline to accept challenges to his present view of things, but at every point he meets them by renewed theological exegesis of relevant passages in the light of the questions that have been asked. (p. 349)

On a sympathetic reading of Packer, the text pushes one into ever truer exegesis as opposed to a subjective realm of deeper self-understanding. Packer is resisting a separation between what God communicates to the individual through scripture and the grammatico-historical meaning of a passage as extracted through exegesis. However, his version of the spiral seems viciously circular. If the exegetical procedure is challenged, the challenge is answered by exegesis. Exegesis uncovers the historical, objective meaning. Since it also confirms one's exegetical procedure, it is not clear how an evangelical interpretation can ever be challenged or corrected.

In an article for Melvin Tinker's *Restoring the Vision*, Packer (1990: 56) disposes of all influence from modern hermeneutics. He claims that the 'current theological debate about hermeneutics, centering on the ideas of Schleiermacher, Heidegger, Bultmann, Gadamer, Fuchs, Ebeling, and Derrida, largely passes evangelicals by'. He does make an exception of Thiselton in a footnote, whom he regards as an Anglican evangelical who has 'contributed masterfully and at length' on the subject (p. 58 n. 2). For the most part, however, he sees evangelicals continuing 'along the old methodological paths' (p. 57). They adhere to the 'historic Christian view that God uses language . . . to tell us things' (p. 56), and their hermeneutical principles are 'inductive from first to last' (p. 48).

Packer, like Stott, emphasizes our common humanity. We find in scripture 'universal and abiding principles of loyalty and devotion' to God, which we detach from their particular situations and cultural frameworks and reapply to the circumstances and conditions of our own lives today (p. 54). Having described this process, Packer, like Stott, ultimately puts the transposition of God's message entirely into God's own hands: 'He speaks from Scripture, read, preached, explained, and applied, across all cultural gaps and barriers, making Christ known and overcoming all muddles of the mind through the power of the Holy Spirit' (p. 57). Cross-cultural communication is depicted simultaneously as a commonsense undertaking and a mysterious transaction.

8.3.3. *The Chicago Statements*

The International Council on Biblical Inerrancy met in Chicago in 1978 to reaffirm the doctrine of the inerrancy of scripture. James Packer and John Wenham were among its members. The Council drafted The Chicago Statement on Biblical Inerrancy.[11] Kathleen Boone (1989: 11–12, 26–7, 29) regards this Statement as representative of fundamentalist attitudes. The Statement did not mention hermeneutics, and dealt directly with biblical interpretation in only one article. It affirmed the traditional evangelical method of grammatico-historical exegesis, and denied 'any treatment of the text or quest for sources lying behind it that leads to relativizing, dehistoricizing, or discounting its teaching, or rejecting its claims to authorship' (Art. 18). Hermeneutics seemed not yet to have posed a significant threat.

Soon after 'Summit I', however, 'it became clear that there was yet another major task to be tackled' (Chicago Statement on

[11] Repr. as an appendix in Geisler (1979: 493–502). Also repr. in Packer (1979: 149–55).

Biblical Hermeneutics). The Council called a further meeting in 1982 to address hermeneutical issues. This resulted in The Chicago Statement on Biblical Hermeneutics, a declaration of 25 Articles of Affirmations and Denials.[12] This document carefully delineates the legitimate use of the term 'hermeneutics' and the correct application of hermeneutical principles:

> WE AFFIRM that the term *hermeneutics*, which historically signified the rules of exegesis, may properly be extended to cover all that is involved in the process of perceiving what the biblical revelation means and how it bears on our lives.
>
> WE DENY that the message of Scripture derives from, or is dictated by, the interpreter's understanding. Thus we deny that the 'horizons' of the biblical writer and the interpreter may rightly 'fuse' in such a way that what the text communicates to the interpreter is not ultimately controlled by the expressed meaning of the Scripture. (Art. 9)

The Statement recognizes the need to apply the text to one's life. However, as Geisler (1984: 894) explains in his Commentary on the Statement, it is the Holy Spirit who 'enables one . . . to understand the spiritual implications' that a passage has for Christian living. Thus, like Stott and Packer, the Council conceives the crucial applicatory stage to be divinely conducted. The former exegetical stage involves 'interpreting the Bible according to its literal, or normal, sense', which is equated with 'the grammatical-historical sense, that is, the meaning which the writer expressed' (Art. 15). Hence, 'the meaning expressed in each biblical text is single, definite and fixed', although the single meaning may have a variety of applications (Art. 7).

Only in Article 12 does it seem that something positive has been accepted from modern hermeneutical theory: 'WE DENY the legitimacy of methods which either are insensitive to the demands of cross-cultural communication or distort biblical meaning in the process.' However, 'cultural and situational factors' are not permitted to determine the distinction between universal and particular mandates. This distinction is indicated by scripture itself (Art. 8). Moreover, even particular injunctions are to be taken as 'normative

[12] Repr. in Radmacher and Preus (1984: 881–7), and McKim (1986: 21–6). Several symposia have been produced by the International Council on Biblical Inerrancy: Geisler (ed.), *Inerrancy* (1979); *Biblical Errancy* (1981); Lewis and Demarest (eds.), *Challenges to Inerrancy* (1984); Hannah (ed.), *Inerrancy and the Church* (1984); Radmacher and Preus (eds.), *Hermeneutics, Inerrancy, and the Bible* (1984).

to the particular situation(s) to which they speak' (Geisler 1984: 893).[13] Article 19 affirms that 'any preunderstandings which the interpreter brings to Scripture should be in harmony with scriptural teaching and subject to correction by it'. The intention of this affirmation is not to acknowledge a process of dialogue but to protect the Bible from accommodation to 'alien preunderstandings, inconsistent with itself, such as naturalism, evolutionism, scientism, secular humanism, and relativism' (Art. 19).

8.3.4. *Evangelical Consensus*

Evangelicals have reacted in varying ways to hermeneutical developments. Some focus on the ability to discern the original meaning, others concentrate on bridging the cultural gap. While members of the Chicago Council resist hermeneutical advances, others such as Stott welcome them. However, many of these differences are only in tone and approach. In content, the more accepting evangelicals concur with the more defensive. Stott is cooperative and considers the benefits to be gleaned from modern hermeneutics, but ultimately his model of interpretation is little affected by modern hermeneutical thought save for the recognition that cultural gaps need to be bridged. The Chicago Council is polemical and warns against the hazards of hermeneutics, but is prepared to accept the insight that cultural boundaries need to be crossed.

From an evangelical perspective, the greatest risk in courting modern hermeneutics is that meaning becomes subjective. Most evangelicals do not allow meaning to be affected by hermeneutical dialogue. The dialogue concerns the significance or application of the text's message. Even then, at the point where the horizons fuse the interpreter is still depicted as essentially passive, save for requesting God's assistance. An element of divine mystery is often introduced into the process, as in Clark Pinnock's (1993: 6) account:

> Fusing the horizons is not a simple operation. What does God's word mean for us today? How do we apply it to pressing issues such as gender,

[13] Contrast with Stott's position summarized in n. 4 above. Geisler, in his interpretation of the Chicago Statement, would not accept that the injunction on women to cover their heads is culturally relative. He would see the injunction as either holding universally or holding timelessly for a particular type of situation.

pluralism, ecology and the like? How do we transcend reader prejudices which silence the text in its power to transform? The only thing a person can do is cry out for understanding with the psalmist: 'Make me to know thy ways, O Lord; teach me thy paths. Lead me in thy truth and teach me' (Ps. 26.4–5).

According to the New Testament, God hears this cry for understanding by giving us his Spirit.

It is God who transposes the text for us so that we perceive its significance in the way God intended. God is, in Packer's (1990: 57) words, 'the Lord of communication'.[14]

At the same time, the ability of people in one culture to understand something from another culture is demystified. Evangelicals qualify the need for hermeneutics by emphasizing that men and women of all cultures are made in the image of God, pose the same sorts of questions about the meaning of life, and recognize universal principles of devotion to the Creator (Kaiser 1979*b*: 32; Stott 1982: 151; Packer 1990: 54). Some evangelicals reject the hermeneutical circle altogether as derived from a 'nonevangelical presupposition . . . that humanity today is radically different from humanity in biblical days' (Lewis 1984: 617).

Evangelicals retain a common-sense ethos. Gordon Fee entitles his discussion of hermeneutical issues 'Hermeneutics and Common Sense' (1980), and Walter Kaiser (1979*a*: 121) claims to take an essentially 'common-sense' approach to the 'art of interpretation'. Kaiser (1979*b*: 31) argues that the principles of interpretation 'are not learned, invented, or discovered by men', but are 'part and parcel of our nature as individuals made in the image of God'. He does not regard his outlook as being itself philosophically informed: 'interpretation is more a native art than it is a science . . . Therefore, we may say without prejudice that it precedes Descartes, Bacon, Common Sense Realism and Gadamer himself!' (1988: 68).

[14] When writing on hermeneutics, evangelicals are pleased to emphasize the mysterious ways in which the Holy Spirit moves as they read scripture. Pinnock gave the above account in a pentecostal journal, so would not have felt shy in this respect. Nevertheless, they keep the mystical element distinct from the task of discerning the text's meaning. This parallels the situation we noted in Ch. 5, of evangelicals separating their objective from their subjective readings of the text. Moreover, appeals to mystery tend to occur where otherwise evangelicals would need to grapple with difficult hermeneutical theory, which suggests that they are partly an avoidance tactic!

The support for phenomenological hermeneutics in the writings so far considered is both slim and shallow. The evangelical scholars have not wrestled with the full implications of hermeneutical philosophy. They have not confronted its radical challenge to classical epistemology and the 'myth of neutral observation' (Lundin, Thiselton, and Walhout 1985: 22). They continue to attack non-evangelical presuppositions as though their own approach were true and objective because rooted in human nature. They remain preoccupied by fears of subjectivism while embracing aspects of a philosophy that is redefining the subject–object relation. Hermeneutic philosophers locate truth intersubjectively. In Richard Rorty's words, they think 'of truth horizontally—as the culminating reinterpretation of our predecessors' reinterpretation of their predecessors' reinterpretation . . .'. Evangelicals tend to retain a largely passive account of the subject. They carry on thinking of truth as, in Rorty's terms, 'a vertical relationship between representations and what is represented'[15]—as is consistent with their realism and their general support for a correspondence theory of truth. In accommodating insights from phenomenological hermeneutics they arrive at a composite, spiral image. Even their spiral makes few concessions to inter-subjectivity, for it is a spiral not of truth or meaning but of understanding, in which one's appreciation of the significance of biblical passages is enhanced. Truth itself remains unchanged: 'WE AFFIRM . . . that biblical truth is both objective and absolute. We further affirm that a statement is true if it represents matters as they actually are, but is an error if it misrepresents the facts' (Chicago Statement on Biblical Hermeneutics, Art. 16).

Thus, by their conception of the nature of biblical truth evangelicals continue to set themselves apart from others. In his commentary on the second Chicago Statement, Geisler (1984: 892) writes: 'in contrast to contemporary relativism it is declared that truth is absolute . . . as opposed to subjectivism it is acknowledged that truth is objective', and 'in opposition to existential and pragmatic views of truth . . . truth is what corresponds to reality'.

[15] Richard Rorty, 'Philosophy as a Kind of Writing: An Essay on Derrida', *New Literary History*, 10 (1978), 143, quoted in Maddox (1985: 518).

8.4. Kuyperians and Hermeneutics

Kuyperians clearly recognize the role of presuppositions in interpretation. They reject the expectation that grammatical-historical exegesis will yield the kind of objectivity traditionally sought by evangelicals. They do not mind that phenomenological hermeneutics implies subjectivity, they object that it makes way for human autonomy.

Cornelius Van Til is militant in his rejection of modern philosophical hermeneutics, which he regards as substituting self-interpretation for the objectivity of God's revelation. Objectivity for Van Til means not that the biblical narratives correspond to brute fact, but that history and scripture alike are interpreted by God. In his book *The New Hermeneutic* (1974) he particularly addresses the hermeneutic of Fuchs and Ebeling. However, he considers the new hermeneutic to be just one trend in modern theology as a whole, all of which is tarnished with the same brush of Kantian philosophy. He continues his theme that a truly Reformed theology cannot be synthesized with the philosophy of Kant (Preface). He regards the new hermeneutic as primarily an attempt to make the message of the New Testament respectable to modern man (p. 1 *et passim*). He therefore sees it as a hermeneutics of accommodation, and one which protects modern man from the offence of the Gospel. Being rooted in Kantian philosophy it is committed to the autonomy of man and the denial of the possibility of knowing anything about God in an intellectual sense. It is primarily experiential, making human experience, or existential encounter, constitutive of the meaning of a text. Thus the authority of scripture is replaced by the authority of human tradition.

> Modern science, modern philosophy and modern theology [repress the biblical message] by means of an epistemology in which the revelation of God to man is turned into a revelation from man to himself. In its desire to be genuinely scientific and philosophical modern theology weaves every word it uses into a pattern of revelation and response that amounts to ventriloquism. The *New Hermeneutic* is the currently most popular method of reinterpreting the significance of Jesus the Christ so as to make it fully acceptable to the natural man. (p. 53)

Others are less hostile, and attempt to forge a connection between Kuyperian and hermeneutical thought in the mutual recognition of presuppositions. Harvie Conn (1984: 316) of Westminster Theological Seminary, who regards Van Til as his 'mentor', attempts to equate Van Til's 'presuppositions' with culturally orientated beliefs (ibid. 15). This move is misleading, for Van Til's presuppositions are more like Kuyper's fundamental life-principles from which a person's thinking unfolds. Van Til (1961: p. ii) talks of 'the presupposition of the God of Christianity'. Hermeneutical philosophy is concerned with culturally and historically conditioned assumptions, which occasion diversity even among those who share a presupposition of the Christian God. Elsewhere, Conn merges the presuppositional element in interpreting scripture with the transforming work of the Holy Spirit. The Spirit furnishes human beings with a universally true set of presuppositions:

> In our turning to God, we are increasingly drawn by the Holy Spirit into a new cultural world. Our way of perceiving the cosmos, our worldview, begins to undergo reshaping. We are given a spiritual disposition to understand the things of the Spirit (I Cor. 2: 14). He makes over our values and perspectives. We become, in this process called conversion, increasingly familiar with the structure of biblical narrative. What seemed like nonsense before now becomes the only sense we can make of things. We see more and more the world as God wants us to see it, from creation to fall to redemption to consummation. (Conn 1987: 31)

It is suggested above that appeals to the Spirit do not suffice to relieve evangelicals of their hermeneutical responsibility. So far we have discovered evangelicals who believe that the Spirit informs them of how scripture is to be applied within their own particular culture. Kuyperians differ in that they tend to speak of 'culture' as something akin to 'world-view'. Conn, in the quotation above, conceives of the Holy Spirit bringing Christian minds into conformity with biblical culture, by which he means not first-century Palestine but the biblical framework of creation, fall, and redemption. According to Kuyperians, the role of the Spirit in the hermeneutical process is not so much to convey the contemporary and personal significance of a passage, but to bring the reader's world-view in line with the world-view of the Bible. 'The unbeliever's preunderstanding must be fundamentally *redirected* by the regenerating power of the Holy Spirit. A believer's preunderstanding may require *reformation* (re-forming) within the regenerated heart through the Spirit's illumination' (Klooster 1984: 464).

Kuyperians have difficulty accepting the image of dialogue between the text and the interpreter. The text cannot challenge the presuppositions of one who is disposed against it when those presuppositions determine how the words of the Bible will be received. The Holy Spirit testifies to and interprets scripture, but scripture itself remains passive. A reader with an inhospitable world-view will simply fail to interpret scripture with the eyes of faith. Hermeneutics grants no autonomy to the text, but provides a new tool for attacking unbiblical presuppositions: 'Faithful interpretation of Scripture requires that one approach it with a preunderstanding that conforms to Scripture. Unbiblical presuppositions will short-circuit the interpretative process' (ibid.).

8.4.1. *James H. Olthuis and Henry Vander Goot*

James H. Olthuis and Henry Vander Goot are Kuyperians who are particularly influenced by Dooyeweerd's philosophy (and have inherited his *penchant* for creating difficult vocabulary). They retain a Dooyeweerdian approach to scripture while considering the positive and negative aspects of phenomenological hermeneutics.

James Olthuis, a senior member of the Institute for Christian Studies, has produced a fairly complex synthesis of Kuyperian and hermeneutical thought. He presents his theory in a book entitled *A Hermeneutics of Ultimacy: Peril or Promise* (1987) with responses from Clark Pinnock, Donald Bloesch, and Gerald Sheppard. This publication comes out of a conference on 'Interpreting an Authoritative Scripture' held in 1981 in Toronto, and jointly sponsored by the Institute for Christian Studies and Fuller Seminary.

Olthuis (1987: 27) makes common cause with modern hermeneutics in dispelling the 'illusion' of presuppositionless exegesis and '*Methodically secured* objectivity'. His neo-Calvinism is evident in his acceptance of 'the foundational role of faith commitment in human cognition' (p. 14). He also manifests an influence from those whom Bloesch describes as 'modern existentialists', i.e. Heidegger, Gadamer, Fuchs, Ebeling, and Ricœur.[16] He recog-

[16] Bloesch (1987: 8, 9) realizes that Gadamer and Ricœur '*have been critical of certain thrusts in existentialism*' but says that they '*nevertheless remain within this general orientation*'.

nizes that our existential surrender to the God of scripture occurs in a particular time and place, and so is culturally conditioned. He distinguishes our 'in-faith-acceptance of the Scriptures from the way we conceptualize and articulate it' (p. 12), the latter being time-conditioned and subject to human fallibility. Combining neo-Calvinist and hermeneutical ideas, Olthuis suggests that the 'faith orientation' by which one is 'attuned to Scripture' enables one to discern the message of scripture 'even as it comes in a variety of culturally-specific and time-bound expressions' (p. 25).

Olthuis describes 'a dialogic process of hermeneutic spiral' between interpreter and text (p. 28). Like other evangelicals, he is critical of 'overly psychologistic and subjectivistic' conceptions of this spiral (p. 29). Unlike most other evangelicals, however, he is not primarily worried about the subjectivity of the interpreter. As we know from Chapters 6 and 7, Kuyperians regard subjectivity as an inherent part of human knowledge, and as not in itself bad. Rather, Olthuis objects to attempts to recover the subjectivity of the author, which can never be fully apprehended. He rejects the common evangelical emphasis upon authorial intention because it ignores the nature of dialogue as an exchange between 'visions of life' (pp. 29–30). Hermeneutical dialogue is a 'confrontation of visions' rather than 'an emphatic re-experiencing of the inner life or cultural situation of the author' (p. 30).

He also points to the danger of assuming that the spiral 'is all there is to reality'. This assumption can lead 'to a side-stepping of the final question of whether or not the message or vision presented in the text is true' (ibid.). He retains for scriptural truth a transcendence above the dialogue, criticizing a 'Heideggerian-Bultmannian hermeneutic' which reduces 'the meaning of the text . . . to its meaning for me'. He thus shares with other evangelicals the need to separate response from discernment of the text's meaning. The decisional moment is important in completing the process of interpretation but should never replace the text as the meaning to be interpreted (p. 40).

As a Kuyperian, he differs from most others in the modern hermeneutical enterprise, evangelical or otherwise, by considering the hermeneutical process as a 'dialogue between worldviews'. He thinks not of cultural distance but of 'the ultimate claims which are implicit in the text confront[ing] the ultimate beliefs of the interpreter' (p. 36). When a text challenges our pre-understanding, our entire vision or world-view may need to be reconsidered. 'For it is not Jeremiah's view, Paul's opinions or the situations of Ruth and Rahab that we share. Nor is it necessary that we do, any more than we need to share David's feelings and Mary's emotions. But we can—and ought to—share their integrating vision, their overarching perspective, their faith certitudes.' If we consequently have to give up our world-view and accept a new ultimate, this is conversion (p. 31). Olthuis changes the metaphor from a 'fusion of horizons' to a 'clash of horizons' (p. 30). Conversion rather than dialogue would have been the more appropriate image for his account: 'An appropriate response to a certitudinal text is of the order of: Yes, I receive that as the Truth, and commit myself to live by it, or, No, I reject that as False, and commit myself to fight against it' (p. 36).

As professor of religion and theology at Calvin College, Henry Vander Goot was a member of a research team in the Calvin Center for Christian Scholarship which in the academic year 1982–3 took as their project 'Theory and Praxis of Hermeneutics'. From this research he produced the book, *Interpreting the Bible in Theology and the Church* (1984).

Vander Goot synthesizes the thought of Dooyeweerd and Gadamer to present the Bible as 'a standard against which the horizon of the reader must be normed' (1984: 47). The reader 'must be ready to let his own previous world, including his own previous world view, be taken over by the world-transforming world view of the Bible' (p. 38). Vander Goot takes Gadamer's most important contribution to hermeneutics to be his stress on the inevitability and desirability of subjectivity, which destroys the illusion of a 'contextless human subject'. This enables Vander Goot to ask about appropriate subjectivity, which he describes as being 'under the power of the Bible's Word'. Such a relationship with the Bible must precede any scientific investigation of scripture (pp. 14, 15).

The presuppositions with which Vander Goot deals are not cultural presuppositions. He rejects Gadamer's depiction of tradition and culture as merely the historical accumulation of human products, and instead looks for 'man's *response* to a "law" of God for culture and history' (p. 16). He wants a 'more fundamental, ontological view of the world context of the human subject' (p. 17).

Gadamer's philosophy offers no vantage point from which to establish such a view, but Vander Goot finds that the 'Bible gives its recipients a privileged look at things' (p. 70):

> In faith we insist that the historical and cultural point of view is not to be considered the rationally certain one in comparison to the perspective of faith . . . Even for the scientific study of the Bible what is central, determining the content of the Bible, is that the Bible's events are presented from the high ground from which they address us. Because we have the Bible we assume, and rightly so, that we are privileged to know God's deeds *from his vantage point*. (p. 24)

Vander Goot interprets 'general hermeneutical theory' as holding that text and reader are 'mutually corrective and interdependent' (pp. 32–3). He shares the familiar evangelical fear that modern hermeneutical practice accommodates the text 'to the wrong prejudices of the reader' (p. 32). In his own theory, he grants priority to the text and denies autonomy to the interpreter. He rejects 'the notion of a dialogue' between horizons and looks for the meaning of scripture 'in the light of the horizon of its internal structure' (pp. 40, 32). He does not think in terms of our 'coming to Scripture with our own questions' (p. 39), but rather of:

> 'listening in' because the world and time of the Bible are so extensive that they include all times and places and thus *in faith* also the time and place of the reader. There is therefore no dialogue, no multiplicity of horizons, because in faith there is no real distantiation. In faith the horizon of the text *is* the horizon of the reader. (p. 40)

Olthuis and Vander Goot share the reluctance of their fellow Kuyperians to allow that interpreters approach scripture with any presuppositions other than biblical presuppositions. They accept the circularity of the Kuyperian method: that one's presuppositions must be informed by scripture before they can appropriately aid interpretation. This circularity cannot complement the 'hermeneutical circle'. The hermeneutical circle operates with all interpreters, whatever their presuppositions. The circle implicit in Olthuis's and Vander Goot's work is for the regenerate only, whose presuppositions have already been brought into line with scripture. Vander Goot sees this incompatibility more clearly than does Olthuis. Olthuis wants both dialogue and Yes/No decisions, a spiral of understanding and conversion from one ultimate to another.

8.5. Remaining Fundamentalist

Evangelicals will draw on philosophically incompatible traditions if the different traditions provide tools for preserving biblical authority. This is a pragmatic measure. They employ phenomenological hermeneutics to enable them to deal with culturally problematic passages while retaining a level of meaning which remains constant and authoritative. Gadamer's insights are utilized only for the 'decisional' or 'application' level in the hermeneutical process, that is, in making the text relevant for today. Even then, Gadamer's contribution is depreciated first by a denial of any really significant lack of understanding between people of different cultures, and second by the ultimate conviction that it is the Holy Spirit who conveys God's message to different cultures. It would be to the benefit of many were evangelicals to develop a defensible position which succeeded in presenting and protecting these sentiments while also acknowledging the reality of cultural conditioning. As it is, evangelicals have not probed deep enough to discover and address the tensions in their composite hermeneutical theories. The majority of evangelicals continue to excavate meaning through grammatico-historical exegesis, and many also locate meaning in the original author's intention. This enables advocates of inerrancy to preserve scripture from error at the level of meaning.

Kuyperians, particularly those influenced by Dooyeweerd, find meaning residing in the all-encompassing biblical story or vision, rather than in the intention of particular biblical writers. They equate the hermeneutical process with the work of the Holy Spirit in bringing the reader's presuppositions into line with the biblical vision. Since the biblical vision, where meaning resides, provides the norm to which the reader must conform, meaning itself is not subject to change and is not vulnerable to the reader's unreformed presuppositions.

The differences in philosophical orientation between evangelicals who reflect common-sense assumptions and those who follow a Kuyperian, neo-Calvinist philosophy do not override the essential similarities between them. While all are concerned to slough off their rationalistic image, all perceive biblical authority to be threatened by either subjective or autonomous interpretative procedures. Either way, evangelicals continue to resist the suggestion that human consciousness is in any way constitutive of truth or meaning. Since phenomenological hermeneutics are rooted in precisely this suggestion, evangelicals seem to be misguided or to be acting in bad faith when they claim to take hermeneutics on board.

These problems of inconsistency are easily contained because evangelicals are in fact inclined to make only trivial use of hermeneutics. This is evident from their treatment of what they euphemistically term the Bible's 'difficult passages' on women. Women wearing hats and keeping silent in church are the issues most commonly interpreted as culturally relative (Stott 1984: 234–57; 1992: 202–4; Goldingay 1977*a*: 351; Conn 1987: 29), and evangelicals could and did so interpret these injunctions before they had a hermeneutical spiral. James Packer takes up the question of women teaching. However, his conclusion that women should not teach is not reached through the hermeneutical process he is supposed to be demonstrating. Rather, it is based on an old theological argument that the possibility of deception is increased when women teach because Eve was deceived in a way that Adam was not (1988: 114).

It would be a radical move for evangelicals really to take phenomenological hermeneutics on board. The philosophy is so alien to their tradition, so unfriendly to the concepts of objective truth and 'plain meaning', so fundamentally Kantian, and it offers no protection to the historicity of critical biblical narratives. As it is, evangelicals are resistant to its transforming power. They bring to the hermeneutical process a presupposition which consists of, to repeat Packer's (1983: 349) words, 'an overall view of Christian truth and of the way to approach the Bible'. They leave very little open to challenge, and can continue to operate with the same formalized view of scripture to which Barr has objected all along. Thus their present use of hermeneutics will not save them from charges of fundamentalism. Lest we lose sight of the complexity of this situation, it should be added that evangelicals anyway sense that a strongly subjectivist hermeneutic which sacrifices the perspicuity of scripture is the wrong horse to back, which brings them finally into agreement with Barr.

Conclusion

The term 'fundamentalism' denotes several things in a study of Protestant Christianity: a historical movement of the 1920s; an identity still assumed by old-style separatist fundamentalists, politicized neo-fundamentalists, and occasionally also by evangelicals; and a mentality which has affected much of mainstream evangelicalism. This mentality connects many of the diverse movements within contemporary evangelicalism to one another, to the original fundamentalist movement, and to its separatist offspring. The persons, groups, and movements considered in this study have been placed in their particular historical and social contexts, with attention paid to their own criticisms of fundamentalist and evangelical thought. Most are not militant, and they differ from one another in their theories of scripture: its inspiration, inerrancy, and interpretation. Yet in their diversity they are in agreement that a 'high' view of the Bible is essential to their evangelical identity. (Even most Dooyeweerdian critics of evangelicalism express a wish to remain identified with the evangelical wing of the church and they fit most naturally there.)

My contention is that the 'high' view of scripture is often essentially fundamentalist. I have described the fundamentalist mentality in terms of the following attitudes: a commitment to a priori reasoning that scripture cannot contain any error because it is inspired by God; an almost contrary commitment to demonstrating empirically that scripture is indeed inspired because it contains no error; a feeling that in moving away from either commitment one is making concessions to modern scholarship; and a hesitancy to make such concessions lest they detract from the authority of the Bible and so threaten the very foundations of the Christian faith.

Much of this study has focused on the inconsistency of evangelicals who retain the first two attitudes simultaneously. Evangelicals are not unaware of this tension. Many see themselves as rejecting a deductive in favour of an inductive approach, or *vice versa*, although usually their reasoning still contains elements of both approaches. However, the larger problem is a persistence to regard the Bible as proof in either of these ways, as though the Christian faith will stand only if the Bible's authority can be rationally or empirically verified. This is an attitude prevalent in evangelical apologetics, but one which does not do justice to wider aspects of evangelical faith. The general criticism from both Barr and Barton is that it distorts scripture to read it within such a framework. It also distorts Christianity by making it seem that 'Jesus need not really have existed'. That is to say, fundamentalist reasoning implies that 'it is the text that reveals the truth about God, not Jesus himself as he actually lived and died and rose again' (Barton 1988: 37).

The fundamentalist influence exists among evangelicals in varying aspects and degrees. It is possible for an evangelical to share some and not others of these attitudes, or to share some explicitly and others implicitly. Kuyperians introduce a lot of variety in that they criticize both a priori and inductive reasoning where the reasoner's presuppositions are not taken into account. Whether or not Kuyperians manifest a fundamentalist mentality depends on their failure or success in relating the authority of scripture to the context of one's life-relation to Christ. A number of Kuyperians have been considered in this study, many of whom attack inerrantist ways of thinking. Yet they have not been Christocentric in their discussions of scripture. Nor have they demonstrated convincingly that their interpretations of scripture would, at important points, look different from fundamentalist interpretations. Like other evangelicals, they sometimes circumvent tricky historical issues and overlook inconsistencies in their composite apologetic arguments.

Not all evangelicals manifest a fundamentalist mentality, so what characterizes those who do not? Evangelicals in their different traditions decide which beliefs ought to be paramount, and indeed whether belief should be prioritized over practice. I have not described the breadth and diversity of the evangelical lineage outside considerations of the fundamentalist mentality. Hence I have said very little about evangelicals in the Wesleyan tradition because for the most part they have remained free of inerrancy debates and do not define themselves by a conservative attitude towards scripture; rather, they give priority to holy living. For a wider picture, readers should look to historical studies of evangelicalism, to European evangelical theology and history, to the growing number of evangelical missionaries and theologians from the two-thirds world, and to writings from Black evangelicals, Lutherans, Methodists, Mennonites, and others.

I have restricted my discussion to attitudes towards scripture. In this respect, non-fundamentalist evangelicals read scripture as the central aspect of their spirituality, and as that which more than anything else mediates their relationship to Christ. They do not regard the factual accuracy of scripture as necessary to keep the Christian faith intact. However, were they to put this disclaimer centre-stage they would probably be harbouring residual anxieties about inerrancy. They insist that historical reality underlies the religious significance of central Christian motifs, notably Jesus' resurrection, and that the Bible is the primary and sufficiently reliable record of the events which make up this reality. At the same time, they acknowledge spiritually rich interpretative elements in the biblical narrative, because 'that narrative is dynamically related to the Holy Spirit, who not only inspires the writing of scriptures but continues to be related to their usage by the people of God' (Samuel 1996: 54). The Bible is their major source for preaching and teaching, not because it provides 'proof' but because it yields life. To use Samuel's phrase, the world of the biblical narrative becomes, for Jesus' disciples down the ages, the 'meaning-giving, life-directing world' (ibid.).

Dave Tomlinson (1995) represents a post-evangelical position which, in the light of this study, might be regarded as anti-fundamentalist. Post-evangelicals have rejected the cultural world of modernity as the environment in which they must contend for the integrity of their faith. They relate more naturally to the world of post-modernity, where they seek 'the spirituality which had been squeezed out by materialism and rationalism' (ibid. 10). They frame their concept of truth in terms of poetry and symbol rather than of scientific language, and in place of evangelical absolutes they develop a sacramental theology. Tomlinson is keen to stress that such believers are not ex-evangelicals but are following on from evangelicalism (p. 7). Whether their position is continuous or discontinuous with the evangelical tradition is no straightforward matter. As we discovered in Chapter 4, evangelicals disagree over the nature of their heritage. Some evangelicals attempt, mistakenly in my view, to trace an inerrancy-style apologetic as far back as the Reformers. Tomlinson's rejection of inerrancy as '*A Monumental Waste of Time!*' (p. 105) is no rejection of evangelicalism, but his sacramental emphasis is a distinctly new way of expressing the evangelical experience of reading scripture.

The roots of the fundamentalist mentality are not the same as the roots of evangelicalism. Evangelicalism is a longer-established and more inclusive phenomenon than the fundamentalist mentality which has come to pervade it. This I take to be Barr's argument when he distinguishes fundamentalism from real evangelicalism. However, Barr also asserts that the basis of fundamentalism is the experience of the Evangelical Revivals (*Fundamentalism*, pp. 11, 345 n. 1). I find this hard to reconcile with his general criticism that fundamentalist rationalism has eclipsed the personal, experiential side of evangelicalism. Sometimes Barr comes close to equating evangelicalism with fundamentalism, even though one of his major contentions is that evangelicalism does not have to be fundamentalist in nature.

I take Barr's principal point to be that much of contemporary evangelicalism has been affected by fundamentalist reasoning. In this respect his critique has been a major inspiration for this study. My initial intention was to reject Barr's arguments as too sweeping, but on re-readings I came to regard them as presenting perceptive and legitimate challenges to the way that many evangelicals think today. Barr's analysis of fundamentalism involves more than an assessment of its rationalism, and in that sense it is a wider account than the one offered here. This study has concentrated on the charge that fundamentalism is rationalistic. I have qualified that charge and identified both rationalist and evidentialist strands in fundamentalist apologetics. These different strands create their own problematic tension, rendering evangelicals guilty of the kind of inconsistency Barr finds in the maximal-conservatism. I have taken the empirical-rationalist framework to be so significant as to provide an explanation for the major features of the fundamentalist mentality as it has impinged upon evangelicalism. In order to question the extent of the fundamentalist influence, I have considered a wider and more diverse range of evangelicals than those featured in Barr's writings.

Barr traces the roots of fundamentalist rationalism to eighteenth-century philosophies of reason. I have focused on

Scottish Common Sense Realism, which religious historians have identified as especially significant in informing fundamentalist thought. Through the theology of Old Princeton, the dispensationalist and holiness movements, and the fundamentalism of the 1920s, a distinctive fundamentalist understanding of scripture emerged which associated the Bible's authority with its perfect factual truthfulness.

The combination of Common Sense philosophy and turn-of-the-century American evangelicalism consolidated doctrines and practices that had long existed in the Christian tradition, such as verbal inspiration and proof-texting. Since the eighteenth century such features have come increasingly to be defended within an empirical-rationalist framework. Prior to this time it would not be appropriate to regard them as fundamentalist. I associate fundamentalism with an attempt to base Christian truth on the authority of scripture while biblical authority is itself defended wholly in terms of reason and evidences. (At least this form of defence is the intention, if not the reality, of a fundamentalist biblical apologetic.) Where the demonstration is intended to be inductive, evidences come to play a foundational rather than a supporting role. This puts a very heavy burden on scripture, for it becomes difficult to dismiss inconsistencies and minor factual errors as insignificant. Without an empirical-rationalist framework and the semblance of inductive reasoning, we would not have fundamentalism. Instead we might have a more direct heir to Protestant scholasticism.

At the same time, empirical rationalism is not a natural ally of these elements from the Christian tradition, and does not typically lead in a fundamentalist direction. It is not even a common-sense reading of Reid to think that his philosophy is supportive of verbal inspiration, of proof-texting, or of strongly realist interpretations of biblical narratives. Reid argued that revelation ought to be subject to the tests of reason. He was a strong advocate of the Baconian scientific method but gave no indication that he regarded the biblical verses as equivalent to the facts of nature. He introduced into his philosophy the principle of credulity; a constitutive principle by which people learn as they get older to discern reliable testimony, and so to control how they respond to reports. Reid said nothing to support a view of biblical testimonies as straightforward factual accounts.

Fundamentalist and evangelical scholars have diversified in confusing ways. Some continue to insist that biblical truth remains fully in harmony with historical and scientific discoveries. Creation scientists are the most extreme in this respect. They question the scientific nature of any theory which threatens their reading of scripture. More commonly though, evangelicals adopt figurative interpretations of biblical passages when historical or scientific 'counter-evidence' becomes too strong to resist. This enables them to preserve scripture from accusations of error in the light of new discoveries. Others affirm inerrancy only in 'religious' matters. They clearly retain the ideal of inerrancy while questioning the notion of truth that that doctrine implies. They have accepted the fundamentalist assumption that the Bible's authority is dependent on its inerrancy, but they are moving away from the fundamentalist conception of truth as direct correspondence to facts.

Distinctions have been drawn between American and British movements at various places in this study, with the suggestion that British evangelicals have been less directly influenced by fundamentalism. The fundamentalist–modernist controversies of the 1920s are not in their bloodstream, and they have received the Princeton doctrine of inerrancy largely via James Packer. American evangelicalism has been dominated by new evangelicals who were direct descendants of the fundamentalist movement. British evangelicals have interacted with the new-evangelical movement, but have themselves absorbed fewer aspects of fundamentalist thought. If pressed, they defend the inerrancy of scripture, but such a defence does not dominate their scholarship. They have retained an emphasis upon the witness of the Holy Spirit within their biblical apologetic more successfully than have their American counterparts, and they are less intent on defending their doctrine of scripture inductively. In this sense they are closer to Gaussen and Orr than they are to Warfield, believing that scripture is accepted as inspired and authoritative because of its effects upon believers.[1]

[1] As David Kelsey illustrates, Warfield has two different types of argument to defend his doctrine of inspiration, the first being that the Bible is used as a holy or numinous object so that the church receives its statements of fact. The second argument is the more familiar one that the Bible itself teaches the doctrine of plenary verbal inspiration. As regards the first, Kelsey justifiably interprets Warfield as saying, in effect, that no other view of the Bible could make sense of the church's numinous experience when she uses scripture. Much in the second argument depends on the force of the first argument (Kelsey 1975: 17–28). This

Evangelicals throughout the twentieth century have been influenced by neo-Calvinism and since the 1970s by phenomenological hermeneutics. These philosophies challenge certain assumptions of the early Enlightenment which affected fundamentalism, particularly that human thought is capable of autonomy and neutrality. They have the potential to restore to evangelical apologetics the centrality of faith in Christ, and an emphasis upon the work of the Holy Spirit. Evangelicals who make use of either influence criticize what they themselves call the rationalism of fundamentalist and evangelical apologetics. Barr recognizes the Dutch and hermeneutical strands within evangelicalism without emphasizing their incompatibility with the rationalist heritage he describes. However, evangelicals on the whole have not accepted any significant challenge to their assumptions about biblical truth and authority from these strands. The neo-Calvinist and hermeneutical philosophies therefore do not seriously undermine Barr's critique.

Neo-Calvinist thought originated with Abraham Kuyper, who argued that biblical authority is recognized through one's faith-relation to Christ. His position has not been adopted by the majority of evangelicals, since they cannot accept that one may have faith in Christ without first knowing that the biblical testimony to Christ is true. Kuyper challenged the apologetics of Princeton Theological Seminary. His followers criticize the rationalism of the Princeton position, which they regard as a vice infecting much of evangelicalism. They reject the assumption that all human beings think alike such that a demonstration of reason and evidences could alone convince someone of the truth of Christianity. Instead, they emphasize subjective factors in the way in which a person reasons and perceives evidence. Therefore, unlike most evangelicals, they do not regard subjectivity as bad in itself. Kuyperians above all reject the assumption of human autonomy, that human beings can contemplate truth unaided by the regenerating work of the Holy Spirit. Evangelicals who are dissatisfied with a Warfieldian apologetic would benefit from a closer reading of Kuyper. Kuyper could in fact supply a solution to the problem

might seem to move Warfield closer to Gaussen and Orr. However, Warfield does not fully acknowledge the role of his own experiential argument. In the article in question, 'The Church Doctrine of Inspiration', he states that 'the church-doctrine of inspiration was the Bible doctrine before it was the church-doctrine, and is the church-doctrine only because it is the Bible doctrine' ([1894*b*]: 114).

noted by Barr that evangelicals have no well-established doctrine of scripture with which to identify other than the fundamentalist one. The majority of evangelicals have not recognized this possibility, since they have assumed that Kuyper and Warfield are essentially in agreement.

The greatest effect that neo-Calvinism has had upon evangelicalism has been via the cultural and social mandate of Kuyper and Herman Dooyeweerd. Evangelicals have been keen to make their religious commitments apparent in all areas of life. They have been less ready to revise their biblical apologetics and to abandon an evidence-based approach. Cornelius Van Til's presuppositionalist apologetic has proved divisive. Van Til anyway endorses the Princeton doctrine of scripture with only the modification that biblical evidences should be understood within a presuppositional framework. Dooyeweerd's approach to scripture is more radical. He regards scripture as a 'supra-theoretical ground-motive' which affects the heart more than the mind. This view has not found favour among many evangelicals. Those who have adopted Dooyeweerd's ideas have moved away from an emphasis upon inerrancy. They remain biblically conservative by protecting scripture from any readings based upon non-biblical presuppositions. We are insufficiently informed as to how they would tackle apparent errors and inconsistencies in scripture, partly because this has not been the major focus of their writings, but also because when they do address inerrancy they refute it by choosing the easiest of targets. We have little reason to believe that their actual interpretations of biblical passages would differ greatly from fundamentalist-evangelical interpretations, since they reveal the same tendency to retain factual readings until the discoveries of science demand some revision.

Recently, evangelicals who are aware of their rationalist past and want to shed their fundamentalist image have intimated that their interest in hermeneutics takes them away from fundamentalism. Hermeneutical philosophy has been introduced to evangelicals largely through the work of Anthony Thiselton. It has alerted them to the role of their cultural presuppositions in interpreting scripture. Where evangelicals have accepted Gadamer's circular image of the fusion of horizons, they have usually merged it with Hirsch's linear concept of a two-step process in interpretation. Hirsch locates the meaning of the text in authorial intention.

Thus he suggests that meaning can be discerned independently of the text's significance for the reader. Evangelicals employ his distinction between meaning and significance. They continue to apply the old arguments about inerrancy and the nature of biblical truth to the level of meaning, and restrict the fusion of horizons to the task of discerning the text's significance. This suggests that an escape from fundamentalism along the hermeneutical route is unlikely.

Implicit throughout this study is a preference for positions which emphasize the personal effects of scripture and the witness of the Holy Spirit to the Bible's authority. Warfield gave priority to a rational and empirical defence of biblical authority. His apologetic does not reflect the way in which one comes to accept scripture as true. Although he was aware of the power of internal testimony, his rationalist framework and his fear of mysticism prevented him from incorporating it apologetically. Evangelicals today are under a similar strain: the highly experiential nature of their faith is not apparent in their apologetics; their personal interaction with scripture cannot be detected in their defence of inerrancy and their 'objective' readings of the biblical text; from a fear of subjectivism they have subordinated religious experience to empirical and rational demonstration. These tensions reflect the age-old faith and reason problem, made more intense by the extreme rationalism and evidentialism of the fundamentalist mentality and the highly personal nature of evangelical experience.

Evangelicals need to explore theoretically the relation between the experience of believers and the rational and historical grounding of their faith. Their major emphasis is on the role of scripture and of the reading of scripture in maintaining that link. They fear that the vitality of their faith will be sapped if they modify their view of scripture, a fear they regard as justified in view of those who have left the evangelical fold. There is a sense of grieving among evangelicals who can no longer read scripture in a precritical way. An argument they commonly use is that they cannot have faith in Christ unless they know that what scripture says of him is true. Thus inerrancy assumes importance. However, the doctrine of inerrancy is an inadequate expression of the simple trust in scripture which evangelicals desire to have. It conflates trust with intellectual submission, as though swallowing the seeming inaccuracies in scripture manifests the appropriate attitude towards God.

It is not from a conviction of factual accuracy that evangelicals get life from the scriptures. Evangelicals testify to growing in a love for the scriptures as they grow in their love for Christ. Their sense that God speaks to them through scripture is an essential element in that dynamic. This sense takes various forms, from feeling that passages leap out at them from the page, to being taken on a long journey of discernment. Their experience of the spiritual and practical benefits of biblical living, for example, of taking a sabbath rest, of paying a tithe regularly, of fasting, of aiming for a holiness of the heart, further informs their conviction of the Bible's authority, as do answers to prayer which seem to accord with their reading of scripture.

We have discovered an anxiety among evangelicals that to stress the functional over the cognitive side of scripture smacks of subjectivism. Yet the way in which scripture functions in their lives is one of their primary joys. Dave Tomlinson (1995: 67) speaks of the 'deep love and respect for the Scriptures' which he gained from an evangelical heritage, in which the scriptures 'exist as a sacrament, or a means of God communicating himself to us'. The Bible enables one to encounter someone who cannot be encountered directly. This is why one's interpretation of scripture and the significance that scripture comes to have in one's life is affected by one's faith-encounter with Christ. Personal faith and the appreciation and understanding of scripture grow together and are not pulling in opposite directions.

Those who feel more sympathetic to a Warfieldian apologetic may well be asking: how far can one question the factual nature of scripture before losing the grounds for faith? How can one know to trust the Bible if its narratives are not straight factual reports? Such questions presuppose that scripture has a purpose to lay out the facts by which faith can be justified. If evangelicals retain some notion of the inspiration of the biblical writings these problems should fade, because if the writings are inspired they are worthy of our trust. However, it impoverishes the trustworthiness of scripture to present it in terms of the reliability of a factual resource. Evangelicals intend by their doctrine of inspiration to communicate an attitude of respect worthy of the God who speaks through scripture. The high regard in which they hold scripture is more complex than their biblical apologetics generally suggest. The value of a doctrine of inspiration is not to assure us that the authors got the facts right, but to express how they are able to convey divine insight into the meaning of the events and experiences they describe.

It is one thing to suppose that real historical events lie behind the biblical writings, another to suppose that the narratives we have are, or need to be, factually precise depictions of these events. The fundamentalist mind would like to take certain biblical verses as statements of bare fact. It conceives of truth as correspondence to the facts, where facts are conceived, in Alasdair McIntyre's (1988: 357–8) words, as entities 'independent of judgement or of any other form of linguistic expression'. 'But', McIntyre says, 'facts, like telescopes and wigs for gentlemen, were a seventeenth-century invention'. The modern world endures the legacy of a shift in the concept of fact: from what a judgement states, to something prior to judgement. The fundamentalist mind treats the biblical writings themselves as free from judgement or interpretation in this way. Yet the scriptures are inspired writings which came out of faith-communities, and the faith from which they came is itself both evidence and the context in which to understand the evidence. This in itself does not make it impossible to speak about historical reality, but it does make our access to that reality less direct than fundamentalists would wish.[2] At the same time, it means that deeper understanding of that reality is gained through participating in the life of the Spirit which has directed the community of believers down the ages.

Even if scripture were inerrant, or close to being so, it would not provide fundamentalists with the sort of proof they desire. Their major anxiety is that of losing proof for the resurrection. However, Jesus' resurrection cannot be proven. It must be accepted on faith. The inerrantist and non-inerrantist alike have the same biblical accounts to reason by: of the empty tomb, of Jesus' post-resurrection appearances to his disciples, of the sending of the Holy Spirit, and the beginnings of the church. We might agree with James McClendon (1994: 246) that the empty tomb, the

[2] Cf. Hagner (1995) who reflects on writing biblical commentary as an evangelical. Similarly to Gundry, he interprets Matthew's Gospel in terms of historical core and theological overlay.

appearances, pentecost, and the founding of the church are not themselves to be equated with the resurrection but rather point to the resurrection, since they are what we might expect if the resurrection were itself true. The majority of evangelicals would concur that the best sense is made of these accounts by positing a physical resurrection as the reality that lies behind them. They thus take a contrary line to theologians who feel that the physicality of the resurrection is not what is being communicated. The inerrancy of the accounts would not enhance a case for the physical resurrection, nor in any way provide proof for it. A preoccupation with inerrancy simply leaves the biblical scholar worrying over whether the resurrection accounts can be made to cohere.

This study of the fundamentalist mentality will be perceived as presenting various challenges to evangelicalism, especially to its apologetic methods, and readers will differ over which of these challenges they find legitimate. I shall end with a set of questions that lies behind all my querying. Do evangelicals recognize the mentality to which I have given the name 'fundamentalist', and if they do, how would they wish to respond to that recognition? From my conversations with many different evangelicals I have become confident that they recognize the mentality and acknowledge weaknesses in it. Do they wish to discuss their identity in ways that have nothing to do with this mentality? If so, how do they wish to portray themselves? If not, what sorts of justification do they think is proper for this way of thinking? The justification must be one which is fully coherent: free of maximally conservative tendencies, properly excavated for inconsistencies which result from a composite conservative apologetic, and as open and critical with respect to its own presuppositions as evangelicals expect others to be.

APPENDIX

Comparative Fundamentalism

Within the Protestant setting, when the term 'fundamentalism' is used to cover militant separatists and tolerant but conservative evangelicals, it indicates some theological similarity between these diverse types. Comparative usage of the term, by contrast, suggests similar activist sentiments among groups which 'necessarily and inevitably have nothing in common with respect to theological substance' (Marty 1992: 4). Today the term 'fundamentalism' connotes less a defence of doctrine than it does 'religiopolitical activism' (Marty and Appleby 1992: 4).

This expansion of the term began in the late 1970s, when the political mobilization of American evangelicals coincided with the revolution in Iran. One recent study felt it necessary to point out that, unlike 'the widely held British stereotype, fundamentalism is not peculiar to Islam' (Sahgal and Yuval-Davis 1992: 1). Today numerous forms of religious resurgence occurring globally and represented in every major world religion are named 'fundamentalist'. The appropriateness of such labelling is the subject of ongoing debate. Jürgen Moltmann (1992: 109) argues that we must accept the term:

> the old Protestant expression has long since become a sociological and psychological category in everyday speech, used in an attempt to understand comparable movements from otherwise incomparable religions and world-views. So we must accept the emigration and extensions of the word 'fundamentalism' from its Protestant origin as it has taken place. We cannot reverse history here.

However, the label has never been extended unquestioningly and is contended as much as it is used. Moreover, it is possible to compare resurgent movements in different religions while reserving the term 'fundamentalism' solely for the Protestant context, as is shown by Gilles Kepel's recently acclaimed study *The Revenge of God* (1991, Eng. trans. 1994).

Comparative studies have appeared since the late 1980s. First, Lionel Caplan edited an anthropological volume, *Studies in Religious Fundamental-*

An earlier version of this appendix appeared as 'Comparative Fundamentalism', *Oxford International Review*, 6/1 (1994), 40–5.

ism (1987*b*). Then Bruce Lawrence produced an account of Jewish, Christian, and Islamic movements in *Defenders of God* (1989*a*), as did Gilles Kepel in *The Revenge of God.* Norman J. Cohen compiled internal and external perspectives on various fundamentalisms in *The Fundamentalist Phenomenon* (1990). Lawrence Kaplan edited a historical and sociological study on *Fundamentalism in Comparative Perspective* (1992*b*). Hans Küng and Jürgen Moltmann devoted an edition of *Concilium* (June 1992) to *Fundamentalism as an Ecumenical Challenge*, investigating Jewish, Islamic, and Christian manifestations. Niels C. Nielsen Jr.'s *Fundamentalism, Mythos, and World Religions* (1993) is a philosophical and theological study which finds among fundamentalists of the major faiths a 'common premise: that religious truth is essentially timeless and unchanging' (p. 24). More recently, volumes which relate fundamentalism to gender issues have appeared: *Refusing Holy Orders: Women and Fundamentalism in Britain* (Sahgal and Yuval-Davis 1992), *Fundamentalism and Gender: 1875 to the Present* (Bendroth 1993), *Fundamentalism and Gender* (Hawley 1994), and *Women and Fundamentalism: Islam and Christianity* (Gerami 1996).[1]

The most ambitious and comprehensive comparative study to date is The Fundamentalism Project. This was a five-year research project running from 1988 to 1993, funded by the American Academy of the Arts and Sciences. Scholars representing a variety of academic disciplines and a diverse range of religious traditions participated. They produced case-studies of a multitude of religious movements and developed theoretical frameworks for interpreting the data collected. Martin E. Marty and R. Scott Appleby of the University of Chicago chaired and directed the Project and published its findings in five major volumes (1991–5). The Project has also overseen the production of two smaller publications: *The Glory and the Power* (Marty and Appleby 1992), a companion to a series of film and radio documentaries,[2] and *Islamic Fundamentalisms and the Gulf Crisis* (Piscatori 1991), which examines the internal crises of various Islamic fundamentalist movements incurred by Saddam Hussein's call for a *jihad.*

Part of the function of comparative studies has been to debate the appropriateness of the term 'fundamentalism', and to suggest criteria for identifying a fundamentalist movement. Generally it is not thought important that one be bound by fundamentalism's original historical refer-

[1] Recent studies of religion, globalization, and world politics include assessments of fundamentalist movements around the world. Within such studies commentators tend to conflate evangelicalism and Christian fundamentalism. See esp. Beyer (1994); Haynes (1995); Juergensmeyer (1993); Sahliyeh (1990); Swatos (1989).

[2] 'The Glory and the Power: Fundamentalisms Observed', William Benton Broadcast Project of the University of Chicago in association with the BBC and WETA-TV, Washington, DC.

ent. At the same time, many commentators reserve the term 'fundamentalism' for the Abrahamic religions. They do not all fully attempt to justify this decision. The majority of studies mentioned above are of Jewish, Christian, and Muslim movements, and the importance of biblical revelation to these movements is emphasized. With the exception of Nielsen's book, the volumes which do include non-Abrahamic religions give a relatively small amount of space to them. The peruser of these studies could well come away with the impression that it is certainly appropriate to extend the term 'fundamentalism' but that it is problematic to do so beyond Christianity, Islam, and Judaism. Both sides of this impression would need to be examined.

The Fundamentalism Project proceeded to test the hypothesis that 'family resemblances' exist among movements commonly perceived as 'fundamentalist' (Marty and Appleby 1991*a*: 816). Throughout the Project the term 'fundamentalism' was used in a temporary and exploratory way, with judgement as to its usefulness postponed until the end. The final verdict is that cases can be categorized as fundamentalist, fundamentalist-like or non-fundamentalist depending on their share of certain characteristics. Project veterans Gabriel Almond, Emmanuel Sivan, and Scott Appleby identify nine recurring characteristics (1995: 399–424). Five of these are ideological: reactivity to the marginalization of religion, selectivity, moral dualism, absolutism and inerrancy, millennialism and messianism. Four are organizational: elect membership, sharp boundaries, charismatic and authoritarian leadership, and behavioural requirements. They conclude that many movements within the Abrahamic religions manifest these characteristics, and that Sikh radicalism shares most of them, and so may be termed fundamentalist.

Since fundamentalism is defined 'from an examination of Abrahamic cases', it is to be expected that some 'movements in other religious traditions, which do not share important features of Abrahamic theology and practice' will be found to be only fundamentalist-like or to be non-fundamentalist (ibid. 416). Sikh radicalism is a deviant case because it 'acquired Abrahamic qualities' through the historical and cultural contact of Sikhism with Islam (p. 423). In an earlier publication Marty and Appleby (1992: 5, cf. 21) argued that Christianity, Judaism, and Islam have the '"natural resources" of fundamentalism, including revealed doctrines, canonized texts, and a linear view of history'. This does not mean that all the Abrahamic movements studied are regarded as fundamentalist. Those which reverse the fundamentalist priority of religion to politics, such as Ulster Protestants and Guatemalan Pentecostals, are categorized as fundamentalist-like, along with the Hindu RSS and Sinhala Buddhist extremists. United States Catholic traditionalism and some Islamic groups are classed as non-fundamentalist because they rate low in the nine characteristics. The Project resolves overall that fundamentalisms are distinct from other religious movements in that they are inherently interactive, reactive, and oppositional, and so inevitably political, and yet distinct from political or social protest movements because they are genuinely religious.

Jeff Haynes (1995), in a document for the United Nations, gives a more inclusive account of fundamentalism which embraces religious movements which are primarily politically motivated. He distinguishes two broad categories of religious fundamentalism. The first category comprises groups based on Abrahamic 'religions of the book' for whom scriptural revelations relating to political, moral, and social issues form the corpus of demands. The second consists of nationalist-oriented derivatives of Hinduism and Buddhism which in the absence of clear scriptural norms are indistinguishable from movements with aspirations for national or cultural purity. He is in basic agreement with the Fundamentalism Project, which emphasizes the 'militant nation- and state-building nature of Hindu fundamentalism' (p. 467), but he retains the ascription 'religious fundamentalist'.

In effect, Haynes suggests an alternative approach to comparing fundamentalisms. He begins firmly in the present, and assumes the perspective that movements from within any religious tradition can be religiously fundamentalist. He therefore bypasses a problem that plagues most comparative studies: how to justify their choice of criteria when moving from one tradition to another. He works with a single definition rather than with a range of variable characteristics. This achieves simplicity at the cost of flexibility. His definition demonstrates how difficult it is to locate Protestant fundamentalists, other than the relatively recent breed of right-wing political activists, within an account of world fundamentalism: 'Religious fundamentalist movements aim to reform society by changing laws, morality, social norms and political configurations in accordance with religious tenets, with the goal of creating a more traditional society' (p. ii). In particular, Haynes is inattentive to early Protestant fundamentalism and its present quietist and separatist forms, and therefore cannot accommodate those who most wish to be called fundamentalist.

The Fundamentalism Project has half an eye on the past, on the origins of fundamentalism and the history of its development. This approach is more common but it too is problematic: there is no obvious point, between the United States in 1920 and the present global situation, at which to begin characterizing fundamentalism for the purposes of a comparative study. The Project's starting-point—a definition of fundamentalism from the Abrahamic religions—appears somewhat arbitrary. The Abrahamic faiths are religiously alike in some respects and different in others, and will have some points of contact with non-Abrahamic religions. Almond, Sivan, and Appleby (1995: 416) argue that fundamentalism 'was first observed and studied in these [Abrahamic] traditions'. However, fundamentalism occurred first in Protestantism and was not observed in Judaism or Islam until about sixty years later, after which the term was applied to other faiths with relative rapidity. Roman Catholic integralism developed simultaneously with Protestant fundamentalism in reaction to Darwinism and higher criticism, but was labelled 'fundamentalist' only after the term had already been extended beyond Christianity. Before that, its absolutism towards magisterial pronouncements was not described as fundamentalist, since such absolutism does not share the attitude of Protestant fundamentalism towards biblical truth and authority.

William Shepard argues that if 'fundamentalism' is taken to mean scriptural absolutism or a focus on a few doctrinal assertions, comparison outside of Protestantism is not justified. He refers to the Islamic phenomenon as 'Islamic radicalism' (1987: 368; 1992: 282), and for comparative usage he suggests the term 'radical neotraditionalism' (1987: 368). Even William Montgomery Watt, despite entitling his 1988 study *Islamic Fundamentalism and Modernity*, prefers to call his subjects 'conservatives and traditionalists' (1988: 2; cf. 1991: 119–21).[3]

The closest point of similarity between Jews, Christians, and Muslims lies in their shared identity as 'people of the book'. Bruce Lawrence criticizes James Barr for assuming 'that only Protestant Christians give unqualified priority to scripturalism in their religious outlook'. Lawrence (1989*a*: 5, 6) asserts that 'the potential for scriptural absolutism among both Muslims and Jews is at least as high as it is among Protestant Christians'. J. D. Hunter (1990: 67–9) goes further and argues that scripturalism is a feature of fundamentalists in any religion, since all indulge in a literal reading of sacred texts.

Lawrence and Hunter, however, betray a lack of sensitivity to the difference between theological studies of Protestant fundamentalism and sociological studies of comparative fundamentalism. In comparative studies, scripture is significant for its social function in setting boundaries of belief, practice, and membership for the fundamentalist community

[3] Several commentators have rightly argued that neither 'traditionalism' nor 'conservatism' are useful alternatives to 'fundamentalism'. Fundamentalists are innovative. They do not simply reassert tradition, but are selective and regard some aspects of their religious tradition as the product of compromise and error (Marty and Appleby 1991*a*: 825; Parekh 1992: 40; Marty 1992: 7). Elshahed (1992), Salim Abdullah (1992), and Shepard (1992) prefer 'Islamism' over 'Islamic fundamentalism'. This has the virtue of being a new term for a new sort of movement. It should not be taken to imply a straightforward return to traditional Islam.

(e.g. Hunter 1990: 68). In theological studies, the doctrine of scripture and the theology of interpretation are of more consequence than is scripture as a social entity. Having faulted Barr (1989: 5) for offering no definition of scripture, Lawrence fails to define 'scripturalism', which cannot but take different forms within different religions. The Fundamentalism Project is similarly lacking in theological analysis, which is a serious weakness in a programme which emphasizes religious and theological characteristics of fundamentalism. Almond, Sivan, and Appleby (1995: 432) ask, for example, whether the host religion's beliefs are 'explicit and coherent, codified in texts as in the case of the Abrahamic religions—in Judaism, Christianity, Islam—and in Sikhism?' A theological study would have investigated different ways of judging religious coherence or of honouring sacred texts.

Within a Protestant context, fundamentalism could not endorse vigorous reinterpretation of the fundamentals of scripture as it does in Islam, or strict adherence to particular rabbinic interpretations as it does in Judaism. Protestant fundamentalists undermine the role of interpretation in their apprehension of scripture. Realizing this, Hassan (1990) and Wieseltier (1990) resist the fundamentalist label for Muslims and Jews respectively, because it implies a suspicion of the interpretation of scripture which is peculiar to Protestant fundamentalism. James Barr (1977: 7, 182, 284–6) would agree.

Similarly, Catholic integralists are less resistant to the notion of biblical interpretation than are Protestant fundamentalists.[4] While some use the Bible in a fundamentalist way, employing passages as proof-texts, they do so in support of papal authority or papal dictates which they regard as the sources of absolute truth (Arnold 1990: 184). They are 'constrained by their orthodoxy to be papal legitimists', and so would follow the Pope in all matters including biblical interpretation (Coleman 1992*a*: 88).

An oppositional stance is cited as a common feature of fundamentalist groups. This criterion takes us beyond the fold of religious movements to positing a fundamentalist 'potential in every movement or cause' (Caplan 1987*a*: 22). It becomes possible to speak only of 'family resemblances' and not of a single phenomenon (ibid. 4). The family resemblances could be stretched so far as to include Germaine Greer and Schumacher's circle on a 'modernity-resistance model', suggests Andrew Walker (1987: 197–8), so indicating the inadequacies of fundamentalism

[4] However, Martin Marty (1992: 5) considers American Roman Catholic fundamentalists to be very similar to Protestant fundamentalists in this respect. He argues that although they have 'never heard of Scottish common sense realism . . . they share with the Protestants the claim that a text, however difficult and mysterious, because it is a revelation of God, is accessible and admits of but one meaning'.

as a unifying paradigm. Jay M. Harris (1994: 156) reasons that only because we are sympathetic to the African National Congress are we not prepared to 'label their transcendent and authoritarian politics as fundamentalist'. Richard Webster (1990: 45–67) regards liberalism as a 'fundamentalism-without faith' which is no less zealous and authoritarian than its religious counterpart. Günter Hole (1992: 24–5) considers that since we all harbour 'hidden fanatical elements', we all have 'tendencies towards fundamentalist attitudes within us', and Caplan (1987*a*: 22) finds 'all of us, to some degree and in some senses, fundamentalists'.

In expounding the oppositional nature of fundamentalism, comparative accounts have emphasized political activism and potency (e.g. Caplan 1987*a*: 5–9; Kaplan 1992*a*: 5). Movements of religious resurgence worldwide have allied themselves with a variety of political ideologies. It would be overstating the case to suggest that any particular political ideology, such as nationalism, is essential to fundamentalism. A more pertinent question is whether politicization itself is essential. Most scholars and practitioners of Protestant fundamentalism regard political activism as an anomaly within the movement.

Premillennialist preoccupation with the end-times has dominated Protestant fundamentalist attitudes towards the world for much of this century. Predicting that chaos will reign until Christ comes to restore order, premillennialist fundamentalists have mostly thought it their duty to separate themselves from worldly entanglements and await his return. During and immediately after World War II premillennialists were somewhat politicized, especially against the Bolshevik threat and perceived degenerative trends in American culture (Marsden 1980: 141–64). Nevertheless, fundamentalism was not primarily a response to social and political issues but to the perceived spread of false doctrine (ibid. 157–9). A few early fundamentalists were engaged directly in political affairs. Most notably, William Jennings Bryan, who was not a premillennialist, was leader of the Democratic Party in the United States during the first two decades of the century. However, he also declared a greater interest in religion than in government (ibid. 132). Those who actively worked towards reform focused principally on the moral realm and on the individual. They believed that the reform of the individual through personal conversion was necessary to the reform of the nation. Then, from the mid-1920s onwards, weary from their battles in the denominations and against evolution, fundamentalists withdrew from the political arena.[5]

[5] Separatist fundamentalist Carl McIntire became politically active in the 1950s in combating communism but his political involvement caused a split among his followers (Beale 1986: 325–6).

Protestant fundamentalists who in the last couple of decades have become politicized have had to denounce the 'older, pietistic, "don't get involved in worldly affairs" version of American fundamentalism' (North 1984: 32). Jerry Falwell (1980: Author's Note), a leading founder of the Moral Majority, laments that 'we, the American People, have allowed a vocal minority of ungodly men and women to bring America to the brink of death'. He calls for withdrawal from 'the silent majority in order to defend and maintain the freedoms that allow us to live and believe as we so choose'. Pastor Muller, a fundamentalist Baptist, described to Alan Peshkin (1986: 4–5) the turn-around in thinking:

> so many Christians didn't vote [in 1964]. It's not because we're not patriotic; see, we feel that our citizenship is in heaven and consequently we're more involved with spiritual entities. It's too easy for us to get the idea that, well, the Lord is coming one of these days and we're on our way to heaven, and just forget about this whole world. Here's the way we finally began to think: We've got leaders that have caused our problems, and governments that have created difficulties for us in the operation of our ministries. So, as leaders we got together and said, 'We've got to do something about this.'

The tendency to 'forget this whole world' has not been fully quashed among Protestant fundamentalists. Bob Jones III (1980: 1) criticized the Moral Majority for attempting to correct the immorality of the nation when it should have been attacking sin as the root cause of immorality: 'the immorality of our nation is not our debilitating disease; it is merely a symptom of our disease. Sin is the disease or causal factor in our nation's decline'. Another withdrawal from political engagement remains a possibility for Protestant fundamentalists:

> Even when the activist element has been dominant there have been those who decry social and political involvement as a diversion, a waste of the energy which should be directed to the primary task of saving souls. It needs very little by way of disillusionment with the active mode to swing the pendulum back to pietistic retreat.
>
> (F. F. Bruce 1988: 175)[6]

The Moral Majority disbanded in 1989, although Pat Robertson's Christian Coalition remains a force in the 1990s.[7]

Ervand Abrahamian (1992: 110) denies that 'fundamentalism' is a

[6] Writing on the inefficacy of the NCR, S. Bruce (1993: 63) notes polls which suggest that Pat Robertson's 1988 campaign for the presidency was hindered by the discomfort fundamentalists felt at the overt mixing of religion and politics.

[7] For reflection on the past and future of evangelical and fundamentalist politics see Noll 1994: 149–75, 221–8.

suitable term for Muslim groups precisely because 'the term fundamentalism implies otherworldliness rather than this-worldliness':

It conjures up doctrinal obsessions with 'moral' concerns—such as abortion, man's creation, and Judgement Day—rather than with such political issues as revolution, imperialism, and social justice. In fact, Khomeini and his disciples succeeded in gaining power in most part because in their public pronouncements they did not dwell on such 'fundamentalist' concerns.

Indeed, Pastor Muller regards the Devil as the ultimate target of fundamentalist political involvement: 'We look around us and see Satan. He's prince and power of this age and he has stronger involvement with this world than Christians do' (Peshkin 1986: 6). The political ambitions of today's American fundamentalists are not comparable to the territorial concerns of Gush Emunim, the revolutionary aspirations of various Islamic movements or the nationalist drive of *Hindutva* (Hindu 'fundamentalism'). Clark Pinnock (1990: 49–50) argues justifiably that the political aim of American fundamentalists 'is not to take over the United States and turn it into a religious theocracy . . . but to be responsible Christian citizens in a democracy'.

As Marty and Appleby (1992: 4) argue, the 'best case against the word *fundamentalism* comes from those who say it represents a Western linguistic encroachment'. This objection is complicated, however, by the possibility that resurgent movements within Hinduism, Sikhism, and Buddhism (and now Shinto) have imitated fundamentalism. The Indian religions are non-exclusivist, and Hindus and Buddhists are proud to have no single source or authority upon which to draw. Marty and Appleby (ibid. 21) cite these as 'cases in which fundamentalist inventiveness extends to the construction of fundamentals—of "doctrines" from vast bodies of teaching, of "scriptures" from epics or historical accounts, and of "founders" of contemporary movements from mythical or legendary figures'. *Hindutva* ideology embodies an interesting tension in celebrating the 'irreducibly non-fundamentalist nature of Hindu thinking' (Ram-Prasad 1993: 292). The religious philosophies of the Hindu schools are pluralist, community-minded, and conduct-orientated (Ram-Prasad 1993; Parekh 1992: 42–5). The very will to assert self-identity against the encroachment of Western culture and the decline of their own traditions betrays some influence from Western thought.

'Modernism' is most commonly cited as that against which fundamentalism asserts itself (e.g. Caplan 1987*a*: 9–14; Lawrence 1989*a*: *passim*; 1992).[8] Although resurgent religious movements around the world may

[8] Some more carelessly suggest that fundamentalists object to 'modernity' itself rather than to a modernist ideology (e.g. Hunter 1990: 57).

have imitated a fundamentalist reaction to modernism, it is sensed that the concept of fundamentalism is not at home outside the culture of Western secular modernity (e.g. Shepard 1989: 290). This cultural sensibility is different from the reasoning by which commentators restrict fundamentalism to the Semitic religions. Protestant fundamentalists do not react to Western modernity in the same way as either Jewish or Muslim fundamentalists because Western modernity has been a creation of Christian culture: 'One has to search hard among evangelical and fundamentalist sources to find much about the core practices and values of the modern world which they reject, which is perhaps not surprising given the important role that conservative Protestantism played in bringing such a world into being' (S. Bruce 1990: 174).

American Protestant fundamentalists are, George Marsden (1993: 37) argues, committed to many aspects of modernity in that they are committed to American culture—its regard for science, its Constitution, its nationalism, and the separation of church and state: 'Although some of their theocratic rhetoric may be at odds with these traditions, their philosophy is, nonetheless, enough a product of the American heritage to be a long way from most other militant religious traditionalists'. American fundamentalists remain fiercely pro-democratic, committed to the freedom of the individual, and supportive of church–state separation. Jewish and Islamic resurgent groups reject the ideal of democracy and the suggestion that individuals possess characteristics independently of the community or of God, and they condemn the false separation of religion and politics (S. Bruce 1988: 174–5; Garvey 1993; Harris 1994: 155–6; Kepel 1994: 196–9; Juergensmeyer 1993: 187). Hence opposition to modernity takes a different form among Christian and non-Christian fundamentalists.

None the less, if correctly understood, the fundamentalist relation to modernity could illuminate a link between Protestant and comparative studies. The fundamentalist war is not against modernity, but it takes place within it: 'Although it revolts against some aspects of the modern world, it is an essentially modern phenomenon competing with secular ideologies on *their* terrain and in *their* terms' (Parekh 1992: 39, cf. 30–1; cf. Coleman 1992*b*: 38–41). It is now largely recognized that fundamentalists positively accept certain features of the modern, scientific age:

> They like many of its products—rapid transportation, telecommunications, electricity, medical science—but are wary of the values that seem to accompany these technological and scientific marvels. One such value of secular modernity is the superiority of human reason to all other means of knowledge, including religious revelation . . . When people agree that only rational discourse is permissible in a society, something of even greater value is lost, say the fundamentalists . . . [namely] spirit, an

animating force that cannot be comprehended by human reason alone . . . To deny spirit . . . is to threaten the very humanity of the person and of society. (Marty and Appleby 1992: 15)

Fundamentalists live in the modern world and use some aspects of modernity, some forms of Enlightenment thought, and some technological inventions to refute other aspects of modernity, secular Enlightenment philosophies, and what they see as destructive and immoral uses of modern technology. They oppose not modernity, but 'secularism' or 'secular modernism' (Kepel 1994: 192; Harris 1994: 156), or 'secular modernity' (Pinnock 1990*b*: 42; Marty and Appleby 1992: 15–18).

The Protestant fundamentalist mentality reflects early-modern as opposed to late-modern thought. Francis Schaeffer (1968*a*: 30–2, 36–40), for example, sides with early-modern science, by which he means the science of Bacon, over and against 'modern modern science' and 'modern modern morality'. This reaction against late-modern thought may provide a clue to a fundamentalist mentality within non-Protestant movements of religious resurgence.

Just as fundamentalists have made use of modernity's main carrier, mass media, they also have appropriated the very heart of Enlightenment reason and rationalism. The near hysteria associated with some mass movement fundamentalist scenes on the Asian subcontinent, in the Middle East, and elsewhere, leads many to conclude that fundamentalisms are essentially antirational, opposed to reason. Some of them may be, but in those we have studied—and the sweep of them is vast—it is clear that fundamentalists often fight modernity by seizing the concept of reason and 'throwing it back,' using not unreason but a different modality of rationalism. (Marty and Appleby 1992: 32)

Marty (1992: 6) describes fundamentalism as 'very rationalistic', and also appreciates that 'its rationalism counters the more regularly supported post-Enlightenment academic rationalisms'. This reflects the paradox in Protestant fundamentalism, that it strongly opposes rationalism while it is itself described in primarily rationalist terms. Roman Catholic integralism bears some relation to Protestant fundamentalism in this respect. It shares a 'strongly rationalistic' orientation where 'religion is based on a standardized objective knowledge of God' (Dinges 1991: 82). Hans Küng ([1970] 1994: 133–9) finds in neo-scholastic thought a Cartesian *naïveté* about the subject's apprehension of the object. Protestant fundamentalist thought endorses the same basic epistemology and reflects a similar *naïveté*. It is modernist in its acceptance of '*scientific rationalism*'—'a science of early modernity—a Baconian model of science based on common sense' (Volf 1992: 102).

Those who describe fundamentalism from a comparative perspective as 'irrational' or 'anti-rational' (Moltmann 1992: 111), or even as a 'child of the late Enlightenment' (McCarthy Brown 1994: 192, 194–8), must either be misjudging the phenomenon or describing developments in the late twentieth century which differ significantly from Protestant fundamentalist ways of thinking. The search for 'family resemblances' among movements which are commonly termed fundamentalist would benefit from more thorough investigation of their philosophical frameworks, and reactions to late modern thought. Nielsen offers such an analysis, though he presents fundamentalism as reflecting a pre-Enlightenment paradigm rather than early Enlightenment patterns of thought. The argument presented in this book is that Protestant fundamentalism is strongly empirically rationalist and, moreover, that its mentality in this respect has dominated twentieth-century evangelicalism.

GLOSSARY OF FUNDAMENTALIST AND EVANGELICAL INSTITUTIONS

ACCC: American Council of Christian Churches, founded in 1941 by Carl McIntire as a fundamentalist alternative to the Federal Council of Churches.

ASA: American Scientific Affiliation, founded in 1941 by evangelical scientists.

Banner of Truth Trust: established in 1957 with the aim of advancing the Reformed faith. The Trust was based first in London and is now in Edinburgh. It issues a magazine and publishes Reformed and Puritan writings.

BCMS: Bible Churchmen's Missionary Society, founded by conservatives in the Church of England who separated from the Church Missionary Society in the 1920s because they demanded a stronger stand against higher criticism.

Campus Crusade for Christ International: founded in 1951 by ex-businessman Bill Bright, originally as a ministry for students at UCLA.

CICCU: Cambridge Inter-Collegiate Christian Union, founded in 1877.

CiS: Christians in Science, a branch of UCCF which began as the Research Scientists Christian Fellowship in 1943.

Christian Coalition: a right-wing political lobbying movement which through Pat Robertson inaugurated a second wave of NCR activity in the late 1980s and 1990s.

CMS: Church Missionary Society, a Church of England society founded in 1799.

CRS: Creation Research Society, formed in 1963 to promote creation science.

CSM: Creation Science Movement, a British Creation Science organization based in Portsmouth. It is the Evolution Protest Movement renamed, and has connections with American creation science groups.

EA: Evangelical Alliance, the first ecumenical evangelical organization, founded in 1846 in London. EA has been much revived since World War II, and especially since the early 1980s.

EFTL: Evangelical Fellowship for Theological Literature, founded by Max Warren in 1942.

ETS: Evangelical Theological Society, an American society of evangelical theological scholars, founded in 1949.

GARBC: General Association of Regular Baptist Churches, founded in 1932 by conservatives who separated from the Northern Baptist Convention.

ISAE: Institute for the Study of American Evangelicals, founded in 1982 by evangelical historians Mark A. Noll and Nathan O. Hatch and based at Wheaton College.

ICCC: International Council of Christian Churches, founded by Carl McIntire in 1948 as a fundamentalist alternative to the World Council of Churches.

ICR: Institute for Creation Research, founded in 1972 by Henry Morris and Duane Gish, and based in San Diego.

ICS: Institute for Christian Studies, a graduate school in Toronto, Canada, founded in 1967 and inspired by the Dutch neo-Calvinist philosophy of Kuyper, Dooyeweerd, and Vollenhoven.

IVCF: Inter-Varsity Christian Fellowship, the American equivalent of UCCF.

IVF: Inter-Varsity Fellowship of Evangelical Christian Unions, formally established in 1928 and now known as UCCF. An American branch was established in the 1940s, with headquarters in Chicago.

MM: Moral Majority, a coalition of religious conservatives prominent in the NCR, who engaged in political lobbying. MM was founded by Jerry Falwell in 1979 and disbanded in 1989.

NAE: National Association of Evangelicals, founded in 1942 as a less separatist alternative to McIntire's ACCC, whose founders pioneered the new-evangelical movement.

NCR: New Christian Right, not an institution but an umbrella term for fundamentalists and evangelicals who ally themselves with the political right. The NCR was particularly prominent in the 1980s.

NEAC: National Evangelical Anglican Congress, held at Keele University in 1967, and at Nottingham University in 1977.

OICCU: Oxford Inter-Collegiate Christian Union, founded in 1889.

Operation Rescue: an activist coalition of Protestants, Catholics, and Jews campaigning against abortion, founded by Randall Terry in 1988.

SCM: Student Christian Movement, the name given in 1905 to the British College Christian Union which had emerged in the 1890s to co-ordinate student Christian groups. Within a few years it ceased to be predominantly evangelical, and in 1928 the more conservative IVF was founded.

TSF: Theological Students' Fellowship, organized by IVF in 1933. Until 1946, TSF was known as the Theological Student's Prayer Union. A North American branch of TSF was founded in 1974.

UCCF: Universities and Colleges Christian Fellowship, which changed its name from IVF in the 1970s having expanded its role beyond universities.

WCFA: World's Christian Fundamentals Association, founded in 1919 by William Bell Riley, and credited as the first fundamentalist organization. It was interdenominational.

YFC: Youth for Christ International, founded in 1944 for ministry to high schools. Billy Graham was its first full-time worker. Its headquarters are in Wheaton, Illinois.

REFERENCES

Tracts, Leaflets, and News Sheets

BRIGHT, BILL (1965), 'Have You Heard of the Four Spiritual Laws?', Campus Crusade for Christ.

Campus Crusade for Christ (1986), 'How Can I Turn the Tables in Witnessing?', Leväsjoki, Finland: Myllykummun kirjapaino.

Christians in Science, News-Sheet, July 1994.

Home Time: A Christian Newsletter for Home-Schooling Families, 3, Spring/Summer 1993.

Independent Baptists in Britain, 'Perhaps To-day! What the Bible Teaches About the Return of Christ', Independent Baptist Tract Ministries, The Elms, Windmill Farm, Clanfield, Oxon.

'L'Abri Fellowship', information leaflet, L'Abri Fellowship, The Manor, Greatham, nr. Liss, Hants.

Perspective, 27/1, Newsletter from the Institute for Christian Studies, Toronto, March 1993.

Scripture Gift Mission, 'Four Steps to Life', 3 Eccleston Street, London.

Scripture Publications, 'God, Christ and Me', 71 Viaduct Road, Brighton.

You Are Here, Muthena Paul Alkazraji, Samizdat, 1992.

General Publications

ABRAHAM, WILLIAM J. (1981), *The Divine Inspiration of Holy Scripture* (Oxford: Oxford University Press).

ABRAHAMIAN, ERVAND (1992), 'Khomeini: A Fundamentalist?', in Kaplan (1992*b*: 109–125).

ACHTEMEIER, PAUL J. (1986), 'The Authority of the Bible: What Shall We Then Preach?', *TSF Bulletin*, Nov./Dec., 19–22.

AHLSTROM, SYDNEY E. (1955), 'The Scottish Philosophy and American Theology', *Church History*, 24: 257–72.

——(1972), *A Religious History of the American People* (New Haven: Yale University Press).

ALEXANDER, ARCHIBALD [1808], *A Sermon Delivered at the Opening of the General Assembly of the Presbyterian Church in the United States, May 1808* (Philadelphia: Hopkins & Earle), repr. with commentary in Noll (1983: 51–4).

—— [1812*a*], *The Sermon, Delivered at the Inauguration of the Rev. Archibald Alexander, D.D., as Professor of Didactic and Polemic Theology, in the Theological Seminary of the Presbyterian Church, in the United States of America. To Which are Added, the Professor's Inaugural Address and the Charge of the Professor and Students* (New York: J. Seymour), repr. with commentary in Noll (1983: 72–91).

—— [1812*b*], 'Theological Lectures, Nature and Evidence of Truth, October 1812', repr. with commentary in Noll (1983: 61–71, 317–91).

ALMOND, GABRIEL A., SIVAN, EMMANUEL, and APPLEBY, R. SCOTT (1995), 'Fundamentalism: Genus and Species'; 'Explaining Fundamentalisms'; and 'Examining the Cases', in Marty and Appleby (1995: 399–424; 425–44; 445–82).

AMMERMAN, NANCY TATOM (1987), *Bible Believers, Fundamentalists in the Modern World* (New Brunswick: Rutgers University Press).

ANDERSON, J. N. D. (1979), *The Fact of Christ: Some of the Evidence* (Leicester: IVP).

ANDERSON, ROBERT (n.d. [1909?–15]), 'Christ and Criticism', *The Fundamentals*, ii. 69–84.

ANDERSON, STANLEY E. (1955), 'Verbal Inspiration Inductively Considered', in Youngblood (1984: 13–21).

ARNOLD, PATRICK M., SJ (1990), 'The Reemergence of Fundamentalism in the Catholic Church', in Cohen (1990: 172–91).

ASHCRAFT, MORRIS (1982), 'The Theology of Fundamentalism', *Review and Expositor*, 79/1: 31–43.

AUSTIN, PERCY (1930), *Letters to a Fundamentalist* (London: SCM).

BACON, FRANCIS (1889), *Novum Organum*, ed. Thomas Fowler, 2nd edn. rev. (Oxford: Clarendon Press).

BALMER, RANDALL H. (1982), 'The Princetonians and Scripture: A Reconsideration', *Westminster Theological Journal*, 44: 352–65.

—— (1993), *Mine Eyes Have Seen the Glory: A Journey into the Evangelical Subculture in America*, expanded edn. (New York: Oxford University Press).

BARCLAY, OLIVER R. (1977), *Whatever Happened to the Jesus Lane Lot?* (Leicester: IVF).

—— (1984), *Developing a Christian Mind* (Leicester: IVP).

BARKER, WILLIAM S., and GODFREY, ROBERT (eds.) (1990), *Theonomy: A Reformed Critique* (Grand Rapids, Mich.: Zondervan).

BARR, JAMES (1966), *Old and New in Interpretation: A Study of the Two Testaments* (London: SCM).

—— (1973), *The Bible in the Modern World* (London: SCM).

—— (1977), *Fundamentalism* (London: SCM; Philadelphia: Westminster, 1978).

BARR, JAMES (1980*a*), *Explorations in Theology, 7: The Scope and Authority of the Bible* (London: SCM) (= *The Scope and Authority of the Bible* (Philadelphia: Westminster, 1980)).

——(1980*b*), 'The Fundamentalist Understanding of Scripture', *Concilium*, Sept.–Oct., 70–5.

——(1980*c*), 'Childs' *Introduction to the Old Testament', Journal for the Study of the Old Testament*, 16: 12–23.

——(1981), 'Foreword to the Second Edition', *Fundamentalism* (London: SCM).

——(1984), *Escaping from Fundamentalism* (London: SCM) (= *Beyond Fundamentalism* (Philadelphia: Westminster, 1984)).

——(1986*a*), 'Fundamentalism and Biblical Authority', in Andrew Linzey and Peter J. Wexler (eds.) (1986), *Heaven and Earth: Essex Essays in Theology and Ethics* (Worthing: Churchman), 23–37. This article first appeared under the title 'Religious Fundamentalism', *Current Affairs Bulletin*, 59/1, University of Sydney, June 1982, and repr. in *St. Mark's Review*, Mar. 1988.

——(1986*b*), 'Exegesis as a Theological Discipline Reconsidered, and the Shadow of the Jesus of History', in D. G. Miller (ed.) (1986), *The Hermeneutical Quest: Essays in the Honor of James Luther Mays on his Sixty-Fifth Birthday* (Allison Park, Pa.: Pickwick), 11–45.

——(1988), 'The Theological Case against Biblical Theology', in Gene M. Tucker, David L. Petersen, and Robert R. Wilson (eds.), *Canon, Theology and Old Testament Interpretation: Essays in Honor of Brevard Childs* (Philadelphia: Fortress), 3–19.

——(1989), 'Literality', *Faith and Philosophy*, 6/4: 412–28.

——(1991*a*), ' "Fundamentalism" and Evangelical Scholarship', *Anvil*, 8/2: 141–52.

——(1991*b*), 'Fundamentalism—A Challenge to the Church', *Quarterly Review*, 11/2: 30–9.

BARTON, JOHN (1988), *People of the Book?: The Authority of the Bible in Christianity* (London: SPCK).

BAVINCK, HERMAN (1909*a*), *The Philosophy of Revelation*, Stone Lectures for 1908–9 delivered to Princeton Theological Seminary (New York: Longmans, Green, & Co.).

——(1909*b*), 'Calvin and Common Grace', in Doumergue (1909).

——(1951), *The Doctrine of God* (*Gereformeerde Dogmatick*, ii (4 vols., 1895–9)), trans. William Hendriksen (Grand Rapids, Mich.: Eerdmans).

——(1956), *Our Reasonable Faith* (*Magnalia Dei* (1909), a synopsis of the 4-vol. *Dogmatick*), trans. Henry Zylstra (Grand Rapids, Mich.: Eerdmans).

BAXTER, TONY (1991), 'Postmillennialism', *Calvinism Today*, 1/4: 24–5.

BEALE, DAVID O. (1986), *In Pursuit of Purity: American Fundamentalism Since 1850* (Greenville, SC: Unusual Publications).

BEANBLOSSOM, RONALD E., and LEHRER, KEITH (eds.) (1983), *Thomas Reid's Inquiry and Essays* (Indianapolis: Hackett).

BEATTIE, FRANCIS R. (1903), *Apologetics or the Rational Vindication of Christianity* (Richmond, Va.: Presbyterian Committee of Publications).

BEATTIE, JAMES (1771), *An Essay on the Nature and Immutability of Truth in Opposition to Sophistry and Scepticism*, 2nd edn. (Edinburgh: A. Kincaid & J. Bell).

——(1786), *Evidences of the Christian Religion Briefly and Plainly Stated* (2 vols.; Edinburgh: W. Creech).

BEBBINGTON, D. W. (1988), 'The Advent Hope in British Evangelicalism since 1800', *Scottish Journal of Theology*, 9: 103–14.

——(1989), *Evangelicalism in Modern Britain: A History from the 1730s to the 1980s* (London: Unwin Hyman).

——(1990), 'Baptists and Fundamentalism in Inter-War Britain', in Robbins (1990: 297–326).

——(1993), 'Martyrs for the Truth: Fundamentalists in Britain', in Diana Wood (ed.) (1993), *Martyrs and Martyrologies: Papers Read at the 1992 Summer Meeting and the 1993 Winter Meeting of the Ecclesiastical History Society* (Oxford: Blackwell), 417–51.

——(1994), 'Evangelicalism in Its Settings: The British and American Movements since 1940', in Noll, Bebbington, and Rawlyk (1994: 365–88).

——(1995), 'The Decline and Resurgence of Evangelical Social Concern 1918–1980', in Wolffe (1995: 175–97).

BECK, DAVID W. (1991), 'Introduction: Designing a Christian University', in Beck (1991: 9–23).

——(ed.) (1991), *Opening the American Mind: The Integration of Biblical Truth in the Curriculum of the University* (Grand Rapids, Mich.: Baker).

BELLAH, ROBERT N., and GREENSPAHN, FREDERICK E. (eds.) (1987), *Uncivil Religion: Interreligious Hostility in America* (New York: Crossroad).

BENDROTH, MARGARET LAMBERTS (1993), *Fundamentalism and Gender: 1875 to the Present* (New Haven: Yale University Press).

BERKELEY, GEORGE ([1734] 1975), *A Treatise Concerning the Principles of Human Knowledge, in George Berkeley: Philosophical Works including the works on vision*, with Introduction and notes by M. R. Ayers (London: J. M. Dent & Sons).

BERKOUWER, G. C. ([1966] 1975), *Holy Scripture*, trans. Jack B. Rogers (Grand Rapids, Mich.: Eerdmans).

——(1971), 'The Authority of Scripture (A Responsible Confession)', in Geehan (1971: 197–203).

BETTEX, F. (n.d. [1909?–15]), 'The Bible and Modern Criticism', *The Fundamentals*, iv. 73–90.
BERRY, R. J. (ed.) (1991), *Real Science, Real Faith* (Eastbourne: Monarch).
BEYER, PETER (1994), *Religion and Globalization* (London: Sage).
BISHOP, GEORGE S. (n.d. [1909?–15]), 'The Testimony of the Scriptures to Themselves', *The Fundamentals*, vii. 38–54.
BLAMIRES, HARRY (1963), *The Christian Mind* (London: SPCK).
BLOESCH, DONALD G. (1973), *The Evangelical Renaissance* (London: Hodder & Stoughton).
——(1978), *The Essentials of Evangelical Theology*, i. *God, Authority, and Salvation* (San Francisco: Harper & Row).
——(1983), *The Future of Evangelical Theology: A Call for Unity Amid Diversity* (Garden City, NY: Doubleday).
——(1985), 'A Christological Hermeneutic: Crisis and Conflict in Hermeneutics', in R. K. Johnston (1985: 78–102).
——(1987), 'Foreword', and 'Promise with Peril: A Response to James Olthuis', in Olthuis (1987: 7–10, 61–9).
——(1992), *A Theology of Word and Spirit: Authority and Method in Theology* (Downers Grove, Ill: IVP).
——(1994), *Holy Scripture: Revelation, Inspiration and Interpretation* (Carlisle: Paternoster).
BOONE, KATHLEEN C. (1989), *The Bible Tells Them So: The Discourse of Protestant Fundamentalism* (Albany, NY: State University of New York Press; London: SCM, 1990).
BOZEMAN, THEODORE DWIGHT (1977), *Protestants in an Age of Science: The Baconian Ideal and Antebellum American Religious Thought* (Chapel Hill, NC: University of North Carolina Press).
BRADLEY, F. H. (1914), *Essays on Truth and Reality* (Oxford: Clarendon Press).
BRATT, JAMES (1984), *Dutch Calvinism in Modern America: A History of a Conservative Subculture* (Grand Rapids, Mich.: Eerdmans).
BRIGHT (1965), see Tracts section.
BROADBENT, E. H. (1931), *The Pilgrim Church: Being some account of the continuance through succeeding centuries of churches practising the principles taught and exemplified in the New Testament* (London: Pickering & Inglis).
BROMILEY, G. W. (1959), *David Henry Charles Bartlett, M.A., D.D.: A Memoir* (Burnham-on-Sea: Dr Bartlett's Executors).
BROMLEY, DAVID G., and SHUPE, ANSON (1984), *New Christian Politics* (Macon, Ga.: Mercer University Press).
BRUCE, F. F. (1988), *The Book of Acts*, rev. edn. (Grand Rapids, Mich.: Eerdmans).
BRUCE, STEVE (1987), 'The Moral Majority: The Politics of Fundamentalism in Secular Society', in Caplan (1987*b*: 177–94).

——(1988), *The Rise and Fall of the New Christian Right: Conservative Protestant Politics in America 1978–1988* (Oxford: Oxford University Press).
——(1990), *A House Divided: Protestantism, Schism and Secularization* (London: Routledge).
——(1993), 'Fundamentalism, Ethnicity, and Enclave', in Marty and Appleby (1993*b*: 50–67).
Bush, Russ (1978), Review of James Barr's *Fundamentalism, Southwestern Journal of Theology*, 21: 100–1.
Buswell, James Oliver (1948*a*), 'The Arguments from Nature to God, Presuppositionalism and Thomas Aquinas', *The Bible Today*, 41/8 (May), 235–48.
——(1948*b*), 'The Fountainhead of Presuppositionalism', *The Bible Today*, 42/2 (Nov.), 41–64.
——(1949), 'Warfield vs. Presuppositionalism', *The Bible Today*, 42/6 (Mar.), 182–7, 192.
Butler, Christopher (1977), 'Jesus in Later Orthodoxy', in Green (1977: 87–100).
Calver, Clive (1995), 'Afterword', in Wolffe (1995: 198–210).
——Coffey, Ian, and Meadows, Peter [n.d.], 'Who do Evangelicals Think They Are?' (London: Evangelical Alliance).
Cameron, Nigel M. de S. (1984), 'Inspiration and Criticism: The Nineteenth-Century Crisis', *Tyndale Bulletin*, 35: 129–59.
——(1985), 'Incarnation and Inscripturation: The Christological Analogy in the Light of Recent Discussion', *Scottish Bulletin of Evangelical Theology*, 3/2 (Autumn 1985), 35–46.
Campbell, R. J. (1907), *The New Theology* (London: Chapman & Hall).
Caplan, Lionel (1987*a*), 'Introduction', in Caplan (1987*b*: 1–24).
——(ed.) (1987*b*), *Studies in Religious Fundamentalism* (Albany, NY: State University of New York Press).
Capps, Walter H. (1990), *The New Religious Right: Piety, Patriotism, and Politics* (Columbia, SC: University of South Carolina Press).
Carnell, Edward John (1957), *Christian Commitment: An Apologetic* (New York: Macmillan).
——(1958), 'Fundamentalism', in Marvin Halverson and Arthur A. Cohen (eds.), *A Handbook of Christian Theology* (Cleveland: World), 142–3.
——(1960), *The Kingdom of Love and the Pride of Life* (Grand Rapids, Mich.: Eerdmans).
——(1965), *The Burden of Søren Kierkegaard* (Exeter: Paternoster).
Carpenter, Joel A. (1980), 'Fundamentalist Institutions and the Rise of Evangelical Protestantism 1929–1942', *Church History*, 49: 62–75.
——(1984), 'The Fundamentalist Leaven and the Rise of an Evangelical United Front', in Sweet (1984: 257–88).

CARPENTER, JOEL A. (ed.) (1988), *Fundamentalist Versus Modernist* (New York: Garland).

——and SHIPPS, KENNETH W. (eds.) (1987), *Making Higher Education Christian: The History and Mission of Evangelical Colleges in America* (Grand Rapids, Mich.: Christian University Press).

CARSON, ALEXANDER, *Works* (6 vols.; Dublin: William Carson, 1847–64).

——(1847), *Faith the Foundation of the Greater Part of Human Knowledge*, ibid. i. 401–4.

——(1863), *Examination of the Principles of Biblical Interpretation of Ernesti, Stuart, and other Philologists*, ibid. v. 221–423.

CARSON, D. A., and WOODBRIDGE, J. D. (eds.) (1983), *Scripture and Truth* (Grand Rapids, Mich.: Zondervan).

CARTER, GRAYSON L. (1990), 'Evangelical Seceders from the Church of England c. 1800–1850', D.Phil. thesis, Oxford.

CARTER, PAUL A. (1968), 'The Fundamentalist Defense of the Faith', in J. Braemen and D. Brody, *Change and Continuity in Twentieth Century America: The 1920s* (Columbus: Ohio State University Press).

CAVEN, WILLIAM (n.d. [1909?–15]), 'The Testimony of Christ to the Old Testament', *The Fundamentals*, iv. 46–72.

CHAPLIN, JONATHAN (1995), 'Dooyeweerd's Notion of Societal Structural Principles', *Philosophia Reformata*, 60: 16–36.

CHAPMAN, JOHN C. (1981), *Know and Tell the Gospel: Help for the Reluctant Evangelist* (London: Hodder & Stoughton).

CHEVREAU, GUY (1994), *Catch the Fire* (London: Marshall Pickering).

Chicago Statement on Biblical Inerrancy (1977), repr. in Geisler (1979: 493–502), and Packer ([1965] 1979: 149–55).

Chicago Statement on Biblical Hermeneutics (1982), repr. in Radmacher and Preus (1984: 881–7), and McKim (1986: 21–6).

CLABAUGH, GARY K. (1974), *Thunder on the Right: The Protestant Fundamentalists* (Chicago: Nelson-Hall).

CLARK, GORDON H. ([1973] 1977), *Three Types of Religious Philosophy* (Nutley, NJ: Presbyterian and Reformed).

——(1990), 'Fifty Years of Infidelity', *Trinity Review*, May/June.

CLARK, KELLY JAMES (1990), *Return to Reason: A Critique of Enlightenment Evidentialism and a Defense of Reason and Belief in God* (Grand Rapids, Mich.: Eerdmans).

CLARK, MATHEW S., and LEDERLE, HENRY I., *et al.* (1989), *What is Distinctive about Pentecostal Theology?* (Pretoria: University of South Africa).

CLOUSER, ROY A. (1991), *The Myth of Religious Neutrality: An Essay on the Hidden Role of Religious Belief in Theories* (Notre Dame, Ind.: University of Notre Dame Press).

COHEN, NORMAN J. (ed.) (1990), *The Fundamentalist Phenomenon: A View from Within; A Response from Without* (Grand Rapids, Mich.: Eerdmans).

COLE, STEWART G. ([1931] 1963), *The History of Fundamentalism* (Hamden, Conn.: Archon Books).

COLEMAN, J. A. (1992*a*), 'Catholic Integralism as a Fundamentalism', in Kaplan (1992*b*: 74–95).

——(1992*b*), 'Global Fundamentalism: Sociological Perspectives', in Küng and Moltmann (1992: 36–45).

COLLINS, VARNUM LANSING (1925), *President Witherspoon, A Biography* (Princeton: Princeton University Press).

CONN, HARVIE M. (1984), *Eternal Word and Changing Worlds: Theology, Anthropology, and Mission in Trialogue* (Grand Rapids, Mich.: Zondervan).

——(1987), 'Normativity, Relevance and Relativism', *TSF Bulletin*, Jan./Feb., 24–33; also in Conn (1988: 185–209).

——(ed.) (1988), *Inerrancy and Hermeneutic: A Tradition, A Challenge, A Debate* (Grand Rapids, Mich.: Baker).

COSTAS, ORLANDO E. (1983), 'Proclaiming Christ in the Two Thirds World', in Vinay Samuel and Christopher Sugden (eds.) (1983), *Sharing Jesus in the Two Thirds World* (Bangalore: Partnership in Mission—Asia), 1–15.

COWDELL, SCOTT (1992), 'All This, and God Too? Postmodern Alternative to Don Cupitt', *Heythrop Journal*, 33/3: 267–83.

COX, HARVEY (1984), *Religion in the Secular City: Toward a Postmodern Theology* (New York: Simon & Schuster).

CRISWELL, W. A. (1982), *Great Doctrines of the Bible*, i. *Bibliology* (Grand Rapids, Mich.: Zondervan).

CROWE, PHILIP (1967), *Keele '67: The National Evangelical Congress Statement* (London: Falcon).

CUNNINGHAM, JAMES D., and FORTOSIS, ANTHONY C. (1987), *Education in Christian Schools: A Perspective and 'Training Model'* (Whittier, Calif.: Association of Christian Schools Int.).

DANZIG, DANIEL (1962), 'The Radical Right and the Rise of the Fundamentalist Minority', *Commentary*, 33/4: 291–8.

DAVIS, D. CLAIR (1984), 'Princeton and Inerrancy: The Nineteenth-Century Philosophical Background of Contemporary Concerns', in Hannah (1984: 359–78).

DAVIS, JOHN JEFFERSON (1985), *Let the Bible Teach you Christian Doctrine* (Carlisle: Paternoster Press).

DAVIS, STEPHEN T. (1977), *The Debate About the Bible: Inerrancy Versus Infallibility* (Philadelphia: Westminster).

DAYTON, DONALD W. (1976), *Discovering an Evangelical Heritage* (New York: Harper & Row).

——(1991), 'The Limits of Evangelicalism: The Pentecostal Tradition', and 'Some Doubts about the Usefulness of the Category "Evangelical"', in Dayton and Johnston (1991: 36–56, 245–51).

Dayton, Donald W., and Johnston, Robert K. (1991), *The Variety of American Evangelicalism* (Downer's Grove, Ill.: InterVarsity Press).

Dean, Tim, and Porter, David (1984), *Art in Question*, London Lectures in Contemporary Christianity (Basingstoke: Marshall Pickering).

Descartes, René (1984–91), *Philosophical Writings*, 3 vols.: i (1985); ii (1984), trans. John Cottingham, Robert Stoothoff, and Dugald Murdoch (Cambridge: Cambridge University Press).

Dinges, William D. (1991), 'Roman Catholic Traditionalism and Activist Conservatism in the United States', in Marty and Appleby (1991: 66–141).

Dockery, David S. (1981), Review of James Barr's *Fundamentalism, Grace Theological Journal*, 2/1: 146–7.

Dollar, George W. (1973), *A History of Fundamentalism in America* (Greenville, SC: Bob Jones University Press).

Dooyeweerd, Herman (1953–8), *A New Critique of Theoretical Thought*, 4 vols. (Philadelphia: Presbyterian and Reformed), i.

——([1959] 1979), *The Roots of Western Culture: Pagan, Secular, and Christian Options*, trans. John Kraay (Toronto: Wedge).

——([1960] 1980), *In the Twilight of Western Thought: Studies in the Pretended Autonomy of Philosophical Thought* (Nutley, NJ: Craig).

——(1971), 'Cornelius Van Til and the Transcendental Critique of Theoretical Thought', in Geehan (1971: 74–89).

Doumergue, Émile, *et al.* (1909), *Calvin and the Reformation* (New York: Revell).

Draper, James T., Jr. (1988), 'Response to Packer's "The Challenge of Biblical Interpretation: Women"', in *Proceedings of the Conference on Biblical Interpretation*, 122–8.

Duffield, Guy P., and Van Cleave, N. M. (1983), *Foundations of Pentecostal Theology* (Los Angeles: LIFE Bible College).

Dunn, James D. G. (1982), 'The Authority of Scripture According to Scripture', *Churchman*, 96/2: 104–22; 96/3: 201–25.

——(1987), *The Living Word* (London: SCM).

Eddison, R. J. B. (1975), *Newness of Life: An Introduction to Daily Bible Reading* (London: Scripture Union).

Edgar, William (1977), Review of James Barr's *Fundamentalism, Westminster Theological Journal*, 40: 154–6.

Edwards, David L., and Stott, John (1988), *Essentials: A Liberal-Evangelical Dialogue* (London: Hodder & Stoughton).

Ellingsen, Mark (1985), 'Common Sense Realism: The Cutting Edge of Evangelical Identity', *Dialog*, 24/3: 197–205.

——(1988), *The Evangelical Movement: Growth, Impact, Controversy, Dialog* (Minneapolis: Augsburg).

ELSHAHED, E. (1992), 'What is the Challenge of Contemporary Islamic Fundamentalism?', in Küng and Moltmann (1992: 61–9).

ELWELL, WALTER (ed.) ([1991] 1993), *The Concise Evangelical Dictionary of Theology* (London: Marshall Pickering).

ESTES, DANIEL J. (1986), Review of James Barr's *Fundamentalism*, *Journal of the Evangelical Theological Society*, 29/1: 93–4.

Evangelical Alliance: A Million People Standing Shoulder to Shoulder [n.d.] (London: Evangelical Alliance).

Evangelical Belief: A Short Explanation of the Doctrinal Basis of the Universities and Colleges Christian Fellowship (1988) (Leicester: IVP).

FALWELL, JERRY (1980), *Listen America!* (New York: Doubleday).

——(1981), with Ed Dobson and Ed Hindson, *The Fundamentalist Phenomenon: The Resurgence of Conservative Christianity* (Garden City, NY: Galilee-Doubleday).

FEE, GORDON D. (1976), 'Hermeneutics and Historical Precedent', in R. Spittler (ed.) (1976), *Perspectives on the New Pentecostalism* (Grand Rapids, Mich.: Baker).

——(1980), 'Hermeneutics and Common Sense: An Explanatory Essay on the Hermeneutics of the Epistles', in Nicole and Michaels (1980: 161–86).

FEINBERG, JOHN S. (1984), 'Truth: Relationship of Theories of Truth to Hermeneutics', in Radmacher and Preus (1984: 1–50).

FEINBERG, P. D. (1993), 'Bible, Inerrancy and Infallibility of', in Elwell ([1991] 1993: 62–3).

FIEDLER, KLAUS (1994), *The Story of Faith Missions* (Oxford: Regnum Lynx).

FRANCE, R. T. (1991), 'James Barr and Evangelical Scholarship', *Anvil*, 8/1: 51–64.

——(1993), 'Evangelicalism and Biblical Scholarship (2) The New Testament', in France and McGrath (1993: 47–56).

——and MCGRATH, A. E. (eds.) (1993), *Evangelical Anglicans: Their Role and Influence in the Church Today* (London: SPCK).

FRANK, DOUGLAS W. (1986), *Less Than Conquerors: How Evangelicals Entered the Twentieth Century* (Grand Rapids, Mich.: Eerdmans).

FULLER, DANIEL (1968), 'Benjamin B. Warfield's View of Faith and History', *Bulletin of the Evangelical Theological Society*, 11/2: 75–83.

——(1972), 'The Nature of Biblical Inerrancy', *Journal of the American Scientific Affiliation*, June, 47–51.

——(1973), 'Daniel Fuller and Clark Pinnock: On Revelation and Biblical Authority', *Christian Scholar's Review*, 2/4: 330–5.

The Fundamentals (1909(?)–15), ed. A. C. Dixon, L. Meyer, and R. A. Torrey (Chicago: Testimony Publishing Co.).

FURNISS, NORMAN (1954), *The Fundamentalist Controversy, 1918–1931* (New Haven: Yale University Press).

GADAMER, HANS-GEORG (1976), *Philosophical Hermeneutics*, trans. and ed. David E. Linge (Berkeley: University of California Press).

——([1975] 1989), *Truth and Method*, 2nd rev. edn., trans. Joel Weinsheimer and Donald G. Marshall (London: Sheed & Ward).

GARVEY, JOHN H. (1993), 'Fundamentalism and American Law', in Marty and Appleby (1993*b*: 28–49).

GASPER, LOUIS (1963), *The Fundamentalist Movement* (The Hague: Mouton & Co.).

GASQUE, W. WARD (1973), 'Evangelical Theology: The British Example', *Christianity Today*, 10 Aug., 49–50.

GAUSSEN, FRANÇOIS, and LOUIS, SAMUEL R. (1841), *Theopneustia: The Plenary Inspiration of the Holy Scriptures* (London: Samuel Bagster & Sons).

GAUVREAU, MICHAEL (1985), 'Baconianism, Darwinism, Fundamentalism: A Transatlantic Crisis of Faith', *Journal of Religious History*, 13/4: 434–44.

——(1994), 'The Empire of Evangelicalism: Varieties of Common Sense in Scotland, Canada, and the United States', in Noll, Bebbington, and Rawlyk (1994: 219–52).

GAY, CRAIG M. (1991), *With Liberty and Justice for Whom? The Recent Evangelical Debate over Capitalism* (Grand Rapids, Mich.: Eerdmans).

GEEHAN, E. R. (ed.) (1971), *Jerusalem and Athens: Critical Discussions on the Theology and Apologetics of Cornelius Van Til* (Nutley, NJ: Presbyterian and Reformed).

GEISLER, NORMAN L. (ed.) (1979), *Inerrancy* (Grand Rapids, Mich.: Zondervan).

——(1981), *Biblical Errancy: An Analysis of its Philosophical Roots* (Grand Rapids, Mich.: Zondervan).

——(1982), with A. F. Brooke, and J. Mark Keough, *The Creator in the Courtroom: 'Scopes II'* (Milford, Miss.: Mott Media).

——(1984), 'Explaining Hermeneutics: A Commentary on The Chicago Statement on Biblical Hermeneutics Articles of Affirmation and Denial', in Radmacher and Preus (1984: 889–904).

GERAMI, SHAHIN (1996), *Women and Fundamentalism: Islam and Christianity* (New York: Garland).

GERSTNER, JOHN H. (1974), 'Warfield's Case for Biblical Inerrancy', in Montgomery (1974: 115–42).

——(1979), 'The View of the Bible Held by the Church: Calvin and the Westminster Divines', in Geisler (1979: 383–410).

——(1984), 'The Contributions of Charles Hodge, B. B. Warfield, and J. Gresham Machen to the Doctrine of Inspiration', in Lewis and Demarest (1984: 347–81).

GITT, WERNER (1986), 'The Biblical Teaching Concerning Creation', in E. H. Andrews, W. Gitt, and W. J. Ouweneel (eds.) (1986), *Concepts in Creationism* (Welwyn: Evangelical Press), 13–45.

GLOVER, WILLIS B. (1954), *Evangelical Nonconformists and Higher Criticism in the Nineteenth Century* (London: Independent).

GOLDINGAY, JOHN (1977*a*), 'Expounding the New Testament', in Marshall (1977: 351–65).

——(1977*b*), 'James Barr on Fundamentalism', *Churchman*, 91/4: 295–308.

Gospel and Spirit (1977), published jointly by Fountain Trust and the Church of England Evangelical Council.

GRAHAM, BILLY (1956), 'Biblical Authority in Evangelism', *Christianity Today*, 15 Oct., 5–7, 17.

GRAVE, S. A. (1960), *The Scottish Philosophy of Common Sense* (Oxford: Clarendon Press).

GREEN, MICHAEL (1977), 'Jesus in the New Testament', in Green (1977: 9–57).

——(ed.) (1977), *The Truth of God Incarnate* (London: Hodder & Stoughton).

GUINNESS, OS (1973), *The Dust of Death: A Critique of the Establishment and the Counter Culture—and a Proposal for a Third Way* (London: IVP).

GUNDRY, R. H. (1982), *Matthew: A Commentary on His Literary and Theological Art* (Grand Rapids, Mich.: Eerdmans).

HAGNER, DONALD A. (1995), 'Writing a Commentary on Matthew: Self-Conscious Ruminations of an Evangelical', *Semeia*, 72: 51–72.

HAGUE, DYSON (n.d. [1909?–15]), 'History of the Higher Criticism', *The Fundamentals*, i. 87–122.

HALDANE, ROBERT ([1830] 1853), *The Books of the Old and New Testament Proved to be Canonical, and Their Verbal Inspiration Maintained and Established; With an Account of the Introduction and Character of the Apocrypha*, 6th edn. enlarged by A. Haldane (Edinburgh: Johnstone & Hunter).

HALL, DAVID (1986), *Dirty Hands* (Eastbourne: Kingsway Publications).

HALL, JAMES H. ([n.d.] *a*), 'Modern Science and Biblical Inerrancy' (Lynchburg, Va.: Museum of Earth and Life History, Liberty University).

——([n.d.] *b*), 'Spotlight on Science and Scripture' (Lynchburg, Va.: Museum of Earth and Life History, Liberty University).

HAMMOND, T. C. (1925), 'The Fiat of Authority', in Howden (1925: 156–206).

HANDY, ROBERT T. (1954), 'Fundamentalism and Modernism in Perspective', *Religion in Life*, 381–94.

HANNAH, JOHN D. (ed.) (1984), *Inerrancy and the Church* (Chicago: Moody).

Harris, Jay M. (1994), '"Fundamentalism": Objections from a Modern Jewish Historian', in Hawley (1994: 137–73).

Hart, Hendrik, van der Hoeven, Johan, and Wolterstorff, Nicholas (1983), *Rationality in the Calvinist Tradition* (Lanham, Md.: University Press of America).

Hassan, Riffat (1990), 'The Burgeoning of Islamic Fundamentalism: Toward an Understanding of the Phenomenon', in Cohen (1990: 151–71).

Hastings, Adrian ([1986] 1991), *A History of English Christianity 1920–1990* (London: SCM).

Hatch, Nathan O., and Noll, Mark A. (1982), *The Bible in America: Essays in Cultural History* (New York: Oxford University Press).

Hawley, John Stratton (ed.) (1994), *Fundamentalism and Gender* (New York: Oxford University Press).

Haynes, Jeff (1995), *Religion, Fundamentalism and Ethnicity: A Global Perspective* (Geneva: United Nations Research Institute for Social Development).

Heagle, David (n.d. [1909?–15]), 'The Tabernacle in the Wilderness: Did it Exist?', *The Fundamentals*, iv. 7–48.

Hebert, Gabriel (1957), *Fundamentalism and the Church of God* (London: SCM).

Helm, Paul (1983), 'Thomas Reid, Common Sense and Calvinism', in Hart, van der Hoeven, and Wolterstorff (1983: 71–89).

Hennell, Michael (1988), 'Patterns of Development in Anglican Evangelicalism', *Anvil*, 5/1: 71–8.

Henry, Carl F. H. (1947), *The Uneasy Conscience of Modern Fundamentalism* (Grand Rapids, Mich.: Eerdmans).

——(1976*a*), *God, Revelation and Authority*, i. *God Who Speaks and Shows, Preliminary Considerations* (Waco: Word Books).

——(1976*b*), *God, Revelation and Authority*, ii. *God Who Speaks and Shows, Fifteen Theses, Part One* (Waco: Word Books).

——(1978*a, b, c*), 'Those Incomprehensible British Fundamentalists', *Christianity Today*, 2 June, 22–6; 23 June, 22–6; 21 July, 29–32.

——(1979*a*), *God, Revelation and Authority*, iii. *God Who Speaks and Shows, Fifteen Theses, Part Two* (Waco: Word Books).

——(1979*b*), *God, Revelation and Authority*, iv. *God Who Speaks and Shows, Fifteen Theses, Part Three* (Waco: Word Books).

Heslam, Peter Somers (1993), 'Abraham Kuyper's *Lectures on Calvinism*: An Historical Approach', doctoral thesis, University of Oxford.

Hinson, E. Glenn (1978), Review of James Barr's *Fundamentalism, Review and Expositor*, 75: 635–6.

Hirsch, E. D., Jr. (1967), *Validity in Interpretation* (New Haven: Yale University Press).

HODGE, A. A., and WARFIELD, B. B. (1881), 'Inspiration', *The Presbyterian Review*, 2: 225–60.

HODGE, CHARLES [1850], 'The Theology of the Intellect and That of the Feelings', *Biblical Repertory and Princeton Review*, 22, repr. with commentary in Noll (1983: 185–207).

——(1871–3), *Systematic Theology*, 3 vols.; i (1871); iii (1873) (London: Thomas Nelson).

HOEVELER, J. DAVID, Jr. (1981), *James McCosh and the Scottish Intellectual Tradition* (Princeton: Princeton University Press).

HOFFECKER, W. ANDREW (1981), *Piety and the Princeton Theologians: Archibald Alexander, Charles Hodge, and Benjamin Warfield* (Phillipsburg, NJ: Presbyterian and Reformed).

HOLE, GÜNTER (1992), 'Fundamentalism, Dogmatism, Fanaticism: Psychiatric Perspectives', in Küng and Moltmann (1992: 22–35).

HOLIFIELD, E. BROOKS (1978), *The Gentleman Theologians, American Theology in Southern Culture 1795–1860* (Durham, NC: Duke University Press).

HOOYKAAS, R. (1960), *The Christian Approach in Teaching Science*, published for the Research Scientists' Christian Fellowship (London: Tyndale).

HOWDEN, J. RUSSELL (ed.) (1925), *Evangelicalism* (London: Chas. J. Thynne & Jarvis).

HUGHES, RICHARD T. (1991), 'Are Restorationists Evangelicals?', in Dayton and Johnston (1991: 109–34).

——and ALLEN, C. LEONARD (1988), *Illusions of Innocence: Protestant Primitivism in America 1630–1875* (Chicago: University of Chicago Press).

HUME, DAVID ([1777] 1975), *An Enquiry Concerning Human Understanding*, with Analytical Index by L. A. Selby-Bigge, 3rd edn., rev. P. H. Nidditch (Oxford: Clarendon Press).

——([1739–40] 1978), *A Treatise of Human Nature*, with Analytical Index by L. A. Selby-Bigge, 2nd edn., rev. P. H. Nidditch (Oxford: Clarendon Press).

HUNTER, JAMES DAVISON (1987), *Evangelicalism: The Coming Generation* (Chicago: University of Chicago Press).

——(1990), 'Fundamentalism in Its Global Contours', in Cohen (1990: 56–72).

HUTCHISON, WILLIAM R. ([1976] 1992), *The Modernist Impulse in American Protestantism* (Durham, NC: Duke University Press).

HYLSON-SMITH, KENNETH (1988), *Evangelicals in the Church of England, 1734–1984* (Edinburgh: T. & T. Clark).

IANNACCONE, LAURENCE R. (1993), 'The Economics of American Fundamentalists', in Marty and Appleby (1993*b*: 342–66).

Jacobsen, Douglas (1987), 'From Truth to Authority to Responsibility: The Shifting Focus of Evangelical Hermeneutics, 1915–1986', *TSF Bulletin*, Mar./Apr., 8–15, May/June, 10–14.

James, Robison B. (1987), 'Is Inerrancy the Issue? The Lessons of Ridgecrest 1987', in James (ed.), *The Unfettered Word: Southern Baptists Confront the Authority-Inerrancy Question* (Waco: Word Books), 177–84.

Jansma, Sidney J., Sr. (1985), *Six Days* (Grand Rapids, Mich.: the author).

Jeffery, Peter, and Milton, Owen (1981), *Firm Foundations: Great Chapters of the Bible* (Bryntirion: Evangelical Press of Wales).

Johns, Jackie David, and Johns, Cheryl Bridges (1992), 'Yielding to the Spirit: A Pentecostal Approach to Group Bible Study', *Journal of Pentecostal Theology*, 1: 109–34.

Johnson, Douglas (1955), 'The Word "Fundamentalist"', *Christian Graduate*, 8/1: 22–6.

——(1979), *Contending for the Faith: A History of the Evangelical Movement in the Universities and Colleges* (Leicester: IVP).

Johnson, Ranklin (n.d. [1909?–15]), 'Fallacies of the Higher Criticism', *The Fundamentals*, ii. 48–68.

Johnston, Robert K. (1979), *Evangelicals at an Impasse* (Atlanta: John Knox).

——(1984), 'Pentecostalism and Theological Hermeneutics: Evangelical Options', *Pneuma*, 6/1: 51–66.

——(ed.) (1985), *The Use of the Bible in Theology: Evangelical Options* (Atlanta: John Knox).

——(1987), 'The Vocation of the Theologian', *TSF Bulletin*, Mar./Apr., 4–8.

——(1988), 'How We Interpret the Bible: Biblical Interpretation and Literary Criticism', in *Proceedings of the Conference on Biblical Interpretation* (1988), 51–63.

Jones, Bob, Sr. (1957), Letter, Mar. 6 1957, from the Bob Jones University Fundamentalism File.

——(1978), 'What is "Second-Degree Separation"?', *Faith for the Family*, Nov., 4.

A Statement from the Chancellor of Bob Jones University [n.d.], Fundamentalism File document 657, Bob Jones University archives.

Jones, Bob, III (1980), 'The Moral Majority', *Faith for the Family*, Sept., 1, 27–8.

Juergensmeyer, Mark (1993), *The New Cold War? Religious Nationalism Confronts the Secular State* (Berkeley: University of California Press).

Kaiser, Walter C., Jr. (1979*a*), 'Legitimate Hermeneutics', in Geisler (1979: 116–47).

——(1979*b*), 'Meanings from God's Message: Matters for Interpretation', *Christianity Today*, 5 Oct., 30–3.

——(1988), 'Interpreting the Old Testament', and Panel Discussion, in *Proceedings of the Conference on Biblical Interpretation* (1988), 65–91, 205–20.

KALSBEEK, L. (1975), *Contours of a Christian Philosophy: An Introduction to Herman Dooyeweerd's Thought* (Toronto: Wedge).

KANT, IMMANUEL ([1783] 1953), *Prolegomena to any Future Metaphysics*, trans. Peter G. Lucas (Manchester: Manchester University Press).

KANTZER, KENNETH S. (1975), 'Unity and Diversity in Evangelical Faith', in Wells and Woodbridge (1975: 38–67).

——(ed.) (1978), *Evangelical Roots: A Tribute to Wilbur Smith* (Nashville: Thomas Nelson).

KAPLAN, LAWRENCE (1992*a*), 'Introduction', in Kaplan (1992*b*: 3–14).

——(ed.) (1992*b*), *Fundamentalism in Comparative Perspective* (Amherst, Mass.: University of Massachusetts Press).

KELSEY, DAVID H. (1975), *The Uses of Scripture in Recent Theology* (London: SCM).

KENDALL, R. T. (1976), 'The Influence of Calvin and Calvinism Upon the American Heritage' (London: Evangelical Library, Annual Lecture).

KEPEL, GILLES (1994), *The Revenge of God: The Resurgence of Islam, Christianity and Judaism in the Modern World*, trans. Alan Braley (Cambridge: Polity).

KLAPWIJK, JACOB (1983), 'Rationality in the Dutch Neo-Calvinist Tradition', in Hart, van der Hoeven, and Wolterstorff (1983: 93–111).

KLOOSTER, FRED H. (1984), 'The Role of the Holy Spirit in the Hermeneutic Process: The Relationship of the Spirit's Illumination to Biblical Interpretation', in Radmacher and Preus (1984: 451–72).

KUITERT, H. M. ([1992] 1993), *I Have My Doubts: How to Become a Christian Without Being a Fundamentalist*, trans. John Bowden (London: SCM).

KÜNG, HANS ([1970] 1994), *Infallible?*, trans. John Bowden (London: SCM).

KÜNG, HANS, and MOLTMANN, JURGEN (1980), *Conflicting Ways of Interpreting the Bible* (Edinburgh: T. & T. Clark; New York: Seabury).

——(eds.) (1992), *Fundamentalism as an Ecumenical Challenge, Concilium*, 1992/3 (London: SCM).

KURTZ, PAUL WINTER (1988), *Neo-Fundamentalism: The Humanist Response* (Buffalo: Prometheus).

KUYPER, ABRAHAM ([1898] 1932), *Calvinism: Being the Six 'Stone' Lectures Given at Princeton Theological Seminary, U.S.A.* (London: Sovereign Grace Union).

——([1898] 1968), *Principles of Sacred Theology*, trans. J. Hendrik de Vries (Grand Rapids, Mich.: Eerdmans).

LACEY, MICHAEL J. (ed.) (1989), *Religion in Twentieth-Century American Intellectual Life* (Cambridge: Cambridge University Press).

Lausanne Committee for World Evangelisation (1982), *Evangelism and Social Responsibility: An Evangelical Commitment* (Exeter: Paternoster Press).

Lawrence, Bruce B. (1989), *Defenders of God: The Fundamentalist Revolt Against the Modern Age* (San Francisco: Harper & Row).

——(1992), 'Reply to William Shepard's Comments on *Defenders of God*', *Religion*, 22: 284–5.

Leibman, Robert C., and Wuthnow, Robert (eds.) (1983), *The New Christian Right: Mobilization & Legitimation* (New York: Aldine).

Letis, Theodore P. (1991), 'B. B. Warfield, Common-Sense Philosophy and Biblical Criticism', *American Presbyterians*, 69/3: 175–90.

Lewis, C. S. ([1952] 1977), *Mere Christianity* (London: Fount).

Lewis, Gordon R. (1984), 'A Response to Presuppositions of Non-Evangelical Hermeneutics', in Radmacher and Preus (1984: 615–26).

——and Demarest, Bruce (eds.) (1984), *Challenges to Inerrancy: A Theological Response* (Chicago: Moody).

Lindsey, Hal, with Carlson, C. C. ([1970] 1990), *The Late Great Planet Earth* (London: Marshall Pickering).

Lindsell, Harold (1976), *The Battle for the Bible* (Grand Rapids, Mich.: Zondervan).

——(1979), *The Bible in the Balance* (Grand Rapids, Mich.: Zondervan).

Linnemann, Eta (1990), *Historical Criticism of the Bible: Methodology or Ideology?*, trans. by Robert W. Yarbrough (Grand Rapids, Mich.: Baker).

Lipset, Seymour Martin, and Raab, Earl (1981), 'The Election & the Evangelicals', *Commentary*, 71/3: 25–31.

Livingstone, David N. (1987), *Darwin's Forgotten Defenders: The Encounter between Evangelical Theology and Evolutionary Thought* (Grand Rapids, Mich.: Eerdmans; Edinburgh: Scottish Academic Press).

Lloyd-Jones, D. M. (1958), *Authority* (London: IVP).

——([1971] 1992), *What is an Evangelical?* (Edinburgh: Banner of Truth).

Locke, John ([1689] 1979), *An Essay Concerning Human Understanding*, ed. Peter H. Nidditch (Oxford: Clarendon Press).

Longfield, Bradley J. (1991), *The Presbyterian Controversy: Fundamentalists, Modernists, and Moderates* (New York: Oxford University Press).

Lundin, Roger, Thiselton, Anthony C., and Walhout, Clarence (1985), *The Responsibility of Hermeneutics* (Grand Rapids, Mich.: Eerdmans).

McCarthy, Rockne, Oppewal, Donald, Peterson, Walfred, and Spykman, Gordon (1981), *Society, State, & Schools: A Case for Structural and Confessional Pluralism* (Grand Rapids, Mich.: Eerdmans).

McCarthy Brown, Karen (1994), 'Fundamentalism and the Control of Women', in Hawley (1994: 175–201).

McClendon, James Wm., Jr. (1994), *Systematic Theology: Doctrine* (Nashville: Abingdon), ii.

McCosh, James (1875), *The Scottish Philosophy, Biographical, Expository, Critical, From Hutcheson to Hamilton* (London: Macmillan).

McDowell, Josh (1972), *Evidence that Demands a Verdict: Historical Evidence for the Christian Faith* (San Bernadino, Calif.: Campus Crusade).

McGrath, Alister E. (1987), *The Intellectual Origins of the European Reformation* (Oxford: Blackwell).

——(1993*a*), 'Evangelical Anglicanism: A Contradiction in Terms?', in France and McGrath (1993: 10–21).

——(1993*b*), *The Renewal of Anglicanism* (London: SPCK).

——(1994*a*), *Christian Theology: An Introduction* (Oxford: Blackwell).

——(1994*b*), *Evangelicalism and the Future of Christianity* (London: Hodder & Stoughton).

McGrath, Alister, and Wenham, David (1993), 'Evangelicalism and Biblical Authority', in France and McGrath (1993: 22–36).

——and Green, Michael (1993), *Springboard for Faith* (London: Hodder & Stoughton).

Machen, J. Gresham (1923), *Christianity and Liberalism* (New York: Macmillan).

——(1925), *What is Faith?* (London: Hodder & Stoughton).

——(1936), *The Christian Faith in the Modern World* (London: Hodder & Stoughton).

MacIntyre, Alasdair (1988), *Whose Justice? Which Rationality?* (Notre Dame: University of Notre Dame Press).

McIntyre, David M. (1902), *The Divine Authority of the Scriptures of the Old Testament* (Stirling: Drummonds Tract Depot).

——(1908), *The Spirit is the Word* (London: Morgan & Scott).

McKim, Donald K. (1985), *What Christians Believe About the Bible* (Nashville: Thomas Nelson).

——(ed.) (1986), *A Guide to Contemporary Hermeneutics: Major Trends in Biblical Interpretation* (Grand Rapids, Mich.: Eerdmans).

McLean, Mark D. (1984), 'Toward a Pentecostal Hermeneutic', *Pneuma*, 6/2: 35–56.

McLoughlin, William G., Jr. (1959), *Modern Revivalism: Charles Grandison Finney to Billy Graham* (New York: Ronald Press Co.).

McQuilkin, J. Robertson (1984), 'Problems of Normativeness in Scripture: Cultural Versus Permanent', in Radmacher and Preus (1984: 219–40).

MacRae, Allan A. (1991), 'The Antecedents of Biblical Theological Seminary', Biblical Theological Seminary's records [n. pub.].

Maddox, Randy L. (1985), 'Contemporary Hermeneutic Philosophy and Theological Studies', *Religious Studies*, 21: 517–29.

MANLEY, G. T. (1925), 'The Inspiration and Authority of the Bible', in Howden (1925: 121–55).
——(1926), *'It Is Written'* (London: Religious Tract Society).
——(ed.) ([1934] 1949), *Search the Scriptures: The I.V.F. Bible Study Course*, 3 vols., rev. edn. with H. W. Oldham (London: IVF).
MARSDEN, GEORGE M. (1971), 'Defining Fundamentalism', *Christian Scholar's Review*, 1: 141–51.
——(1973), 'The Christian and the Teaching of History', *Christian Scholar's Review*, 2/4: 311–24.
——(1977), 'Fundamentalism as an American Phenomenon: A Comparison with English Evangelicalism', *Church History*, 46: 215–32.
——(1979*a*), 'J. Gresham Machen, History, and Truth', *Westminster Theological Journal*, 42: 157–75.
——(1979*b*), Review of James Barr's *Fundamentalism, Theology Today*, 35: 520–2.
——(1980), *Fundamentalism and American Culture: The Shaping of Twentieth Century Evangelicalism 1870–1925* (Oxford: Oxford University Press).
——(1983*a*), 'The Collapse of American Academia', in Plantinga and Wolterstorff (1983: 219–64).
——(1983*b*), 'Roots of the New Fundamentalism', *Bulletin of Westminster Theological Seminary*, Winter, 1–3.
——(ed.) (1984*a*), *Evangelicalism and Modern America* (Grand Rapids, Mich.: Eerdmans).
——(1984*b*), 'Introduction: The Evangelical Denomination', in Marsden (1984*a*: pp. vii–xix).
——(1984*c*), 'Understanding Fundamentalist Views of Science', in Montagu (1984: 95–116).
——(1987), *Reforming Fundamentalism: Fuller Seminary and the New Evangelicalism* (Grand Rapids, Mich.: Eerdmans).
——(1988), *The Fundamentals, A Testimony to the Truth*, Introduction (New York: Garland).
——(1989), 'Evangelicals and the Scientific Culture: An Overview', in Lacey (1989: 23–48).
——(1990), 'Defining American Fundamentalism', in Cohen (1990: 22–37).
——and DAYTON, DONALD W. (1977), 'Demythologizing Evangelicalism: A Review of Donald W. Dayton's *Discovering an Evangelical Heritage*', *Christian Scholar's Review*, 7/2–3: 203–11.
MARSHALL, I. HOWARD (1977*a*), 'Introduction', and 'Historical Criticism', in Marshall (1977*b*: 11–18, 126–38).
——(ed.) (1977*b*), *New Testament Interpretation: Essays on Principles and Methods* (Exeter: Paternoster Press).

——(1992), 'Are Evangelicals Fundamentalists?', Laing Lecture for 1991 delivered in the London Bible College, *Vox Evangelica*, 22: 7–24.

MARTIN, LINETTE (1979), *Hans Rookmaaker: A Biography* (Downers Grove, Ill.: IVP).

MARTY, M. E. (1992), 'What is Fundamentalism? Theological Perspectives', in Küng and Moltmann (1992: 3–13).

——and APPLEBY, R. SCOTT (1991*a*), 'Conclusion: An Interim Report on a Hypothetical Family', in Marty and Appleby (eds.) (1991*b*: 814–42).

——(eds.) (1991*b*), *Fundamentalisms Observed* (Chicago: University of Chicago Press).

——(1992), *The Glory and the Power: The Fundamentalist Challenge to the Modern World* (Boston: Beacon).

——(eds.) (1993*a*), *Fundamentalisms and Society: Reclaiming the Sciences, the Family, and Education* (Chicago: University of Chicago Press).

——(eds.) (1993*b*), *Fundamentalisms and the State: Remaking Polities, Economics, and Militance* (Chicago: University of Chicago Press).

——(eds.) (1994), *Accounting for Fundamentalisms: The Dynamic Character of Movements* (Chicago: University of Chicago Press).

——(eds.) (1995), *Fundamentalisms Comprehended* (Chicago: University of Chicago Press).

MATHEWS, SHAILER (1924), *The Faith of Modernism* (New York: Macmillan).

MAURO, PHILIP (n.d. [1909?–15]), 'Modern Philosophy', *The Fundamentals*, ii. 85–105.

MAVRODES, GEORGE I. (1973), 'Christian Philosophy and the Non-Christian Philosopher', *Christian Scholar's Review*, 2/4: 325–9.

MOLTMANN, J. (1992), 'Fundamentalism and Modernity', in Küng and Moltmann (1992: 109–15).

MONTAGU, ASHLEY (ed.) (1984), *Science and Creationism* (Oxford: Oxford University Press).

MONTGOMERY, JOHN WARWICK (1965), 'Inspiration and Inerrancy: A New Departure', in Youngblood (1984: 59–90).

——(ed.) (1974), *God's Inerrant Word: An International Symposium On The Trustworthiness of Scripture* (Minneapolis: Bethany Fellowship).

MORISON, FRANK (1930), *Who Moved the Stone?* (London: Faber & Faber).

MULLER, RICHARD A. (1987), *Post-Reformation Reformed Dogmatics*, i. *Prolegomena to Theology* (Grand Rapids, Mich.: Baker).

MURCH, JAMES DE FOREST (1952), *Cooperation Without Compromise* (Grand Rapids, Mich.: Eerdmans).

MURRAY, IAIN H. (1993), 'The Story of the Banner of Truth Trust', *The Banner of Truth*, Nov., 15–23.

NASH, RONALD N. (1969), *The Case for Biblical Christianity* (Grand Rapids, Mich.: Eerdmans).

NEILL, STEPHEN (1977), 'Jesus as Myth', in Green (1977: 58–70).

NELSON, JOHN OLIVER (1935), 'The Rise of the Princeton Theology: A Genetic Study of American Presbyterianism until 1850', unpub. doctoral dissertation, Yale University.

NELSON, RUDOLPH L. (1982), 'Fundamentalism at Harvard: The Case of Edward John Carnell', *Quarterly Review*, 2: 79–98.

——(1987), *The Making and Unmaking of an Evangelical Mind: The Case of Edward Carnell* (Cambridge: Cambridge University Press).

NEUHAUS, RICHARD JOHN, and CROMARTIE, MICHAEL (eds.) (1987), *Piety and Politics: Evangelicals and Fundamentalists Confront the World* (Washington: Ethics and Public Policy Center).

NICOLE, ROGER (1983), 'The Inspiration and Authority of Scripture: J. D. G. Dunn versus B. B. Warfield', *Churchman*, 97/3: 198–215.

NICOLE, ROGER, and MICHAELS, J. RAMSEY (eds.) (1980), *Inerrancy and Common Sense* (Grand Rapids, Mich.: Baker).

NIEBUHR, H. RICHARD (1932), 'Fundamentalism', *Encyclopaedia of the Social Sciences* (London: Macmillan), vi. 527–57.

NIELSEN, NIELS C., Jr. (1993), *Fundamentalism, Mythos, and World Religions* (Albany: State University of New York Press).

NOLL, MARK A. (ed.) (1983), *The Princeton Theology 1812–1921: Scripture, Science, and Theological Method from Archibald Alexander to Benjamin Breckinridge Warfield* (Grand Rapids, Mich.: Baker).

——(1985), 'Common Sense Traditions and American Evangelical Thought', *American Quarterly*, 37/2: 216–38.

——(1986), *Between Faith and Criticism: Evangelicals, Scholarship and America* (Grand Rapids, Mich.: Baker).

——(1989), *Princeton and the Republic, 1768–1822: The Search for a Christian Enlightenment in the Era of Samuel Stanhope Smith* (Princeton: Princeton University Press).

——(1994), *The Scandal of the Evangelical Mind* (Grand Rapids, Mich.: Eerdmans; Leicester: IVP).

——and WELLS, DAVID F. (eds.) (1988), *Christian Faith and Practice in the Modern World: Theology from an Evangelical Point of View* (Grand Rapids, Mich.: Eerdmans).

——BEBBINGTON, DAVID W., and RAWLYK, GEORGE A. (eds.) (1994), *Evangelicalism: Comparative Studies of Popular Protestantism in North America, the British Isles, and Beyond, 1700–1990* (New York: Oxford University Press).

NORTH, GARY (1984), *Backward, Christian Soldiers?: An Action Manual for Christian Reconstruction* (Tyler: Institute for Christian Economics).

——(1991), *Westminster's Confession; the abandonment of Van Til's Legacy* (Tyler, Tex.: Institute for Christian Economics).

NOTARO, THOM (1980), *Van Til and the Use of Evidence* (Phillipsburg, NJ: Presbyterian and Reformed).

The Nottingham Statement (1977) (London: Falcon).

NUMBERS, RONALD L. (1992), *The Creationists: The Evolution of Scientific Creationism* (Berkeley: University of California Press).

NUTTALL, A. D. (1983), *A New Mimesis: Shakespeare and the Representation of Reality* (London: Methuen).

——(1992), *Openings: Narrative Beginnings from the Epic to the Novel* (Oxford: Clarendon Press).

OCKENGA, HAROLD J. (1978), 'From Fundamentalism, Through New Evangelicalism, to Evangelicalism', in Kantzer (1978: 35–46).

OLIVER, W. H. (1978), *Prophets and Millennialists: The Uses of Biblical Prophecy in England from the 1790s to the 1840s* (Auckland: Auckland University Press; Oxford: Oxford University Press).

OLTHUIS, JAMES H., PINNOCK, CLARK H., BLOESCH, DONALD G., and SHEPPARD, GERALD T. (1987), *A Hermeneutics of Ultimacy: Peril or Promise* (Lanham, Md.: University Press of America).

ORR, JAMES (1905), *God's Image in Man and Its Defacement in the Light of Modern Denials* (London: Hodder & Stoughton).

——(1910), *Revelation and Inspiration* (London: Duckworth).

——(n.d. [1909?–15]), 'Science and the Christian Faith', *The Fundamentals*, iv. 91–104.

——(n.d. [1909?–15]), 'The Early Narratives of Genesis', *The Fundamentals*, vi. 85–97.

——(n.d. [1909?–15]), 'Holy Scripture and Modern Negations', *The Fundamentals*, ix. 31–47.

OSS, DOUGLAS A. (1989), 'The Interpretation of the "Stone" Passages by Peter and Paul: A Comparative Study', *Journal of the Evangelical Theological Society*, 32/2: 181–200.

OSWALD, JAMES (1768), *An Appeal to Common Sense in Behalf of Religion*, 2nd edn. (London: J. Hughs), i.

——(1772), *An Appeal to Common Sense in Behalf of Religion* (Edinburgh: A. Kincaid & W. Creech), ii.

PACKER, JAMES I. (1955), '"Keswick" and the Reformed Doctrine of Sanctification', *Evangelical Quarterly*, 27/3: 153–67.

——(1958*a*), *'Fundamentalism' and the Word of God* (London: Inter-Varsity Fellowship).

——(1958*b*), 'The Fundamentalism Controversy: Retrospect and Prospect', *Faith and Thought*, 90/1: 35–45.

——(1958*c*), 'Fundamentalism: The British Scene', *Christianity Today*, 29 Sept., 3–6.

——(1971), 'Biblical Authority, Hermeneutics, and Inerrancy', in Geehan (1971: 141–53).

Packer, James I. ([1965] 1979), *God Has Spoken*, rev., enlarged edn. (London: Hodder & Stoughton).

——(1983), 'Infallible Scripture and the Role of Hermeneutics', in Carson and Woodbridge (1983: 325–56).

——(1984*a*), 'John Calvin and the Inerrancy of Holy Scripture', in Hannah (1984: 143–88).

——(1984*b*), 'Exposition on Biblical Hermeneutics', in Radmacher and Preus (1984: 905–14).

——(1988), 'The Challenge of Biblical Interpretation: Creation', 'The Challenge of Biblical Interpretation: Women', 'The Challenge of Biblical Interpretation: Eschatology', in *Proceedings of the Conference on Biblical Interpretation* (1988), 21–45, 103–15, 191–204.

——(1990), 'Understanding the Bible: Evangelical Hermeneutics', in Tinker (1990: 39–58).

Padilla, Rene, and Sugden, Chris (eds.) (1985), *Texts on Evangelicals and Social Ethics* (2 vols.; Nottingham: Grove Books).

Parekh, Bhiku (1992), *The Concept of Fundamentalism* (Meghraj Lecture 1991), Occasional Papers in Asian Migration Studies, 1 (Leeds: Peepal Tree Books).

Parker, Stephen E. (1996), *Led by the Spirit: Toward a Practical Theology of Pentecostal Discernment and Decision Making* (Sheffield: Sheffield Academic Press).

Pawson, J. David (1988), *Leadership is Male: A Challenge to Christian Feminism* (Crowborough: Highland Books).

——(1993), *Fourth Wave: Charismatics and Evangelicals, Are We Ready to Come Together?* (London: Hodder & Stoughton).

Peele, Gillian (1984), *Revival and Reaction: The Right in Contemporary America* (Oxford: Clarendon Press).

Percy, Martyn (1996), *Words, Wonders and Power: Understanding Contemporary Christian Fundamentalism and Revivalism* (London: SPCK).

Perks, Stephen C. (1992), *The Christian Philosophy of Education Explained* (Whitby: Avant Books).

——(1993), 'Christianity and Law: An Enquiry into the Influence of Christianity on the Development of English Common Law' (unpub.).

Peshkin, Alan (1986), *God's Choice: The Total World of a Fundamentalist Christian School* (Chicago: University of Chicago Press).

Phillips, Timothy Ross (1986), *Francis Turretin's Idea of Theology and Its Bearing Upon his Doctrine of Scripture* (Ann Arbor: University of Microfilms International).

Pimenta, Leander R. (1984), *Fountains of the Great Deep* (Chichester: New Wine).

Pinnock, Clark H. (1971*a*), *Biblical Revelation—The Foundation of Christian Theology* (Chicago: Moody).

——(1971*b*), 'The Philosophy of Christian Evidences', in Geehan (1971: 420–5).
——(1973), 'Daniel Fuller and Clark Pinnock: On Revelation and Biblical Authority', *Christian Scholar's Review*, 2/4: 330–5.
——(1974), 'The Inspiration of Scripture and the Authority of Jesus Christ', in Montgomery (1974: 201–18).
——(1979), Review of James Barr's *Fundamentalism*, *Sojourners*, 8 Jan., 31–3.
——(1984), *The Scripture Principle* (San Francisco: Harper & Row).
——(1987), 'Peril with Promise: A Response to James Olthuis', in Olthuis (1987: 53–60).
——(1990*a*), *Tracking the Maze: Finding Our Way Through Modern Theology From An Evangelical Perspective* (San Francisco: Harper & Row).
——(1990*b*), 'Defining American Fundamentalism: A Response', in Cohen (1990: 38–55).
——(1993), 'The Work of the Holy Spirit in Hermeneutics', *Journal of Pentecostal Theology*, 2: 3–23.
——and Brown, Delwin (1990), *Theological Crossfire: An Evangelical/Liberal Dialogue* (Grand Rapids, Mich.: Zondervan).
Piscatori, James (ed.) (1991), *Islamic Fundamentalisms and the Gulf Crisis* (The Fundamentalism Project, American Academy of Arts and Sciences).
Plantinga, Alvin (1985), 'Advice to Christian Philosophers', *Truth: An International, Inter-disciplinary Journal of Christian Thought*, 1: 11–23.
——(1990), *The Twin Pillars of Christian Scholarship* (Grand Rapids, Mich.: Calvin College and Seminary).
Plantinga, Alvin, and Wolterstorff, Nicholas (1983), *Faith and Rationality: Reason and Belief in God* (Notre Dame: University of Notre Dame Press).
Plass, Adrian (1987), *The Sacred Diary of Adrian Plass (aged $37\frac{3}{4}$)* (Basingstoke: Marshall Pickering).
Pollock, John Charles (1953), *A Cambridge Movement* (London: John Murray).
Preus, Robert D. (1955), *The Inspiration of Scripture: A Study of the Theology of the Seventeenth Century Lutheran Dogmaticians* (Edinburgh: Oliver Boyd).
——(1970), *The Theology of Post-Reformation Lutheranism: A Study of Theological Prolegomena* (Saint Louis, Mo.: Concordia).
Priestley, Joseph (1775), An Examination of Dr. Reid's *Inquiry into the Human Mind on the Principles of Common Sense,* Dr. Beattie's *Essay on the Nature and Immutability of Truth,* and Dr. Oswald's *Appeal to Common Sense in Behalf of Religion*, 2nd edn. (London: J. Johnson).
Prince, Derek (1986), *Foundation Series*, rev. 3-vol. edn. (Chichester: Sovereign World).

The Proceedings of the Conference on Biblical Interpretation (1988) (Nashville: Broadman Press).

QUEBEDEAUX, RICHARD (1978), *The Worldly Evangelicals* (San Francisco: Harper & Row).

RADMACHER, EARL D., and PREUS, ROBERT D. (eds.) (1984), *Hermeneutics, Inerrancy and the Bible* (Grand Rapids, Mich.: Zondervan).

RAMADAN, TARIQ (2004), *Western Muslims and the Future of Islam* (Oxford: Oxford University Press).

RAMM, BERNARD L. (1956), *Protestant Biblical Interpretation: A Textbook of Hermeneutics for Conservative Protestants* (Boston: Wilde).

——(1973), *The Evangelical Heritage* (Waco: Word Books).

——(1983), *After Fundamentalism: The Future of Evangelical Theology* (San Francisco: Harper & Row).

——*et al.* (1987), *Hermeneutics* (Grand Rapids, Mich.: Baker).

RAM-PRASAD, C. (1993), 'Hindutva Ideology: Extracting the Fundamentals', *Contemporary South Asia*, 2/3: 285–309.

REID, THOMAS, WORKS (1863), ed. William Hamilton, 6th edn. (Edinburgh: Maclachan & Stewart).

RENNIE, IAN S. (1994), 'Fundamentalism and the Varieties of North Atlantic Evangelicalism', in Noll, Bebbington, and Rawlyk (1994: 333–50).

RICE, JOHN R. (1969), *Our God-Breathed Book—The Bible* (Murfreesboro, Tenn.: Sword of the Lord).

RICHARDSON, ALAN ([1950] 1955), 'Fundamentalism', *Chambers' Encyclopaedia*, new edn. (London: George Newnes), vi. 114.

ROBBINS, JOHN W. (1986), 'Cornelius Van Til', *The Trinity Review*, May/June.

ROBBINS, KEITH (ed.) (1990), *Protestant Evangelicalism: Britain, Ireland, Germany and America, c.1750–c.1950: Essays in Honour of W. R. Ward* (Oxford: Blackwell).

ROBERTS, VAUGHAN (1992), 'Reframing the UCCF Doctrinal Basis', *Theology*, 95: 432–46.

ROBINSON, DANIEL N. (1989), 'Thomas Reid's Critique of Dugald Stewart', *Journal of the History of Philosophy*, 27/3: 405–22.

ROGERS, JACK B. (1971), 'Van Til and Warfield on Scripture in the Westminster Confession', in Geehan (1971: 154–65).

——(1974), *Confessions of a Conservative Evangelical* (Philadelphia: Westminster).

——(1977), *Biblical Authority* (Waco: Word Books).

——and MCKIM, DONALD K. (1979), *The Authority and Interpretation of the Bible* (San Francisco: Harper & Row).

ROOKMAAKER, H. R. (1970), *Modern Art and the Death of a Culture* (London: IVP).

RUNNER, H. EVAN (1982), *The Relation of the Bible to Learning* (Jordan Station, Ont.: Paideia Press).

RUSHDOONY, ROUSAS JOHN (1959), *By What Standard? An Analysis of the Philosophy of Cornelius Van Til* (Philadelphia: Presbyterian and Reformed).

——(1973), *The Institutes of Biblical Law* (Nutley, NJ: Craig).

RUSSELL, RICHARD A. (1973), 'The Growing Crisis of the Evangelical World-view and its Resolutions', unpub. master's thesis, Bristol University.

——[n.d.], 'Social Concern: Cancer or Maturity of the Evangelical Movement', unpub.

RYRIE, CHARLES C. (1983), 'Some Important Aspects of Biblical Inerrancy', in John F. Walvoord and Roy B. Zuck (eds.), *The Bib Sac Reader* (Chicago: Moody), 3–12.

SAHGAL, GITA, and YUVAL-DAVIS, NIRA (eds.) (1992), *Refusing Holy Orders: Women and Fundamentalism in Britain* (London: Virago).

SAHLIYEH, ÉMILE (ed.) (1990), *Religious Resurgence and Politics in the Contemporary World* (Albany: State University of New York Press).

SALIM ABDULLAH, M. (1992), 'What Shall Be the Answer to Contemporary Islamic Fundamentalism?', in Küng and Moltmann (1992: 70–8).

SAMUEL, VINAY (1996), 'The Holy Spirit in Word and Works: A Study in John Chapters 14 to 16', in Stott, *et al.* (1996: 50–6).

SANDEEN, ERNEST (1962), 'The Princeton Theology: One Source of Biblical Literalism in American Protestantism', *Church History*, 31: 307–21.

——(1967), 'Toward a Historical Interpretation of the Origin of Fundamentalism', *Church History*, 36: 66–83.

——(1970*a*), 'Fundamentalism and American Identity', *The Annals of the American Academy of Political and Social Science*, 38: 56–65.

——(1970*b*), *The Roots of Fundamentalism: British and American Millenarianism 1800–1930* (Chicago: University of Chicago Press).

——(1971), 'Defining Fundamentalism: A Reply to Professor Marsden', *Christian Scholar's Review*, 1: 227–32.

SCHAEFFER, EDITH (1981), *The Tapestry: The Life and Times of Francis and Edith Schaeffer* (Waco: Word Books).

SCHAEFFER, FRANCIS A. (1968*a*), *Escape from Reason* (London: IVF).

——(1968*b*), *The God Who Is There: Speaking Historic Christianity into the Twentieth Century* (London: Hodder & Stoughton).

——(1969), *Death in the City* (London: IVP).

——(1975), *No Final Conflict* (Hodder & Stoughton).

——(1981), *A Christian Manifesto* (Westchester, Ill.: Crossway Books).

——(1984), *The Great Evangelical Disaster* (Eastbourne: Kingsway).

SCHOULS, PETER A. (1990), 'John Locke and the Rise of Western Fundamentalism: A Hypothesis', *Religious Studies and Theology*, 10: 9–22.

SCOFIELD, C. I. (ed.) (1909), *The Scofield Reference Bible* (New York: Oxford University Press).

Scopes Trial Transcript, Billy Graham Center Archives, Collection 244–2, Wheaton College, Ill.

SEERVELD, CALVIN (1985), 'Dooyeweerd's Legacy for Aesthetics: Modal Law Theory', in C. T. McIntire (ed.), *The Legacy of Herman Dooyeweerd* (Lanham, NY: University Press of America), 41–79.

SHAW, STEVE (1994), 'Modal Theory: A Personal Testimony', unpub.

SHEIKH, BILQUIS (1978), *I Dared to Call Him Father* (Eastbourne: Kingsway).

SHEPARD, WILLIAM (1987), '"Fundamentalism" Christian and Islamic', *Religion*, 17: 355–78.

——(1989), '*Response to the Critiques of "'Fundamentalism' Christian and Islamic"* by Bruce Lawrence and Azim Nanji', *Religion*, 19: 285–92.

——(1992), 'Comments on Bruce Lawrence's *Defenders of God*', *Religion*, 22: 279–85.

SHEPPARD, GERALD T. (1983), 'Barr on Canon and Childs: Can One Read the Bible as Scripture?', *TSF Bulletin*, Nov./Dec., 2–4.

SIDER, RONALD J. ([1978] 1990), *Rich Christians in an Age of Hunger*, expanded edn. (London: Hodder & Stoughton).

SKILLEN, JAMES W. (1990), *The Scattered Voice: Christians at Odds in the Public Square* (Grand Rapids, Mich.: Zondervan).

SLOAN, DOUGLAS (1971), *The Scottish Enlightenment and The American College Ideal* (New York: Columbia University, Teachers College Press).

SMAIL, TOM, WRIGHT, NIGEL, and WALKER, ANDREW (1993), *Charismatic Renewal: The Search for a Theology* (London: SPCK).

SMALLEY, STEPHEN S. (1977), 'Redaction Criticism', in Marshall (1977*b*: 181–95).

SMITH, GARY SCOTT (1989), *God and Politics: Four Views on the Reformation of Civil Government* (Phillipsburg, NJ: Presbyterian and Reformed).

SMITH, H. SHELTON, HANDY, ROBERT T., and LOETSCHER, LEFFERTS A. (1963), *American Christianity: An Historical Interpretation with Representative Documents*, ii. *1820–1960* (New York: Charles Scribner's Sons).

SPONG, JOHN SHELBY (1991), *Rescuing the Bible from Fundamentalism: A Bishop Rethinks the Meaning of Scripture* (San Francisco: Harper).

SPYKMAN, GORDON J. (1992), *Reformational Theology: A New Paradigm for Doing Dogmatics* (Grand Rapids, Mich.: Eerdmans).

STEWART, DUGALD (1792), *Elements of the Philosophy of the Human Mind* (London: A. Strahan & T. Cadell), i.

——(1810), *Philosophical Essays* (Edinburgh: William Creech & Archibald Constable).

——(1814), *Elements of the Philosophy of the Human Mind* (Edinburgh: Archibald Constable), ii.

——(1827), *Elements of the Philosophy of the Human Mind* (London: John Murray), iii.

——(1828), *The Philosophy of the Active and Moral Powers of Man* (2 vols.; Edinburgh: Adam Black).

——([1802] 1863), *Account of the Life and Writings of Thomas Reid*, in Reid (1863: 3–38).

STONEHOUSE, NED B. (1954), *J. Gresham Machen: A Biographical Memoir* (Grand Rapids, Mich.: Eerdmans).

STORKEY, ELAINE (1985), *What's Right with Feminism?* (London: SPCK).

STOTT, JOHN R. W. (1956), *Fundamentalism and Evangelism* (London: Crusade).

——(1977*a*), 'Obeying Christ in a Changing World', in Stott (1977*b*: 9–31).

——(ed.) (1977*b*), *Obeying Christ in a Changing World*, i. *The Lord Christ* (Glasgow: Collins).

——(1978), 'Are Evangelicals Fundamentalists?', *Christianity Today*, 8 Sept., 44–6.

——(1982), *I Believe in Preaching* (London: Hodder & Stoughton) (= *Between Two Worlds: The Art of Preaching in the Twentieth Century* (Grand Rapids, Mich.: Eerdmans)).

——(1984), *Issues Facing Christians Today* (Basingstoke: Marshalls).

——(1992), *The Contemporary Christian* (Leicester: IVP).

——(1996), 'The Anglican Communion and Scripture', in John Stott, *et al.* (1996: 13–49).

——and COOTE, ROBERT (1980), *Down to Earth: Studies in Christianity and Culture: The Papers of the Lausanne Consultation on Gospel and Culture* (London: Hodder & Stoughton).

——*et al.* (1996), *The Anglican Communion and Scripture: Papers from the First International Consultation of the Evangelical Fellowship in the Anglican Communion, Canterbury, UK, June 1993* (Carlisle: EFAC and Regnum).

STRAUB, GERARD (1986), *Salvation for Sale: An Insider's View of Pat Robertson's Ministry* (Buffalo, NY: Prometheus Books).

SUGDEN, CHRISTOPHER (1989), 'Evangelicals and Wholistic Evangelism', in Vinay Samuel and Albrecht Hauser (eds.), *Proclaiming Christ in Christ's Way: Studies in Integral Evangelism* (Oxford: Regnum), 29–51.

SWATOS, WILLIAM H., Jr. (ed.) (1989), *Religious Politics in Global and Comparative Perspective* (New York: Greenwood).

SWEET, LEONARD I. (1984), *The Evangelical Tradition in America* (Macon, Ga.: Mercer University Press).

TAPPER, RICHARD, and TAPPER, NANCY (1987), '"Thank God we're Secular!" Aspects of Fundamentalism in a Turkish Town', in Caplan (1987*b*: 51–78).

THISELTON, ANTHONY C. (1970), 'The Parables as Language-Event: Some Comments on Fuch's Hermeneutics in the Light of Linguistic Philosophy', *Scottish Journal of Theology*, 23: 437–68.

——(1974), 'The Supposed Power of Words in the Biblical Writings', *Journal of Theological Studies*, NS 25/2: 283–99.

——(1977*a*), 'The New Hermeneutic', in Marshall (1977*b*: 308–33).

——(1977*b*), 'Understanding God's Word Today', in Stott (1977*b*: 90–122).

——(1980), *The Two Horizons: New Testament Hermeneutics and Philosophical Description with Special Reference to Heidegger, Bultmann, Gadamer and Wittgenstein* (Carlisle: Paternoster).

——(1985), 'Reader-Response Hermeneutics, Action Models, and the Parables of Jesus', in Lundin, Thiselton, and Walhout (1985: 79–113).

——(1988), 'Speaking and Hearing', in Noll and Wells (1988: 139–51).

——(1992), *New Horizons in Hermeneutics* (London: HarperCollins).

THOMAS, KEITH (1971), *Religion and the Decline of Magic: Studies in Popular Beliefs in Sixteenth and Seventeenth Century England* (London: Weidenfeld & Nicolson).

THOMAS, W. H. GRIFFITH (n.d. [1909?–15]), 'Old Testament Criticism and New Testament Christianity', *The Fundamentals*, viii. 5–26.

TIDBALL, DEREK J. (1994), *Who Are the Evangelicals?: Tracing the Roots of Modern Movements* (London: Marshall Pickering).

TINKER, MELVIN (ed.) (1990), *Restoring the Vision: Anglican Evangelicals Speak Out* (Eastbourne: MARC).

TOMLINSON, DAVE (1995), *The Post-Evangelical* (London: Triangle).

TRACY, DAVID (1975), *Blessed Rage for Order: The New Pluralism in Theology* (New York: Seabury).

TRAVIS, STEPHEN H. (1977), 'Form Criticism', in Marshall (1977*b*: 153–64).

TREMBATH, KERN ROBERT (1987), *Evangelical Theories of Biblical Inspiration: A Review and Proposal* (New York: Oxford University Press).

TORREY, REUBEN A. ([1898] 1957), *What the Bible Teaches: A Thorough and Comprehensive Study of What the Bible has to Say Concerning the Great Doctrines of Which it Treats* (London: Oliphants).

——(1920), *How to Study the Bible for Greatest Profit* (London: Pickering & Inglis).

TURRETTIN, FRANCIS (1688–9), *Institutio theologiae elencticae* (Geneva: Apud Samuelem de Tournes).

VANDER GOOT, HENRY (1984), *Interpreting the Bible in Theology and the Church* (New York: Edwin Mellen).

VANDERLAAN, ELDRED C. (1925), *Fundamentalism versus Modernism* (New York: H. W. Wilson).

VANDER STELT, JOHN C. (1978), *Philosophy and Scripture: A Study in Old Princeton and Westminster Theology* (Marlton, NJ: Mack).

Van Til, Cornelius (1948), 'Introduction', in Warfield (1948: 3–68).
——(1949), 'Presuppositionalism', *The Bible Today*, 42/7 (Apr.), 218–28; 42/9 (June–Sept.), 278–90.
——(1950), *The Intellectual Challenge to the Gospel* (London: Tyndale).
——(1955*a*), *The Defense of the Faith*, 1st edn. (Philadelphia: Presbyterian and Reformed).
——(1955*b*), *Christianity and Idealism* (Philadelphia: Presbyterian and Reformed).
——(1961), *Christian-Theistic Evidences*, Teaching Syllabus for Westminster Theological Seminary.
——(1963), *The Defense of the Faith*, 2nd edn. rev. and abridged (Philadelphia: Presbyterian and Reformed).
——(1967), *In Defense of the Faith*, i. *The Doctrine of Scripture* (Phillipsburg, NJ: Presbyterian and Reformed).
——(1969), *A Christian Theory of Knowledge* (Phillipsburg, NJ: Presbyterian and Reformed).
——(1971*a*), 'My Credo', in Geehan (1971: 3–21).
——(1971*b*), 'Response' to Dooyeweerd, in Geehan (1971: 89–127).
——(1974), *The New Hermeneutic* ([Phillipsburg, NJ (?)]: Presbyterian and Reformed).
——[n.d.], 'The Apologetic Method of Francis A. Schaeffer', paper written for Westminster students [n. pub.].
Vine, W. E. (1923), *The Divine Inspiration of the Bible* (London: Pickering & Inglis).
Volf, Miroslav (1992), 'The Challenge of Protestant Fundamentalism', in Küng and Moltmann (1992: 97–106).
Wacker, Grant (1985), *Augustus H. Strong and the Dilemma of Historical Consciousness* (Macon, Ga.: Mercer University Press).
Walker, Andrew (1987), 'Fundamentalism and Modernity: The Restoration Movement in Britain', in Caplan (1987*b*: 195–210).
Wallis, Jim (1981), *The Call to Conversion* (San Francisco: Harper & Row).
Walvoord, John F., and Zuck, Roy B. (eds.) (1983), *The Bib Sac Reader: Commemorating Fifty Years of Publication by Dallas Theological Seminary 1934–1983* (Chicago: Moody).
Warfield, Benjamin B. [1893], 'The Real Problem of Inspiration', *Presbyterian and Reformed Review*, 4: 177–221, repr. in Warfield (1948: 169–226).
——[1894*a*], 'The Divine and Human in the Bible', *Presbyterian Journal*, 3 May, repr. with commentary in Noll (1983: 275–9).
——[1894*b*], 'The Church Doctrine of Inspiration', from *Bibliotheca Sacra*, 51: 614–40, repr. in Warfield (1948: 105–28).

WARFIELD, BENJAMIN B. [1895], 'The Latest Phase of Historical Rationalism', *Presbyterian Quarterly*, 9: 36–67, 185–210, repr. in Warfield ([1932] 1988: 585–645).

——[1899*a*], ' "It Says:", "Scripture Says:", "God Says" ', *Presbyterian and Reformed Review*, 10: 472–510, repr. in Warfield (1948: 299–348).

——[1899*b*], Review of R. A. Torrey's *What the Bible Teaches, Presbyterian and Reformed Review*, 39: 562–4, repr. with commentary in Noll (1983: 299–301).

——(1903*a*), Review of Herman Bavinck's *De Zekerheid des Geloofs, Princeton Theological Review*, 1: 138–48.

——(1903*b*), 'Introduction' to Beattie 1903: 19–32.

——[1908], 'Apologetics', in Samuel Macauley Jackson (ed.), *The New Schaff-Herzog Encyclopedia of Religious Knowledge* (New York: Funk & Wagnalls), 232–8; repr. in Warfield ([1932] 1988: 3–21).

——(n.d. [1909?]), 'The Deity of Christ', *The Fundamentals*, i. 21–8.

——[1911*a*], 'On the Antiquity and the Unity of the Human Race', *Princeton Theological Review*, 9, repr. in Warfield ([1932] 1988: 235–58).

——[1911*b*], 'On Faith in its Psychological Aspects', *Princeton Theological Review*, 9: 537–66, repr. in Warfield ([1932] 1988: 313–42).

——[1915], 'Calvin's Doctrine of Creation', *Princeton Theological Review*, 13, repr. with commentary in Noll (1983: 294–8).

——[1917], 'Mysticism and Christianity', *Biblical Review*, 2: 169–91, repr. in Warfield ([1932] 1988: 649–66).

——([1932] 1988), *Studies in Theology* (Edinburgh: Banner of Truth).

——(1948), *The Inspiration and Authority of the Bible*, (ed.) Samuel G. Craig (Phillipsburg, NJ: Presbyterian and Reformed).

WATSON, DAVID C. C. ([1975] 1989), *The Great Brain Robbery* ([n.p.]: the author).

WATT, W. MONTGOMERY (1988), *Islamic Fundamentalism and Modernity* (London: Routledge).

——(1991), *Muslim-Christian Encounters: Perceptions and Misperceptions* (London: Routledge).

WEBER, TIMOTHY P. (1982), 'The Two-Edged Sword: The Fundamentalist Use of the Bible', in Hatch and Noll (1982: 101–20).

——(1987), *Living in the Shadow of the Second Coming: American Premillennialism 1875–1982*, enlarged edn. (Chicago: University of Chicago Press).

——(1991), 'Premillennialism and the Branches of Evangelicalism', in Dayton and Johnston (1991: 5–21).

WEBSTER, RICHARD (1990), *A Brief History of Blasphemy: Liberalism, Censorship and 'The Satanic Verses'* (Southwold: Orwell Press).

WELLS, DAVID F. (1994), 'On Being Evangelical: Some Theological Differences and Similarities', in Noll, Bebbington, and Rawlyk (1994: 389–410).

WELLS, DAVID F., and WOODBRIDGE, JOHN D. (eds.) (1975), *The Evangelicals: What they Believe, Who they Are, Where they are Changing* (Nashville: Abingdon).

WELLS, WILLIAM W. (1978), 'Blasting Bible Believers', *Christianity Today*, 2 June, 30–4.

WENHAM, JOHN ([1972] 1993), *Christ and the Bible*, 2nd edn. (Guildford: Eagle).

——([1984] 1992), *Easter Enigma*, 2nd edn. (Guernsey: Paternoster).

——(1989), 'Fifty Years of Evangelical Biblical Research: Retrospect and Prospect', *Churchman*, 103/3: 209–18.

WIESELTIER, LEON (1990), 'The Jewish Face of Fundamentalism', in Cohen (1990: 192–6).

Willowbank Report (1978), in Stott and Coote (1980: 308–42).

WIMBER, JOHN, with KEVIN SPRINGER (1985), *Power Evangelism: Signs and Wonders Today* (London: Hodder & Stoughton).

——(1987), *Power Healing* (San Francisco: Harper & Row).

WITHERSPOON, JOHN ([1753] 1763), *Ecclesiastical Characteristics, Or, the Arcana of Church Policy. Being an Humble Attempt to open up the Mystery of Moderation wherein is shewn a plain and easy way of attaining to the Character of a Moderate Man, as at present in repute in the Church of Scotland* (Edinburgh: pub. unknown).

WOLFFE, JOHN (ed.) (1995), *Evangelical Faith and Public Zeal: Evangelicals and Society in Britain 1780–1980* (London: SPCK).

WOLTERS, ALBERT M. (1985), *Creation Regained: Biblical Basics for a Reformational Worldview* (Grand Rapids, Mich.: Eerdmans).

WOLTERSTORFF, NICHOLAS (1976), *Reason within the Bounds of Religion* (Grand Rapids, Mich.: Eerdmans).

——(1981), 'Is Reason Enough?', *The Reformed Journal*, 31 (Apr.), repr. in R. Douglas Geivett and Brendan Sweetman (eds.), *Contemporary Perspectives on Religious Epistemology* (New York: Oxford University Press, 1992), 142–9.

——(1983), 'Thomas Reid on Rationality', in Hart, van der Hoeven, and Wolterstorff (1983: 43–69).

——(1987), 'Teaching for Justice', in Carpenter and Shipps (1987: 201–16).

WOODBRIDGE, J. D. (1982), *Biblical Authority: A Critique of the Rogers/McKim Proposal* (Grand Rapids, Mich.: Zondervan).

——(1993), 'Carl F. H. Henry: Spokesperson for American Evangelicalism', in Carson and Woodbridge (eds.) (1993), *God and Culture: Essays in Honor of Carl F. H. Henry* (Grand Rapids, Mich.: Eerdmans), 378–93.

——and BALMER, R. H. (1983), 'The Princetonians and Biblical Authority: An Assessment of the Ernest Sandeen Proposal', in Carson and Woodbridge (1983: 251–79).

WRIGHT, DAVID F. (1980), 'Soundings in the Doctrine of Scripture in British Evangelicalism in the First Half of the Twentieth Century', *Tyndale Bulletin*, 31: 87–106.

WUTHNOW, ROBERT (1988), *The Restructuring of the American Religion: Society and Faith Since World War II* (Princeton: Princeton University Press).

YOUNG, E. J. (1957), *Thy Word is Truth: Some Thoughts on the Biblical Doctrine of Inspiration* (Grand Rapids, Mich.: Eerdmans).

YOUNG, WILLIAM (1952), *Toward a Reformed Philosophy: The Development of Protestant Philosophy in Dutch Calvinist Thought Since the Time of Abraham Kuyper* (Grand Rapids, Mich.: Piet Hein).

YOUNGBLOOD, RONALD (ed.) (1984), *Evangelicals and Inerrancy* (Nashville: Thomas Nelson).

ZIMMERMAN, WENDELL (1984), 'The Inerrant Infallible Word of the Living God', in Raymond Barber, *et al.* (eds.), *Baptist Fundamentalism 84 Sermons* (Washington: pub. unknown), 187–99.

ZYLSTRA, BERNARD and JOSINA (1975), 'Introduction' to Kalsbeek (1975).

INDEX